Recovery Rising

A Retrospective of Addiction Treatment and Recovery Advocacy

William L. White

Amazon/CreateSpace Edition
Book Cover Art by
Jeremy Reddington © 123rf.com

ISBN-13: 978-1976051869

I have tried to recreate events, locales, and conversations from my
memories of them. In order to maintain their confidentiality and
anonymity, I have, in some instances, changed the names and
identifying characteristics of individuals.

Dedication

For Alisha, Stewart, Troy, and Kim. This one's for you. And to Rita Chaney for your emotional and technical support in getting this book to press.

"A radical recovery movement is now rising in America. That movement is flowing from the realization that addiction and its progeny of problems are visible everywhere, while recovery from addiction lies hidden. It is rising in the recognition that the stigma attached to AOD problems has increased in recent decades and has fueled the demedicalization and recriminalization of these problems....It is in this regressive climate that a style of recovery advocacy is emerging that is radical in its scope (focus on environmental as well as personal transformation), radical in its inclusiveness (celebration of multiple pathways and styles of recovery), and radical in its synthesis of social responsibility and personal accountability."

White, W. (2004). Recovery rising: Radical recovery in America. *Let's Go Make Some History: Chronicles of the New Addiction Recovery Advocacy Movement.* Washington, D.C.: Johnson Institute and Faces and Voices of Recovery, pp. 121-134.

Introduction

While researching *Slaying the Dragon: The History of Addiction Treatment and Recovery in America,* I discovered the ephemeral nature of oral history. The story of several critical episodes in the history of addiction treatment and recovery could not be told simply because all of the key actors within those incidents had died, leaving no documents, recordings, or fragments of memory behind. Such historical episodes exist only as fleeting rumors that all too quickly fade into nothingness. This candle-in-the-wind quality of historical information was also revealed when key people I interviewed for *Slaying the Dragon* died shortly after they were interviewed. If those interviews had been delayed, in some cases by only a few weeks, the stories of key chapters in the modern history of addiction treatment and recovery could not have been fully told and might have been forever lost. Such potential losses have been magnified by the closing of some of the largest addiction studies libraries in the country—their historically important and priceless collections scattered to the winds.

Those of us who work in the addiction and recovery arenas are by nature creatures of action and speech, capturing few if any of our thoughts and experiences on paper or in the many new digital formats. The resulting vacuum risks leaving future generations entering the addictions field without the experience and guidance of those who came before. The possibility that crucial chapters in the modern history of addiction treatment could be lost prompted me to consider writing a memoir of my professional life. It took time and the encouragement of others to overcome resistance to such a venture. I am by nature a private person and have tried, not always successfully, to keep my ego out of my professional contributions.

My decision to capture the stories that fill the following pages was prompted by a growing conviction that using my life as a laboratory of lessons learned—the good, the bad, and the ugly—would benefit those addiction professionals who will inherit and shape the future of this field. The resulting document was thus crafted not as a celebration of self, but an act of service to a field that has enriched my life beyond measure. As you will quickly see, many incidents contained in this book would not have been included if I had wanted to present myself in the best possible light. What I have included is as much about my failures as my successes and the relationship between the former and the latter.

In the movie *Forrest Gump*, the protagonist, without conscious intent, participated in some of the most important historical milestones of the late 20th century. There is a Forrest Gump quality to my professional career and the stories contained in these pages. Partially out of the many roles I occupied in the addictions field and partially out of my attraction to the field's pioneers, I occupied a Gump-like bystander role to critical events in the modern history of addiction treatment and recovery. Others have played far more central roles in the field than I, but much of what they did, witnessed, and learned will likely be lost. The absence of memoirs by addiction professionals is striking.

I have attempted to do two things in these pages: 1) use personal stories from my own life's work to document what it was like within the soul of this field over the closing decades of the 20th century and the opening decades of the 21st century, and 2) extract lessons from these experiences that might stimulate reflection among current and future generations of addiction treatment professionals and recovery support specialists. It is both a personalized history of the modern world of addiction treatment between 1967 and 2016 (and counting) and a collection of reflections about how to conduct oneself amid the promises and pitfalls of this most unusual occupation. Many of the most important episodes recalled in these pages include encounters with individuals and families seeking my help. Real names have been changed and identifying details have been stripped from these stories to protect confidentiality and privacy.

The presentation of this material is organized sequentially (I will forever hear the mantra of my mentor, Ernie Kurtz: "tell the story chronologically") and organized topically in what I hope are engaging and easily digestible vignettes. I have tried to write the kind of book I wish my professional elders had prepared and placed in my hands the first day I entered the field. And I have tried to provide the reflective questions I wish I had pondered BEFORE finding myself in the situations I describe in these pages. I hope the questions at the end of many of these stories will provide a stimulus for personal reflection, an aid in educational and training settings, and a tool in supervision. The reader should also be aware that nearly all of the papers and monographs referenced in this text are available for free download at www.williamwhitepapers.com

Some will think these pages the musings of a hopeless romantic, with all the talk of passion and calling and destiny, but the field of addiction treatment was built by people whose lives were guided by the power and meaning of such words. If such a thing as calling exists, I have been blessed to experience it. If destiny is a possibility, I have lived it, willingly if not perfectly. Perhaps some readers will feel the stir of that calling or reconfirm a calling that came long ago as we proceed on this journey together. The pages that follow are my gifts to those who are considering entry into the field of addiction treatment and to those who have long-labored in this unique ministry. As you turn the pages, I hope you feel a torch being passed into your hands or feel your own life's work being honored, because, as you will quickly see, this book is ultimately more about you than about me.

Contents

Chapter One
Prelude to a Career: Recovery and Calling
(1965-1972)

Our story opens in the 1960s. It was a decade of rapidly changing drug patterns—the country's ever-pervasive alcohol problems, a maturing of the juvenile narcotic epidemic of the 1950s, rampant but invisible prescription drug dependence, and a rising youthful polydrug phenomenon, the likes of which no country in the world had ever witnessed. Growing numbers of people with drug problems brought the country's lack of recovery support resources to a detonation point. The cultural resolve to build a national network of addiction prevention and treatment programs emerged at a policy level. Only a few recovery support resources existed in most communities—a few (by today's standards) AA groups, very few if any NA groups, no widely available secular or religious alternatives to AA and NA, fledgling alcoholism programs and halfway houses, and a smattering of newly rising therapeutic communities and methadone maintenance programs. Science-based addiction treatment was decades away, as was research on prevalence, pathways, stages, and styles of addiction recovery.

Few recovery support resources existed in the communities I served. These were the days before the National Institute on Alcohol Abuse and Alcoholism (NIAAA), the National Institute on Drug Abuse (NIDA), and the Center for Substance Abuse Treatment (CSAT). This chapter is about the pathways of people entering professional work in the world of addiction treatment during this era and how those respective pathways shaped what evolved from a fledgling social movement into a multi-billion dollar addiction treatment industry.

In the Beginning

Each of us brings a personal palette to our work with others. I brought experiences from a large service-oriented family (a tribe of 20 plus blood/adopted/foster brothers and sisters); experiences growing up in a small rural Illinois community; an early Protestant religious orientation that evolved through the civil rights movement into a

1

sustained and more secularly-oriented social activism; my privileged status and socialization as a white heterosexual American male; no particular sense of ethnic identity or heritage; youthful energy and immaturity; working class and union-centered social sensitivities; marginal survival to exceptional success in my pre-college school years; and a precocious involvement in the world of work since my early teens. Such influences, unique for each of us, are as invisible as the air we breathe, but they exert profound influences on how we perceive, think, feel, and act, as well as how we perceive and relate to those who seek our guidance. The first tasks of clinicians and recovery support specialists are to identify their own unique influences and increase their conscious awareness of how these factors enter the helping process, for good or bad.

I have had to challenge every developmental filter over the course of my career, exploring the sensitivities and insensitivities that were part of my whiteness, my maleness, my heterosexuality, my social class, my stage of life, and all the other factors that influenced how I perceived the world and people in it at any moment in time. In these pages, we will explore how each of us must identify and in some cases remove or diminish these filters if we are to serve our clients and this field with distinction. Especially important is the need for every addiction professional to examine his or her personal relationship with alcohol and other drugs and the ways that relationship shapes one's perception of people seeking help for alcohol and other drug problems. Such past experiences can be a source of great insight and instinct in the clinical setting, but they can also be a source of blindness and bias. We must also explore and resolve the depths of our own developmental wounds to keep them from unconsciously contaminating our helping relationships. "Know thyself!" is a most fitting mantra to guide the work we have chosen or been called to pursue.

What are the most significant experiences that have shaped who and what you are at the deepest levels? What developmental experiences or accidents of circumstance brought you to the doorway of entry into this field? What is your personal and family history with alcohol and other drugs? How have these influences shaped your views of alcohol and other drug (AOD) problems, your

2

attitudes toward individuals and families experiencing such problems, and your perceptions of the prospects and methods of long-term recovery?

The Soil and Seeds of Addiction

I'm not sure when I crossed the precise line that marked my status as an addict, but that line was likely crossed long before I would come to see myself as an addict. Blood connected me to generations of addicted men and women in my father's family, but I offer no genetic justification of my addiction career. Drug use was as much a political as personal statement in the 1960s, but *my* drug use was not a symbol of such protest. The emotional wounds of my early developmental years—wounds we all share in different forms and degrees—provided fertile exploration during years of therapy, but their role in my drug use is indistinct and, at most, an indirect influence.

Like so many people who later pursued addiction careers, I have distinct memories from my youth of walking mechanically among people I did not feel a part of, longing for some transformative potion or ritual that would instill life and banish the feeling of masquerading as a human being. Today, I know that such disconnectedness from self and others has a multitude of roots and that such haunting feelings of imposterhood are referenced in addiction and recovery stories across the globe and across generations of addiction narratives.

One of the many things that separate drug users from drug addicts is the magical quality addicts feel in their relationship with drugs, often from the first contact. With my family history of alcoholism, I was consciously temperate in my early relationship with alcohol. In my teens, the sight and smell of alcohol evoked images and feelings of revulsion—memories of my father coming home drunk, the verbal fights between him and my mother on such occasions, and his innumerable infidelities. That was a path I was committed not to follow. Nor did I feel any special connection to alcohol during my early drinking experiences. This lack of magical effects was also true in my response to cannabis and a variety of other substances. These early, rather unremarkable experiences left me unprepared for my response to stimulants. It seems some people are vulnerable to every manner of excess and every manner of drug while others experience dramatically heightened vulnerability to a narrow spectrum of substances. Stimulants alone gave me, and then nearly took from me, everything I had ever wanted in my young life.

Daily lists of things I wanted to accomplish have been part of my life as far back as I can remember. Ideas constantly whirled in my mind. I wanted to do everything, and was often frustrated by my inability to do it all and do it with perfection. The personal context of my love affair with amphetamines broke all the prevailing stereotypes about addicts. I was not a person whose character and lifestyle would be associated with addiction. I was simultaneously enrolled in a private college and a state university, making grades that would allow me to graduate magna cum laude. I had a 20-hour per week psychology fellowship through which I tutored students, graded papers, and gave occasional lectures. On top of that, I was working additional part-time jobs to pay for my education, and I was politically active on and off the campus. (It was the '60s!) My life as I and others saw it was one of unceasing activism and achievement. I viewed my relationship with life as one of confrontation and would have considered ridiculous the suggestion that any aspect of my character or lifestyle was escapist. And of course with such boundless energy and motivation, I considered sleep a waste—the enemy.

Between the worlds of normalcy and innumerable varieties of madness lie frontiers of excess that are the birthplace of great possibility and pain. Many great artists see and experience the world more intensely than others. Such hypersensitivity is a source of their art and their vulnerability for depression. I lived on the other end of this continuum in a state of sustained hypomania—a state that could have tilted, and at times did tilt, into a clinical state. When I later met people suffering from severe forms of mania, I always felt a sense of kinship and a recognition that we differed not in nature but in degree. The gifts that can flow from this zone of hyper-arousal include heightened pleasure, achievement, and meaning. This same zone is also filled with fertile soil in which considerable trouble can grow.

What vulnerabilities do you bring into your role as a professional helper that will need to be actively managed? What past

4

curses in your life might serve as bridges for empathic identification with those you counsel? What excesses might form the grounds for unique contributions to the field? What gifts do you possess that might have a shadow side that you will need to consciously monitor and manage?

Brain Candy

The first hint of what was to come was my early addiction to nicotine (two-plus packs a day). It provided an embryonic shadow of the stimulant effects that I would come to cherish. A second hint was the massive quantities of caffeine I consumed, first in the form of caffeinated beverages and later in the form of caffeine tablets. (In my early days in college, I taped empty boxes of No-Doz to frame the mirror of my dorm room as if they were awards.) My access to the first amphetamine tablet was serendipitous—a gift from a nurse at my place of employment who was concerned about my long drive back to school after working a double shift. (Readers aghast at such an offering need to be reminded that amphetamines had not yet been demonized and criminalized and were viewed benignly by most health care personnel in the 1960s.)

The physical and psychological response to my first contact with amphetamines was instantaneous and unequivocal: "Where have you been all my life?" It was not a sense of euphoria—I never considered amphetamines an intoxicant. It wasn't even the energy that amphetamines provided, although I would later come to think of them as a chemical battery pack. The magic of amphetamines was a degree of focus, clarity of thinking, and a sense of personal power beyond anything in my previous experience.

In later years when steroids became something of a rage, I was reminded of how I felt during the early years of my regular amphetamine use. I viewed amphetamines as a brain steroid—a form of "academic doping" that inadvertently morphed into addiction. The insidiousness of the slide from use into addiction wasn't just what the drug gave me; it was what it drew out of me. The "you" in the "Where

5

have YOU been all my life?" was far more than the drug; it was the revelation of a previously unknown self within my body whom I liked far more than my own fragmented self.

In the weeks before my first consumption of amphetamine, I had been struggling through repeated diversions and false starts in meeting a deadline for a paper in one of my classes. In that 90-minute drive from work to school under the influence of my first Dexedrine tablet, I wrote in my head what I knew was the best paper of my college career. When I reached the dorm, I sat down and quickly typed the paper as if the words were being dictated by an omniscient god. And I felt wonderful— not high, not intoxicated, but infused with a warm, flowing sense of power and well-being. I immediately fell in love with what seemed to promise it could make all things possible and fuel any journey I chose to embark upon. Most importantly, I felt a level of unprecedented self-comfort and self-confidence. Was it possible that I had discovered the potion of my dreams?

I resolved immediately that I had to have more of these magical pills. It was not difficult in the mid-1960s to find an almost unlimited supply of Dexedrine, Benzedrine, Desoxyn, Methedrine, and other amphetamine compounds—pills later christened in the illicit culture by their distinctive appearance—*white crosses, robin eggs, black beauties, pink hearts, purple subs, purple hearts, footballs, Christmas trees*, to name just a few. Presenting symptoms of fatigue, depression, or narcolepsy, or posing as a wrestler needing to lose weight, generated regular supplies of amphetamines from physicians who at best were naïve and at worst were little more than "script doctors." One of my physician suppliers was aged and impaired. He personally answered the locked door when I rang the bell at his office and religiously asked me for a urine sample but never tested it. He kept no records that I could see and never remembered (or didn't care) that I had been there days earlier. Subsequent complaints of "jitteriness" or "sleeplessness"—both real and feigned—also generated supplies of pills that combined amphetamines and barbiturates—concoctions such as Dexamyl, Desbutal, and Ambar. All of these so-called medicines were dispensed at these physicians' offices from large brown gallon jugs for costs I could easily afford. An early warning of what was to come was a dream I had early in my drug use career of living in an apartment with shelves lined with those brown gallon jugs.

My pill-hoarding increased over time in the knowledge that my legal drug connections could die, lose their medical licenses, or be arrested—all of which later occurred. By using physicians located in cities between where I was going to school and where I worked on weekends, I made sure my drug procurement activities remained secretly compartmentalized from both my school life and my work life. I lacked any premonition of the twist of fate that would a few years later place me working professionally in these precise cities and afford me the opportunity to witness the broad effects of such indiscriminate prescribing practices. I later faced periods of panic when some of these physicians were arrested after I had begun working in the addiction treatment field. I feared disclosure of my record of drug purchases would discredit me and cast a shadow on the organizations with whom I was working, but no such public disclosures ever occurred, probably because of the mountains of patients within which my name was so deeply buried.

The effects of continued amphetamine use were subtle in the first year, and I recall no one voicing any suspicions of such use. Consciousness about drug use was not what it is today. I had always had an excess of energy; it likely seemed I had even more. That these drugs would later be called "speed" was quite apt and particularly fitting for me. I was speed before I used them and became speed from their effects—walking, talking, thinking, and feeling fast both before and after. The racing thoughts, distractibility, and physical restlessness that had always been part of my personality actually mellowed out initially (at least by my standards of excess) under the focusing effects of amphetamines. I had always had rapid, pressured speech and the gradual increase in this seemed to go unnoticed by those close to me. I had always been behaviorally hyper—always on the move, always needing to be doing something, always fidgeting if I was required to contain myself for any length of time—always multitasking years before it became a cultural trend. I was known in college for being able to get by with little sleep, and that reputation, not surprisingly, grew in tandem with my amphetamine consumption. Whatever struggles I had keeping up with the competitive demands imposed on me during the day, I knew in my small college world that I alone owned the night.

I suspected a few other "night owl" friends of mine also using stimulants, but this was never discussed among us—something not talked about in the milieu of a small, religious-affiliated Illinois college in the mid-1960s. I kept my sustained pharmaceutical research to myself, partly out of the sense that these pills were my own secret weapons. My secretiveness was not due to any shame related to illicit drug use or the condition of addiction; I did not then think of myself in those terms. The secrecy of my drug use was instead related to the sense that I was cheating—the academic version of a corked bat in a home run race or Olympic medals acquired under the influence of performance-enhancing drugs.

I did have troubling thoughts about such cheating, but rationalized my drug use as an "equalizer" on a stage where the odds were stacked against me. I saw academic performance in those years as a form of class warfare waged against people of privilege who brought far more resources to the battlefield than I possessed. The pills were part of my edge. When my construction worker father asked if I was "giving the rich kids a run for their money," I assured him with great bravado that I was kicking their asses. That's how I saw it—academic achievement as an expression of class struggle, an act of aggression. At least that's what I told myself. In reality, the many academic honors I achieved during my years of drug use were always accompanied by a sense of illegitimacy. Each time I looked out on audiences when I received those awards I did so through the eyes, not of a self-identified addict, but through the eyes of an impostor.

Several protective rules governed my early drug-taking: use only legal, pharmaceutical product; never go more than two days without sleep; take vitamins every day; drink plenty of fluids; eat even when you feel no hunger; and, the most frequently broken rule, don't take more than "X" number of pills a day—an ever-shifting number. In spite of such rules, my life, like amphetamine addicts before and after me, eventually was reduced to a blurred series of "runs" and "crashes."

My dependence on amphetamines, and particularly the methamphetamine that was then available by prescription, built gradually for most of my college career and reached a climax the end of my senior year. What had once given me power began to drain that power. What had once helped hold the pieces of my fragile self together

8

gradually threatened to disintegrate that self. A thing apart from me that had been a tool—not a problem, but a wonderful solution—gradually came alive and threatened to consume me, become me. Signs of that coming crisis would have been evident to anyone who looked closely, but few did.

My detached aloofness from all but a small circle of people with a high threshold for deviance made such recognition unlikely. But the signs were there: the dilated eyes, insomnia followed by respites of Jim Beam- or sedative/opioid-induced sleep (the latter acquired from the same "script doctors" who provided the amphetamines), weight loss, bruxism (teeth grinding), perpetual dry mouth and deteriorating dental health, dry skin, physical restlessness, a frenetic flight of ideas and rapid speech, and the growing presence of chest pains and headaches. There was also the auto accident from falling asleep at the wheel while driving from classes at Illinois State University to work after two days of no sleep. And there was that creeping paranoia that for some unexplained reason was never as severe for me as I would later witness in my clinical work with others addicted to methamphetamine.

One ironic effect of my drug use was a preoccupation with conserving my energy—an effect incongruent with the requirement of my small liberal arts college that I complete two years of physical education classes. I completely blew off or dropped out of these classes shortly after my drug use began and took failing grades in "phys ed" multiple times before I finally got my act together enough to pass a final class that allowed me to meet the physical education graduation requirement.

Addiction professionals are in a unique position to witness all of the things that drugs do to people, but it may be harder in that role to understand what drugs do for these same people before the crash and burn experiences that bring them to us. Understanding that "doing for" dimension is critically important for within it can be found the seeds of addiction and the ingredients that must be discovered or forged to sustain recovery. The same needs met through drug use must be met in recovery even as these needs change through the recovery process. Addictive behavior in its final destructiveness is inexplicable to self and others without an understanding of what it gave before what it took. We must remind ourselves of this dimension when we encounter those who

9

continue their alcohol and drug use in the face of the most devastating consequences.

Bargain with an Unknown God

I felt myself moving gradually toward some crisis point, but I had no premonition of whether that crisis would be one of body or mind. It turned out to be both. The crisis came on a day that began like many others in the spring of 1969. It was the end of my senior year in college and one more prolonged run of amphetamine use. I hadn't slept in some time—not unusual for this period—and had made it through a day of classes, work, and a visit with my girlfriend without incident. I had taken no more or no fewer pills on this day than any other (although my escalating tolerance had brought me to an excessive maintenance dosage). I continued to work into the late night, not knowing that some cumulative point of drug intake was about to propel my life into a new direction.

The first thing out of the ordinary was a rise in anxiety that lacked any identifiable source and what felt like a cramping in my stomach and chest—the latter a tightening band far worse than anything previously experienced and that I feared might be a heart attack. Simply attributing all of this to lack of sleep, I decided to lie down for a while. Over the next few hours my condition deteriorated and by 2:00 AM my heart felt like it was beating out—no, tearing out—of my chest. This was by no means the first severe, drug-induced chest pain I had experienced, but its intensity was beyond the pale of anything I had experienced before. I also remember being drenched in sweat and experiencing muscle tremors in my arms and hands that I feared might signal impending seizures—something I had often witnessed in my work on psychiatric units.

A deep realization flowed over me. I knew beyond a shadow of doubt that I was going to die that night—that I had crossed a point of no return. My mental status was deteriorating. I felt I was losing my mind—that my whole being was dissolving. I was anything but a religious person at that point in my life—having abandoned both the church and my belief in God, but in desperation I recall simply thinking, "God, if you get me through this night, I will stop this shit and try to do something with my life." I saw no white light, nor heard any voice from heaven in response to my plea. It seemed as if I was suspended in time—

awaiting the decision on my plea cast to the universe. Somewhere in that waiting, I lost consciousness, but I can still recall a brief moment of wrenching clarity wondering if it was sleep or death I was entering.

I awoke more than twelve hours later feeling completely emptied and hyperaware of my surroundings and myself. I remember trying to decide if I had escaped death or had died and been resurrected—the latter thought propelled by the fact that I did not feel at all like myself. Remaining from the night before were two things: a deep sense of reprieve and the memory of that proffered promise. Grateful beyond words and fearing revival of my morning ritual, I quickly emptied pill bottle after pill bottle into the toilet, hesitating only for a moment before I pushed the handle. As I watched the swirling rainbow of pills disappear, I had the panicked feeling that the core of my own self was being flushed away.

I think in retrospect that my recovery began before this first day of no drug use, but that day held a catalytic breakthrough that jump-started what would be a long process of transformation. I would never again use amphetamines of any variety, but my recovery was a long way from being stable, and, unbeknownst to me at the time, my life would be forever marked by physical legacies from my addiction career. A few months later, I was informed by my physician, Dr. Edward Livingston that I had damaged my heart, although what this would mean for my future health and longevity was unclear. My regular heart checkups since have continued to reveal several heart abnormalities, though my cardiologists over the years have differed in their opinions on the role my past drug use may have played in these abnormalities. What has not changed is that every new physician listening to my heart for the first time frowns and calls for an immediate electrocardiogram and stress test. As a result, I have long risen each morning with a sense that this day is a gift that must be lived purposely and fully.

Don't think that this is one of those "addiction left me and I lived happily ever after" stories. It's not. My drug use had filled me up—given me confidence, assertiveness, power, focus, and a feeling of greater human connectedness. Without it, I experienced an emptiness that could have easily pulled me back to using. My drug use had emptied out what natural resources I had and turned me into a machine posing as a human being. As that sense of internal emptiness intensified, I attempted to maintain some picture of external normalcy. A detached part of me watched this play-acting with blunted emotion and an occasional sense of impending dread—a most harrowing form of depersonalization. On

11

the positive side, this sense of emptiness co-existed with an inexplicable faith that some process had begun that would all work out in the end. What I didn't know was how long it would take to fill that emptiness.

Although I now use the terms *addiction* and *recovery* to describe this period, I had no consciousness of being "addicted." I knew I had become physically dependent upon methamphetamine—but even this physical dependency differed in character from what I would later witness as a streetworker and addictions counselor. I was acutely aware of my inability to stop or cut down my use in spite of innumerable resolutions to do so, but there was no self-identification as an "addict," nor was there an immediate identification of myself as a "person in recovery" following my cessation of methamphetamine use. As I experienced it, I saw this transition as a change in behavior—not a change in identity. There was little cultural consciousness about addiction and recovery in those days—no local Narcotics Anonymous (NA) meetings (NA was only then rising from its near collapse), no Dr. Drew shows, no celebrities on TV heading off to rehab, no recovery sections in bookstores, no "Clean and Sober" movies, no highly visible educational campaigns on addiction and recovery, no national or local recovery celebration events, no campus recovery programs.

The cultural images of addiction and addicts that did exist were such warped caricatures that they offered nothing with which I could identify. Like many of my era, the challenge of those earliest days of recovery was to change my life without an available set of words, concepts, rituals, and role models to guide us. Prior to the closing decades of the 20th century, many addicted people got lost without any map or personal guides out of this labyrinth. I was fortunate to survive until such resources came into my life.

Styles of recovery initiation vary. The most common style is one of self-driven, other-supported stages of incremental change, sometimes marked by numerous false starts preceding the achievement of stable recovery. For others, the entry into recovery is marked by an experience of sudden transformative change that is dramatic, positive, and enduring in its effects. My recovery journey had started through the latter experience but, as we shall see, what would be required to solidify and maintain that recovery was quite different than the experience that had kindled it.

In retrospect, I was indeed very fortunate. My addiction career was atypical in that it was shorter—spanning several years rather than decades—and less severe than many. This was due to several factors: 1) the combination of my drug choice and my rapidly accelerating pattern of use was unsustainable, 2) other drugs offered little appeal to me at that time so I avoided the common pattern of quickly cycling into opiate or alcohol dependence, 3) I sustained my drug use in virtual isolation so was not enmeshed in a social world of drug use that could have repeatedly pulled me back into "the life," and 4) I brought a higher level of assets and fewer obstacles to my recovery initiation than those I would later encounter as a streetworker and therapist. I also ended my addiction career outside the sanctuary of professional addiction treatment or a mutual aid fellowship, although both of those institutions would later play roles in my long-term recovery. What these experiences did give me were recovery at a young age and, given my already established propensity for activism, a direction for my life. Initiating my recovery at such an early age provided a long period of gestational learning that would make my later contributions to the addictions field possible.

My dark night of reckoning is what in today's scientific literature is called *quantum change* or *transformational change*—a breakthrough of awareness or self-perception so profound that it can forever alter one's life course (see Bill Miller and Janet C'de Baca's book, *Quantum Change*). Such experiences can be of the religious, spiritual, or secular variety, but they share the qualities of suddenness, high intensity, positivity, and permanence. What experiences in your own life or those close to you confirm the potential and enduring power of such experiences? Are the personal and professional experiences you have had part of a similar gestational process? Do you have any inkling of what callings, challenges, and opportunities are coming? Do you have any sense that you are being prepared for something? Are you open to the power of such experiences in the lives of those you are helping?

The Monkey and the Circus

The comedian George Carlin once reflected, "Just cause you got the monkey off your back doesn't mean that the circus has left town." In May of 1969, I shed the methamphetamine monkey, but in the months that followed I was still living within the circus of my own character excesses. Through most of the tenure of my drug use, pills had been more of a strategic solution than a problem. When I abandoned my drug use, I was left with the same problems (and some new ones) for which drugs had been my solution and simultaneously left with less natural abilities to respond to these challenges. Those capacities had atrophied during the years of my drug use like muscles no longer used. The issue of stopping any pattern of compulsive drug use is not in the act of stopping; it is in answering within one's daily life the subsequent question, "Now what do I do?"

The vacuum left when drugs are abandoned is a circus in which much mischief can brew. All manner of excesses are possible and likely until one can redefine oneself and one's relationship with the world and refine and solidify those definitions over time. Getting professional help or working a structured program of recovery can accelerate what can be a long search for sanity and serenity. In my case, it was not an initial treatment experience that helped me get the monkey off my back, but treatment experiences to come did help me figure out how to shed the monkey and find a world outside the circus. And yet, in my case, I tried to hide my treatment and my need for it as carefully as I had hid my drug use. In your work with individuals and families wounded by addiction, don't get so focused on the monkey's absence that you forget the circus is still in town.

Bootleg Therapy

Just as my addiction process began before my drug use, my recovery process began before I stopped such use. The recovery germination period that predated my drug cessation was not conscious. As my addiction was burning itself into ash, new experiences were opening the doors to recovery. Without knowing it, I was preparing for my recovery career at the same time my addiction was reaching its most severe state.

My interest in psychology grew in tandem with my drug use. My accumulating psychology courses were a form of bibliotherapy that paved the way for other therapies. I rapidly migrated toward clinically-oriented courses in psychology, and, within the chapters on alcoholism and addiction, I first suspected the possible diagnoses of many of my extended family members while still denying my inclusion in this group. (As is typical of most psych students, I applied innumerable labels on myself as I plowed through chapters on the varieties of mental illness.) These studies led me to seek employment as a student worker at a state psychiatric facility where I volunteered to work on every unit that provided contact with alcoholics and addicts.

Ironically, I spent my addiction career working for the Illinois Department of Mental Health. In the coming chapters, we will explore my professional career as it continued along with my recovery. In the early years, I used everything I absorbed from the work environment to work out the bumps of my early recovery and young adulthood. The vogue in training in the late '60s and early '70s was highly experiential, and that suited me just fine. I volunteered for every experiential training session I could worm my way into, gravitating quickly to training in psychodrama, transactional analysis, Gestalt therapy, and an unending list of others.

By choosing to work with alcoholic patients who had been admitted to the psychiatric units, I was also able to work with volunteer members of Alcoholics Anonymous. One volunteer in particular, Lynn J., befriended me and taught me a great deal about alcoholism. Lynn had a warm magnetism. I wasn't sure what that indefinable quality was, but I knew that I wanted some of it. None of the AA members I met between 1967 and 1969 were on staff—all were there as volunteers as part of their recovery service work. No formal alcoholism or addiction treatment programs existed in the community in which I was working, but the training experiences at the Adolf Meyer Zone Center served an unintended recovery priming function. I'm sure without this germination process, my bargain with God would have been quickly forgotten and those exiled pills would have gone into me instead of the toilet, with many more to come. All this bootlegged therapy and support was but a prelude to my coming of age at Gateway House.

Deriving such personal benefit from our professional work is not inherently unethical as long as those benefits don't come at the expense of those we counsel. What personal wounds have been healed as a positive side effect of your own service work with others? What insights from your training and clinical experience have enhanced the quality of your own life?

Gateway and "the Game"

Gateway House is a direct descendent of Synanon, the first ex-addict-directed therapeutic community (TC) in the United States founded in California by Charles Dederich in 1958. Graduates of

Synanon started Daytop in New York City, and Daytop graduates, under the leadership of Carl Charnett, came to Chicago in 1968 to open Gateway House at 4800 South Ellis Street in Hyde Park. After entering my embryonic recovery and graduating from college, I accepted a job to work full time for the Illinois Department of Mental Health in a role that combined crisis intervention services and organizational efforts to develop community-based alcoholism and addiction services. To deepen my knowledge of such services, I explored various training opportunities and chose one that required me to enter a treatment facility as a client as part of my training experience—an extension of my pattern of bootlegging therapy! I entered Gateway Foundation in late 1969 for my planned "treatment/training" experience, spending time at both the Ellis Street and Cregier Avenue facilities.

It was an exotic world I stepped into by the standards of today's treatment centers. Here are my memories of the first few hours. People walking around with shaved heads. A person wearing a diaper and a sign reading, "I'm a baby. Help me grow up!" Shouts and piercing profanities coming through closed doors. Someone prostrate on a couch in what I instantly recognized as withdrawal sickness. People of all colors and cultures (the most racially integrated living environment I had ever encountered). The beautiful and the street-worn crowded into a century-old Chicago mansion. Two aging men talking with a female heroin addict who couldn't have been older than 12 or 13 who had just arrived from New York City. An emaciated man sitting on the "prospect chair" awaiting an interview to enter "the family." A man dressed in a silver shark-skin suit, looking pale and shaken from his just completed intake interview. People bustling here and there within an impeccably clean facility that seemed to be operating with military efficiency. Everyone speaking a language I did not understand—TC-ese filled with references to people's roles (e.g., *ramrods*, *expediters*) and status (e.g., *strength*, *splitees*), people being verbally confronted (*pullups* and *haircuts*) for being *dead wood, tipping out, stuffing their feelings*, or *selling wolf tickets,* and people being complimented for *showing their ass* or *growing balls*. After barely mastering the new language of psychiatry, it was clear I was now awash in a new world with its own language and inexplicable etiquette. And this new world was distinguished at first contact by its almost raw level of honesty and authenticity. In this alien environment, I felt like I had come home.

Gateway brought me three things. First, Gateway provided the building blocks to forge a life narrative (of addiction and recovery) that made sense of otherwise inexplicable experiences. Second, it brought me into deep fellowship with a community of recovering people, many of whom went on to distinguished careers in addiction treatment. My connection with that community offered important friendships and sources of support that would span more than four decades. Those early relationships later opened doors of great opportunity for me. Third, Gateway was my introduction to the "Game"—a powerful experience I later described in *Slaying the Dragon* as a "synergy of leaderless group therapy, confrontational theatre, verbal riot, group confessional, and improvisational comedy." The Game—both in its short form (a few hours) and longer formats (8-24+ hour *probes*, *stews*, *trips*, *reaches,* and *marathons*) emotionally opened me like a can opener and forced me into a level of honest disclosure I had never experienced or witnessed. It was a form of emotional and behavioral surgery that marked the beginning of my maturation in recovery and the deepening of my commitment to do something positive in the world.

I explored entering the Gateway community on a longer term basis, but was told by Gateway leaders that I had important work to do outside and that I needed to go do it. I also faced being drafted into military service within days of leaving a job for which I was granted a deferment from the draft—more about this later. As a result, it was suggested that I continue my full-time job and remain a member of the Gateway community by regularly returning for groups and other community events. Part of that recommendation may have also reflected the pecking order within Gateway and other TCs in the late 1960s. Just as alcoholism programs were designed for "real alcoholics" and often patronized younger and female clients entering treatment ("I spilled more booze than you ever drank."), the TC of this period was designed for "real dope fiends" (defined as street-sophisticated, jail-hardened heroin addicts). My second-class status as a young "pill head" (or "jelly bean freak"/"garbage head") didn't place me high on the list of desirable admissions. If you hadn't shot dope, you were viewed as a burnt out "hippie," not an addict. Some of the former ("dope fiends" or "junkies" in the street and TC vernacular of the day) were quite unimpressed and even bored with my story, although they did perk up a bit when I talked about using Percodan and other prescription opiates to end my speed runs.

I returned for many visits to Gateway in the following years to get myself emotionally recharged. Those regular pilgrimages helped keep me grounded during my early days of recovery, and created a debt

17

of gratitude I feel toward Gateway that will never be fully repaid. People like Joe Difiore, John Sabora, Michael Darcy, Chuck and Linda Schwartz, Bobby Matuszak, and too many others to name here touched my life in ways more profound than I can describe. My Chicago-based network of Gateway relationships remained my primary recovery support network for years, but I needed a source of support closer to where I lived and worked. A source of such support appeared serendipitously when a group of recovering alcoholics invited me to talk with them about the work I was doing with alcoholics and addicts.

Invitation from Friends of Bill W.

My work with alcoholics through the jails and hospitals was beginning to bring me in contact with local Alcoholics Anonymous (AA) groups. I had great respect for AA based on my earlier encounters with AA volunteers who visited the psychiatric units in which I'd worked while I was in school, but I had not yet attended AA meetings. I started dropping into a few open meetings to better orient myself to the AA program (and to find support within a community in which Narcotics Anonymous had not yet arrived). I wasn't sure what to expect from my first AA meeting so I did what the people next to me were doing. I ended up smoking about 20 cigarettes and drinking 10 cups of coffee during the meeting. I hadn't been that wired since I had stopped using methamphetamine. In spite of my acute caffeine intoxication, I was impressed with the people I met and began referring even greater numbers of people to AA. At a personal level, I didn't know where I belonged, so I sampled everything, including Al-Anon.

Sometime during this period, Tom H., one of the local AA patriarchs, invited me to come to a closed AA meeting to talk about my work and how they might be of help in my service to alcoholics. I had to get special dispensation to attend, as announcing I was a recovering addict in a closed AA meeting in those years would have been greeted more by calls for my expulsion than greetings of welcome. Many factors split these worlds of recovery in the early 1970s, including differences of age, social class, ethnicity, and politics. All this occurred at a time young people were, for a brief moment, rhetorically rejecting alcohol and viewing the use of marijuana, LSD, and other drugs as a symbol of being hip. When those 45- to 75-year-old AA members invited this young, bearded, bushy-headed "hippie" streetworker into their meeting, a great cultural divide was crossed.

18

Those early meetings and growing relationships with local AA members and AA groups—several years before the first NA meeting in Illinois—exerted a profound influence on my personal and professional life. Most important for this opening chapter is the fact that a group of older AA members adopted me as a "work in progress." I am particularly indebted to a then-young AA member, Wayne S., whose friendship and support during this period meant more than I have ever been able to express to him. I didn't exactly fit in the AA social world with my talk about pills and potions, but I was recognized as some kind of distant kindred spirit, and these men and women served as a personal support group and advisory committee on my professional work until my feet were planted firmly on more solid ground. My relationships with some of these individuals, including Wayne S., evolved into sustained friendships that continue to this day. Years later, my writings on the history of AA and participation in film documentaries about AA were, in part, a means of expressing gratitude for that early support.

What I learned at a professional level through these first contacts with AA was the power of a sustained sense of community—peer-based recovery supports that could never be found in the professional consulting room. The potential transforming power of AA's Twelve Steps became clearer to me as I watched their effects on those I was introducing to AA and as I inevitably applied the Steps in my own life. I also learned a great deal about the variety of personalities within AA, the great variation in the character of AA groups and meetings, and the need to match people in need to particular AA members and AA meetings.

What We Have Here is a Failure to Identify

Like Gateway, I used much from AA to guide my early recovery, but in both cases I felt I existed in those days on the boundaries of these communities—a misfit among groups of misfits. I did not fully identify with the heroin addicts whose lives before and during addiction were so different from my own. Nor did I fully identify with the older alcoholics whose stories only partially resembled my own. I recall thinking that my recovery would be so much easier if my poison of choice had been heroin or alcohol. Over the coming decades, I would have contact with numerous recovery mutual aid societies—religious, spiritual, and secular—and take much of value from each of them. Paradoxically, I felt myself at times in kinship with all, but a

19

member of none. I remained for some time on their boundaries, feeling an affinity with them, but always the stepson and never the son. This was not just a case of the self-perceived terminal uniqueness of the addicted personality; it was a case of the genuine differences in the content of our stories.

This failure of mutual identification would be shared by many others and contributed to the subsequent growth of recovery mutual aid alternatives in the United States. My early contact with the whole spectrum of recovery groups filled my life with enriching ideas, experiences, and relationships, but at that time failed to provide the exclusive claim of the true believer or the sense of full membership in a single closed community. In fact, I came to have great affection for groups that spent a lot of time criticizing each other.

What I did not know was that this early marginality and growing participation in and affection for quite diverse recovery mutual aids groups would afford entrance to the inner workings of many groups without the blinding biases that can come from devotion to only one. What I didn't know at the time was that this strange combination of connectedness and estrangement was preparing me for a day when I would call for people within these groups to transcend their group identities and stand together publicly not as members of Alcoholics Anonymous, Narcotics Anonymous, Cocaine Anonymous, Women for Sobriety, Secular Organizations for Sobriety, LifeRing Secular Recovery, or Celebrate Recovery, but as "people in recovery." But that day would not come for a quarter of a century. Is it possible that your own unique combination of assets and experiences are preparing you for such a mission in the future? Do you have any premonition of what that mission might be?

Use of Self in Service to Others

The point here is not that I was unique, but that we are all simultaneously unique and the same. None of us are perfectly equipped to facilitate the process of addiction recovery. We will all find ourselves mismatched to those with whom we seek to help if we add enough qualifiers. We will all encounter others who make us feel like impostors posing as helpers. The key is to find a way to use what we have to build avenues of connection. We have to find a foundation of experience from which we can reach across whatever barriers separate us from those we serve. The emotional core of addiction is a mixture of isolation (in the end, only the drug exists), desperation (over rapidly fading power and control), and shame (over the loss of control of the drug and ourselves and the damage we are inflicting on ourselves, our loved ones, and the world). Each of us must reach into ourselves and find the imprinted memory of such feelings if we are to enter into relationships with our clients from a position of moral equality and emotional authenticity.

The issue is not whether we share or don't share an addiction history or a particular drug choice; the issue is whether we can connect with our own experiences of isolation, desperation, and shame with the hope that infuses all communities of recovery. The issue is whether we have witnessed parts of ourselves die so other parts could be born. The issue is whether we can reach into our own broken state as passage to accept the woundedness of others, and then reach again to find the hope that today burns within us that others so desperately need. What I thought was my uniqueness turned out to be the ground upon which I would connect with people across the recovery spectrum. That is the ground that each of you in your own way must find.

For those who do bring recovery experience to the field, my story underscores why it is advisable for people in recovery to have a few years of recovery behind them before they enter the professional service arena. I entered the field early in my own recovery, which was common at that time. The reason that this first chapter is more about me than the clients I worked with is that the opening chapter of my career was focused more on me than anything else. This is not to say that everyone working in this field cannot grow personally through what they experience in the professional arena. But it does suggest that one must have sufficient maturity to separate one's own needs from the needs of individuals, families, and communities. Like many of my peers in communities around the country in the 1960s and early 1970s, I used what was available to me in an era when Narcotics Anonymous was unavailable in most communities, when AA meetings were closed to "drug addicts," and when few other resources were available for long-term recovery support. The enmeshment of my personal life and work life sometimes created problems for me, my clients, and the organizations for which I worked, but I was fortunate to have supervisors who gracefully and skillfully guided me through these difficulties. Many others in that era who tried to mix these personal and professional journeys were not so fortunate.

21

What I know today is that we must build our service to others on a foundation of personal healing, if not health. I also know that only a few bring such optimal health when they enter the addictions field and even fewer continually sustain such health throughout their careers. This is not about recovery experience or the lack of it. No one enters this field without personal wounds that they bring to their helping relationships with others. Our wounded imperfection is the very source of the empathy, authenticity, and moral equality that is so crucial to our work with others. We all bring some past or current relationship with alcohol and other drugs that creates blind spots and distorting filters. We have all experienced breakthroughs of self-perception, unexpected windows of opportunities, crossroads, and turning points of profound significance.

The ideal helper is not a therapist or recovery support specialist with a blank slate, but a person who recognizes the nature of his or her woundedness, understands the healing process, and separates his or her own experiences from those with whom they work. The goal is not perfection, but assurance that our imperfections do not injure those we are pledged to serve. We achieve that by entering clinical work at a time (and only at a time) that we are ready for such responsibility and by seeking outside-of-work professional help to manage issues that could impede our therapeutic effectiveness. We also achieve that goal by seeking supervision to help us stay grounded in our service work, and by continually self-monitoring our own health and its relationship to our helping activities. The latter includes removing ourselves from helping relationships or work with particular types of people during periods of heightened vulnerability or impaired effectiveness. Each of us brings to each helping encounter a smorgasbord of life experiences, attitudes, beliefs, character traits, emotional baggage, knowledge, and skills. The skilled, self-aware therapist and recovery coach learns to actively manage these dimensions. They find a way to keep their "stuff" out of their client's "stuff" (pardon the highly technical language here.)

Those Other Drugs

My near-brush with death had convinced me that amphetamines were now my enemy, but other psychoactive drugs were not even on my radar screen of consciousness. No broad concept of addiction or chemical dependency existed in the cultural stew of this period. And smoking several packs of cigarettes a day and consuming unfathomable quantities of coffee were almost a required ticket of admission to work in the alcoholism and "drug abuse" fields of the 1960s and 1970s. Recovering alcoholics walked around dying of emphysema while strapped to oxygen tanks, chain-smoking cigarettes—all while proclaiming the joys of sobriety and drug-free living. Some alcoholics "in recovery" who would have died before taking a drink also experimented with marijuana and hallucinogens during their period of celebrated use in the 1960s. The "drug abuse field" of the late 1960s and early 1970s did not consider alcohol a drug—with the exception of Narcotics Anonymous, but NA was not present or visible in most communities during this period.

The open and excessive consumption of alcohol at drug abuse conferences was the norm. At the time I was involved with Gateway, "drinking privileges" were earned in second phase by the mostly heroin-addicted clientele being treated there—a practice that started at Daytop and was the norm in many therapeutic communities of the late 1960s. And the treatment centers (TCs) of that era were based on a philosophy quite different than that found in AA and NA. TCs viewed themselves as superior to AA and NA, as its members were not viewed as destined for a process of lifelong recovery but instead seen as achieving a reconstruction of character that allowed one to achieve the status of ex-addict. Abstinence from alcohol and tobacco was not included as a requirement for the ex-addict status. It would be years, the subsequent alcoholism of many "ex-addict" counselors, and greater TC-NA/AA connections before this conceptual blindness was overcome. It wasn't until the alcoholism and "drug abuse" fields came together under such conceptual umbrellas as "chemical dependency," "substance abuse" and "addiction" that such categorical thinking began to break down. (Gateway, and particularly longtime Gateway CEO Michael Darcy, played a leadership role in this national awareness process.)

My story was not atypical. Following my bargain with God, I permanently shed the amphetamines and periodic sedatives and narcotics that had helped me come off methamphetamine runs. I continued (and then increased) my addiction to nicotine. I used little alcohol during my speed days (other than to induce sleep or periodically justify my status as a college student) and did continue alcohol use—as was the norm for Gateway graduates of that era. My drinking increased in the early 1970s, primarily from the influence of the heavy-drinking professional and social milieu within which I was then nested. I was also desperately trying to gain weight following my amphetamine-

23

related emaciation (being 6'1" and 138 pounds) and my physician (who knew all the details of my past drug dependence) recommended two food supplements to help me gain weight: milk shakes and BEER. I continued some brief marijuana use into 1970 as part of my street work within the opiate and polydrug street culture of this era. Part of my rationale for this was that accepting a passed joint was a means of establishing credibility in the streets and a signal that I was not what some suspected me to be—an undercover narcotics agent. Volumes of caffeine continued to pour into my body all the while.

Recovery was defined narrowly in these days to a specific substance or substances to which one had been addicted. To be an ex-addict in those days meant you were no longer dependent on those substances to which you were once addicted. There was no broader concept of addiction at that point within the worlds I occupied—an awareness that would come only with the eventual spread of NA and the maturation of addiction treatment as a professional field. As the definition of recovery expanded in tandem with consciousness about concurrent and sequential drug problems, I, along with many of my peers, peeled these drugs out of our lives in what I later described in my writings as a process of *serial recovery*.

I watched this process closely in a whole generation of recovering alcoholics and addicts through my roles in the treatment field and my membership in diverse communities of recovery. I learned several lessons from these observations. First, vulnerability for addiction can vary from person to person, with some being vulnerable to addiction to a single drug or category of drugs while others bring vulnerability for addiction to all psychoactive drugs and to a broader arena of excessive behaviors. I have known heroin addicts who recovered from heroin addiction in the 1960s who drank socially without problems all of their lives, and I have known others that went on to prematurely die of alcoholism. In the future, we may be able to identify the scope of such individual vulnerability the way we currently identify the scope of allergies. I also witnessed people using secondary drugs to manage acute withdrawal, post-acute withdrawal, and the stressors of early recovery. Such use had three distinct trajectories: a progressive deceleration leading to cessation, subclinical (non-problematic) maintenance, or escalation to a primary dependence. I've watched many poly-addicted individuals peel drugs out of their lives in onion-like layers over an extended span of time. I shed methamphetamines, sedatives, opiates, marijuana, alcohol, nicotine, and caffeine in that order over a span of years—with the last of these drugs shed January 1, 1988. (More on this later.) My motivations differed for giving up each drug and the experiences and stages of letting go of each also varied. I have great hope that new understanding and the experienced lessons of those who came before, will condense this timeline for new generations of people entering recovery.

What we take from our own experience and absorb from our social and professional cultures shape what we see and fail to see. I was slow to recognize the potential for cross-addiction because I had been professionally indoctrinated in a world split into alcohol and "drugs" and because alcohol and non-stimulant drugs had never held the attraction to me that stimulants did. Our personal, professional, and cultural experiences can enrich what we bring to the helping process, but they can also create blind spots of gargantuan proportions and filters that horribly distort reality.

My experience also confirms that recovery is a multi-layered experience. Most of us are recovering from multiple drugs, conditions, and experiences: "serial recovery" is the norm, not the exception. Each layer revealed and healed opens a new layer in the unfolding metamorphosis of recovery. Addiction counseling is not just about matching the best helping strategy to the right person; it is also about helping each individual in different ways through the stages of his or her recovery career and remaining freshly open to the surprise of what that next layer reveals. This does not mean that recovery is a process of unending drudgery and angst from which there is no escape. Once we begin taking the process seriously and ourselves less seriously, recovery actually takes on the quality of an adventure in which we are able to relish the moment while eagerly anticipating the unexpected experiences that lie ahead. That's not a bad lesson for all of us—regardless of our recovery status.

What's My Motivation Here?

This opening chapter explored some of the roots of how I entered the field of addiction treatment. It is interesting to note that my motivations for getting into the field were quite different from the motivations that would later emerge to sustain my involvement in the field. This parallels the recovery process itself, where the motivations that sustain recovery are often different than the motivations that spark the beginning of the recovery process. Such motivations are not a determinant of professional effectiveness, but they can exert influences on our work with others. (For example, repeated studies have demonstrated that addiction counselors in recovery are not more or less effective than those who do not bring personal or family recovery experience.) What brought you into this field or is pulling you toward this field? What motivations have sustained your involvement in this field? Like the actor in a new role, regularly checking the source of our motivation is a useful exercise.

With the foundation of personal reflections laid about what brought you and me into the addictions field, it is time for our journey through the modern history of addiction treatment to proceed.

Chapter Two
Back Wards and a Vision of Community
(1965-1971)

Three human service movements crested in the 1960s. The community mental health movement successfully pioneered legislation that led to the closing of hundreds of large state psychiatric hospitals and transferred responsibility for treatment of the mentally ill to a newly emerging network of local, comprehensive community mental health centers. The advocates within what has been christened the "modern alcoholism movement" brought the advances of the 1940s-1960s to passage of a federal law (the "Hughes Act") in 1970 that filtered federal money through the states to local communities for the planning, construction, staffing, operation, and evaluation of community-based alcoholism programs. Advocates within the American Medical Association and the American Bar Association laid similar groundwork for new federal legislation that created a parallel structure to support the development of local treatment for drug addiction.

This was the world of heightened optimism that I entered in the late 1960s. I had arrived in time to witness what had existed before and the new structures that were rising to alter the history of addiction treatment and recovery in America. A valuable exercise is to ponder at what point of history we have entered a field and how our own destiny is shaped by and can in turn positively influence the momentum of that history. I hope the reflections below will stimulate your own thinking about these questions.

Five Minutes that Opened a Career Path

In the summer of 1965 I was working construction and looking forward to my freshman year in college. As fate would have it, I was helping build a new state psychiatric facility—Adolf Meyer Zone Center in Decatur, Illinois. One day that summer, several dignitaries waded through the dust and debris to monitor progress on the facility. One of the psychiatrists, perhaps seeing the novelty of one so young working among far more tenured construction workers, stopped and greeted me. When I explained that I was working to get money for college, he said, "When this building is done, we will be hiring students to work on some of the units. If helping people with mental illness would be of interest, you should consider applying here." I later fell in love with my first few psychology classes and would recall the memory of that invitation. In June of 1967, I was among the first student workers hired (at a robust salary of $255 a month—before deductions!) to work at the newly opened Adolf Meyer Zone Center—yes, the same facility I had helped build.

But this story is not about me; it is about a psychiatrist who took a few moments out of a busy day to greet and encourage a young kid. Those few moments opened a doorway into a world unimaginable to a working class kid nestled in the farm fields of Central Illinois. Joseph Campbell, the famed mythologist, once noted that doors open where only barriers existed when we align ourselves with that which we are meant to do and be. On a summer day in 1965, a door was opened in the span of five minutes that turned into a lifetime journey. In the intervening years, I've tried to take moments to pass on such encouragement to others—a small repayment for that unexpected gift I received on a construction site in 1965.

What blessings have you received that need to be passed on? How might you increase your opportunities for such service? To whom have you yet to say "thank you" for a gift that they knowingly or unknowingly bestowed on you? Perhaps today is the day to express that gratitude.

"One Flew over the Cuckoo's Nest"

The decade of the 1960s was the heyday of de-institutionalization of the mentally ill. Thousands of large, decaying state psychiatric hospitals were systematically dismantled as the care of mental illness shifted from these virtual cities of the insane, some warehousing thousands of highly institutionalized patients, to treatment in the community. My first paid job (student worker / psychiatric technician position) in the field was within the Illinois Department of Mental Health's efforts at de-institutionalization. The lack of alternative care and the conceptualization of alcoholism and drug addiction as superficial symptoms of mental illness had placed a large number of late-stage alcoholics and addicts in the state's psychiatric hospitals. Late-stage alcoholics (many suffering from Korsakoff psychosis,

28

Wernicke syndrome, and other chronic brain syndromes produced by prolonged alcoholism) were warehoused while earlier stage alcoholics and addicts detoxed and provided months-long respites from active addiction. One of my responsibilities was to serve as a member of several teams who traveled from state hospital to state hospital screening patients for potential discharge into the community. That role allowed me to see the last years of how alcoholics and addicts had been treated for decades within state psychiatric hospitals. Here are some vivid images that remain from those visits.

Daily Life on the Wards To say that alcoholics and selected addicts (most addicts were in prisons or jails rather than in state hospitals) were warehoused is not an understatement. State hospitals were larger than many towns, with some literally and figuratively containing thousands of patients. The grey or tan buildings seemed to have the life drained from them. Bland buildings. Bland rooms. Bland clothes. Bland food. Everything was bland except the smells—wards reeking with disinfectant and fouled with the odor of urine, feces, and sweat; and alcoholism units filled with the pungent smell of paraldehyde—the sickening sweet liquid sedative then used to aid detoxification. The extreme and enduring social isolation (often measured in years and decades), the endless nothingness of daily institutional life, and the rarity of anything but the most stereotyped and patronizing interactions between patients and staff slowly elicited its devastating effects. The sustained isolation from the community and institutional drudgery was so complete it left one questioning whether past memories of family, community, work, and play were themselves hallucinations. What I remembered the most from those visits were the eyes of those who had wasted years of their lives in such wards. It was a place that ground down every shred of individuality and personhood of those who entered—patients and staff—and too often left both with beating hearts but dead eyes.

Alcoholics in the state hospitals fell into three groups. Most of those suffering from organic psychoses related to their alcoholism became highly institutionalized and passively lived out their lives, dying within and often being buried on the grounds of the state hospitals. Others, following detoxification and physical renewal, were among the brightest and highest functioning patients and were often recruited to become surrogate staff of the institution. A third group had used their manipulative powers and street smarts to escape outside consequences by entering the state hospital. Members of this group spent most of their

29

time entertaining themselves at the expense of other patients and the staff. Ken Kesey's engaging tale, *One Flew Over the Cuckoo's Nest,* accurately depicts how horribly invasive "treatments" could be used in the power struggle between these alcoholic patients and their psychiatric caregivers. Continued intoxication inside the facility from alcohol and a myriad of pills pilfered from other patients, sexual acting out (with other patients and staff), humiliating pranks, and other challenges to the authority of the staff could and did spawn reactive methods of control, pacification, and retaliation by institutional staff.

Mandatory Sterilization The eugenics movement of the early 20th century set forth the proposition that many of the world's health and social problems were a function of bad breeding. This evolved into proposals to eliminate defective stock from the race through the mechanism of mandatory sterilization laws that targeted the mentally ill, developmentally disabled, and other perceived defectives, including those chronically addicted to alcohol and drugs. While these laws did not have a dramatic effect on men (most men were done conceiving children and many were impotent by the time they were identified as chronic alcoholics), they did affect women as they were more likely to enter state hospitals at an earlier age. A pattern began to develop as I reviewed the medical files of women I was screening at the state hospitals. A high percentage of these women had been surgically sterilized while hospitalized. (Many of the state hospitals I visited were self-contained cities with their own medical infirmary, surgical suite, and morgue.) The source of this anomaly became clear when I ran across file after file that actually named the process: "discharge contingent upon voluntary sterilization." Throughout much of the early and mid-20th century, there was a pervasive philosophy within mental health institutions that alcoholic women—erroneously and stereotypically perceived as oversexed creatures—should be sterilized on therapeutic grounds and on the assumption that in the community they would bear unhealthy children who would, in turn, receive incompetent care and become a burden on society. Such perceptions and practices were deeply rooted in American history.

> Granting the [alcoholic] woman has been given treatment, proper, persistent, and prolonged, without avail, she should be desexualized...It might be curative; it surely would be preventive, and better, by far, unsex the woman, than have her beget a brood tainted with this

30

curse of the world. Dr. Agnes Sparks, *Journal of Inebriety*, 1898.

ECT, Psychosurgery, and Drug Therapies The professional belief that addiction was a symptom of underlying psychiatric illness meant that alcoholics and addicts were subjected to prevailing fads of psychiatric treatment in the first half of the 20th century. The records of those I screened in the 1960s, some with decades-long histories of state hospital admissions, revealed a long history of invasive treatments. Alcoholics were treated with chemo- and electro-convulsive (ECT) therapies on the grounds that their alcoholism was a manifestation of untreated depression. Variations of this rationale were similarly used to justify psychosurgery (primarily prefrontal lobotomies) on alcoholics and opiate addicts. While ECT and psychosurgery were not uncommon in the treatment histories of those I screened, exposure to exotic drug therapies were near universal. These drugs included the sickly sweet-smelling liquid sedative (paraldehyde) used to aid detoxification, barbiturates and amphetamines (commonly used in the mid-20th century as treatments for depression), anti-psychotic medications (particularly Thorazine and Haldol), and LSD.

The episodes I have described were my first realization that grievous injuries can be masked by benevolence. I later learned that harm done in the name of help had a name ("iatrogenic illness") and that the history of addiction treatment in America was filled with such insults. My initial reaction to such invasive and harmful treatments was one of moral outrage, but then it occurred to me that those delivering these insults did so without awareness of the injury they were inflicting and with a perception of themselves as compassionate and competent caregivers. It became clear to me that iatrogenic insults are often invisible to those who perpetrate and witness them, and only become visible through the grace of historical hindsight. That realization led to my resolve to regularly ask myself over a long career two important questions: 1) Are there unforeseen, potentially harmful consequences of this intervention into the life of an individual, family, organization, or community? 2) How will historians of the future judge what I am doing today?

What most confounded me about such "closed cities of the insane," as I then thought of them, was that they were birthed with the noblest of intentions. The vision was to remove the mentally ill from their stressful living environments, or the jails and almshouses to which their care had been delegated (an oft-used euphemism for being *dumped*), and provide them a quiet sanctuary within which their jangled nerves could heal themselves and which, with proper care, they could be returned to wholeness and a life in the community. I left these institutions questioning how such a noble experiment had mutated into something so ghastly. And I also wondered how those who worked within such an institution could no longer see it for its true self—as if day by day the deformed nature of these places had become invisible, the aberrant slowly transformed into the normal. An institution designed as an instrument of rehabilitation had become one through which people were regressed to the subhuman. A culture of care had mutated into a culture of custodial control—more prison than hospital.

What practices of today in the world of addiction treatment do you feel will be judged harshly by historians of the future? What practices in your immediate work environment elicit the most gut-level discomfort within you? Is it time you tried to express your feelings about those practices? How and to whom could this best be communicated? In my later career, I attempted to personally answer such questions in a 2008 paper co-authored with Dr. Herbert Kleber entitled, *Preventing Harm in the Name of Help: A Guide for Addiction Professionals.*

Deinstitutionalization

To dismantle its aging network of state psychiatric hospitals, the State of Illinois built a network of zone centers in the 1960s. These centers served multiple purposes: they offered treatment designed to transition people from state hospitals to the community, they provided emergency care and stabilization to keep people out of the state hospital system, and they served as the base of operation for numerous professionals whose job was to help build mental health services in local communities across the state. The vision was that the zone centers would serve as a temporary transition on the way to treating the mentally ill, the developmentally disabled, and the alcohol and drug dependent within their local communities. If successful, it was theorized that the zone centers would work themselves out of existence.

The zone centers' vision and the realities of what unfolded tell an important story for the uninitiated service worker. It is a story about how a vision can be partially fulfilled at the same time the forces that shape the design and fate of institutions change. The zone centers in Illinois did make significant achievements. They transitioned thousands of patients from the state hospitals to the community, laying the groundwork for the closure of many of the state hospitals. They provided the safety net that kept many individuals out of the state hospital system. And they supported the community organizers who were building community mental health services across the state. But there is another side to this story.

The patients left the state hospitals but much of the money to support their care remained with the institutions and did not transition to community supports. What started out as a focus on the needs of the mentally ill and their families rapidly shifted to needs of those linked to the institutional interests of the state hospitals. The dollars that should have shifted from the state hospitals to community-based services were slowed by the influence of labor unions, cities, and businesses dependent upon the dollars generated by the state hospitals, as well as a host of politicians responsive to those constituencies. While a growing number of people discharged from state hospitals ended up in local communities where services were needed, a large portion of the dollars that could have supported those individuals remained with the state hospital. It was my first lesson about how personal and institutional interests could corrupt systems of care that were theoretically designed to respond to the needs of service consumers. Years later, I would witness the same process unfold with the zone centers. What were supposed to be temporary institutions took on a life of their own via the interests of those who worked within them and who profited from their existence.

As a result of my time working at the zone centers, I learned about the factors that shape the design and operation of service systems. The principle is that service systems set up to meet the needs of service recipients often lose responsiveness to those needs over time. What this means is that we must constantly struggle to keep personal and institutional needs in the background and the needs of clients and families in the foreground. When clients' and families' needs are first, such systems are renewed or dismantled. The greatest stressors I've experienced over my career did not come from contact with clients and families; they arose from battling the conflicting interests and needs of the institutions and clients and families. To serve in this arena, you must be prepared to wage such battles and to recognize when your own interests are getting in the way of serving clients and families. Remaining faithful to that responsibility is a significant challenge.

Professional Pecking Order

The life of most organizations is structured around the delineation of power and responsibility across roles. I kept a daily journal the summer of 1967 to record my first experiences working as a psychiatric technician—the bottom rung of the pecking order in the various units I worked on that summer. It was through this role that I first learned that psychiatric institutions (and service organizations as a whole) had a life of their own. I learned some special lessons working in this role. One lesson I learned was the importance of people who work at the bottom of the organizational hierarchy. I learned that the more power staff held in the institution, the less time they spent relating to the recipients of services. This fact seemed quite a paradox to me and was evident every day. The unit administrators, psychiatrists, psychologists, and social workers spent most of their time with each other and only a few hours or minutes a day interacting with "residents." (As I entered the field, they had just stopped being "patients," although this designation would later return.) In contrast, the nurses, techs, housekeeping staff, and kitchen staff spent most of each shift relating with residents. My most enduring lesson from this time in my career was if you really want to know about people in residential care, ask the people who spend the most time with them—those who work at the bottom of the organizational hierarchy.

Another advantage people in less empowered roles provide is that of clear observation uncluttered by theoretical filters and professional jargon. I once asked a man whose job was to help clean the ward each day what he thought of a particular resident who had been on the ward for the past two months. He responded, "I think he is an asshole"—a term not found in any diagnostic manual but which said a great deal about this resident's character and why his family and community so regularly expelled him. I realized that staff in the least powerful roles had an extensive and sophisticated network of communication about the happenings in the life of the organization. I was amazed at how quickly this network could ferret out the most closely-guarded secrets of the institutional leaders.

As my career advanced, I found that each upward progression tended to further isolate me from the residents and removed me from

34

the informal informational networks of staff having less organizational status. I began to feel "disconnected" and had a sense that I needed to do things that countered these tendencies. As a result, I tried to consciously find ways to sustain contact with people in the earliest days of recovery, and I have actively cultivated relationships with those staff and volunteers at the bottom of the organizational pecking order. So, as an administrator or clinical director, I worked an occasional night shift, did periodic intakes, did regular lectures to clients, periodically sat in on groups, filled in for a sick staff counselor, and, perhaps most importantly, structured time in each day to interact informally with clients and staff. My role was not to lead, but to listen—really listen. Perhaps leading and listening are the same things. What actions could you take to increase your listening opportunities and to remain connected to the frontlines of addiction recovery support?

Early Mentoring

The universe had conspired to bring an extremely bright and energized group of people together in the early years of Adolf Meyer Zone Center, whose vision was nothing short of revolutionizing the treatment of mental illness in the United States. That vision attracted some of the best and brightest psychiatrists, psychologists, social workers, rehab counselors, and psychiatric nurses. This created a learning laboratory that could not have existed in earlier years nor been replicated in later years. As a twenty-something kid, I had arrived at the right place at the right time. My assigned responsibilities were mundane, but I came to work early and left late, seeking every learning opportunity I could find. What is most interesting as I reflect on this period was that, rather than a dominant mentor in my life, I had many mentors in the institution. Everyone seemed open to my questions; everyone was responsive to my requests to be part of various experiences. My work at Adolf Meyer Zone Center was one of the few times in my life when I was mentored by a whole institution. By assertively seeking out learning opportunities, I was able to work on multiple units, visit innumerable psychiatric hospitals and community clinics, work at a camp for people with developmentally disabilities,

35

and participate in training on everything from psychopharmacology to psychodrama.

Long careers have an ebb and flow to them marked by periods of intense refreshment (personal and professional learning) and times of excessive demands in the face of minimal supports. These patterns of receiving and giving need to be recognized and actively managed

As a young professional-to-be, I assumed the rich resources in my early career would continue throughout my professional life. As a result, I took those resources for granted and, at times, failed to avail myself of some opportunities I was sure would come again. They often did not.

One of the regrets I have in my career is not recognizing the preciousness of some of the people around me and not learning more from them when I had the opportunity. I assumed, for example, that the intensity of supervision offered to me in my early career was something that would be forever available as my career progressed, but that was not the case. If I had known that, I would have drawn even deeper from these early supervision experiences. The adage, "He who hesitates is lost" contains a profound lesson. There are times in each of our lives when we hesitate and what we really need to do is just jump.

What people/resources now exist in your environment that you have not fully drawn upon? Who do you need to seek out for more active mentorship? What opportunities do you need to more assertively access?

Hero Mentors

Besides mentors at work, others exerted considerable influence on my young life. These influences presented in two forms— aspirational figures from whom I drew inspiration and people closer to home whom I could closely observe and emulate. For me, the most important of the former included President John Kennedy, Bobby Kennedy, Martin Luther King, Jr., and a legion of young civil rights workers and peace activists. John Kennedy's calls to public service and King's call for racial justice exerted profound influence on my youth and emerging adulthood. In spite of acute awareness of my personal limitations, I vowed to be of service within these traditions. Closer to home, I was able to witness how people pursued such avocations in academic settings (e.g., Eureka College faculty members Dr. Genevieve Langston and Dr. Don Anderson) and community settings (e.g., John Gwynn, Peoria National Association for the Advancement of Colored People [NAACP]). Distant and close associations with such inspirational leaders set examples of how I hoped to live a life of service. The only question was what form such service would take.

What aspirational figures influenced your early and later development?

Chapter Three
Working the Streets (1970-1972)

L andmark legislation was passed in 1970 that laid the foundation of modern community-based addiction treatment, but it would be some years before many communities opened their first addiction treatment programs. Pressure to do so came from three sources: 1) the growing burden alcoholics were placing on jails and hospital emergency rooms, 2) social panic about a rising youthful polydrug experimentation, and 3) fears of heroin-addicted Vietnam veterans returning to the US.

In 1969, I began work in a community that, like most American communities of that era, had no specialized addiction treatment services. This chapter will explore the worlds of addiction and recovery before such resources were widely available.

Vietnam and an Altered Life Path

If a singular coming-of-age issue existed for the men of my generation, it was the Vietnam War. Whether you supported or opposed this war, whether you fought in or escaped the War, it shaped your life in profound ways. I had planned to go straight from college graduation to a PhD program in clinical psychology, but those plans were swept away by the War and my adamant opposition to it. I was convinced the US government was wasting tens of thousands of lives in a war so ill-conceived that it could do nothing but bring needless sorrow and wrenching divisions within the country and the world. I considered several options to resist the war: serving in a non-combatant position, going to jail as an act of civil disobedience against the War, renouncing my American citizenship and leaving family and country forever, or seeking a civilian alternative to military service. That last option occurred in the form of an occupational deferment for my service work in the community. It was as if the whole Bloomington, Illinois community stepped forward to say that the work I was doing could not at that moment be done by others and that the best place for me to serve my country was to continue the service work I was already doing—including my work with addicted veterans. Primarily as a result of the latter, my civilian job was deemed a safety-sensitive alternative to military service.

I have reflected many times on how my life would have been different if I had pursued a PhD in 1969. I loved the life of academia and suspect I would have spent my life there, but the universe had a different plan for me. In some ways, I owe everything I have done in the addictions field to the Vietnam War. Without its diverting influence, it is unlikely I would have ended up in this field. Days into my own isolated recovery, I had no burning desire to help the addicted (I had not yet embraced an addiction recovery identity), but I put myself on a path in which that desire could and would be kindled. And I had a debt to repay for my own survival—both my survival from addiction and my escape from a war that took the lives of so many of my friends. Unbeknownst to me, that debt was about to come due.

I tried to continue school part-time by taking graduate classes in psychology at Illinois State University, but two things thwarted that effort. As the demands of and my love for my work increased, my tolerance for academia diminished. Each day I became more involved in the problems of my community, my classes seemed less and less relevant to the real world. I was not a particularly good sport about this dichotomy. I delighted in challenging my professors with the gap between their theories and the realities I was confronting. (I'm sure my exit from the University provided some of them relief and a cause for celebration.) As work and school demands and related pressures grew, I found myself thinking more about my lost battery pack (methamphetamines). On a day that such preoccupation was particularly intense, I literally walked out of a class and out of the University without looking back. What may have looked like a destructive decision on my part by many close to me turned out to be a wise decision—both for my personal recovery and for my future work in the addictions field. (I do wish I would have taken the time to drop the classes and formally withdraw from the university; not doing that was irresponsible and left a couple of Fs on what was an otherwise stellar academic record.) In the years since, I have met many people who similarly and impulsively left situations from jobs to relationships as a protection against a return to addiction. Such actions exemplify a motto I would later embrace: *recovery by any means necessary*—even when such means may not appear to others as wise choices. In my case, I did not return to school for five years. When I did, I was ready for it and brought stable recovery, greater personal maturity, and a clear understanding of the knowledge and skills I needed to achieve my life goals.

The chain of events that brings each of us into the addictions field varies. Just as the motivations for initiating recovery are different than those that later sustain recovery, the circumstances that keep us in the addictions field differ from those that brought us to this endeavor. The challenge for each of us is to figure out if this is where we are meant to be (at least for right now) and, if so, what precise niche in the field best fits the needs of the field and our unique talents and circumstances. Some are destined to take things from this field to other arenas. Others of us are destined to spend our lives in this field in a role or series of roles that prepare us for the next. I have spent my whole adult life asking what I was meant to do in and for this field. It turned out to be an entire list. I nearly lost my life as a young man, but was given that life back as a precious, undeserved gift. I have since come to believe the adage that to those whom much is given, much is asked.

Everyone has events and circumstances over which we have no control that push us in this or that direction, redirect our life, and close some doors and open others. The trick is to recognize (even belatedly) that a closed door is often not the end of a journey but a detour to a calling and a destiny that awaits us. Some roles must die before a new role can be birthed. Arthur Frank offers some sage advice to guide us through this process: "The Phoenix does not mourn what lies in its ashes; the snake does not mourn its old skin." The trick is to feel and follow what pulls us. It is a mix of our choosing and making ourselves available for destiny to choose us.

What larger events have shaped your life and professional career? What forks in the road have been the most significant in bringing you to this day? Do you have a sense that those events and decisions are preparing you for something? Are you open to that calling? Is it time to shed an old skin and discover what is underneath?

The World of Community Mental Health

The 1960s and early 1970s were the Camelot days of community mental health in the United States. The vision was a clear one: empty the state psychiatric hospitals—a 19th century reform that had evolved into an institution with unfathomable capacities to deform the human spirit. The strategy for emptying the state hospitals involved building community resources to provide sanctuary and support for discharged residents while treating others in the community to avoid such hospitalizations. My initial charge in 1969 was to work with a team of community mental health workers to screen individuals in state hospitals, facilitate their re-entry into local Illinois communities, and help the communities expand mental health services. The work involved multiple tasks: screening patients from my "catchment area" who resided in various state hospitals, arranging for their re-entry into the community, conducting follow-up visits to assure their adjustment, and working with multiple community groups to expand mental health and addiction services.

In the heat of this work, it was hard to realize the profound lesson I was witnessing: the healing power of community connectedness and participation and the danger of inadvertent harm anytime helping professionals isolated people from the community in the name of helping them. I had remarkable teachers who reinforced this lesson. Drs. Lewis Kurke and Matt Parish provided indoctrination in the emerging schools of community psychiatry and community psychology. Matt had worked as a military consultant and discovered the importance of treating what today we call Post-Traumatic Stress Disorder, PTSD, (what was then called "shell shock") by keeping soldiers within their own units when possible and returning wounded soldiers to their units quickly following hospitalization. He explained to me that isolation of people from their natural support systems was often followed by clinical deterioration. He stressed that the only justification for such isolation was when an individual was a threat to that community or when that environment was so pathogenic (illness-inducing) that an alternative community had to be created. It took decades for me to truly understand the healing power of community inclusion.

I worked with Anne Menz and Lem Upchurch, who led a team of mental health workers serving a two-county area of Central Illinois and who applied that emerging philosophy on an hour-to-hour basis. We only rarely saw clients in an office. Our work was conducted wherever the client was, their home, a jail cell, a bar, or a street corner. Hospitalization, even local hospitalization, was the last resort, sometimes needed, but often experienced as a failure on our part. The goals were to support the caretaking abilities of family, friends, and neighbors and engage local institutions from community centers to churches to labor unions in surrounding each client in a web of

41

hospitality and support. Much of this approach was swept away in the wave of biological psychiatry that dominated the 1980s. The same occurred in addiction treatment with the shift from an earlier focus on the community to a focus on expanding inpatient and residential programs. I learned lessons early on about the power of community that would later become the centerpiece of my career.

All advancement is not progress. Change is as likely to represent regression as progression. As you confront significant change in your work environment or in your personal life, try to identify what of greatest value is on the brink of being lost or diminished. As you find situations that need to be changed, you can look to the old as well as the new. Sometimes an old principle applied to new circumstances can generate important breakthroughs.

Alcoholics and Addicts in the Community Mental Health Centers (CMHC)

Legislation was passed in 1963 and 1965 that provided federal funds for the development of comprehensive community mental health centers (CMHC). Each CMHC was expected to develop services for the treatment of alcoholism and drug addiction. Some CMHCs did an excellent job of developing these services, but by the late 1960s growing consensus emerged in the alcoholism and addiction advocacy communities that alcoholics and addicts had not and were not faring well within programs organized under the psychiatric umbrella. The memories of mistreatment of those in the recovery communities of mental health systems were strong—invasive treatments, the contempt in which they were greeted, and dollars that were supposed to support alcoholism services redirected to less stigmatized problems. We needed a specialized, segregated system of care designed for people suffering from addiction. I was hopeful that the system would be based on a set of kinetic ideas that distinguished the addiction field from other service systems for alcoholics and addicts. Those ideas included acceptance of the following premises:

- Severe alcohol and other drug problems constitute a primary disorder rather than a superficial symptom of underlying problems.

42

- The multiple life problems experienced by alcohol and other drug (AOD)-impacted individuals can best be resolved within the framework of recovery initiation and maintenance.
- Many individuals with high problem complexity (biological vulnerability, high severity, co-morbidity) and low "recovery capital" (internal assets, family, and social support) are unable to initiate and sustain stable recovery without professional assistance.
- Professional assistance is best provided by individuals with special knowledge and expertise in facilitating the physical, psychological, socio-cultural, and spiritual journey from addiction to recovery.

Today the field of addiction treatment faces a wave of service integration initiatives that threaten its status as a specialized system of care. The memory of why addiction treatment emerged as a specialized field has been lost, and addiction treatment is getting absorbed into (colonized by?) more powerful systems in its operating environment— the mental health, public health, child welfare, and criminal justice systems. If that colonization is successful, the focus on addiction treatment will be lost and the ability of these systems to support recovery will dissipate. Those unmet needs will, as they have in the past, generate new advocacy efforts, led by recovering people, their families, and visionary professionals. These movements will again seek to rearticulate the kinetic ideas and core clinical technologies that have distinguished the field of addiction treatment.

Community Organizing

My approach to filling gaps in needed services was to first fill the gap myself and then get some existing agency or new service structure to take over that function. The process involved both direct service skills, public education and policy advocacy, and working with existing agencies and community groups to garner the needed resources to take over this service function. For example, I provided 24-hour emergency services at the same time I worked with community groups to organize a crisis center called Providing Access to Help, PATH. When PATH opened, I served as an advisor and trainer for the volunteers, which then freed time to organize other services. The social workers in my network of support—particularly Jo Major, Frank Stark, Jim Galbraith, and Richard Evans—exerted a great influence on my early professional development. I remember long conversations with them about the activist roots of social work and how what I was doing was in the spirit of that tradition. I also remember their sadness that such roots had been abandoned as social workers sought the status and income of more clinically-oriented work. I did not know at the time that thirty years later I would be mourning the same loss of activism within the field of addiction treatment.

In the Heat of the Day

One of my first jobs was to set up systems (crude systems by today's standards) of intervention that would divert people from entering state hospitals into the local services I created to respond to their needs. Since the jails and community hospitals were the first doorway of eventual extrusion from the community, I developed relationships with these institutions via a process of daily rounds and being available 24 hours a day for psychiatric and addiction-related emergencies. Establishing relationships with the hospitals and city jails and intervening in such crises went relatively smooth and were producing exactly the results we hoped for: decreased state hospital admissions and the expansion of community-based services. However, rather than a story of success, this is one of an unquestionable failure for which I take responsibility.

The county jail in McLean County in 1969 was a dungeon-like structure that had been built in the 1800s and looked like it. It was one of the most foreboding and dehumanizing places I had ever encountered. And it was run with an iron fist by a sheriff who looked like his counterpart in the movie, *In the Heat of the Night*. He was my worst nightmare, and I'm sure I fit that same description for him. It was only the interventions of the chief judge and the local states attorney that opened the jail for me to interview prisoners who were in need of treatment services. Such intervention got me in the doors, but only worsened an already deteriorating relationship between myself and the sheriff. To him, I was a hippie communist drug addict masquerading as a social worker—a probable source of drugs getting into his jail and a port of exit for messages from inmates to their lawyers and family members (the latter was true). To me, he was a racist bully who relished the brutality and control he wielded over others. I told anyone who would listen that the jail was a culture of corruption and abuse—a lawsuit waiting to happen. Yeah, it was an old-fashioned, testosterone-driven pissing contest, and neither of us would back down.

The fact is that both of us were wrong in putting our egos before the needs of the community we were pledged to serve. I went to war with him when this was a war I could not win and should not have fought. The casualties of that war were people inside the jail who needed services they were not getting because of the arrogance of two so-called servants of the community. Today I reserve most of the blame for this situation for myself. I should have known better. I should have been mature enough not to get caught up in this struggle for dominance. I should have kept my focus on the service goal rather than my feelings about the sheriff and his jail. Like countertransference gone haywire in a clinical relationship, this was a situation I should have resolved before it escalated out of control or I should have arranged for someone else to organize these desperately needed services. It is a chapter in my early career I would like to forget, but it offers some important lessons.

Each of us will encounter others with whom we must work professionally that at best we do not like and at worst wish we could banish from the planet. The question is whether we take the high road or the low road in our management of those feelings and their consequences. What separates professional from unprofessional, mature from immature, effective from ineffective responses to such feelings are our abilities to rise above such feelings and to remain focused on the needs of our clients and our communities. One of my consultants from this period said it all: "Whether what you say about him (the sheriff) is true or untrue is irrelevant. This is about you and whether you can respond strategically rather than emotionally to your feelings about him. This isn't about who's right; it's about what approach is going to work getting services into that awful place." The consultant was right.

An interesting footnote to this story is that the sheriff and I encountered each other decades later. He had lost his re-election for sheriff much earlier—defeated by a young progressive policeman who brought the sheriff's office and jail into the 20th century. The now former sheriff had received a politically appointed post in a state agency in which I was brought in as an expert trainer. There we were, two old combatants, both wiser and both a bit embarrassed by our past history. I still wouldn't invite him over for dinner, but in this last encounter, we were able to let go of a struggle that had earlier elicited the worst from each of us.

Recall the most negative relationship in your professional career. What does your response to that person tell you about yourself? If you were to encounter another situation similar to this one, how would you handle your role differently in such a relationship?

The Art of Alliances

Notwithstanding the toxic chemistry between the sheriff and I, the work I accomplished in the Bloomington-Normal community between1969-1971 would not have been possible without innumerable people. To do my job effectively, I needed access to people at the lowest points in their lives, and I needed informal resources at a time few formal resources were available for alcoholics and addicts. A small band of physicians, most notably Dr. Seymour Goldberg and Dr. Ed Livingston, provided me access to local hospitals and outpatient medical treatment for those I would refer. Paul Welch and Hal Jennings in the states attorney's office and two local police chiefs provided access to the city jails. Ed Beveridge and Ken Simmons provided access to the adult and juvenile probation departments. Key judges opened the doors for me to provide expert testimony and link defendants to treatment— before I had gone back to school and acquired the educational credentials that would normally allow such a role. And the list continues of those who provided access to their organizations. I found and forged alliances with people of good will who were able to transcend prevailing attitudes and bend rules to get help for those who needed it. Those informal relationships I forged would later go out of style and be replaced with formal interagency agreements, but I have never forgotten the importance and power of those personal alliances.

Each of those alliances required a period of testing. What I found most important was to get to know each person personally, commit to only what I knew I could deliver, keep them informed, let them share in the successes, and commiserate together on the failures. In the end, all that we do boils down to the quality of relationships we can forge—both with those we serve and with the allies we can mobilize on their behalf. With every success, we build social and professional credit in the community and eventually are rewarded with a status that no educational institution or professional credentialing body can grant. To be vetted by the community and deemed a healer is the highest compliment one can receive. Are there needed alliances you could form that would help you achieve or maintain such a status?

A Different Kind of Hustle

There can be a shadow side to this art of forging professional alliances and mobilizing a local community. It is easy to pass from establishing relationships based on shared or complementary goals to acts of deception and manipulation. There was a definite period in which I drifted into the latter—where I saw myself "hustling" for a good cause, but hustling none the less. There was a period when I was willing to do anything and be anything to move progress forward on the services I was trying to create in the communities I served. The hustling skills one acquires in active addiction can be recast in new roles, but such masquerades and manipulations are best shed for more authentic and lasting collaborations. It took some time for me to learn that lesson. The manipulative psychopath masquerading as a healer is still at heart a psychopath. Such qualities must be shed in both recovery and in authentic community service.

Becoming a "Streetworker"

My work as a streetworker evolved out of my jail and hospital rounds and the emergencies I was responding to. Following up on people with such chaotic lives was not easy. Even finding them was not easy. Two things happened in tandem. First, as I followed up more and more clients, I became a known quantity within the local drug and street cultures and began to meet many others who were in need of psychiatric and addiction counseling services. Second, it became apparent to me that the people I was seeing in crisis were at late stages of problem development, and that much could have been done for them if I could have intervened in their lives at an earlier point. I proposed developing a formal streetwork program in which I could work with those individuals who were highest risk for addiction-related psychiatric hospitalization or incarceration. I argued for what I called the "Willie Sutton Principle." (Willie Sutton was a famous bank robber who, when asked why he robbed banks, responded, "Because that's where the money is.") I argued that if we were really serious about doing something about addiction, we should take services to the very heart of local drug cultures.

My supervisor at the Illinois Department of Mental Health in Bloomington, Illinois, Anne Menz, agreed to experiment with such a model with the proviso that I keep her and myself "out of the newspapers and out of jail." Within months, I was making daily rounds at bars, pool halls, rescue missions, and houses where heavy alcohol and drug users congregated, including "after hours" joints and what were then delicately described as "houses of ill-repute." My goals were clear: identify people with alcohol and other drug problems who were in need of services, motivate them to seek help, open doors for them to the formal service system, provide stopgap services where such services were not available, monitor individuals' responses during and following delivery of those services, and, when necessary, re-intervene and do it all over again. I also took responsibility for organizing services that were needed but not available.

"Daily rounds" were about establishing myself as someone who could be trusted and someone with connections to resources, e.g., access to lawyers, doctors, hospitals, "VD clinics," cheap housing, and other resources. I floated through the community each day doing a kind of triage to locate those individual who were in most desperate need of help, while building relationships with others that would help them get their lives together before becoming a casualty. I also tried to enlist the support of the healthiest to care for the sickest—a process that ended with some returning to school and building distinguished careers in the helping professions. A level of untapped service exists within all communities that can be activated only by invitation. When I asked, many responded. This network of indigenous helpers would let me know when someone needed my immediate attention (e.g., "You better check on Jerry today; he's getting pretty ripe."), visit someone who needed support but whom I couldn't get in the hospital, put someone up for a few days, or pass on information about adulterated drugs that were generating adverse reactions. It was an incredible network that could move information through a community in a few hours and offer support in a world few formal service providers were aware of, cared about, or could enter. This work took me deep into the subterranean subcultures that exist invisibly in most communities.

How could you enhance your knowledge of such subcultures within your own community? What indigenous resources do you need to use more frequently in your work with those you serve?

Life on Skid Row

In the mid-20th century, most communities of any size had what was commonly known as a "Skid Row" area. Before these areas were rooted out by urban renewal and redevelopment, they were occupied by a mixture of the poor, the homeless, the transient, the mentally ill, and those in the latest stages of addiction. These were "my people"—one of my primary constituents as a streetworker. They lived on streets dotted with warehouses, empty storefronts, cheap hotels whose hallways stank of urine and worse, down-and-out bars, package liquor stores that sold poisons in their most concentrated forms, soup kitchens, rescue missions, day labor offices, pawn shops, pool halls, and an assortment of shelters and social service agencies. The inhabitants of "the Row" cycled from these streets to the city drunk tanks to the county jails (where they were sentenced a portion of each year for chronic public intoxication and related charges) and to the hospital emergency rooms (when they could get into them). They lived off the proceeds of petty crime, social security disability checks, and handouts. It was a world that seemed to have no exit doors. My job was to build relationships inside this world and then help create portals of egress.

The despair that pervaded the streets of Skid Row masked other more subtle dimensions of daily life there. Agencies saw the despair in bold relief because they always encountered the Skid Row alcoholic at a point of real or feigned crisis. But a closer look at life on the Row revealed a kind of brotherhood/sisterhood of the damned—relationships that were based on mutuality (even if the most visible evidence of that was the passed bottle), a bawdy sense of humor, and tales of past triumphs and pipe dreams that one could still pretend were possible. Men and women alienated from nearly every mainstream institution found membership in this society of the ostracized. I had two primary jobs in this world: 1) intervening with the new arrivals and getting them reconnected to life outside the Row before the Row became their whole world, and 2) rescuing those imbedded within the Row when they were in crisis and using such crises as opportunities for access to acute medical and psychiatric care and, on occasion, to sources of recovery initiation and maintenance.

The World of the Righteous Dope Fiend

The secrecy, isolation, and efficiency of my own addiction had left me ill-prepared for the elaborate lifestyle and drug culture in which heroin use had become nested in most American cities. I began building relationships within this culture one addict at a time—helping one arrange a visit with her children, visiting one recovering from an overdose in an emergency room, finding one a clinic to treat his gonorrhea, helping another find housing, and on and on. Following up every contact brought me in touch with the cartography of addiction— the shooting galleries, dope-copping corners, the bars and after hours clubs, the pool halls, the houses of prostitution, the dealers, the fences, and the invisible networks that were part of a subterranean subculture with its own language, values, rituals, and status hierarchy.

Popular cultural stereotypes of that time suggested that addiction, particularly heroin addiction, was an escape from reality—a chemical shelter for those ill-equipped to live in the real world. I learned that nothing could be further from the truth. There are few careers with more rigorous and unceasing demands than heroin addiction. My past addiction to pharmaceuticals provided me no status in this culture and shouldn't have. Maintaining my addiction required little effort and skill compared to that required to sustain heroin addiction. The demands of that lifestyle were revealed to me in a curious incident.

I had begun referring a large number of heroin addicts to a few psychiatrists who had agreed to serve as my backup in the treatment of addiction. I opened these doctors to a side of their community they had never seen. One pointedly asked me, "Where do you find these people?" In response, I took him for a brief drive through the neighborhoods where heroin use was most concentrated. When I described the process of working the streets to find and help addicts, he looked out the window of my car and asked, "But how do you know who to talk to? Everyone out here looks like they need help." It was an interesting question that I hadn't even asked myself. After reflecting on it, I responded, "I look for people who are in a hurry."

In the particular streets through which we were traversing, few people moved with speed and purpose. The pace was not one of relaxation, but timeless despair and hopelessness. In this world, drug addicts were notable for their bursts of manic activity. They had places to go and things to do—all generated by the demands of a habit that offered no holidays or vacation days. The daily lifestyle of many addicts was an exhausting one, fraught with innumerable demands, challenges, threats, and the ultimate daily reward: Junk. I came to respect the rigor of the lifestyle and the skills required to sustain it. In fact, an interesting pecking order pervaded this culture—from the "gutter hype" who was disdained by most addicts for his or her depravity to the "righteous dope fiend" whose oft-flashed money roll, stylized dress, smooth speech, and daily life was a carefully crafted and highly admired art form. The pecking order also was one based on knowledge, skills, and achievement within the illicit drug markets and related underground economies.

Jackie Casanave did a fascinating study of the early Illinois Drug Abuse Program (IDAP)–one of the first modern programs in the country that recruited recovering addicts into service and management positions in the growing network of treatment clinics. What she found was that the placement of recovering addicts in IDAP's organizational chart reflected their previous positions within Chicago's illicit drug market. It seems that those who had functioned as competent middle managers in the drug culture also performed that role well in IDAP. My point here— and a major early discovery for me—is that there are skills and orientations buried within the addiction experience that can be utilized as building blocks of recovery. To see the 30- or 45-year old heroin addict who has never had a legitimate job as having no assets is a gross mistake on our part. Those assets exist; our job is to find them, acknowledge them, and reframe them to support recovery. When a client without a formal work history reports to you that he has "an extensive background in sales," listen to him!

I slowly came to appreciate that many people were as addicted to the culture of addiction and the needs they got met there as they were to the drugs that were the centerpiece of that culture. It became clear that recovery was more than severing a person-drug relationship. It was often a process of disengaging a person from a culture that had met a broad spectrum of their needs and, in the process, transformed their character and identity. Those discoveries were the beginnings of a book I would write 20 years later on how to facilitate the journey from the culture of addiction to the culture of recovery.

What's in a Name?

Everyone on the streets had a street name and everyone knew "Spike"—a moniker derived from his affection for needles. I met Spike within days of beginning my role as a streetworker. Once we got past the usual street paranoia, Spike would alternately be a major consumer of my services and a self-appointed assistant. Once he figured out what I was doing, he developed the hope that, if he could clean himself up, perhaps he could one day work with other addicts as a streetworker—a position he once told me might be the only career he was qualified to perform. Unfortunately, by the time he did finally get clean, streetwork had gone out of fashion. I liked Spike a lot and anguished over the self-destruct mechanism buried so deeply within him. His intelligence and verbal skills provided hours of engaging conversation on every imaginable topic and his good heart provided a flowing pipeline of referrals.

Spike taught me many things during his addiction years, but one of the most important was the prophetic power of a single word. Spike's migration from self-destruction to sobriety experiments to stable recovery spanned years, and I was able to witness one of his turning points. Spike tracked me down one day to share a kind of epiphany that he had experienced a few hours before during one of his many dark nights of the soul. It was hard to sort through his manic, speed-fueled speech but the gist of his message was that he had been "Spike" all his life even before he took on the street name. His new insight was that his name was a metaphor for being born to destroy himself.

What he had confronted was the contradiction of how he could continue to be "Spike" when he was finally trying to, in his words, "get his shit together." His dilemma was one of how to shed a long-held damaged identity and forge a new healthier one. He had reached a point where he could no longer strive for a future with a name that chained him to his past and that seemed to define his destiny. What he told me was, as of that day, he was no longer "Spike"—the only name I and others knew him by. In the days that followed, he re-introduced himself with the admonition that he would no longer respond to his old name. I knew in that act that he would recover.

The man who used to be Spike never entered professional service work. His was not the kind of spirit that could be contained by a job description or dress code. The profane expletives could never be erased from his vocabulary. His developing passion to respond to the wounds of others was so genuine and so direct that he could have never been constrained by any set of policies or procedures. But he became an incredible folk healer (sponsor) who brought rough bikers and businessmen alike through their early days of recovery. I'm grateful to him for giving me my first lesson about the power of language—the power of a single word whose embrace or rejection can define one's destiny. In the years that followed, I spent considerable time reflecting on the power of words to wound and to heal.

Street Safety

I was often asked, "Isn't it dangerous doing what you're doing?" The answer was "yes" and "no," and it changed over time. My streetwork brought me into different worlds. The "junkie world" of the 1960s in the communities where I worked was a predatory one, but one in which status came from slickness rather than brutality. In the world of the "righteous dope fiend," committing an act of violence was seen as a sign of incompetence and an indication of one's lack of cool. It was also a world of bargaining chips. My status as a potential helper—a person to call in crisis, a person who could open doors of hospitals, visit you in jail and carry messages to family members and lawyers—provided a shield of safety in what might have otherwise been an unsafe environment. The young polydrug subculture was safer, but it took much testing to convince the hard-core elements of this culture that I was not a "narc" or any other threat to their existence. That task took time and consistent service presence.

My most serious encounters with threats of violence occurred in the "speed freak" days of 1971-1972. That was the first time I encountered armed, paranoid people experiencing stimulant psychosis. My intimate personal knowledge of stimulants and my pre-existing relationship with these individuals helped lower my feelings of threat and get many of them desperately needed help.

My work regularly took me into all of the public housing projects in my community, but once I was known within those smaller, self-contained communities, I had few safety concerns in my work there. But some environments like the down and out bars and after hours joints and "flop houses" required caution. The danger was sometimes just a matter of timing and location. I had been to a particular house many times to visit two individuals who had been discharged from state psychiatric hospitals. My job was to offer what support I could to keep

53

them from being re-hospitalized. Recovery for them at that moment was too far away to even dream of. The house was always filled with an assortment of the most exotic characters, including an interracial gay couple who were always fighting each other during bouts of intoxication. I offered what I could to those living in and passing through this home. One day on my regular rounds, I received a message at a pool hall to stop by this residence as soon as I could. Apparently trouble of some sort was brewing. When I pulled up to the house, police cars were just arriving and one of the men was lying in the front yard with a hole in his chest from a .45 caliber pistol as a result of a fit of jealous rage. Only minutes had separated me from being in the middle of this altercation—only minutes from possibly saving a life or putting my own in harm's way. Sometimes, it's just about the seconds, the place, and the luck—good and bad.

The media link between illicit drugs and violence at the user level has been long overplayed. The presence of alcohol in the environments I entered was always a signal of a greater threat of violence than the presence of other drugs. Several things worked to protect me. First, I knew most of the bartenders well through work with some of their customers and through getting help for some of their own friends and family members. Second, I had helped some scary people through my interventions in the jails and hospital emergency rooms and these past debts sometimes protected me when threats arose from others within the bars and dives I regularly frequented as part of my outreach rounds. Today's cell phone technology and practice of working high risk areas in teams has enhanced personal safety, but there is no substitute for knowing the underbelly of a community and having relationships with those who live and work there.

In my first months as a streetworker, I interviewed a man in jail who under other circumstances would have terrified me, given his intimidating physical presence and his long history of brutality. The day I first met him, he was withdrawing from heroin and I was able to talk the county physician into medicating him until he could be bailed out of jail. At his release, I talked to him about treatment options and gave him my contact info, but I didn't expect or receive any calls in the following days. A few weeks later, I was called to a client emergency in a public housing project that I was visiting at night for the first time. With nothing but the unit number in hand, I walked on that warm evening toward my destination past people sitting in chairs clustered outside their front doors. The silent eyes marking my progress were interrupted by four young men approaching me on the sidewalk who introduced themselves via the alpha leader with words projected for all to hear, "Mothaf***a, what'ya doing here?" Before I could respond, I heard challenging words from someone approaching from behind me: "He's my motherf***er! You sissies got a problem with that?" Those words from the man I had helped in jail elicited rapid apologies and my blessing to enter this community.

In the years of service in that housing project that followed, I never experienced another threat to my safety and came to be warmly welcomed during my frequent visits. Interestingly, those who first confronted me always seemed to go out of their way to offer a special welcome and even became my protectors, I'm sure all the while wondering the source of my connection to the man they and so many others justifiably feared. You work your way into a community one relationship at a time, but some incidents can bestow instant and sustained credibility. Some would suggest these are God's gifts to those trying to do His work; others might argue for the luck of fools.

There is one additional and important chapter in my rescue story above. I continued to encounter my rescuer and he much later called for help to arrange entry into a methadone program. But what is significant is that our relationship changed after he came to my defense. He was not comfortable in the helpee role but was able to start a relationship with me once our relationship had been put on an equal footing by him helping me. A few years later, sociologist, Frank Riessman would write about the "helper principle"—that those helping benefited from the helping process—and 30 years later an extensive body of scientific evidence would emerge on the therapeutic effects of helping in groups such as AA. Sometime we help most by encouraging people out of the helpee role and into the helper role. Historically, letting those we serve help us would be considered a boundary violation and a breach of professional ethics. Do you think there are circumstances in which that position needs to be re-evaluated?

Street Culture

A new drug culture was rising in the 1960s. Incorporating elements of the '50s' "beat culture," it began with a celebration of marijuana and hallucinogens (washed down with a new menu of pop wines). This culture soon began to generate casualties from adverse

55

drug reactions, and I found myself quickly extending my work with heroin addicts to these new polydrug casualties. I built relationships in this world like I had done in the heroin culture—through contacts in jails and hospitals. As I became known inside this polydrug culture, I became a link between the "freak"/"head" and "straight" institutions. Over time, I began to make daily rounds in this culture moving from house to house—what the newspapers were calling "communes," and through regular afternoon stops at head shops (filled with smoking paraphernalia, dope-themed books and magazines, black lights and posters, and the obligatory incense, candles, clothing, and jewelry) and evening rounds at newly opening dance clubs.

Each of the houses I visited—some 25-30 per week—had its own character. Some were devoted solely to drugs, sex, and Rock n' Roll. Others were centers of new left politics, fringe religions, mystical cults, or local community activism. The doped "hippie" image masked the fact that many of those living there were drowning in alcohol. Many marginal people were drawn to these countercultural institutions. As one of my clients once disclosed, "I was a 'freak' long before I became one; when people started calling themselves 'freaks', I knew I'd found my home." Part of my job was to link the weakest and strongest within these cultures and serve as a safety net when the natural supports within those cultures were insufficient to sustain their most fragile members.

On a typical day of rounds, I would dispense information on adulterated or mis-dosed drugs that were creating "bad trips," pick up tips on people who were in need of help, link one person to the "VD Clinic" and another to a needed job, admit a person to a local hospital for detox or treatment of acute psychosis, visit others in a hospital room or jail cell, chastise one dealer for their "bad drugs," and simply greet many others. Much of my time was spent listening, participating in the political and cultural "raps" of the day, and offering encouragement to people to do something positive with their lives. I saw myself as a kind of safety net for these loosely defined street cultures. My goal each day was to interact widely within these cultures, leaving those I had touched feeling better as a result of my presence. I was glad to see each of them. I was interested in their lives. I spent most of my time questioning, listening, and encouraging. That posture created a foundation of respect and trust so I could offer help when it was needed.

One of the places I regularly frequented was a music/dance club called the Red Lion. It was middle ground for the "dopers" and "juicers" and a central gathering place for many of the people I had seen or would

56

see in the local hospitals and jails. The bouncers knew my role, waived the cover charge for my nightly entry, and often cued me at the door that I needed to talk to this person or that person (e.g., "Man, you better talk to Marcy; she's really f***ed up tonight.") The Red Lion was later closed and remodeled to house the local mental health center—a move many community members considered an ironic and appropriate transition.

Seeing people in their natural drug-using environments offered insights never available in the counseling office. Like the world of the righteous dope fiend, this culture drew people because it offered something they could not get elsewhere. I came to understand that you could not disengage people from a drug culture unless you could offer entrance into an alternative culture capable of meeting the same needs met in the drug culture. That insight was crucial to my thinking about cultures of recovery and their role in the long-term recovery process.

What cultures are your clients enmeshed within? What needs get met within those cultures? What cultural alternatives do you have to offer those clients?

A Day/Night in the Life of a Streetworker

I was paid the huge salary of $655 a month before taxes for working as a streetworker nearly around-the-clock during those years. Such a lifestyle was possible and enjoyable because I was single and exhilarated by the work.

A typical day for me began with morning rounds at jails and local hospitals to visit with the previous night's casualties. Interviewing people in these institutions and conducting follow-up visits upon their discharge was a remarkably effective intervention and an excellent way to build relationships within the culture of addiction. Since few local addiction treatment services existed, part of my role was serving as a linkage to such services outside the community. So, some of my daily routine was disrupted by transporting people to the VA's alcoholism unit (a two-hour drive), the state hospital alcoholism unit (a two-hour drive), or to a therapeutic community in Chicago (a three-hour drive). Those rides provided a decompression chamber where I could get to know people when they were at their most vulnerable. Such opportunities cemented relationships with difficult-to-engage individuals and created a foundation that allowed me to continue to serve them in the months and years following their return from treatment.

After completing early morning jail and hospital rounds, I made "street rounds"—walking a beat visiting bars, pool halls, flop houses, welfare hotels, houses of prostitution, and other subterranean institutions on a regular schedule to check for or leave messages for people who had no permanent locations. The consistency of contact and positive regard I expressed to the gatekeepers and others who occupied these worlds was an art form that is difficult to describe. And my contact with some of these institutions provoked questions I explored later in my career. For example, my daily rounds on Front Street included stops at the Commercial Hotel and the Hamilton Hotel. These two hotels contained such a high concentration of addicted and mentally ill men and women and those on their way to bearing such wounds that I could have spent whole days just serving those who resided there. I sometimes whimsically wondered whether the community should support a service office within these hotels. I wish now I had turned that whimsical thought into a reality, but that type of outreach was rare in those days and the idea would have seemed a strange one to those seeking to professionalize and beautify human service offices.

Finishing street rounds by late morning, I worked out of my Bloomington, Illinois office for a few hours—responding to phone messages, brokering resources by phone, and attending clinical supervision meetings and meetings with other agency representatives. By mid-afternoon, I usually spent a few hours doing follow-up visits on individuals whom I was working with more intensely.

During the late afternoon and evenings, I made rounds at the earlier described "communes" and "drug houses," bars and dance clubs, and the coffee shops where AA members frequently gathered after meetings. The long evenings usually occurred three to four times a week. Emergencies could be interspersed anywhere during that daily schedule, with most, as might be expected, occurring at night and on weekends.

In retrospect, I was most effective in this work when few people in the mainstream and professional communities knew about what I was doing. As word got out about the role I was performing, I spent more time talking about it and less time doing it—a common occupational hazard among the most dynamic streetworkers of that period. The media attention my work garnered brought kudos to the institutions I worked for but actually worked against my own effectiveness.

58

Beyond Boundaries of Competence

As I became more engaged with local cultures of addiction, I was frequently called upon to intervene in medical as well as emotional crises—from drug emergencies to threatened suicides. The former illustrate the challenges faced in trying to fulfill a newly emerging role that had yet to be clearly defined and whose limits remained uncharted. The street climate in those days was one of chronic paranoia—a distrust of mainstream institutions that was often well-deserved because of the contempt and injury that could be inflicted on the addicted by those claiming the title of public servants. It was a climate, for example, in which hospital emergency rooms could and did deny services to addicts or simply called the police to remove what they saw as human refuse from their medical facility. In this climate, I was called upon when drug-related medical emergencies arose—ranging from an overdose, a needle abscess, jaundice from hepatitis, and a host of other health problems. What I provided at the most basic level was what I came to think of as *safe passage*—reducing the risks of service denial and arrest, increasing access to services, and decreasing the contempt one could encounter within such service experiences. By building relationship capital with physicians and hospitals, I could use that capital to assure admission and a higher quality of care than would have otherwise been available. The real dilemma came when people in acute medical distress refused to seek mainstream medical care.

Some emergency calls I responded to were ill-defined—the caller's paranoia precluded sharing details over the phone. So I often encountered an individual in acute drug intoxication who was in extreme distress but refused to go to the emergency room. Some of these situations could be and were handled without immediate professional medical care, but my limited medical knowledge at that point in my life often left me as distressed as the person in crisis, particularly when the refusal to see a doctor or call a rescue squad was adamant. More than once, I spent the night comforting someone through such a crisis, but more often I was able to convince others present that immediate medical care was the only way to avoid the threat of death. It is the former situations that today still trouble me as I look back on them. Who was I to make such calls that went so far beyond the boundaries of my education, training, and experience? I never had anyone die in such circumstances, but that possibility was present in such crises. Today, I

59

would handle such situations differently and bring a more enlightened knowledge and skill set. But the hindsight of 50 years was not available to me in the early days of my outreach work. I was, however, fortunate to have physicians I could call to walk me through some of those decisions.

The ultimate professional mandate is to practice within the boundaries of our education, training, and experience, but in the pre-professional days within any role, those boundaries are not yet drawn. In such circumstances, one's commitment to help can lead to the unintended infliction of harm. Are you currently working in any undefined territory? Pioneers enter such territory when there are no alternatives, but it is best to have some comrades with you. Find shadow consultants to contract with to support you in such situations.

Rock Festival Medicine

The "happening" known as "Woodstock," was more an evolving movement than a historical moment. What is often portrayed as a singular and transforming moment within the youth culture of the 1960s and early 1970s was actually part of hundreds of large "rock festivals" during this period—including McLean County's own Kickapoo Creek Festival in 1970. Thousands of people (many of whom had little prior experience with drugs) gathered in locations far from medical facilities and usually undersupplied with food, water, and sufficient sanitation. Under such circumstances, festivals could spell trouble, particularly for attendees intoxicated on high dosages of multiple drugs. Those circumstances led to a unique innovation: teams of physicians, nurses, paramedics, and folk healers (individuals trained in the psychological management of acute drug intoxication) who staffed the medical tents of the rock festival circuit. Because of my experiences as a streetworker responding to adverse drug reactions, I was invited into this world of rock medicine and had the opportunity to work in the medical tents at a number of large rock festivals in the early 1970s. (Dr. David Smith and his colleagues at Haight Ashbury Free Clinic in San Francisco developed "rock medicine" as a medical specialty that continues to the present.)

Work in the world of rock festival medicine provided a unique window into the rapid evolution of the youth drug culture during this period. In the span of three years, we went from mostly treating cut feet, sunburn, bee stings, poison ivy, dehydration, and a small number of drug reactions to treating thousands of adverse reactions to hallucinogens. Later, we were confronted with opiate overdoses, alcohol and barbiturate overdoses, the delivery of babies, as well as the treatment of acute trauma, including gunshot and stab wounds. When the latter arrived, it was a symbolic announcement that a youth culture brimming with optimism was burning itself out. The question of what, if anything, might rise from the ashes of this collapse took years to answer, but there were immediate lessons from the evolution of these events that could help others and provide much food for later thought.

First, adverse drug reactions were increasing in communities across the country and what we had learned in the rock festival medical tents could benefit those communities. At the behest of the Illinois Youth Network Council, I collaborated with Len Unterberger and Eric Rogue to write a manual on the management of adverse drug reactions. That manual was my first professional publication and my first realization that I could serve the larger field through reflection and writing. My role as a writer in the addictions field had begun—a role I had no way of suspecting would one day surpass all others.

Second, the complex relationships between person, drug, and environment were never more evident than at these festivals. Drug emergencies were sometimes clearly a product of the drug—a synergy of excessive dosage, adulteration, and shifting methods of administration. Other emergencies brought on by drug intoxication were clearly a product of pre-existing emotional wounds and psychiatric illnesses. And I recall incidents that clearly revealed the power environment could exert on drug experiences. At one Midwest festival, a number of neophyte drug users wandered by the medical tents to let us know how wonderful certain drugs were. At this particular festival, the attributes of a particular brand of marijuana being widely sold under the name "Vietnamese Black" were being greatly extolled. This product turned out to be little more than horse manure and oregano, but its lack of tetrahydrocannabinol (THC) did not lower its powerful placebo effects within the intoxicating milieu of the rock festival. Particularly striking were reports from some young users that it was the best marijuana they had ever smoked. This was a powerful lesson that the pull of any drug (or alleged drug) involves symbolic meanings that far transcend its pharmacological properties.

Jail Rounds

As earlier noted, part of my job in 1969-1971 was to keep the alcoholics and addicts in my community from entering the state's psychiatric hospitals where they risked floundering for years and becoming institutionalized. In hopes of avoiding such fates, I provided emergency services to the jails and local hospital emergency rooms—the points at which people were often shipped to the state hospitals, and I also developed local service alternatives to state hospital care. The front lines of this work involved being on call for emergencies and making daily rounds at the local jails and hospitals. That work provided a window of perception into how communities responded to alcohol and other drug problems in the days before detoxification centers and addiction treatment programs were opened.

In the mid-20th century, it was hard for an alcoholic/addict to get into a hospital and easy to get into a jail cell. What made hospital admission difficult were two things. First, many hospitals at that time had by-laws that precluded the admission of people of morally questionable character. Such restrictions prevented admitting anyone with a primary diagnosis of alcoholism or drug addiction. The second obstacle lay in the attitudes of physicians and nurses—most of whom had seen alcoholics and addicts at their worst, but had no experience with people in long-term recovery. These twin barriers required subterfuge in finding physicians who would help me "bootleg" an admission behind an acute medical problem or behind some vague psychiatric diagnosis.

Two different circumstances made jail a common experience for those addicted. The first was the practice of repeatedly arresting alcoholics for public intoxication and then turning them into trustees once they were sober. Temporarily sobered alcoholics were a source of free labor for county jails throughout the country. It took only serial sentences ranging from 30 days to a year to assure this labor supply. A second quirk was the presence of "loitering addict" laws that made it illegal for known addicts to associate with each other in public and, of course, there was the sheer volume and array of petty crimes required to sustain heroin addiction during those years.

The "drunk tank" in the city jails and the presence of alcoholics and addicts in the county jails and work farms provided temporary reprieves in addiction careers of this era, but experiences within these institutions hastened the development of one's self-transformation from a human being to a social outcast. Worse was the fact that many alcoholics and addicts died inside these institutions. My job in making jail rounds was to throw a life raft to men and women who were drowning of hopelessness inside these wretched places. But as I would come to learn, hope can also be a dangerous intoxicant.

Commitment from a Hanging Cell

Early in my rounds at the jails, I met a man who was on the brink of losing everything to his drinking. Jim's family had left him, he had lost his job, and the spirals of drinking, sickness, remorse, more drinking, and drunkenness escalated in spite of repeated promises to those who had not yet given up on him. On successive interviews in the local police department's "drunk tank"—a sparse eight-foot square cell with nothing but a built-in steel bunk and urinal, I spoke with him about his life and the prospects of his recovery. My discussions with him at the jail and at the cheap hotel where he was staying elicited the conclusion that staying sober by his own resolve had failed and would likely continue to fail. If it had been five years later, I would have admitted him to treatment, but no local treatment resources existed then, only a small number of AA meetings.

The linkage to AA was easily made and Jim began his first serious effort at sobriety. After a few weeks of struggle getting himself fully sober (I could not get a physician or hospital to admit him for detox), Jim enmeshed himself in AA and within two months had been invited to move back in with his family and had physically rehabilitated himself enough to plan his return to construction work. Things looked promising for Jim and his family until Christmas week.

On Christmas Eve, Jim's feelings about what he had done to his family, his financial dependence on his wife, his lack of presents for his wife and children reached an unbearable point. Jim exited his home to a neighborhood where a passed bottle awaited him, and six hours later he was arrested once again for public intoxication. Early the next morning, I received a call from the desk sergeant at the police department stating that he needed me to come down to the station. When I arrived I was told that Jim had hung himself in his jail cell during the night. Seeing Jim's body in that cell and talking with his wife that day was the lowest emotional point of my young career, but that low point was a catalyst for all that was to come in the years ahead.

When I stared at Jim's body, I was enraged that his last hours were spent in a place reeking with such despair. I felt overwhelmed by the paucity of resources available to me to help Jim and his family. I was wounded by my own sense of futility and ineptness. I didn't know at the time that this darkest moment of my young career would be one of the most important. In the months before first meeting Jim, I had met others whose lives were devastated or ended by addiction. Through these encounters came a growing sense that I was saved from my own addiction for some yet-to-be-revealed purpose. I had begun to wonder if perhaps I was destined to play a role in helping other addicted people who brought far fewer resources to their recovery efforts. As I turned from Jim's body and walked out of the jail cell that morning, I vowed to use my life to help end the days of the "drunk tanks" and to spend my life creating resources for widening the doorways of addiction recovery. On the worst day of my young professional life, what was once a vague sense of calling had now come into sharp focus. There would be other bright and dark days in the future that would provide opportunities to recommit myself to that mission.

Jim's fate was not unique. Suicides by alcoholics and addicts while incarcerated were the bane of city and county jails in the early to mid-20th century and added momentum to the drive for decriminalization of public intoxication. What I didn't know at the time was that others were making vows similar to mine all across the country and that our collective commitments would stir the American conscience and lead to the banishment of the "drunk tank" and the creation of community-based detoxification and treatment programs. But those resources did not arrive in time for Jim and his family and many like them.

The lessons in this story are numerous, including the tragedy of placing desperately sick people in systems of control and punishment. For those of us on the front lines of addiction treatment, it reinforces the deadly seriousness of our work. We can never forget that recovery and addiction are life and death issues where the scales can be tipped by what we individually and collectively do or fail to do. In spite of our best efforts, some will die, and we must find ways to rise above such losses and transform our pain into a positive force for personal and social change. I took one other lesson from Jim's death: The need to avoid raising hope for recovery too quickly when inadequate resources exist to support that hope. More bodies have hung in jail from the suddenly crashing hope of a failed sobriety effort than the slow accumulation of pain from addiction. We must be careful in stimulating hope where insufficient resources exist to help people reap the harvest of that hope.

Addicts, Doctors, and Hospitals

During my early work with alcoholics and addicts in the jails and on the streets, one of the most critical backup resources I needed was medical care. I needed physicians who could treat needle abscesses, serum hepatitis, venereal disease, and a host of alcohol-related medical disorders. I needed hospitals that would admit alcoholics and addicts for detoxification and treatment of everything from toxic psychosis to acute trauma. (Most alcoholics I was identifying were in late stages of addiction where the interaction of acute withdrawal and compromised health could be life-threatening.) Those needs posed a significant challenge in the communities where I worked. Physicians did not want to work with alcoholics and addicts for a variety of reasons: moral distaste, poor self-pay histories, few, if any third party payers for addiction-related care, and poor post-treatment compliance with continuing care recommendations.

The fact that doctors who openly treated alcoholics became suspect among their peers and their other patients is testimony to the social stigma pervading alcoholism and addiction in the mid-20th century. But pioneer physicians stepped forward in most of these communities to care for these individuals and who lobbied to open the doors of local hospitals for alcoholics and addicts. These were the days before rapid hospital expansion programs. Hospitals were frequently full and could be quite selective about who they admitted.

My initial approach to opening doors of local hospitals was to appeal to the consciences of the leaders of these organizations. I was surprised and initially angered at the ineffectiveness of this strategy. It took some time to come to the stark realization that few institutions could be said to have a conscience. They exist to survive and grow and take whatever actions are thought to further their institutional interests. So the trick became creating conditions in which caring for alcoholics met the institutional interests of these hospitals. That was achieved first by working within the state agencies to create funds that could pay for such care and then convincing hospital administrators that alcoholics and addicts could be effectively managed in their hospitals without disrupting other more socially and financially desirable patients. The longer-term strategy was affecting changes in insurance reimbursement for alcoholism and addiction treatment. That success would come, but would bring unexpected consequences with it. Most of my professional life had passed before I truly understood that the most desirable change is often accompanied by unanticipated negative side effects that must be actively managed.

Parents in the ER

My hospital work often involved being called to local hospital emergency rooms to assist with drug emergencies. I helped coax information about drugs taken, reduced the emotional distress of the patient, shared information with the ER personnel about drug doses and adulterants within the local drug culture, and provided linkage to the limited post-emergency treatment and recovery support resources. While these functions had become quite routine, one function that remained technically and emotionally challenging was responding to the distress of parents of the young men and women admitted for adverse drug reactions. For many, these incidents were the first announcement of a drug problem within the family; for others, it was one of a long series of such episodes that would test a family's love and endurance. The emotions expressed within these events were raw: disbelief, shock, confusion, anger, disappointment, fear, profound love and concern, and, for those frequently experiencing such episodes, emotional exhaustion and resignation. The time spent with all those parents marked the beginning of my recognition of the need for family-oriented addiction treatment. It was in those years that I began to formulate a vision of what such care could and should look like, but it would take decades before I saw even the skeleton of that vision emerge as a reality within the treatment field. In the interim, I had made a vow in my heart to those parents to not let their children or that vision die.

The Case of the Missing Joint

A long and checkered history of school-based alcohol and drug "abuse" prevention exists in the United States, beginning with the 19th century temperance education movement. The rise of youthful drug experimentation in the 1960s triggered a frantic and poorly thought out flurry of prevention activities in the schools. Even school administrators tried to scare kids out of experimenting with drugs using portrayals of drugs and their effects that were a throwback to the "Reefer Madness" days of the 1930s. When the information provided in those programs was not confirmed by their experience, young people came to disregard all warnings from such programs. A later phase of "just the facts" assumed young people would make the right decisions if they were given the objective information on drugs. This was followed by approaches that sought to clarify values or teach assertiveness skills. These ill-conceived approaches created a generation of well-informed, assertive drug experimenters who had clarified that their values were not those of their parents.

A formal field of "substance abuse prevention" had yet to emerge in the late '60s and early '70s so those of us in the treatment world were frequently invited into the schools. Schools were under enormous pressure to do something about drug use, and this pressure produced an assortment of one-shot programs that often did more harm than good. My first indication of this was a program at a junior high school in which I was supposed to follow a local narcotics officer as a speaker to a class of eighth graders. The officer had a large, glass-encased display loaded with the kind of pills that he wanted those listening not to take, and he passed around a sampling of drug paraphernalia and three marijuana joints so that those present could recognize them if they were ever offered any. The officer was young, engaging, and seemingly doing a good job when all the trouble began. I was personally nervous sitting close to all those pills I had once worshipped, but it was when only two of the three joints passed around made it back to the front of the room that I knew that drug abuse prevention was going to have a long and checkered history. (The next hour was spent questioning and threatening all the students. I left amid the chaos, but was later told that the missing joint was never found.)

Young ex-addicts were often asked to speak to students as a means of finding engaging and relevant programs. Many of us on that circuit looked like rock stars of that era (one of the women who co-presented with me always showed up wearing skin-tight leather that left young men in the audience totally transfixed). We spoke provocatively and with great passion. The students were riveted by the detailed recounting of the dramatic progression of addiction and our far briefer recovery tales. For our part, it was hard not to be seduced by the adoration of so many young students, and the principals and teachers loved our presentations for the animated responses they drew from the students. But I left such programs troubled that some dynamic was afoot that I could not identify.

The source of that discomfort became clear when a shy student approached me after a presentation and asked for my autograph. Stunned, I looked at his face and knew beyond a shadow of a doubt that he wanted to be me. What I realized at that moment was that I was speaking to a generation of young people hungry to break out of the sterility of their lives and that I was a beacon of something that they desperately wanted. The professional ex-addicts in the schools were viewed by students more as ambassadors of the drug culture than emissaries of recovery. We were unintentionally drawing them to that culture and conveying the idea that if they got in trouble, recovery was simple and always open to them. The medium was the message and that message was one of charisma, honesty, energy, drama, and meaning through community service activism. Too many students wanted what we had, and we inadvertently drew them to the world from which we had escaped in their search for what seemed missing in their lives.

During this same period, another incident occurred that taught me an important lesson. I was speaking to a class of seventh graders. And, after I had begun speaking, the classroom door opened and in wandered a young man that had "deviant" written all over him—all black clothes and boots; long, unkempt hair, fake jailhouse tattoos on his knuckles, and lots of attitude. He sat in the back of the room and made interesting facial gestures and whispered commentary that I could not hear. When I asked for questions at the end of my presentation, his hand shot up and he said the following: "Of all the drugs, which one is the most dangerous?" I responded with some factual information about different dimensions of dangerousness, but suggested that volatile solvents were among the most physically destructive substances consumed to get high. As I finished my brief remarks, I made eye contact with him as his face broke into a gallows smile and he said, "Thanks." In that second, I knew that he was not asking that question to protect his health and that he would choose particular drugs not in spite of their risks but because of them.

My forays into prevention in the late 1960s and early 1970s heightened my awareness of interventions done with the noblest of intentions that produced unintended and often unrecognized harm. The search for and exposure of such interventions would become a theme of my later work in the field. Their existence then and now add weight to the ultimate ethical admonition, "First, do no harm."

Before Boundaries Existed

No ethical issue in my early career was more ill-defined than that of the appropriate "boundaries" (a word/label I had not yet heard) between myself and those I served as a streetworker (outreach worker). I was not a physician, nurse, psychologist, or social worker and the role of addiction counselor had not yet arrived, so the ethical mandates of those roles were not imposed on me nor could the ethics of the clinical consulting room be easily applied to the situations I regularly encountered in the down-and-out bars, pool halls, shooting galleries, houses of prostitution, cheap hotels, and the private residences I entered in my outreach role. Complicating this further was the fact that I did not see myself as an outsider to these institutions, but as someone who was working inside these cultures. The sense that these places represented "my world" and that those I worked with were "my people" (in the sense of co-membership in a community of shared experience) precluded what would later evolve as a widening professional chasm between client and addiction counselor. I had not yet found professional peers doing this work and thus there was no peer consensus on relationship guidelines. I made the ground rules up as I went, and had only the professional supervision I received as a safety net for myself and those I served.

As a streetworker, I was paid for a service-oriented lifestyle in which little distinction existed between when I was "working" or not working. When I was providing non-clinical services of widely varying intensity and duration to hundreds of people within a community where I viewed myself as a member, the line between the personal and professional was close to non-existent. As I recognized the power and status within my role—power that could be potentially exploited for my gain and harm to others, I began to pose the question: What guidelines should govern my service relationships when a whole community was my client? My experiences, concerns, and self-observations during this period were the building blocks of many of my later writings on professional ethics, but this was the "flying blind" period of my professional career. Guidelines would eventually come for the addictions field, but not before the loss of many sacrificial lambs (workers who themselves became casualties within these emerging roles and institutions). I was one of the survivors—a status earned as much by luck as pluck—as the following critical incident illustrates.

Enmeshment in a Subculture and a Panicked Retreat

The counterculture of the 1960s and early 1970s was an amalgam. It was a political culture. It was a social celebration of the largest generation in American history. It was a culture of music, art, and dance. And it was a culture facing the largest menu of intoxicants in the history of the world. I was a member of this culture and saw my role as serving wounded individuals within this culture. As noted, the line between my social relationships and service relationships was thin to non-existent.

At the height of my involvement in this culture, I moved into a house (what others at the time were calling a "commune") with a number of people. It was an interesting mix of highly intelligent, politically involved, and socially engaging people. I shared much of the far left political sympathies of these groups, but made it clear that "no dope in the house" had to be a non-negotiable rule given the nature of my work. All agreed to the "no holding" rule and months unfolded without incident. The house was one of the many local intellectual and social centers of what others were calling the New Left, but it was also a gathering point for leaders of the local women's movement and gay liberation movement.

The judgment I had made to live in the "Taylor Street House" was questionable at best. I enjoyed the friendships there, and while I am sure it enhanced my credibility in the elaborate street and political cultures of the period, it could have strained if not violated my relationships with the larger community in general and with particular institutions (e.g., police departments to local politicians). The risk that I was putting myself in was short-lived because of an incident that occurred on an otherwise quiet Saturday afternoon. I was in my upstairs bedroom reading when I heard a piercing scream coming from below. Running downstairs, I realized that the sound was coming from the basement—an inhabitable, dirt-floored area of the house that I had only seen once when I first moved into the house. The scream was from a housemate who was staring in panic at more than 100 bricked kilos of marijuana. He had gone downstairs to put something in storage and had been curious about the large tarp-covered mound in the center of the floor. The scream was his response to uncovering what was beneath the tarp.

I would have screamed also, but I had no capacity for speech. What I was staring at was the potential end of my career. I had been worried about an occasional joint being brought into the house, but nothing prepared me for such a grotesque violation of the "no holding" rules we had all established for living together. My response was immediate: my name was off the lease in an hour and I moved out before the day was over. To have placed my life and career in such jeopardy was one of the stupidest things I have ever done and a decision that left me forever careful about how I managed my personal and professional life. Everything I achieved afterwards could have been jeopardized by my poor judgment and ill-placed trust in others.

A Marriage of Heads and Hoods

A distinct West to East Coast movement of drug trends continued through the 1960s and 1970s. This awareness was my first experience of anticipating what I would be seeing in the Midwest by studying what was happening in California. Between 1967 and 1968, the California youth polydrug culture was changing. In Haight-Ashbury, lysergic acid diethylamide (LSD) prices dropped and few were buying it. The drug of choice was Methedrine ("speed" / "meth") and more people used booze, barbiturates, and heroin to come down from sustained Methedrine runs. Early members of the Haight had a growing sense that their dream of an alternative culture had turned to a nightmare and even held a "Death of Hippie" ceremony in October 1967. The beats and hippies that brought Haight-Ashbury to national attention gave way in 1968 to young psychopaths who had donned the trappings of their peace-espousing predecessors. These newcomers brought a much greater degree of emotional disturbance that was reflected in growing violence and more destructive drug choices and patterns of drug consumption.

The early innocence of the drug culture gave way to headlines of drug-related casualties, such as the report in October 1969 that the daughter of prominent television entertainer, Art Linkletter, had plunged to her death from an apartment window while under the influence of LSD. While many point to the 1969 Woodstock rock festival in Bethel, New York as the literal and metaphorical high point of the '60s drug culture, other events revealed a darker omen of things to come. Four people died at a Rolling Stones Concert at the Altamont Raceway, including one who was stabbed to death by the Hell's Angels

71

security force while "Sympathy for the Devil" reverberated in the background. Sharon Tate, wife of film director, Roman Polanski, and six others were slain before the arrest of well-known Haight-Ashbury figure, Charlie Manson, and the young female members of his commune. The deaths of Jimi Hendrix (from barbiturates) and Janis Joplin (from heroin) were added to other prominent drug-related deaths from this period.

This more ominous turn in the polydrug culture reflected changes in drug tastes. Between 1969 and 1972, increased medical complications due to injection and needle sharing became common. Drug users seen in health clinics suffered from needle abscesses, bacterial endocarditis, needle-transmitted hepatitis, malaria, and syphilis. The Haight Ashbury Free Medical Clinic that had in 1967 treated "bad trips" through new "talking down" techniques and "calm rooms" was by the end of 1969 treating young people strung out on heroin. A street youth culture espousing peace and brotherhood had been abandoned to the paranoid ravings of the speed freak and the detached, predatory proclivities of the junkie. These personal transformations and transformations of the American drug culture replicated themselves in a westward to eastward movement through American communities in the late 1960s and early 1970s.

We are at the present enamored by biological models of addiction in the treatment field, but this early history reminds us of the enormous importance cultural context plays in alcohol and other drug related problems. Those of us working on the front lines of this problem must closely monitor the changes in the American drug culture and what it means for the treatment of addiction. For years I have thought of this as a form of clinical anthropology. What we can do is regularly ask ourselves what a personal story or event tells us about the larger picture that is unfolding culturally and what that larger picture portends for the future. How are the clients you saw this week different from the clients you saw two years ago? What does this tell us about the evolution of the problem and the needed evolution of treatment as a system of care? What does it tell us about how we need to treat today's clients differently from those we saw two years ago? What do we need to anticipate in the future? These are the questions for the clinical anthropologist.

The Dangers of Self-Infatuation

One of the employees of the Department of Mental Health who had exhibited a fascination with my work asked me one day if he could visit for a day to get a feel for what my "streetwork" was all about. I readily agreed and after coaching him to dress down for the day so he wouldn't stand out, we set a time for his visit. After his arrival, we set out on an extended tour of pool halls, bars, wino hotels, a few dope houses, and a house of prostitution. At each stop, he was able to witness me working with individuals in these naturalistic environments— questioning, informing, praising, encouraging, linking (to community resources), and playfully chastising. He witnessed people at all stages of problem development and people struggling with early stages of recovery. It was quite an education for him, and I knew that stories of my work would grow from his visit. But that was the problem.

Everything about the day was wrong. His presence was not about his education; it was about my aggrandizement. It was a tour of the "jungle" and my clients were objectified and displayed as if they were exotic animals. I picked the sites not because they were representative of my work or because they were stops I needed to make that particular day. I picked them because I knew they would be the most titillating to him and make my work look more glamorous and dangerous than it really was. No client I saw that day benefited from his (and probably my) presence. I'm sure some people we saw that day sensed the true purpose of our visit and were demeaned by it. Bringing this particular individual into the world I occupied every day did much to enhance my professional reputation, but it was one of the low points of my professional career. That day was reflective of a larger problem. The focus of my work was shifting from my clients to myself.

I was becoming fascinated by the novelty of my role and the recognition it was bringing me. I was infatuated with my own image— the wild bushy hair, the beard, the exotically patterned shirts, the vests, and the bell-bottom jeans and boots. I looked more like a character from *Easy Rider* than a service professional. I was intoxicated by the exoticness of what I was doing. I had ceased reaching out as an act of service and instead pursued my work as an assertion of my own self-importance. When that realization struck home to me, I knew it was time to organize systems to do what I had been doing as a lone worker. It was time to get out of the limelight of this frontier role, time to get less focused on myself and re-focused on the experience of my clients, and time to focus less on the dramatic rescue and more on the nuances of the on-going recovery process. The need for such shifts opened a pathway from the world of streetwork to a world of addiction psychotherapy.

Kindred Spirits

My service and survival as a streetworker was not an act of isolated achievement. I had wonderful supervisors who guided me through this work, but, equally importantly, I had a few peers who walked in my shoes through related work.

My first relationship with Jo Major was at Eureka College where he was instructing a class I was taking. Jo also worked at the Family Counseling Center in Bloomington, Illinois and he and I became good friends when I also ended up working in Bloomington. He invited me to teach a class at Eureka. We both become involved in community outreach efforts in Bloomington, and we worked for several years as co-therapists with families and in running groups for young addicts.

Jo and I have always been kindred spirits. We both brought great passion to our work, considerable skill, and great but not always fulfilled potential. The relationship we forged was based on mutual collaboration and respect, but it was also based on recognition of our mutual vulnerability. It was a relationship that helped us both maintain personal and professional balance—two imperfect parts that in collaboration could at least partially transcend our imperfections. That relationship has now spanned more than four decades.

The mantra in all recovery mutual aid is that people can achieve together what they have been unable to achieve in isolation. That mantra equally applies to the professional arena. That is best achieved by finding kindred spirits with whom you can professionally collaborate. Have you found your kindred spirits? Have you lost touch or are you losing touch with them?

"I guess I am just tired."

My sojourn as a streetworker was one of the most intense learning periods of my life. I remember it today with fond memories of all I drew from it, with scant recall of the emotional toll of the work. While recently cleaning out decades of files and miscellaneous writings,

I uncovered among this detritus of my life handwritten pages penned in 1971 that capture some of the latter. Below is an excerpt from my reflections on my experience of this role that is written in the language of those days.

> Most of all, it [streetwork] means a tightrope—walking a tightrope between the streets [drug culture] and the community at large. If I take half a step toward the community, I lose credibility on the streets; if I take half a step towards the streets, I lose credibility in the community. My inclination to leave this role means I refuse to walk that tightrope any more. It means I'm tired of getting hate mail and threatening calls from both right and left wings. I'm tired of dopers saying I don't have any credibility because I won't use any drugs; I'm tired of community people saying I don't have any credibility because they are sure I'm on drugs. I'm tired of catching hell for being rough on drug dealers; I'm tired of police who think I'm selling drugs. I'm tired of being suspected of being a narcotics agent by drug users. I'm tired of right wingers who think I am a communist and left winger militants who think I am a reactionary. I'm tired of people who will talk to me about what drugs are contaminated but refuse to talk to me about my garden or the really nice old couple that lives behind me. I'm tired of people who will spend hours talking about their good and bad trips but won't talk about how lonely and frightened they are and how empty they feel. I'm tired of doped up parents who don't give a damn about their kids; I'm tired of doped up kids who don't give a damn about their parents. I'm tired of doped up people who don't give a damn about anything. I guess I am just tired. When I took on this role, I predicted that no one person could maintain the pressure of such a role for more than a year. I am about to reach the two year mark. I think my original estimate was correct.

As I exhausted what I could give and learn in this role, a new role beckoned that would again test the limits of my competence and my character. Sometimes you just have to empty yourself into a role and then move on to something that fills you up again. This is not an abandonment of mission; such transitions are a necessity if one is to forge a sustained contribution to changing the world or even a small part of it. Such transitions can be mined for lessons for others. I later addressed the issue of personal and organizational burnout—a topic of critical interest since my early days as a streetworker (see Chapter Ten). Everything in your career—the good, the bad, and the ugly—is grist for learning and future contributions.

Chapter Four
Becoming a Therapist (1971-1973)

As the non-stop intensity and isolation of streetwork took its inevitable toll, an opportunity arose that opened the next chapter in my professional life. In my life, I have often experienced well-timed opportunities that seemed part of an unknown evolving master plan. This next step was a perfect synergy of personal and community need that occurred at a time the darker side of street life was asserting itself and leaving people deeply wounded. The question at a personal level was whether I could acquire skills that, in partnership with numerous other individuals and organizations, might help heal such wounds. In my streetwork days, I had never viewed myself as an *addictions counselor* or *therapist*, but that was about to change. Below are stories that highlight this transition in identity and service that may have personal meaning to you.

From Streetworker to Therapist

In 1971, I was invited to organize adolescent and outpatient addiction services at the McLean County Mental Health Center in Bloomington, Illinois. It was a remarkable opportunity because of the unique nature of the agency. Dr. Robert Chapman had come to Bloomington with a vision of replicating a community mental health clinic modeled on his training experiences at the famed Menninger Foundation in Topeka, Kansas. To fulfill that vision, he recruited Dr. Douglas Bey, another Menninger-trained psychiatrist, and three Menninger-trained psychiatric social workers (Jim Galbraith, Richard Evans, and Frank Stark) and recruited psychiatric consultants from the Chicago Institute of Psychoanalysis (including Drs. Kenwood, Gilhoff, Richmond, and Elkin). What opened this opportunity was a relationship I had developed with Dr. Chapman during my regular rounds at the Brokaw Hospital psychiatric unit.

The transformation from streetwork and crisis interventionist to a therapist was not an easy one. First, the roles overlapped for some period creating considerable tension in the evolution of my work and identity. Second, my appearance (long, bushy hair and goatee; bell-bottom jeans, leather boots, and vest) worked well on the streets but not in the professional offices of a community mental health center. Third, the action-orientation that fueled my work on the streets was ill-suited for the more sedate work of therapy. But my greatest challenge at this time was the need for a massive acquisition of new skills. I achieved this transition by receiving intense teaching and supervision.

If there was a period of peak learning about how to perform "counseling" or "therapy," this was unquestionably my Camelot. What was most unique about this period was that it did not rest on a single mentorship relationship but a complete learning milieu in which all the staff extended themselves to share their knowledge with me while also seeking to learn from me. The latter was a powerful source of legitimization that boosted my sense of what I could achieve in the future. What is most interesting in retrospect was that I did not recognize just how special this period was until reflecting back on it years later. If I had made such realization, I would have sought out even greater opportunities for co-therapy and supervision. I think the lesson from this is to define every opportunity as a potential Camelot (even in the face of a negative work experience) and draw out from that experience everything one possibly can. What previously unrecognized resources exist before your very eyes? Who around you do you need to work with and learn from more intensely than you have? This may be a fleeting opportunity. Take advantage of it! Such Camelot periods cannot last forever. They are not meant to. But we can carry the best of what existed in such a moment of time inside us—if we recognize a moment at the time for what it is.

The Power of Clinical Supervision

Historically, psychoanalysis was not an effective framework for the treatment of alcoholism or other addictions, but there were many things I took from these psychoanalytically oriented psychiatrists and social workers that guided my clinical career. They placed great emphasis on self-knowledge; they had all been through their own analysis and their openness about these experiences made seeking therapy not only okay but a professional must. They taught me to still the roaring voice of my own ego and to listen to clients at a depth unknown to me before then. They taught me about the nuances of transference and countertransference. They detailed how the client and the therapist project their past experiences into the therapy process in

78

ways that can enhance or disrupt the helping process. Their ability to accept their own limitations, to laugh at themselves, while taking the work and their role in it seriously was a style I have since sought to emulate.

The level of clinical supervision that I had was the most intense of my career. I had weekly supervision (one hour) from one of the psychiatrists, weekly group psychiatric supervision of the adolescent therapists (two hours), bi-weekly supervision from a family psychiatrist, and constant daily consults with the psychiatric social workers and psychiatric nurses. What these sessions of true clinical supervision entailed were: 1) a theory-grounded review of the clinical process, 2) feedback on my degree of fidelity to established clinical protocol, 3) a refinement of clinical protocol based on the unique needs of individuals and families, 4) an exploration of how what I personally brought to the helping relationship was helping or impeding the service process, and 5) a cumulative review and goal-setting related to my personal development as a therapist. My personal and professional growth dramatically accelerated under this guidance.

As I watched some of my recovering peers self-destruct in these early days of modern addiction treatment, I sometimes questioned the source of my own resilience. I know today that such resilience was not a function of my character, but a function of the consistency and quality of the supervision and support I experienced during those years. Years later, when I assumed supervisory and management roles, I tried to replicate this climate of intense clinical supervision. I have watched that intensity decline over the years, both in the time devoted to clinical supervision and the content of such supervision. My fear is that the cultural memory of such supervision will die and that young therapists of tomorrow will have no idea what they are missing and the impact of that loss on themselves and their clients. For the supervisors reading this, are you ensuring individual meetings with each clinical staff every week? What type of teaching experiences do you bring to those individual meetings? How do you approach weekly staff meetings to ensure the development of clinical expertise in your staff?

Bootlegging More Therapy

The early 1970s was a vibrant time in community-based mental health and family counseling agencies. Powerful experiential therapies were emerging that, if not always appropriate for clients, were a source of great infatuation with many therapists of this era. From psychodrama to transactional analysis and Gestalt therapy to the latest therapy of the month, therapists were "trained" by working on their own issues in these intense experiential therapies. It was not unusual in this period to work all week and then participate in such experiential training with a dozen other therapists from Friday evening through Sunday afternoon and then return to work on Monday. A generation of young therapists who burned out on changing the world turned toward processes of deep introspection.

It was perfect timing for me. I still needed therapy and there was much therapy to be had—both from the expectation during those years that therapists should undergo their own therapy and from the experiential training that was then the norm. Important lessons emerged during this period that guided much of my career as a clinician and trainer of clinicians. The most important of these was the need to quiet the roar of our own history and our immediate preoccupations to truly listen to each client. Cleaning up some of the emotional baggage of that history and learning to diminish the distorting filters of what remained dramatically improved my effectiveness as a therapist.

While many of my colleagues and I emerged as healthier people and better therapists, there was a shadow side to this period. Some therapists became so caught up in their own "unfinished business" that clients became at best a distraction and at worst a nuisance. Collectively, Christopher Lasch's "culture of narcissism" was indeed emerging. Whole agencies experienced a process of inversion via an intense focusing on the personal and interpersonal problems of staff. In this milieu of constant processing, relationship casualties were high and sexual intimacies between staff in the freewheeling pre-AIDS days of the 1970s turned many a program into an ongoing soap opera. It is not surprising in this climate that clients often got leftovers from the staff's latest growth experiences. What went on in therapy groups on Monday was often determined by and an extension of the workshop the therapist had attended the weekend before.

The first lesson I learned from all of this was that creating powerful emotional experiences for client (and staff) in the context of addiction treatment is not a difficult task. However, such experiences, as impressive as they appear and feel, may have little connection with long-term recovery outcomes and may even compromise such outcomes by leaving an individual emotionally exposed once they leave the treatment setting. Everyone has developmental insults, sins of omission and commission, and "unfinished emotional business." The question is whether disclosing and resolving such issues has anything to do with recovery, and, if so, whether such work is an early, middle, or late-stage recovery task. We have a lot of folk wisdom on this question, but very little science.

Another important lesson I learned was that organizations whose mission is to serve others can get hijacked by the unmet needs of their own service providers. I suspect this tendency is a normal, perhaps inevitable stage in the life of human service agencies, but amenable to processes of renewal that get staff as individuals and as a group refocused on the needs of clients and communities. Where that renewal process does not occur, organizations are vulnerable to incestuous implosion—a process we will explore in a later chapter. Ideally, there is a balance between the energy devoted to service needs of clients and the self-maintenance needs of the individuals and organizations serving those clients. How is that balance in your own organization today? Lean too far one direction, and individuals and organizations self-destruct from lack of self-maintenance. Lean too far the other direction and organizations eventually self-destruct from self-indulgence and lost mission. Is your organization nearing a tipping point?

Adolescent Services in the Early 1970s

When I came to the McLean County Mental Health Center, the goal was for me to transition from my streetworker role to one of developing and delivering addiction counseling and mental health services to adolescents and young adults. Within a year, most of that transition had been accomplished and I had written a grant that allowed me to hire Jolene Kaylor to work as a therapist with adolescent females. Then another opportunity presented itself. Roger Krohe, who had been a student intern at the McLean County Juvenile Probation Office, had just finished his internship. Jolene and I had been impressed with Roger (who remains one of the best therapists I have ever worked with and a good friend) and were hoping we could find a way to bring him on staff at the mental health center to specialize in working with juveniles who were involved with the criminal justice system.

81

We were unsuccessful in our attempts to get what little grant money was available for youth services in those years, but we were able to hire Roger through funds from a local prevention project and through money that Roger, Jolene, and I raised from speaking engagements. We had a bit of a folk hero status in the local community that generated a lot of speaking requests from local civic and religious groups and we used the small fees and begged donations from such groups to support what we were trying to do. Speaking and asking for donations are what it took to expand adolescent services before the funding streams for such services became institutionalized. Today that community has a broad spectrum of youth services, but I suspect few people working in them are aware of how those youth services began decades ago.

I learned two important lessons from those early years. First, you cannot let pipelines of funding or the lack of such pipelines restrict your vision of what is possible, and, second, the community is a well of untapped hospitality that will respond when invited to help with a critical need.

Roger and I also shared a house to reduce our living expenses and offset the meager salaries we were being paid. Our house on Roosevelt Street became something of a 24-hour crisis and drop-in center for a few years. Our home also served as a meeting place for visionary service professionals to gather and share ideas about changing the world. The line between our personal and professional lives was almost non-existent, with our home on Roosevelt Street serving as an annex of the mental health center. Roosevelt Street was a hub of unending conversation about what we were reading and what we were learning from our clinical and community organizing work and our supervision. It was a wonderful period of incubation of much that I would achieve later. The "Roosevelt Street Annex" period came to an end with Urban Renewal's confiscation and demolition of the house we were renting.

The problem with a Camelot period so early in one's career is that you take it for granted, assuming that this is the way it will always be. It was only later that I would realize the good fortune that the forces of the universe coalesced to bring me to that place at that time. What I learned is that you can never take opportunities for granted and that we must draw deeply from such opportunities as they unfold. To have exceptionally bright and talented people who believe in you and who are willing to invest time in your development is more precious than gold.

The Attic: A Case Study in Failure or Success?

I had met hundreds of teenagers during my earlier years of streetwork and had envisioned a place of safety—a sanctuary—where they could flee to for acceptance, support, and encouragement. Many were at high risk for a host of problems but, they also brought fathoms of undeveloped potential. I discussed the possibility of such a sanctuary with my colleagues at the mental health center and they encouraged me to pursue development of such a place. As it turned out, there was a fifth floor attic in the building whose fourth floor housed the mental health center and the family services agency. I found out that we could rent the attic for a nominal fee ($35 a month), but that it would take substantial clean-up and remodeling. I worked with a group of teen volunteers for more than a year before we gave up on the project as impossible due to zoning regulations and the cost of a fire escape that we would have needed to add.

It was probably best that this project didn't succeed in this location—the building was a real fire trap (and a few years later was completely destroyed by fire), but the collapse of the Attic project was a big disappointment to me. I felt I had let down all the kids that had worked for months cleaning the place up and plastering and painting several days a week after school—for those that were in school. We invested far too much work before discovering that this site really wouldn't work. When the decision to abandon the project was final, I shared my disappointment with a sage psychiatrist at the mental health center who offered me these words. "Those kids didn't come here every day to create a drop-in center. They came here to have contact with you and the hope you provided in their lives. The sweeping and the painting were simply the excuses to be with you. What they needed was not a physical place but people who treated them with respect and expanded their vision of what was possible in their lives. Now stop feeling sorry for yourself and go spend some time with those kids. You are what they need." And, of course, he was right. Are there times that, like me, you have been blind to your own power and influence?

A Merger of Professional/Private Relationships

It is hard to maintain relationships with civilians when you work in a stigmatized arena. Persons outside this world view you as either a saint or insane for choosing such work. Both constitute a form of depersonalization and neither is conducive to authentic friendships. So it is little wonder that closed professional/social networks often characterize the worlds of those who work in the mental health and addiction treatment arenas. Such was my life in the early 1970s at the mental health center. The core of the staff worked together, shared innumerable interests, didn't fit well into the larger community, and thus created our own closed social network. Much of this socializing was deeply rewarding, but there was a more destructive side to such intimacy that I would later describe as a process of "incestuous closure." (See Chapter Ten.)

In periods when work was exhilarating and fulfilling, we spent most of our time away from work talking about work—a process that left little room for disengagement and replenishment from stressful demands. In periods when work was draining and demoralizing, we spent more and more time at work talking about what was going on with us as a group outside of work. These actions diminished our ability to support each other professionally to remain engaged in our clinical work. More and more personal conflicts in relationships outside of work spilled into the work setting and strained our interactions with one another. Somewhere along the way, we began to re-establish a healthier distance between ourselves, but the "family" and our individual friendships had somehow been wounded through processes we poorly understood. And those wounds affected how we functioned as a team.

There is nothing inherently wrong with socializing outside of work with one's co-workers. Such relationships are natural and often the basis of life-long friendships. But what we had done at the mental health center was use such relationships to replace rather than supplement non-work social relationships. At that point, it was only a period of time before the work milieu was transformed into a soap opera. It would be years and a few more replications of this process before I fully understood it. The key is one of balance. As you think about your relationships with your co-workers, do you need to increase or decrease distance in these relationships?

"Hard Core Street Women"

Over a number of months I referred a number of women to Jolene in hopes she would be able to engage them in some form of on-going therapy. She in turn suggested that we co-lead a group for these women, which we did in 1971. We had about 7-9 young women aged 18-25 who described themselves as our "Hard Core Street Women Group." They were a difficult-to-engage tip of an iceberg of deeply wounded women who filled the street culture of this era. Most had horrific histories of childhood sexual abuse and abandonment, a long history of toxic and often violent intimate relationships, school failure, occupational transience, and frequent emotional crises—some resulting in hospitalization and all a product of what were then clinically labeled as depression, bipolar disorder, or borderline personality. They were periodically homeless, traded sex for drugs and shelter, and had numerous medical and gynecological problems (included chronic STDs and infections). At the time the group started, no addiction services (other than what we were providing) or specialized services for women or domestic violence services existed in the community. Our group was a desperate attempt to alter the chaotic and crisis-driven lifestyles of these young women. Our office was close to several dope houses, bars, and dance clubs and early on our clients began dropping by our offices on the way to or from these establishments. They stopped to say hi, to talk about things they couldn't share during group, or to seek help with the latest piece of drama in their lives. They somehow managed to make it to the weekly groups and slowly began to get their lives together (relatively speaking).

I learned a lot from my relationships with these deeply wounded but amazingly resilient women and the psychiatric supervision Jolene and I received to guide our work with them. In my initial consultation with Dr. Bey, the psychiatrist who supervised this work, he explained to me that these women would try to replicate their historical pattern of relationships in their relationship with me. In short, they would try to seduce me; they would find a non-sexual, non-exploitive relationship incomprehensible and threatening; their failure to seduce me would provoke anger and acting out—both designed to test my capacity to stay engaged and whether I would reject them. He explained that my challenge as a therapist was to resist their sexual overtures while sustaining consistent emotional contact and respectful regard for them. To use them sexually or reject them would simply confirm their view of themselves and the world. This proffered scenario sounded pretty bizarre to me when I first heard it, but in a matter of a half-hour Dr. Bey had outlined what would unfold over the next two years.

The fact that I was only a few years older than these women, single, and had status in the local street culture in which they were enmeshed all heightened the early sexual tension between us. I later learned that a contest had been created in the early months to see who would be the first to, in the vernacular of the day, "ball me" (add my name to a personal list of sexual trophies). Their provocative sexuality was so extreme that there was a period when I would not see them without Jolene being present. They went through a period of suspecting I was gay and then an angry period in which they felt rejected. They challenged me as to what I wanted from them. In the end, Jolene and I vacillated between the roles of older sibling and parents: nurturing, advising, chastising, encouraging, coaching, but more than anything, staying present in their lives and listening. These wounded women have spent their lives becoming whole. This is not a story about the transformative power of brief intervention. But Dr. Bey was right. Jolene and I had created a therapeutic bubble within which these young women were forced to see themselves and their world differently—a change that opened new possibilities in their lives.

I learned from this that all clients bring historical patterns into their relationships with professional helpers and set us up to play certain roles and act out fixed rituals that continue the destructive patterns within their lives. When we unknowingly play those roles and act out the past in the present, they leave this pageant with less potential for future recovery than when they came to us. When we force a break in that pattern, when we force the client into foreign territory, they enter a world in which recovery resides.

The Rise and Fall of a Super-Ex-Dope-Fiend-Folk-Hero

In the 1960s and early 1970s, traditional helping professionals were not trained to treat alcoholism or drug addiction and their prior contact with alcoholics and addicts had often produced more contempt than either compassion or clinical expertise in the treatment of addiction. This void was filled by hiring thousands of recovering alcoholics and addicts to work as "paraprofessional" counselors on the front lines of newly opened outpatient and residential treatment programs. I was part of that cadre and developed a network of associations with others like myself in communities across Illinois. Some of these individuals worked in virtual isolation and their roles within the community became something of a controversy. The following is an excerpt from my journal in 1971.

> All of a sudden, I have become a person to be loved as a folk hero with some magic wand that mystically pulls people's heads together or hated as an antichrist doing more harm than good. All of a sudden, my work is an issue that few can remain neutral about. The ironic thing is that most of those who defend me the most have no more understanding of me as a person or my work than those who most bitterly attack me.

It did not take long to realize the vulnerability and high casualty rate of individuals who were poorly selected, poorly trained, and poorly supervised to do this work. The following story is drawn from my experiences working with these other early pioneers in addiction treatment during 1970-1975. A network was forming: recovering alcoholics and addicts working as paid staff or volunteers were single-handedly starting outreach programs, running therapy groups, using our homes as drop-in centers, inviting people with days of recovery to stay at our own homes, and working in the schools.

Bob was part of that network of "one-person programs" scattered across the state. He had been hired by a mental health center to develop addiction services. Because he was early in his own recovery with no prior treatment other than state hospital detox, he accepted my suggestion of additional training/treatment at Gateway House. Bob returned after a few weeks deeply converted to the therapeutic community (TC) philosophy and began running TC-like groups for adolescents and adults. Bob's energy was boundless and his personal charisma quickly brought a large clientele of adolescents and adults into services. He became something of a folk hero in his local community, particularly among the troubled youth who nearly worshipped him following their turnaround.

A little more than a year after Bob had been hired, I received a most troubling call from Bob's agency director. The director informed me of the following events that had just broken into visibility. Several months ago, Bob had started smoking marijuana with a number of his adult clients and had recently begun drinking. These events had just been reported by one of Bob's clients to the client's probation officer. Bob was also discovered to be sexually involved with one of the adolescents in his teen group. The director requested that I help confront Bob and help process his relapse with his clients. Over the next 24 hours, I participated in that intervention, helped get Bob admitted to a treatment center, and met with Bob's clients to process his relapse and their needs for continued service. Meeting with the adolescent and adult clients who had idolized Bob and processing their sadness over his relapse, their rage at his perceived betrayal, and their increased fear for their own futures was one of the most emotionally wrenching experiences of my professional career.

Bob was not the only casualty among a growing workforce of alcoholism and drug abuse counselors made up primarily of people in recovery. Here are some lessons that can be drawn from this period.

1. Working in paid or volunteer service work with other alcoholics and addicts is not, by itself, a program of personal recovery.
2. Effectiveness with others rests upon the primacy of personal recovery and the stability and quality of that recovery.
3. The relapse of recovering individuals working in the addictions field flows from personal vulnerability, but it often occurs in an organizational context marked by high stressors (e.g., role-person mismatch, role ambiguity, role conflict, and role overload) and low professional supports (e.g., limited orientation and training, poor supervision, and failure to respond to early warning signs).
4. The passion people in recovery bring to their entrance to the field makes them vulnerable for exploitation, e.g., excessive hours with inadequate compensation and support.
5. The relapse of recovering people working as paid or volunteer helpers injures multiple parties: themselves and their families and friends, their clients and families, their co-workers, their agencies, their professions, and the communities they had pledged to serve. (In Bob's case, it would be years before the families in this rural community would be comfortable

88

requesting help for their children from the agency at which he had worked. Such violations of trust are hard to repair.)

Families as Systems

In 1970, I met Leonard Unterberger at an addictions conference at the University of Illinois. Len was a therapist who was involved with a family therapy training center called The Depot (located in Hyde Park on the South side of Chicago). Len and I became friends and collaborated on a number of projects over the years. Len introduced me to a network of family therapists from around the country who were, unbeknownst to me at the time, the emerging pioneers of family therapy. Through Len, I was able to meet and observe the work of people like Carl Whitaker, Virginia Satir, Salvador Minuchin, Jay Haley, and Ross Speck. Each of these remarkable individuals brought a unique approach to therapy with families, but what I drew from them that would be so invaluable was the ability to see the world in terms of systems rather than its component parts. I spent a couple of years enmeshing myself in their workshops, books, and published articles. Much of the work I would later do with individuals, families, organizations, and communities would draw heavily from this early training. I would also later be blessed with the opportunity to interview some of the pioneers in family-oriented addiction treatment, including Dr. Claudia Black, Dr. Stephanie Brown, Dr. Robert Meyers, Jerry Moe, Sharon Wegscheider-Cruse, and Sis Wenger.

For almost 40 years, I have maintained a sustained meditation on the relationship between personal health and the health or sickness of larger family and social systems. Across what seem like diverse and unconnected roles, the link between personal health and systems health has been an integrating theme within my career. Is there an integrating theme in your own professional life? If you look across all that you have done to date, what are the connecting threads? Identifying such connections may provide hints about your personal destiny. What theme links the fragments of your past? What theme is calling you to be fulfilled?

An Impostor?

I think the feeling of being an impostor is common in one's work in the addictions field. The challenge is to define one's source of competence and credibility in a field where such requirements have been a subject of sustained speculation and debate. Early in my career, I had few educational credentials other than undergraduate psychology courses relevant to what I was doing and found myself intimidated by and needing to prove myself to professionals with advanced degrees. (I later learned to my great surprise that they had similar feelings in their relationships with me.) At that time, I also possessed no addiction counselor certification because such a credential did not yet exist. But the credential of experiential knowledge did carry value. Yet my addiction and recovery experiences were so atypical that I fit neither the profile of the older AA old-timer who had drifted into the alcoholism treatment field nor the ex-addict from the streets who had graduated from a therapeutic community following years of heroin addiction and enmeshment in the criminal justice system. I struggled to define a foundation for my work to progress. I vacillated between believing I was destined to do this work and feeling completely inept.

Resolving this question of legitimacy took time and effort. Several things helped. First, rather than competing with degreed professionals I decided to turn them into my teachers. I didn't always agree with those I learned from but I knew there would be a time and place where I needed what they could teach me and I became an apt pupil. Second, I also used other ex-addict counselors and those in recovery from alcoholism as teachers. I imitated what I thought were the best traits of both groups until I could find a way to refine and personalize this new knowledge and skill. As these unique lessons were absorbed, I seemed to find myself, my voice, and my style. I had to figure out how to transform the imposter into a human being and an effective helper. You may have to do the same. If you aren't there yet, be patient.

Chapter Five
Birthing a Treatment Program (1973-1976)

The early 1970s marked a period of explosive growth in addiction treatment resources in the United States. Within a decade, the foundation of modern addiction treatment was forged though it would take decades to refine it—a process that is still underway. Addiction treatment programs had existed earlier in American history, but never on this scale. In community after community, lone therapists and concerned citizens collaborated to design formal programs of addiction treatment—reflecting widely different operating philosophies and methods.

Making that transition from lone addiction therapist to building a formal treatment program was the next stage of my professional life and one of the most exciting of my career. Join me for some tales and lessons from these early days.

A Grassroots Community and a Vision

Like thousands of other communities in the early 1970s, a vanguard of people within the twin cities of Bloomington and Normal, Illinois came together to create treatment resources for alcohol and other drug problems. The growing numbers of local alcoholism and drug abuse councils were made up of people in recovery, family members impacted by addiction, professionals (physicians, nurses, judges, prosecutors, police, social workers, school administrators, and teachers), local politicians, and local business people and philanthropists. They shared a vision: increase access to hospitals for detoxification, create post-detoxification counseling and rehabilitation services, develop systems of early problem identification in the schools and workplaces, and provide information and referral services to local citizens. The McLean County Alcohol and Drug Assistance Unit (MCADAU) was typical of these local councils in both its membership composition and its goals. Created in 1970, the MCADAU met regularly until it successfully procured a grant from the Illinois Law Enforcement Commission to open the doors of the county's first public funded addiction treatment facility. That facility, christened Project Lighthouse, opened its doors in January 1973 within a beautiful but

91

badly deteriorated, two-story Victorian home. Lighthouse provided social setting detoxification (two beds), short- and long-term residential treatment (seven beds), outpatient treatment and community outreach services, and a variety of public and professional education presentations. These services were delivered by a team of seven staff working within a budget of less than $150,000. I had served as a board member and advisor to MCADAU during its pre-funding years and was hired as a counselor (at the robust annual salary of $9,600) as part of the original Lighthouse team.

The relationship between Lighthouse and the local community was an exceptionally close one. Board members were in and out of the facility on almost a daily basis. Local AA members and AA volunteers dropped by daily to chat with residents and staff over endless cups of coffee, and staff (those with and without recovery backgrounds) were encouraged to attend open or closed AA and Al-Anon meetings. Local politicians championed funds from the City Councils to help support Lighthouse services. Local clergy regularly served on the MCADAU board and heard the Fifth Steps of clients in treatment. Local business people donated materials needed to rehabilitate the facility, and members of local labor unions donated their skills. Local police delivered intoxicated people to Lighthouse as an alternative to arrest. Institutionalizing my earlier work, Lighthouse staff made daily rounds in the jails and hospitals and were on-call for situations that arose within local schools, businesses, and community centers. Our heavy public speaking schedules also kept us in weekly touch with citizens from all over the county. Such connectedness with the community was as much a matter of circumstances and necessity as it was a deep philosophical commitment to community-based services.

Over the next thirty years, Lighthouse evolved into an organization providing services around the world, but I don't think we were ever more connected to the communities we served than in those earliest years. In fact, that growth has forced us to reflect on the meaning of the term "community-based" when evolving into an organization that serves individuals and families from many communities and countries. To what communities do you feel accountable? Are your relationships with these communities strengthening or weakening?

A Program Built on Financial Sand

Lighthouse, like many programs of this period, was supported by a hodgepodge of donations and a single grant of $115,000 that sustained the program. The grants in these years ran for one year and had to be reapplied for every subsequent year. This grant process was filled with problems. First, the application and decision process each year took months and the end of each grant nearly lapsed before you knew whether you would be funded the next year and for how much. Sometimes, at the end of these cycles, I would leave work on a Friday not knowing if we had jobs on Monday. And clients in residential treatment on that same Friday were also unsure of what their status would be on Monday.

The second problem was one of cash flow. These grants paid slowly and both federal and state funders were often months behind in paying invoices, leaving us either praying that the state check would arrive in time to make payroll or forcing the Board to borrow money from a local bank so that service could continue. The meager resources we received in those early days forced us to literally live from check to check, with no cash reserve to buffer any delays in payment. Staff sometimes went without paychecks amidst such delays. Those meager resources also did not allow for hiring extra help for covering vacations and sick time so, when a house manager took vacation or was ill, other staff took turns working evening or night shifts in addition to continuing to work their regular daytime shift.

Funding was slowly stabilized through improved federal and state contracting and reimbursement processes, our success at diversifying funding streams, and greater local contributions. By the mid-1970s, a vision had emerged to get community-based addiction treatment agencies like Lighthouse accredited and all their staff credentialed so that the program would be eligible for insurance reimbursement. Years were put into this effort, and the irony is that the private reimbursement of residential addiction treatment would swell through the mid-1980s and then virtually collapse for a time in the late 1980s and early 1990s.

While Lighthouse had courted this private insurance money, its major resources had gone into assuring a stable flow of federal, state, and local dollars earmarked for the treatment of addiction. In spite of the early dream of treatment services totally funded by private health care insurance, the foundation of the modern treatment system is a federal, state, and local partnership. That partnership replaced the shifting sands upon which earlier efforts had been built. That partnership must be protected at all costs because without it there is no field of addiction treatment accessible to all families. That partnership has sustained Lighthouse and programs across the United States for the past decades. Later, Lighthouse found another creative way to support its core services, but we will wait a while to tell that story.

It would have been impossible to conceive in 1973 that this fledgling organization called Lighthouse would grow into a behavioral health company (at the time of this writing) with an annual budget in excess of $35 million, offices across Illinois serving thousands of clients a year, more than 650 employees, a research division of more than 90 staff, and an employee assistance division providing services around the world to 85 companies and more than 250,000 employees. That reality is still beyond my comprehension. But in that process something happened to the relationship between Lighthouse and its community that was symbolic of changes occurring in the relationship between treatment programs and local communities across the country—a larger story we will return to later.

A Visit to Mecca (Minnesota)

In early 1973, days after the first clients entered Lighthouse, a board member and three staff made the pilgrimage from Bloomington, Illinois to Center City, Minnesota to visit Hazelden. The ritual was replicated thousands of times by newly opening alcoholism programs across the country. These journeys conveyed the essence of the "Minnesota Model" of chemical dependency treatment through exposure to those who had helped create it. We visited with Dan Anderson, Gordy Grimm, Harold Swift, and others. They discussed the philosophy of the Minnesota Model at length and then walked us through the details of their treatment protocol for individuals and families.

Three things remain in my mind from that visit. One was the deep passion these individuals had for their work and their sense of its importance. I was in the presence of people who were changing how alcoholics were treated in the United States, and I recall hoping that someday I could be counted among that company. The second thing that struck me was their openness and lack of any proprietary ownership of what they were conveying to us. They "gave us the store," offering

94

anything and everything that would be of help to us. As the treatment field became highly commercialized in the 1980s, I tried to resist this new business orientation that turned every document into a protected proprietary product that could not be shared with one's competitors. I still believe that the "pass it on" philosophy of the Minnesota pioneers is worthy of emulation. The third thing I recall from that visit is the respect with which I was treated as a "youngster" in a field dominated by older men. Dan Anderson, in particular, took an interest in me and mentioned that maybe one day I would add my own contributions to this embryonic field. I thought the comment a joke until I saw the seriousness in his eyes. It made me think that maybe that was a possibility. I left standing taller than when I had arrived. Dan and the others could have so overwhelmed me with their own knowledge that I would have left feeling less capable. Instead, I walked away believing that I had what it would take to make a difference. It was a precious gift that I have tried to pass on to others in the years that followed.

As we left Hazelden, Dan Anderson encouraged us to visit Lutheran General Hospital in Park Ridge, Illinois where the Minnesota Model was being adapted within an acute care hospital by Dr. Nelson Bradley, Dr. Jean Rossi, and Reverend John Keller, all of whom had helped shape the Minnesota Model through their earlier work at Willmar State Hospital. Following Dan's suggestion, we visited Lutheran General a few weeks later and furthered our indoctrination in the Minnesota Model. It would have been hard to envision on our visit to Lutheran General that this program would evolve into Parkside Medical Services—the largest provider of addiction treatment services in the world in the early 1990s. It would have been impossible for me to envision that twenty years later I would be writing a book on the history of addiction treatment in which I described the forces that had led to the virtual collapse of Parkside in 1993. It would have been impossible for me to envision that more than thirty years later I would have the honor of helping organize the papers that Dan Anderson's family bequeathed to Brown University's addiction studies archives. It would have been impossible to envision that I would one day receive an award bearing the name of Dr. Nelson Bradley from the National Association of Addiction Treatment Providers (NAATP). And yet, looking back there seems to have been a certain order through which these events were connected, raising the question of whether we choose such roles or are instead chosen.

Meccas of addiction treatment exist in every era. Are there such places that call to you? Perhaps your own destiny will be influenced by such pilgrimages. Maybe the time is now.

A Man's World

When I entered the addictions field, it was a man's world—a world of male administrators, male clinicians, and mostly male clients. Treatment milieus were filled with male language, masculine metaphors and rituals, and an understanding of addiction and recovery based almost exclusively on experience with men who were adult, white, working class, and heterosexual (or at least presumed to be). Women rarely entered this environment, and when they did, they didn't stay long. It was an environment in which they were suspect. The machismo of this environment questioned whether any woman could have consumed enough booze to have earned admission to this motley club of drunks. It was also an environment where women could be and were sexually hit on by male staff and clients and sent to predominately male AA meetings where they often faced more of the same.

At its most benign, treatment was an environment filled with information and expectations that bore little relevance to female experience. We taught a physiology of alcohol based on men's bodies. We believed in a progression of alcoholism based on the experience of male alcoholics. We challenged women with metaphors of acceptance, surrender, and powerlessness and recommended rituals such as acts of service that constituted more the story of their lives than catalytic breakthroughs. It is a wonder that any women survived such environments. Many did not, but some recovered in spite of the treatment they received and went on to champion gender-specific treatment. As for me, I understood little about the special needs of adult addicted women at this point in my career, nor was there any awareness that the treatment milieu of this era was male-dominated. It was the invisible air that one neither saw nor questioned.

The ironies of this conceptual blindness include my marriage to a rather liberated and politically active woman at this time and my intellectual support of the blossoming women's movement. How could I consciously work on "getting it" in my personal life and remain so blind to such awareness in my professional life? I don't think we can will away such blind spots because we can't address what we can't see, but I do think we can put ourselves in situations and surround ourselves with people who will invite (or push) us into situations that create perceptual breakthroughs of enormous professional significance. It would take more than a decade before opportunities would present themselves that would allow me to transcend my privileged status as a male professional, the key to which was listening repeatedly to the stories of addicted and recovering women and the women pioneers in addiction counseling. That it took so long for these experiences to become part of my professional learning is testimony to the invisibility of women and their needs at this early stage of my career.

A Recovering World

Many local treatment program staff in the early 1970s knew more about recovery than they knew about treatment. Recovery was everywhere. Most of the staff were in recovery, programs had extensive volunteer programs made up almost exclusively of AA and Al-Anon members, and people from the local recovery community dropped in for coffee and a little Twelve-Step work all hours of the day and night. As a result, people starting treatment entered a community of recovered and recovering people—a culture with its own history, language, values, rituals, and leisure pastimes. I would later refer to this community as a *culture of recovery* and describe recovery for many people as a passage from the culture of addiction to the culture of recovery. In retrospect, I know today that many of the clients who entered recovery through treatment at Lighthouse did so primarily through the power of this healing community. Such power was not a conscious part of treatment in the early 1970s and thus the loss of the connection between treatment and community was not immediately noticed. Such disconnection came slowly in response to regulatory zealousness (e.g., the most extreme confidentiality standards in the health care field), the professionalization of the staff, and the commercialization of treatment. All of these forces pushed treatment towards a medical model mirroring the relationship between "patients," doctors, and hospitals.

As the walls of treatment institutions became thicker and higher, the connection to community was first diminished and then lost. Thirty years later, new models would emerge that would extol the healing power of community. This observation emphasizes the importance of defining the active, potent ingredients in treatment so they can be safeguarded. Without such definition and care, the most essential ingredients of treatment can be lost without such a loss even being recognized. Look around you. Is there anything essential to the recovery initiation and maintenance processes that you see on the verge of being lost?

Death of a Recovering Counselor

Few educational or experiential credentials were required to be hired in the emerging "drug abuse programs" in the early 1970s. If you self-reported being an AA member or could spin yourself as an ex-addict graduate of this or that program, could speak in complete sentences, and express a desire to serve, you had a good chance of employment. This "flying blind" period of the field attracted some incredibly bright and skilled people who went on to give this field its early distinctive character and credibility, but there were casualties on the road to a new profession.

One day I received a call from a friend who worked in a large therapeutic community in a neighboring state. He reported that one of their recent graduates was going to be taking a job in a city a few hours' drive from me, and he wanted to know if it would be okay for him to stop by and see me to get oriented to the field in Illinois. I readily agreed and a few weeks later received my first call from Danny to set a time for him to visit. When he arrived, he explained that he was hired as a "county drug abuse coordinator" and would be doing a variety of things ranging from talks to community groups and the schools and providing counseling to people referred to him for "drug abuse problems." In essence, he was a one-person prevention and treatment program reporting to the county board's human service committee. Such positions were often created in response to the first high profile drug-related casualties via arrest, injury, or death. Politically, they were a way to demonstrate responsiveness to what many perceived as the growing "epidemic of drug abuse."

Danny did have some skills that suited him to the position. He was bright and articulate and entered this position with an enormous passion for doing a good job. And yet, he was hopelessly ill-prepared for what he was about to face. He had spent his whole life in an urban multi-ethnic environment and struggled valiantly to adjust to this rural, white county. His own recovery looked solid within the urban therapeutic community in which he had lived for more than two years, but looked fragile as he entered this remote rural county. He was unprepared for the fishbowl environment he would be operating in, unprepared for questions about his lack of religious affiliation, and unprepared for suspicion from local AA members—the only other people in visible recovery within his environment. He was ill-prepared for criticism of what he did or failed to do.

The fishbowl environment was something that exerted enormous pressure, and no one was available locally to guide him through this process. He called and visited me a few times, always putting the best face on how things were going to elicit my praise for what he was doing. He visited his therapeutic community (TC) on occasion, but the physical distance precluded consistent support in these pre-email days of expensive phone calls. Danny struggled on a salary that barely provided subsistence living and strived to put together a personal life. In the end, the struggle was too much. On a weekend in 1973, Danny visited the largest nearby city and checked himself into a hotel. He was found dead Monday morning; he died of a heroin overdose.

The post-mortems of Danny's death, as they were for others who died under such circumstances, focused on personal character and what he'd failed to do in terms of his recovery program. But the larger lessons of how the field screened, selected, oriented, trained, and supervised recovering people in these new service roles would not be discussed until the number of casualties had reached critical mass and threatened the field's credibility and future. Those who survived this period helped lay the foundation for our field, but the casualties also should be honored, for they also struggled to help birth this field and often did so with virtually no support. Such casualties provided two lessons. First, working in prevention and treatment does not constitute a program of personal recovery. Second, prevention and treatment are not activities that can be sustained in personal and professional isolation. Someday, we should erect a monument to honor Danny and others whose lives were sacrificed in the early days of this field. Then old-timers like myself could visit and touch that monument, whispering to ourselves "but for luck and the Grace of God." Young people in this field could visit this monument to reflect on the importance of self-care and having a network of personal and professional support.

Everything I Know I Learned in Detox

In the treatment world I entered in the 1960s, it was common to work as a detox "tech" or as a detox counselor before being promoted to positions within residential or outpatient programs. At Lighthouse, we provided social setting detoxification within the same large Victorian house that also served as our residential facility. We were only a few hundred yards from the community hospital we closely cooperated with for those persons needing medical detoxification. In these early days, all staff helped with detoxing clients in the house and with visiting clients who were undergoing detoxification in the hospital.

Work in detox provides an opportunity to see aspects of addiction not revealed in other levels of care. In recent years, the specialization within levels of care has created a more antiseptic environment where many counselors know the beast of addiction only by hearsay. If someone is going to work in the world of addiction treatment, it is important that they know the realities of addiction and know it beyond the thresholds of their own personal and family experience. Here's what I learned in detox that no other level of care provided with such clarity.

1. Addiction is filthy. It soils the body and soul, shrouding the human being behind a mask of repulsiveness that would challenge a mother's love.
2. Addiction is profane. It transforms the meek into the brash and obscene.
3. Addiction is poison. It poisons body, mind, and character. The cleaned-up addict entering treatment from detox obscures the physical devastation of the beast that was so apparent only hours or days earlier. In detox, one sees more clearly than any other setting what most addicts fear more than physical death: the fear that personal degradation will evolve into complete disintegration and insanity. Detox can put human faces on such terms as delirium tremens, Wernicke syndrome, alcoholic hallucinosis, Korsakoff psychosis, and methamphetamine psychosis. Addiction deforms character and fuels hatred, jealousy, resentment, rage, and self-pity.
4. Addiction is anguish. A level of despair is expressed at a level of honesty within detox that is rarely seen in other settings.

5. Addiction is unredeemable shame. In detox, raw feelings of shame and self-hatred pour from the addict, revealing the existential position: I am unworthy of the love of others; I am unworthy of recovery.
6. Addiction is about isolation. It destroys the connecting tissue that binds the addicted person to their parents, siblings, intimate partners, children, friends, and co-workers. No one is as utterly alone as the man or woman waking into pained consciousness in their first day in detox. There is no "we" in addiction.
7. The addict in detox is a Mr. Hyde that transforms into Dr. Jekyll in the transition to other levels of care. Staff working exclusively in detox have only a glimmer of the Dr. Jekyll; staff working exclusively in inpatient and outpatient treatment see only a shadow of the deranged Mr. Hyde.

Working in detox is about more than pain; it is about opportunity. It is an opportunity to love the unlovable, respect the disreputable, and, in those acts, force individuals to redefine themselves, the world, and what is possible for them within it. It is about sowing seeds of recovery—priming the recovery process. It is about using this brief window of vulnerability to forge a recovery-inspiring relationship. It is recognizing that there are brief developmental windows of opportunity in all of our lives that can forever change our destiny. It is not so much the words said at those times that make a difference, but being authentically present with the person in those moments. Detox is about an unrelenting message of hope that the future can be different. It is breaking through the shell of addiction in the act of comforting someone who fears they are beyond redemption. Detox is about battling the beast—face to face. It is a special ministry, and those who do it well deserve a special place of honor within our field and within our communities.

Status among the Damned

Stigma seeps into every pore of the stigmatized, creating behavior that is otherwise inexplicable. As hatred of our own characteristics is absorbed by cultural osmosis, we strive to maintain esteem in whatever way we can. Maintaining esteem can involve aggression toward others who are perceived as sharing those stigmatized qualities to a greater degree. This defensive mechanism explains the historically elaborate pecking orders that existed within communities of color based on those qualities that most defined one's identity—skin tone, hair, and facial features. Such pecking orders also existed among the addicted and created status differences between the "righteous dope fiend" and the "gutter hype." These pecking orders also reflected the dichotomized view of celebrated and prohibited drugs in America. In the early days of "combined treatment" at Lighthouse, late stage alcoholics and addicts found themselves sharing the same space. Strange scenarios unfolded out of this mixture.

At intake, we asked about the whole spectrum of possible drug choices. I vividly remember the following scene. A late stage alcoholic with more than 150 arrests for public intoxication was dropped off for detox at Lighthouse by the police. He had been on a few months' jag and looked and smelled like it. Everything precious in his life had been violated and lost from alcoholism. Nothing was left in his life but rotgut wine. It would have been hard at that moment to find a sicker or more depraved individual. And yet, when I asked him about his use of drugs other than alcohol, he expressed moral outrage, "I may be a no-account drunk, but I'm no godda**ed dope fiend!" A short time later I witnessed a late stage heroin addict, equally depraved, react similarly when asked about his drinking—proclaiming with disgust and superiority that he was many things but he wasn't a "f***in' wino." Members of these demarcated, deviant subcultures cloistered on opposite sides of the room with staff gathered in a third group, each looking askance at the other as all chain-smoked a lethal invisible drug widely promoted and universally available in the early 1970s and drank gallons of caffeinated coffee.

Early National Conferences

Lighthouse was emerging in tandem with the births of state and national association of alcoholism and "drug abuse" professionals and programs. The field's birth and coming of age were celebrated at large annual conferences that provided a window into the larger movement of which each of us was a part. The conferences each had their own character—the National Council on Alcoholism conferences, the Alcohol and Drug Problem Association of North America conference, the National Drug Abuse Conference, and the many conferences sponsored by the National Institute on Alcohol Abuse and Alcoholism (NIAAA) and the National Institute on Drug Abuse (NIDA).

My earliest reactions to these conferences were ones of awed reverence and righteous indignation. The awe was elicited in response to the brilliant and charismatic individuals emerging as leaders in the field. The indignation was in response to the amount of drinking and drug use that occurred at many of these conferences. The conference attendees quickly organized themselves within the larger life of each conference. One cluster included those in recovery—we were called paraprofessionals in these early years—cloistered together for support, to share our early experiences working in treatment, and to share our disbelief at some of what was going on around us at the conference. A second cluster was filled with renegade professionals and older administrative types from other fields, many of whom brought heavy drinking rituals into the field with them. Much of their conference time was spent politicking at the closest hotel bars and lounges. A final cluster was populated by the much younger staff working in "drug abuse" prevention and treatment, many working in the field as an extension of their involvement in the youthful counterculture of this period. These attendees were the source of clinging marijuana smoke that one encountered each evening walking through hotel hallways. I saw much of the world in terms of black and white in those days, and what I saw at those conferences was a professional world split between drinkers (some of whom had obvious problems with alcohol), active drug users (whose presence in the field was an absolute puzzle to me), recovering people (whose intense cloistering suggested that these conferences were a threat that required an active plan of support), and a group of very serious and sober service professionals (divided between some who would go on to shape the future of the field and those who didn't have a clue).

One incident forever shaped the consciousness of how I conduct myself in public when representing the field. It was at a national alcoholism conference in 1973 or 1974, and another attendee and I were looking for a cup of coffee. When we found the restaurant closed, we walked into an open bar area across from where our conference presentations were occurring and asked the bartender if we could get coffee there. While he was pouring our coffee, he asked what kind of convention we were having. We explained that it was a conference for people who were working in newly created alcoholism treatment programs across the country. His response was, "You've got to be kidding!" I couldn't understand the look of repugnance on his face until I looked at those seated in the lounge area with their tables filled with empty and half-filled drinks. The incongruity between the good sales day the bartender was having and the realization of who we were was represented in the cynical disgust registered on his face. That brief incident underscored for me that, in our work in a stigma-laden arena, how we conduct ourselves serves to either confirm or counter that stigma. How we conduct our lives within and outside our professional roles is a living message about the integrity of the field, our agency, and ourselves and also influences how people view those we are pledged to serve. The look on the bartender's face said it all: "The way they drink, how the hell could they help anybody with an alcohol problem?"

Another thing that struck me about the conferences was how much time was consumed with talking about the structure of the field (the organizations and personalities) and the funding and regulatory apparatus that was emerging to support the field compared to how little time was spent actually talking about the treatment of alcoholism and addiction. For the latter you had to get into the scheduled presentations and some of these were a wonderful learning opportunity. By today's standards, science played only a minor role in these presentations, but they provided an opportunity to share what was being learned on the front lines of treatment as well as emerging conceptual models about the treatment of addiction. Some presentations exerted a profound influence on my thinking and my career. Here's one example.

In 1974, John Wallace presented a paper at the Alcohol and Drug Problems Association meeting in Minnesota that stunned me in its clarity and implications. Wallace argued that alcoholics develop a preferred defense structure (PDS) (e.g., denial, minimization, projection of blame, and intellectualization) that allows them to sustain their drinking and escape the consequences of that drinking. That starting position was not a new idea, but Wallace went on to say that the same PDS that supports drinking may be used to get through the early stages of recovery and that prematurely confronting this brittle PDS could actually trigger relapse. His idea that denial and minimization (of the problems facing the just-sobered), black-white thinking (e.g., "all of my problems are related to my drinking"; "all I have to do is not drink and everything will be fine"), and other defense mechanisms were actually an ally in the recovery process was a striking concept to me, pregnant with clinical implications. But then Wallace laid out the third paradox of recovery: the same PDS that supported alcoholism and that was reframed to support early recovery must later be abandoned in late stages of recovery.

104

Wallace's presentation changed the way I looked at the recovery process and the way I responded to the defensive machinations of the alcoholic in early recovery, and it also began a lifelong interest in the stages and styles of long-term recovery. Why is it important to go to conferences? Yes, we get to network and develop important mentor relationships. Yes, we get some time for rest and renewal. Yes, we get a sense of the larger professional context in which we are working. But sometimes, we encounter a perfectly timed idea that will change the trajectory of our professional lives and those whose lives we touch. It is an ethical responsibility for each of us to seek out those kinetic ideas and new skills.

A Vision of Legitimacy

The mid-1970s was a heady time in the world of addiction treatment. We had a sense that our time had come, that we were about to take our places alongside more established and mature helping professions. New mechanisms emerged that placed the mantle of legitimacy on treatment organizations and their service personnel. Organizational legitimacy came through two mechanisms: state licensure and independent accreditation. Designated state agencies promulgated regulatory standards for treatment programs, conducted site visits, cited deficiencies, and granted licensure for those programs that met minimal requirements. Most of these early standards focused more on board and administrative structures and compliance with fire and safety standards than on clinical protocol. Independent accreditation bodies encompassed these same areas but focused more on service procedures and granted a stamp of quality to addiction treatment programs. From the day the Joint Commission on Accreditation of Hospitals announced it would develop standards and accredit alcoholism treatment programs, the Lighthouse staff invested enormous energy toward achieving this coveted status. Public funding was unpredictable in these days, and there was promise in the air that JCAH accreditation would open the doors to insurance reimbursement for addiction treatment services. We also had a sense that JCAH accreditation would bestow a level of cultural and professional legitimacy on treatment institutions. And with those aspirations came major changes. Treatment programs residing in old Victorian homes or abandoned hotels in the 1970s built modern new facilities in the 1980s and 1990s. "Program Directors" became CEOs surrounded by a new army of specialists in business, finance, marketing, fundraising, and fee collection. Non-profit organizations began to think and act like private businesses, creating complex corporate structures and new ventures that promised to feed profits into the service divisions, but more often drained such resources and raised all manner of ethical and legal issues related to their operation.

The search for parallel legitimacy for those who worked on the front lines of addiction treatment led to the development of special counselor certification programs. Counselors invested considerable time and money to achieve this new status. We were a messy lot—unpolished, profane, and carriers of stories of backgrounds not usually associated with the status of a professional. We did clean up and weeded out those who couldn't make the transition. We cut our hair. We learned to dress up and even wear ties. We learned professional jargon and eliminated or became more selective in our use of profanity. We learned the art of discretion—now withholding the more lurid chapters of our personal histories—at least in professional and public circles. And after a time, we often withheld our recovery status.

An oft-cited Al-Anon slogan of this period was "Be careful what you wish for, you may get it." We would have been well-served by heeding this warning. Addiction treatment organizations did become more credible through the licensure and accreditation processes and insurance dollars did flow for a time, although never to community-based (versus hospital-based) programs to the extent hoped for and expected. "Alcoholism and drug abuse counselors"—as we were known then—also developed a degree of legitimacy through the processes of counselor certification. What we didn't know was the price we would pay for such legitimacy. We didn't know that we had entered a pathway whose course would transform our organizations from service organizations to businesses and create a day when seasoned old-timers would mourn the field's loss of heart. We didn't know that certification would accelerate educational requirements to the point that many dedicated and skilled workers would be pushed out of the field. We charged blindly ahead without defining the most essential ingredients of these new organizations and roles that could not be compromised. Our blindness to where we were going and what we would inadvertently sacrifice sowed the seeds for a future day when we would have to return to these questions.

Two Fields and a Shotgun Wedding

No addictions field existed in the early 1970s. There was an "alcoholism field" and a "drug abuse field," each viewing the other with considerable suspicion and condescension. The separation in the two fields, which on the surface reflected a difference in drug choice, also reflected deep generational differences and differences in ethnicity and social class. The alcoholism field of this period was dominated by middle-class white men in recovery from alcoholism. The drug abuse field was filled with younger white ethnics, people of color, and a higher percentage of women, with many from these groups drawn from what were then referred to as America's urban ghettos. Where the former had once exemplified and still aspired to the values and status of middle-class America, the latter had spent most of their lives living as outsiders and, even in recovery, often still saw themselves as outsiders. The two fields reflected different people in separate worlds. Separate treatment organizations. Separate federal and state funding and regulatory agencies. Separate counselor credentialing bodies. (Being an alcoholism counselor or a drug abuse counselor were two separate career choices.) Separate professional associations. Bringing these fields together was at best like mixing oil and water and at worst like bringing gasoline and fire together. And yet they did come together—amidst enormous emotional debate and conflict. Well, almost together. We still have the nonsensical federal split between National Institute on Alcohol Abuse and Alcoholism (NIAAA) and the National Institute on Drug Abuse (NIDA).

The debates for and against merger/consolidation of the fields were personal and acrimonious. I don't think the fields could have survived as segregated disciplines and organizations, but the process of moving beyond such separation was messy and painful.

The eventual merger of these separate worlds into an integrated addictions field brought together stakeholders with different motivations for merger. Merger advocates from the drug abuse field hoped to lessen the stigma of illicit drug use by embracing it within a larger addiction or chemical dependency umbrella. (The alcoholism field was having some breakthrough success in the destigmatization of alcoholism.) Merger advocates from the alcoholism side hoped to avail themselves of the larger pool of funding flowing from Nixon's War on Drugs. At the front lines of clinical service, the separation in thinking and practice became untenable for a variety of reasons. Growing numbers of clients were dependent upon alcohol AND other drugs. Too many clients treated for alcohol OR drugs developed a problem with the other that contributed to post-treatment relapses. Too many people who worked in the field out of an alcoholism or drug addiction background developed problems with the other while working in the field. It was only a question of time before the arbitrary separation between alcohol and drugs collapsed at the point of service delivery. Too many communities were too small and had too few resources to maintain separate infrastructures for alcoholism treatment and drug abuse treatment. The dye for consolidation was cast on both clinical and pragmatic grounds. Such an integrated concept of "addiction" and a broadened understanding of "recovery" had been presaged within Narcotics Anonymous in the early 1950s, but it would take much longer for such perspectives to emerge within the modern history of addiction medicine.

A leading voice for integration of alcoholism and drug abuse treatment at the clinical level was Dr. Don Ottenberg of Eagleville Hospital in Pennsylvania. In the early 1970s Don and I regularly presented on what was then called "combined treatment" at the respective alcoholism and drug abuse national conferences. Don was a visionary and one of the most client-focused, recovery-focused administrators I ever met in the field. I was on the integrationist side of the great debate, and I vividly recall Don telling me this fight was for the very future of the field. He assured me that the fate of people for decades would be shaped by the outcome of this debate and that I could personally make a difference by helping wage this battle.

What I learned through all of this is that nothing is more sacred within a professional field than its definitional boundary. Drawn too tightly, professional fields can become what I later christened "closed incestuous systems"; drawn too loosely, a professional field is vulnerable for co-optation or colonization by more powerful forces in its environment. All discussions about what should and should not be included within a field's rubric of responsibility—all discussions about merging organizations are, in the end, discussions that dictate, for good and for bad, the future of a field. How do you view the boundary of the addiction treatment field today? Is that boundary drawn too tightly? Is that boundary being stretched too far?

Lessons from Mama Lou

One of the true characters I met during my Lighthouse years was a woman affectionately known as "Mama Lou." She was hired as the cook at Lighthouse's residential facility, but her title should have been "Mother Earth." She was part of the magic of these early years and literally loved people into recovery. Lacking any formal training other than her own family recovery experience, she provided part of the special chemistry that guided many men and women into recovery. I have often reflected on those unique ingredients she brought to the Lighthouse treatment experience. She was ever-present—much more accessible than the counselors who were often tied up in individual sessions or meetings of innumerable varieties. She hugged everyone whether they needed or wanted it. When asked, she wouldn't hesitate to offer common sense advice—something anathema to the more detached objectivity offered by the professional staff. In responding to such requests, she peppered her responses with stories of her own experiences and those of the many alcoholics who had been part of her life. The other ingredient that she brought was a belly laugh that could shake the rafters of the old Victorian home we occupied. In the years that followed my work with Mama Lou, addiction treatment became professionalized and women and men of Lou's character disappeared from the treatment scene. Today, counselors are less accessible, rarely or never self-disclose or offer advice, don't touch, and rarely laugh in Lou's boisterous style. I still think about Lou and what she represented. I think a lot in my old age about what we lost on the road to professionalization.

Becoming a Clinical Director

The role of a clinical director in the newly opening programs of the early 1970s was unlike that role today. In 1974, the clinical director role I held included such duties as sitting with someone who needed close supervision in detox, interviewing a walk-in, calming an irate family member visiting the facility, soliciting materials from local businesses to renovate the facility, helping paint the facility (most clients were too shaky to paint very far off the ground), in addition to a daily menu of conducting individual and group counseling. I learned many skills working alongside carpenters, painters, masons, plumbers, and electricians that were regularly admitted to Lighthouse. These men rehabbed the facility while they rehabbed themselves. This reciprocity was part of the glue that made us a community. It conveyed that each person had something to offer the community and that this was more about mutual assistance than charity or paid professional service.

Training for clinical supervisors was virtually non-existent in these days. One got to be a supervisor by outlasting those around you. The role of supervisor was more often a badge of survival than of competence. But we did the best we could. We tried to mirror the best of what we had received from others along the way and tried to avoid actions we judged to be mistakes by the supervisors that came before us. My circumstances were somewhat unique because of the intensity of supervision I had experienced in the psychiatric settings where I had worked. I had experienced a structure and depth that was rare in the early treatment field that contributed to what I was able to bring to the clinical supervision process even though the addictions field lacked the stable infrastructure that made such supervision possible. As a result, I tried to replicate a consistent structure for individual and group supervision even though that structure was often superseded by crises of one sort or another. I must say, in retrospect, during my early years as a clinical supervisor, this problem was more characterological than organizational. The truth is that I felt much more comfortable in the throes of a crisis than I did in the trenches of clinical supervision. The former fed the adrenaline rushes that had fueled my success in streetwork and crisis intervention in the years before Lighthouse opened. As a result, I too quickly abandoned a scheduled supervision meeting for a crisis that I could take on my own shoulders. It took a while to realize that the thing that had contributed to my success in one role was sabotaging my success in another. It's impossible to grow professionally without growing personally.

The Resurrection of a Carpenter

Don was brought to Lighthouse by his family shortly after the residential program opened. He could have been a poster for E. M. Jellinek's "Gamma species alcoholism"—a family history of alcoholism, a slow and predictable progression of alcohol problems with a recent escalation in loss of control and radical personality change while drinking, and a rapid escalation of those problems following the death of his wife, all amid intense guilt and remorse. Don was a master

110

carpenter whose skills had eroded in tandem with the deterioration of his body. Following Don's detox in the hospital, he was treated at Lighthouse for more than nine months and physically advanced from an inability to walk due to advanced alcoholic polyneuritis to the point of returning to work. Following his discharge, Don relapsed at the anniversary date of the death of his wife and within three days could no longer walk—a year's work in physical rehabilitation destroyed in 72 hours. Don was re-admitted and later discharged to a productive life in recovery, a remarriage, and his eventual retirement. He remained sober and active within AA the remainder of his life.

Following his discharge from Lighthouse, Don lived a few blocks from me and I used to stop by and have coffee with him on Saturday mornings. These visits took place before formal boundaries existed between counselors and clients. Later, informal contacts like mine with Don were a natural part of what would be called continuing care services. We didn't use that term; we simply saw ourselves—clients and staff—as holding common membership in a mutually supportive community of recovery. I still have a beautiful shelf (now in the Illinois Addiction Studies Archives) that Don built as a gift for me in 1974. (Yeah, I know—another boundary violation, but this was still the time before I knew what a boundary was.)

Requiem for a Lost Soul

Larry was a special client. (Yes, we all have special clients!) He arrived early in the history of Lighthouse and was one of those clients everyone enjoyed. He was a true habilitation project, needing everything (and more) than we had to offer. Some clients spent many months in treatment and Larry stayed for the better part of a year during a time when staff and clients formed a cohesive healing community. I served as Larry's primary counselor and enjoyed being part of his personal transformation. After his lengthy stay, Larry graduated and returned a considerable distance to his home. That distance precluded his attendance to the "aftercare group" then offered to all graduated Lighthouse clients, but he did call during the early months of his return home to say hi to everyone and report that he was doing well. The space that Larry took in my professional life was quickly filled by others with similar problems and needs.

One early evening after I returned home from work, Pete Huffman, who was working the evening clinical shift at Lighthouse, visited my home to tell me he had just received some bad news. The story he revealed was indeed horrific. Larry's parents had just called Lighthouse and reported the following. Larry had done well in the months after his return home. He had gotten involved in local AA meetings, found a good job, and even developed his first serious romantic relationship. After some months of intense courtship, Larry and his girlfriend broke up yesterday and Larry began drinking almost immediately. After drinking to the point of extreme intoxication, Larry crawled into the back seat of an unlocked car and went to sleep. When the car owner returned, Larry was arrested and charged with public intoxication and car theft. Sometime during the night, Larry had used strips of torn clothing to hang himself in his jail cell. He was found not breathing by the jail staff and could not be revived. Before hanging himself, he had pinned a note on his body asking forgiveness for letting me down and asking me to attend his funeral. As you can well imagine, these final details were like an assault on my heart and mind. A few days later, the Lighthouse staff and many of the clients who had known Larry attended his funeral and burial. One more surprise was in store for me. In the months since leaving Lighthouse, he had grown a goatee cut in the precise style as my own. Staring at him in the coffin was like looking at myself.

I walked around for weeks vacillating between emotional distress and numbness. I drew no great insights from this experience, no new vows of heightened commitment to the field. (Those would not come for a long time.) Instead, I spent considerable time assessing whether I could continue as a therapist and keep working in the field. I was most critical during that time of the healing community that Larry had been a part of and I realized he had disconnected from it when he needed it most. That community of staff and clients and the larger recovery community helped me walk through the motions until I could complete my grieving and re-establish my therapeutic confidence. Anyone working in this field for any length of time will encounter crises of faith that will challenge their ability to do this work. Rigorous clinical supervision and a close network of collegial support from professional peers and from peers in long-time recovery are critical to weathering such emotional storms. Those sources of strength helped me get through one of the most significant personal and clinical crises of my career.

As I began to recover from this incident, I did find ways to use it positively. Larry has stood in my mind for more than thirty-five years as my personal image of the devastating lethality of addiction. I still have great respect for his recovery effort. I have long used Larry's life as a source to intensify my work with others. Years later when I was anxious about some presentation I was about to give, I would think of Larry and the importance of the message I was about to give and quietly dedicate that presentation to him. I have tried to give Larry's too-short life some sustained meaning through my work and words.

One other notable lesson lies within this vignette. In a period of ever-briefer interventions, it is important to realize there was a period when we had almost unlimited time in treatment and that such long lengths of stay were not enough for many clients to stabilize and sustain recovery in the community. In the months following Larry's death, I was haunted by an edge-of-awareness sense that something was inherently flawed in the way we as a field were treating individuals like Larry. I was too far inside the acute care model of addiction treatment to see it at that time, but I know today that we did everything we could for Larry in terms of detoxification and stabilization. The acute treatment was fine; what was missing was recovery. We treated Larry like we were mending a broken arm rather than a broken spirit that would take years of support to become whole. We failed to link his treatment to the long-term process of recovery, failed to provide post-treatment monitoring and support, and failed to provide assertive linkage to a community of recovering people within his natural environment.

Thirty years later, I would write about the need for treatment programs to do assertive post-treatment monitoring, support, and early re-intervention with each client in the early months and years following primary treatment. As I wrote those articles, I thought of Larry and wondered if those services would have made a difference in Larry's life. I like to think they would have and regret that my full understanding of their importance came so late in my career. I hope I can pass that understanding on to the next generation of treatment professionals—as a way to honor Larry's life and ease my still painful memory of his death. Are there people you could similarly honor?

"Scars and Stuff"

Precious lessons can come from unusual circumstances. In the early history of Lighthouse, we admitted a number of young men (ages 17-30 years) whose primary drug had been, since their pre-adolescent years, volatile solvents. There are many subpopulations of young people who participate in what in some parts of the country is known as "sniffing and huffing." What distinguished these clients were their singular devotion to solvents (eschewing most other drugs) and the frequency, intensity, long duration, and severe consequences relates to such use. I had the idea that some special benefits could come from segregating these individuals in a specialized treatment group. The following incident occurred at the third meeting of this group.

I was running a few moments late for group. When I opened the door to the group room, I was stunned to see members of this small group in various stages of undress. Two members had their shirts open, another a sleeve rolled up, a third had his pants pulled down enough to expose a good portion of a butt cheek, and a fifth had a bare leg exposed from a rolled up pants leg. My entrance sparked embarrassment and a frantic attempt to reorder their appearance. When I asked what they were doing, I got a sheepish "nothing," as if I was a parent finding all of their arms deep in the family cookie jar. When I pushed, one finally revealed, "We were just comparing scars and stuff." Pulling words out of them as if they were teeth, I asked each, "What scars and stuff?" When I pushed the young man who was exposing his butt cheek, he again pulled a shirt up his side, revealing a rope-like scar receding into his jeans. In explanation, he reported that he got that one the second time he fell out of an upstairs window—the second fall coming at the age of five. This client and the others seemed to take this information as a quite normal story. And then they got into it: show and tell for the therapist. Each revealed scar triggered another story—stories of arms through windows, accidents with tools, burns of many varieties, injuries from fighting (usually someone bigger, meaner, and better at it), and a list of auto and cycle accidents that left several without driving privileges.

The pattern was clear. What I was seeing was not individuals seeking pleasure or seeking sedation, but individuals involved in risk-taking so extreme as to constitute a courtship with death. As I looked at these young men, I realized there was a depth of pathology here that far exceeded any seen in the alcoholics and heroin addicts with whom they shared the treatment milieu. Over the next few weeks, I reconstructed the abandonment and tragic early losses in their lives, and knew at a deeper level than ever before how this history would get played out within the treatment environment. I watched closely over the next few weeks as one split treatment after an intense level of emotional disclosure in group, another cut himself on a knife while washing

114

dishes, and the young man with the rope-like scar injured himself on two consecutive fishing trips (the first a hook in his ear; the second a heavy weight cast into the mud that, when jerked loose, hit him square between his eyes). The fishing trip injuries were followed by my entrance on the second floor and noticing a towel stuffed along the inside bottom of the bathroom door. Our fishing aficionado was in the bathtub with his face buried in a quart of contact cement—an episode that then led to his expulsion from treatment.

In the years that followed, I would meet other such young men and women, and I would have greater success in their treatment— thanks primarily to collaboration with some very good psychiatrists. But it was following the lives of my "scars and stuff" group that taught me just how lethal this pattern was and that these cases should not be treated solely by an addictions counselor. I followed their lives through the hospitals and prisons that would follow and grieved their further injury and premature deaths—from falls, fires, suffocation (falling face-down into a solvent-saturated bag or cloth), an auto accident, and from suicide. Their fixation on solvents was not a self-contained disorder that had grown from the problems in their lives, but part of a much broader pattern of risk-taking in which their drug choice was but one potential source of their demise. At the time I met the members of this group, they were not in a position to learn much from me, but I learned a great deal from them, beginning with the importance of clinical humility.

Becoming an Expert Witness

Hal Jennings served as a McLean County Assistant States Attorney who prosecuted many people addicted to alcohol and drugs. He then ventured into private criminal law where he specialized in defending people facing similar charges. Hal was also a founding member of the board of Lighthouse and a passionate supporter of addiction treatment. After he moved into private practice, he approached me with a request to serve as an expert witness on addiction and treatment in cases he was defending. For the next two years, I periodically testified in circuit and federal court cases. My testimony most often involved presenting the results of a clinical evaluation of someone under indictment for possession or sale of illicit drugs, with related testimony related to the individual's potential needs for treatment and his or her prognosis for recovery.

The process itself was an interesting one with Hal or another defense attorney establishing my experience in the field and then guiding me through my testimony. This would be followed by a prosecuting attorney challenging my expertise and my conclusions that someone needed treatment. The former usually involved a long series of questions intended to emphasize what I was not, e.g., Are you a psychiatrist? Are you a physician? Are you a doctoral-trained clinical psychologist? Are you licensed as an addictions specialist by the State of Illinois? (At that time, there was no such licensure.) Have you written any books on addiction? (At that time, I hadn't.) This series would go on for 15-30 minutes with the goal being to convince a judge or jury—and myself—that I was a worthless human being who had nothing whatsoever to contribute to the legal proceedings that were underway.

This would be followed by rebuttal intending to make it look as if I had been personally appointed by God to do this work: Do you collaborate in your work with psychiatrists, physicians, psychologists, and other licensed professionals? Isn't it true that such professionals refer patients to you? Do you provide training that persons representing these professions attend? Isn't it true that you are on-call for local hospitals and police departments to handle addiction-related crises? How many addicts from this county have you had the opportunity to evaluate or treat in the past three years?

In watching this pageant unfold around me time after time, I came to realize how little the proceedings had to do with the law, public safety, or personal rehabilitation. Most of the people whose interests I represented were there for one reason: their status as addicts. I came to see my role as that of presenting the person behind the stereotype. I knew that if I failed, my client would be thrust even deeper into the culture of addiction. The weight of that responsibility propelled me to prepare myself as best I could for such proceedings. And all of those "no" responses to prosecuting attorneys helped convince me that I really did need more education and professional credentials.

Being Played

You know you are in trouble as a Clinical Director when you get to work and all of your staff members, including those whose shifts ended earlier that morning, are gathered for your arrival. You are in more trouble when most of the current clients are standing behind them also waiting for you. When they have a spokesperson, you can rest

116

assured that this is not going to be your best morning. That's the scene that greeted me on a spring day in 1974. The spokesperson blurted out the problem, "This man has made a mockery of everything this program stands for," and then catalogued the dastardly deeds the referenced client had committed in the four days since his admission. I had to admit the list was impressive. It seemed this client had found a way to break nearly every rule in the house short of those that would have gotten him instantly expelled. As the list of major and minor misdeeds was finally completed, the spokesperson pointedly concluded, "And we want to know what YOU are going to do about it."

Knowing when I am outnumbered, I stood tall and suggested it was time to have, in the vernacular of the day, a little "come to Jesus" meeting with this client. The client was quickly retrieved and a general meeting of the treatment community ensued in which we reviewed the client's nasty behaviors and made our expectations for the client exceedingly clear. In short, we drew a proverbial "line in the sand" and made it clear that the next time the client crossed that line he would be thrown out of the program. Assuring us that he understood, the meeting adjourned. The rest of the day passed quietly until I received a call at home that night about 10:45, reporting that the client refused to go to bed (there was the usual in bed, lights out rule that all were expected to follow). Now, suppose you were the Clinical Director. How would you have responded? I threw him out of treatment, and did so with a fair amount of gusto.

When I arrived the next morning, smiles were on everyone's faces and I received pats on my back for "sticking to my guns." I must confess to feeling pretty good about how I had handled the whole thing—at least until I got the phone call from the local judge who had mandated the just-expelled man to treatment with us. As I recall it today, the judge said something like the following:

> *Let me get this straight. I send you a man who has lived in every manner of deviant culture—a man who has committed every kind of unthinkable crime. And you kicked him out of treatment because he wouldn't go to bed on time?! I sent this man to you for treatment, not for charm school!* (Phone slams).

I still feel sheepish about that call. But things got worse after it. This client had several prior treatments, and we had dutifully obtained releases of information from him to get copies of these earlier records.

Days after his extrusion, these records slowly trickled in—long after we needed them. The discharge summaries indicated four prior residential treatments in which the client had been administratively discharged during the first seven days of treatment for failure to comply with program rules. Who do you think was in control of this man's treatment? It sure wasn't me or my clinical team.

I am convinced that the client I expelled that night walked down the steps of my facility with a bitter smile on his face, muttering, "Just like all the others!" His view of himself and the world was untouched. I believe he left my treatment program with less capacity for future recovery than when he arrived. The client, consciously or unconsciously, played me and everyone else in the treatment milieu. And I played my own scripted role perfectly, if unknowingly.

In your career, you will encounter many clients with chronic self-defeating styles of "doing treatment." Such styles constitute a major source of self-sabotage in early recovery efforts. It is as important to understand such styles, as it is to understand the nature of each client's substance use patterns. By recognizing and understanding such patterns, we can alter the script, refuse to play our programmed roles, and write alternative outcomes. We can avoid being played or therapeutically use the experience of being played as a turning point for the client.

"I'm sober. Now what do I do?"

During my tenure at Lighthouse, I was approached by a number of old-timers in Alcoholics Anonymous and asked if I would consider running a therapy group for people in long-term recovery. I agreed and embarked on one of the most meaningful service processes and rich learning experiences of my life. At that point in time, my entire clinical career had been focused on working with people in the latest stages of their addictions and the earliest days of their recoveries. I knew little, at least from my professional role, about the needs of people in long-term recovery. For almost two years, I met an evening a week with recovering people who had at least five years of continuous sobriety. Each of these remarkable individuals had moved beyond the early struggles of achieving and maintaining sobriety and had shifted their focus to reconstructing their character and interpersonal relationships, as well as redefining the meaning and purpose in their lives.

One of the most powerful lessons I learned facilitating this process was that the things that maintain and enrich sobriety are often different from the things that help first achieve that sobriety. It is a paradox of recovery that the one thing you most want and which seemed so unattainable, once achieved, is no longer enough. Each of the members of my group woke up one morning years into his or her recovery and confronted the question, "I'm sober. Now what do I do?" The pink cloud of early recovery was gone, sobriety had become a hard-won habit, but a dark mid-life recovery crisis loomed. That crisis often involved a more in-depth examination of one's own character, one's relationships, and questions about the ultimate meaning of life. It was as if the recovery gods had played a cheap trick of delivering sobriety while denying the happiness that was promised to accompany it.

In the months after months we met, I had the privilege of watching people who were among the recovery community elders work to shed obsessions with work, money, power, fame, and sex. I watched them break free of shame and achieve a previously unattainable level of self-acceptance. I observed them moving beyond their addictions— using their addiction and recovery experiences to achieve depths of character, personal meaning, and service to their communities. I watched their evaluation of their addiction history move from the status of a curse to the status of a gift—a doorway of entry into authenticity and service.

As service relationships in addiction treatment have become briefer, there is a dimension of the recovery experience that is lost to addiction professionals—the experience of witnessing these late-stage recovery transformations up close. The bottom line is that we cannot prepare people for long-term recovery if we haven't observed that process across a diverse number of people. Staying connected to communities of recovery (regardless of your own recovery status) is remaining in a sustained internship within those communities so you can increase depth of knowledge about the answers to the question, "I'm sober. Now what do I do?" In short, we cannot prepare people for recovery if we don't have knowledge of what comes after stable recovery initiation is achieved. How could you increase your contact with people in long-term recovery?

119

A Road Not Taken

What we choose not to do can be as important as what we choose to do. In the spring of 1978, I entertained the possibility of leaving clinical work for academia. During a brief encounter with Rev. Glenn Riddell, he mentioned that there was going to be an opening in the psychology department at Eureka College and that I should apply. I was subsequently offered a contract to serve as a full-time instructor for the coming school year for an $11,000 salary. I gave this option considerable thought, but in the end decided that my future contributions were to be made outside the academic community. What I didn't know was how much of my future would still involve teaching. What we are drawn toward but think we have forsaken can still reveal what lies ahead. Some fates will simply not let us say no.

Closed Incestuous Systems

The incestuous process I described experiencing earlier at the McLean Country Mental Health Center was replicated and intensified in the early years of Lighthouse. The core of the staff was young, worked all day together, and often spent evenings and weekends socializing with each other and our respective spouses. As staff became physically and emotionally depleted and intimacy barriers dissolved within these relationships, it was only a question of time before the soap opera began. I would later describe us at that point in time as a *closed incestuous system*, and describe this closure process as a stage in the life of an organization in which the professional, social, and sexual needs of the staff are increasingly met inside the boundary of the organizational family. This process exacts a high toll. Of the ten key staff who were most involved in such intense work and play, only one of their marriages survived this period. Lighthouse, like many programs before it, could have easily imploded at that point in time and came close to doing so. (We will discuss some of the lessons from this period a bit later.)

The lesson here is one of wholeness and the importance of meeting one's professional, social, and sexual needs outside of one's immediate workplace. The lesson is also to be careful out there. People who enter this work to help others can get caught up in organizational processes that can leave long-lasting wounds. There are many strategies to respond to such potentially harmful group processes. Completely unaware of these broad strategies in 1973, I chose flight.

Time to Leave

How do you know when it is time to change roles within an organization or move from one organization to another? I've left jobs for many reasons over the course of my career, usually in the collision between my own readiness for a next step and an unexpected opportunity. While the latter seemed to sometimes fall out of the sky, there were warning signs of the former—a gnawing sense of dissatisfaction, a psychological disengagement from clients and professional peers, a longing for an indefinable something just out of reach, and a sense that my relationship with an organization had grown toxic. In the face of such feelings, one can choose to leave or be spared that choice via being scapegoated and forcibly extruded.

For me there is a zone of optimum performance and health in the workplace. Constant adjustments are necessary to stay within that zone over time. I always felt it was time to leave an organization when I could no longer find that zone. "Follow your heart, not your bank account" is the best advice I was ever given on how to make a decision to join, remain with, or leave an organization. My experience is that when you align yourself with the kind of work you truly love, your passion generates such a high level of achievement that the financial necessities take care of themselves. I loved my work, but in 1976, my heart was hurting.

Every professional career has periods when you hit a wall, and I hit mine in 1976. I had worked in the field during my first seven years of recovery and through my evolution from a streetworker to an addictions counselor to a clinical director. Something shifted for me in 1976. The work had not changed, but I had. It became clear to me that I either had to get into the field at a deeper level or get out of the field. I had begun to question whether I could sustain the commitment I had made to myself standing in that jail cell in 1970. Intellectually, I was still committed to help develop a national network of addiction treatment programs, but I was physically and emotionally exhausted from the unrelenting demands of my early years in the field. My life circumstances had also changed and I was wrestling with how to reconcile the demands of the job with a wife and a beautiful young

121

daughter. My discomfort grew to the point that I knew something had to give.

In the end, I could not forsake my commitment to the field, but I did decide it was time for me to leave Lighthouse. My personal stagnation occurred in the context of toxic organizational processes unfolding within Lighthouse that would take me years to understand. In 1976, Lighthouse received the Francis J. Gerty Award presented by the Illinois Department of Mental Health for outstanding addiction services. On the day I traveled to Springfield to accept the award from Governor Dan Walker, the Lighthouse program had never looked better in terms of the veneer it projected to the public. Internally the program was in shambles. We sensed that some ailment had befallen us, but we had no words to name the nature of that ailment or find a quick solution to it. That understanding came for me only after I left and following years of reflection.

I knew that, if I was going to remain in the field in clinical work, I had to be able to understand what had taken a dynamic program and a wonderful group of people and nearly destroyed them. I also felt I needed to know much more about addiction and recovery if I was going to be effective with clients that were appearing with increasingly severe and complex problems. I had reached a point where I was obsessed with the clients who were not making it. Those clients whose lives were being transformed by recovery were no longer enough to offset the personal wounds and sense of inadequacy produced by clients who had started to hopelessly recycle through newly opened treatment centers.

I made two important decisions. I decided to return to school for a master's degree in addiction studies, and I moved my family to Chicago to accept work as a trainer for the Illinois Dangerous Drugs Commission, the agency that then planned, funded, and monitored all drug addiction treatment services in the State of Illinois. Both decisions would open professional vistas beyond my dreams, but also bring unexpected consequences.

Turning points in our lives can come from things we need to run from or things we need to run to. Are you experiencing a need to do either?

Finding an Addiction Studies Program

When I decided to return to school for a master's program in 1976, I began looking for schools that offered a specialty in addiction studies. What I found was pretty bleak. Few, if any, specialized addiction studies programs existed in the United States. (Now, more than 400 programs are linked together in the International Consortium of Addiction Studies Educators. See a listing of such programs at http://www.attcnetwork.org/learn/education/dasp.asp). Only a handful of programs in psychology, social work, or counseling offered a subspecialty in addiction counseling. The more I looked at traditional academic offerings, the more frustrated I became. During this period, a Gateway peer, friend, and mentor, "Joe D.," suggested I consider designing a specialty degree at Goddard College in Vermont. Joe's suggestion was a turning point in my life. In typical Gateway fashion, Joe encouraged and walked me through the entire admission process and his wife Pat typed most of my papers over the next two years.

In the days before wide availability of addiction studies programs, many ex-addicts sought out non-traditional academic programs to build credentials that would enhance their mobility in the addictions field. Joe had completed a master's at Goddard and was enrolled in a PhD program at the time of our conversation. Exploring the option of a "university without walls" seemed like a way I could enhance my learning while continuing to work and support my family. It was one of the best decisions I have ever made.

The Goddard "Experience"

Goddard College was founded in 1938 and went on to develop a reputation as a "radical college" in the tradition of Antioch, Sarah Lawrence, and Bennington. It was a haven for academic mavericks, freethinkers, and political radicals. As one of the early colleges promoting non-traditional graduate education, Goddard's faculty served more as learning consultants than expert teachers. My central point of contact with Goddard was Dr. Alan Walker. In my initial meeting with him, I proudly outlined my proposed plan of study and awaited his admiring comments. He responded as follows: "It feels like you are trying to impress me with what you already know. Goddard doesn't exist to legitimize what you've already accomplished; we're here to push you beyond the boundaries of what you know about yourself and your chosen field. Go home and reflect on your life and your field and come back with a plan that explores those frontiers." That was the beginning of my Goddard experience—one not recommended for the faint of heart or those needing a high degree of structure.

Goddard's program is not for everyone. It sustained a creative tension that many if not most would find intolerable, and it required a level of self-discipline far beyond that required in traditional programs. But Goddard exerted an enormous influence on my life and career; it was a perfect match with my abilities and temperament. I gained two special things from Goddard. The first was a message that my life was about more than what I wanted to do; it was also about what the world (and my professional field) needed that I was uniquely qualified to provide. This was the beginning of an ongoing process of matching my passions with the needs of the addictions field. Answering that question in 1976 allowed me to plan a program of learning that prepared me for the contributions I have sought to make in the more than four decades since. What do you think are the field's greatest needs at this moment in its history? Which of those needs energize and call you? Buried in the answers to these questions may lie your own frontier—your personal destiny and the destiny of the field.

The second thing I learned from Goddard was a process of learning that I've continued to this day. When I outlined to Alan Walker what I needed to know and be able to do, he asked me to reflect on the best people I could think of to help develop these knowledge and skill areas. He emphasized that I should "think big" as I created this list. A list was soon assembled of some of the foremost people in addiction treatment. He then asked me to select one person from the list who could provide general oversight of my studies and who would be geographically accessible to me. When I shared my working list, he then said, "Now go get them." When I looked confused, he explained that a major portion of the tuition I was paying was to pay special learning consultants and that I should contact these individuals and negotiate their support in my learning plan.

After conquering shyness and a nearly paralyzing degree of intimidation, I finally contacted those on my list. None of them knew me and all initially reported that they doubted they would have time for this role. (I had a whole list of busy people: who else would you want?) I convinced each to agree to a brief face-to-face meeting. All eventually agreed to work with me, and, in the end, most even refused financial payment. Dr. Ed Senay, from the Department of Psychiatry at the University of Chicago and a national leader in addiction medicine, agreed to supervise my overall learning process. The quality of the subsequent learning experience was beyond words and culminated nearly two years later in a final meeting with Alan Walker. What he told me in that meeting was that I could have done much of this learning without Goddard and that I could continue this process the rest of my life. He said I could create a "university inside my own life" by continuing to find special people to teach and mentor me in what could be an endless series of structured learning experiences. The least important thing I got from Goddard was a master's degree. The most important thing I got from Goddard was a strategy for lifelong learning. What do you need to know? What do you need to be able to do? Who are the best people who could teach you these things? Is it time you contacted them and asked for their help?

Goddard brought me in touch with the Illinois Drug Abuse Program—the umbrella for the rapidly growing network of Chicago-area addiction treatment programs in the 1960s. It was a laboratory of clinical innovation under the leadership of people like Drs. Jerry Jaffe, Ed Senay, John Chappel, and an army of charismatic ex-addicts. Every field has institutional pockets of innovation where the synergy of place and people set the stage for periods of individual and collective achievement. Those aspiring to leadership roles in the addictions field are advised to locate such centers of innovation and cultivate relationships with them. Are there any such centers in your area? Is it time you took the initiative to work more closely with or within such organizations?

Methadone: A Rant (and a Repentance)

During my Goddard experience, I was forced to rethink much of the holy dogma I had absorbed in my early years in the addictions field. One such example of this involved my feelings about methadone. Notice I said "feelings" and not "thoughts"; I didn't have any thoughts about methadone treatment, but I had a lot of intense feelings. The following experience is typical of the shifts in epistemology I underwent during my Goddard years and the years that would follow.

125

In one of my first meetings with Dr. Ed Senay, the subject of methadone maintenance came up. My views about methadone were scripted by my deep involvement with the therapeutic community and Minnesota Model programs of this period. Not surprisingly, I launched into an anti-methadone rant that focused on the stupidity of using an addictive drug to treat addiction. The rant went on for some time—I had a lot to say about this subject, but it slowly dawned on me that Dr. Senay was looking at me strangely. (I had just presented this rant to one of the leading architects of addiction treatment in the United States and one of the country's leading experts on methadone.) I don't recall Dr. Senay's exact words at that point but he basically pointed out to me that my passion on the subject of methadone was in inverse proportion to my knowledge. (A few years before his passing, Dr. Senay told me that his actual words were much more direct and colorful than this, and he thanked me for cleaning up this story.) Following my rant, Dr. Senay shared with me that there were many problems with methadone maintenance treatment, but that those problems were unrelated to anything that had come out of my mouth in the past ten minutes. I sheepishly left with a pile of books and research studies that began my education about methadone maintenance and medication-assisted recovery.

Methadone maintenance faces many problems more than a half century after its development, (e.g., scientifically indefensible dosing policies; exorbitant clinic fees; inflexible and inconvenient pick-up/take-home schedules; inadequate treatment of co-occurring physical and psychiatric disorders; inadequate integration of psychosocial therapies and recovery support services; arbitrary limitations on length of methadone maintenance treatment (MMT); and inadequate clinical training and supervision of MMT staff, to name some of the more important). But none of those deficits were reflected in the ignorance and bigotry that I and many others so freely spewed on this subject. The stigma attached to methadone extracts a high price on those in MMT-supported recovery, but a day will come when thousands of people whose lives have been saved by methadone will stand together and offer themselves as living proof of the legitimacy of medication-assisted recovery. They will, at the same time, also share the need to elevate the quality of MMT.

The words we speak with greatest passion are sometimes the words that are the most distasteful when we must later eat them. I wish I could erase what I said about methadone before 1978, but I cannot. All

I can do is try to make amends to those my words may have injured and for my role in contributing to the atmosphere of ignorance and bigotry that continues to surround medication-assisted recovery. In April of 2009, I was asked to keynote the annual conference of the American Association for the Treatment of Opioid Dependence—the major association of medication-assisted treatment providers. As I stood that morning at the podium, I could not help but think of Dr. Senay's words (recalled in part due to his presence in the conference audience that day) and my need to repay the debts my ignorance and arrogance had incurred. Do you have such debts? Is it time to repay them? How might they be repaid?

The Tyranny of Friendship

For twenty years, my professional development was nurtured within the mainstream of the field. I absorbed the core ideas of the field from elders and peers for whom I had great affection. Going back to school was a milestone for me in that it marked the elevation of my critical thinking skills. Those skills laid the foundation for my contributions to the field but they also brought unexpected strain. As I learned more, the gap between old ideas and new ideas widened into a gulf. One way for me to handle that strain was to bring the field along with me on this new journey, and I did that for years through my speaking and writing activities. The hardest part of this process occurred when new conclusions I had come to after years of careful research and reflection challenged my own pre-existing beliefs and the ideas of people who were beloved friends and colleagues. I wish I could say that my awareness of their potential reactions did not affect my presentations and writing, but that would not be true. My sense of loyalty to these people slowed the timing of some of what I conveyed and influenced how I communicated what I knew would be recognized as heresy.

As I look back over my professional life, I notice stages when my friendships prevented me from being exposed to new ideas and slowed my acceptance of new ideas. Then later, they influenced how I communicated new ideas to the larger field. While it was important to me to share with the field how my thinking was evolving, my friendships reminded me to communicate such ideas out of a position of humility and respect for those who disagreed with the directions my ideas were moving. New relationships helped spur the evolution in my thinking, but I found it important to retain old friendships and use these as a way to test new ideas. Friendship can be a source of tyranny or liberation. Maintaining integrity of self means that what we think remains independent of, but not disconnected from, the people who matter in our lives.

A Promise Finally Kept

I've met thousands of alcoholics in my life, but Bret was someone special. It took a while to uncover that specialness. When he first presented himself at Lighthouse, Bret was indistinguishable from many other chronic public inebriates we admitted to detox and treatment in those early years. He was in the latest stages of alcoholism, suffering from many alcohol-related medical problems and the social estrangement common to those castigated as winos. But something within Bret came alive through treatment and his enmeshment in AA. He was eventually offered employment as a "house manager" and worked endless hours at Lighthouse over a number of years. I had the joy of working with Bret during his first years of sobriety, but lost touch with him when I relocated to Chicago and then Washington, DC. I had heard through the grapevine that he had later married and left Lighthouse following medical problems that made it difficult for him to perform his job. It was with great distress that I received a call that Bret had relapsed and killed himself following the collapse of his marriage and the worsening of his health problems.

The pain of Bret's passing has stayed with me—even haunted me at times—in the intervening years. I could not shake my sense that Bret's resurrection from alcoholism, his valuable years of service to other alcoholics, followed by his eventual demise from alcoholism, was more than a personal tragedy. I promised myself that I would try to answer the enigma of Bret's death and those with similar stories. It would be years before I could extract the lessons from this loss—years before I would write about our need to understand the long-term stages of recovery and provide professional support across the stages of recovery. On the day I finished an article on the need for research on addiction recurrence after prolonged sobriety, I felt like I had made a down payment on that promise. I still feel there are more payments due on that promise, but I have the sense that through this continuing process I have kept the promise I made to Bret and to myself.

A Ghost from the Past

Have you ever had someone who was important in your life, but from whom you have been estranged for a long time? Perhaps the relationship ended on such a strained note that it has continued to haunt you over the years. I had such a relationship with Tom Hoffman—a man with whom I collaborated in the early 1970s in founding what became Chestnut Health Systems. Tom was the leader of the volunteer community coalition that worked for years to procure the funding to bring addiction treatment services to McLean County, Illinois. When that first funding finally arrived, Tom became President of the Board and I was hired as a counselor at what was then called Project Lighthouse. Tom and I had worked together to help alcoholics and their families in the years before Lighthouse was funded, and he had been instrumental in my being hired at Lighthouse and later promoted to Clinical Director.

Over the three years of my work at Lighthouse, my relationship with Tom became strained, and I left Bloomington for Chicago in 1976 without meeting with him to clear the air. And I didn't speak to him for the next 31 years. That is not to say that Tom remained simply a figure from my past. I thought of him often when returning to visit Bloomington and even more so when I later returned to work for Chestnut Health Systems. And yet I never reached out to him, primarily from the awkwardness of all the time that had passed. Tom kept returning to my memories and those memories were filled with gratitude for our early work together and discomfort over our subsequent estrangement. I felt a sense that Tom had become a ghost from my past who continued to haunt me with regrets.

A series of circumstances occurred in 2007 that allowed me to discover that Tom was still in Bloomington and to get his contact information. On a blustery day in Southwest Florida, I picked the phone up and called Tom. I explained to him that I had wanted to reach him for quite some time to express my gratitude for all he had done for me and for Lighthouse, my affection for him as a person, and my regrets that we had lost touch over the years. We both seemed relieved that the ice had been broken, and we spent considerable time reminiscing, getting caught up with each other's lives, and made plans to get together during my future trips to Illinois. That first call is a source of great satisfaction to me. It was like a decades-long piece of unfinished business in my life had finally been completed. Tom ceased being a

129

ghost and returned as a living presence in my life. Although he died of cancer months after our first face-to-face reunions, he remains a living presence for me. Are there estranged relationships that continue to haunt you? Is it time you made that call or wrote that letter?

Chapter Six
The Chicago Years (1976-1979)

The late 1970s marked a transition period within the history of addiction and addiction treatment in the United States. The country remained concerned about evolving patterns of polydrug use (e.g., Quaaludes, PCP, etc.), shifting heroin trafficking channels (from Asia to Mexico), and the resulting exotic forms of drug substitution (e.g., Ts and Blues). On the treatment front, major efforts were underway to elevate the quality of addiction treatment and to forge the controversies in creating a unified professional field from two fields: an *alcoholism treatment field* and a *drug abuse treatment field*. On the recovery front, the first major mutual aid alternatives to AA and NA were birthed (Women for Sobriety; Secular Organizations for Sobriety), triggering a continuing expansion of formal pathways of long-term recovery support. On the research front, the National Institute on Drug Abuse (NIDA) and the National Institute on Alcohol Abuse and Alcoholism (NIAAA) were expanding addiction research activities and seeking ways to disseminate addiction science and best clinical practices in addiction treatment via separate national training and workforce development systems.

My professional transition from a local to national focus occurred within three wonderful but personally turbulent years in Chicago. To follow are some of my experiences and lessons from those transitional years.

The Power of a Network

My early apprenticeship in the field of addiction treatment occurred in predominately rural and relatively small (less than 100,000 population) urban communities. In addition to feeling it was time to leave Lighthouse, I felt a need to spread my wings in a large urban community such as Chicago. The question was how to make this move. Where would I work? Where within the sprawling city of Chicago would I live? My past experience suggested that networks of people could open doors where none were visible, and that's precisely how I made the move to Chicago.

I had two overlapping networks of support outside my family: a network of ex-addicts (we had yet to define ourselves as people in recovery), most of whom shared linkages to Gateway and a network of professional peer relationships (many were current or former Gateway staff). I contacted several of these individuals in mid-1976 and expressed my desire to relocate and work in Chicago. Within weeks I was being informed of numerous possibilities and in August interviewed for two open positions within the Illinois Dangerous Drugs Commission (DDC)—the state agency responsible for planning, funding, monitoring, and evaluating addiction treatment in Illinois. The ex-addicts I knew who worked for DDC served as professional references for me. They vouched for my expertise with those who interviewed me and prepped me for the interviews via a detailed orientation about DDC and those who were going to interview me, as well as the current state of addiction treatment in Chicago.

When I was offered a position at DDC, these same individuals helped facilitate my transition to Chicago. They guided me to neighborhoods near them and arranged for a small army of "volunteers" from the Gateway community to help move my family into our new neighborhood in Chicago. The volunteers—clients currently in treatment—were assigned to assist me as part of a work detail in exchange for a modest donation to Gateway. Such a practice might raise eyebrows by today's ethical standards, but in the mid-1970s this was part of the reciprocal support that existed within the Gateway extended family.

In my first non-clinical position within the addictions field, there was a lot to adjust to, and this network of exceptionally bright, street-wise ex-addicts continued to guide me through the maze of this new world. Such support was not one way. We were brothers and sisters in recovery and those who had provided such support to me would have later opportunities to receive my support. That's the way the community worked.

I often hear individuals bemoan the lack of opportunities that they have been afforded in the addictions field. Such opportunities take more than preparation and perspiration. They require a network of reciprocal support—being part of a network of people with shared values and aspirations. Nowhere was the power of such a network more evident than in my transition from rural Illinois to Chicago. Networks and the relationships that make them up require care and maintenance. How is your network doing today? Who is on the verge of slipping out of that network who needs to hear from you? Opportunities for service and contribution require working the network. That principle has remained unchanged over the course of my half-century career in the addictions field.

Listening to the Hawk

I worked with people who loved Chicago, including some who had never traveled outside the city. They delighted in my lack of urban sophistication and tried to outdo each other in regaling me with urban tales of mayhem. I was told many such tales but I never knew which were true or contained some kernel of truth. One day over lunch in November of 1976, a few co-workers were warning me about the coming winter. They shared vivid stories about "The Hawk"—the mythical personification of Chicago's notorious winter winds off of Lake Michigan. Each tried to outdo the other in telling me of The Hawk's ferociousness. One pointed out the upper floor windows of Marina Towers where we worked and told me that the Hawk was so strong that the city put ropes up in the winter for people to pull themselves into the buildings so they wouldn't be blown into the Chicago River. I, of course, considered this among the more brazen attempts to "pull my leg," as we would say where I came from. My response was, "How naïve do you they think I am?" I delighted in having caught them in having fun at my expense. So imagine my surprise some weeks later when I looked out my 16th floor office window and saw ropes strung from the bridge over the Chicago River leading into the IBM office building. And along the ropes were people literally pulling themselves through the wind from an icy State Street to the IBM building entrance. I was stunned. The Hawk was real, and it was indeed ferocious.

For me, The Hawk became a metaphor for my readiness to take on new risks and challenges and for when I needed to slow that process down. My experience of moving to Chicago was a stretching process, and the stretching seemed endless. The trick was to pace such stretching. When new challenges occurred too quickly, I felt overwhelmed. When they occurred too slowly, I stagnated and grew restless. Like most everything else in my life, work was, and remains, a process of finding balance. Listening to The Hawk became my personal metaphor for my need to listen to my own inner voice. How about you?

Feeling overstretched professionally? Feeling a need to stretch? What's The Hawk trying to tell you?

New Mentors

Two new mentors entered my life at the Dangerous Drugs Commission. The first was Deputy Director, Carl Akins. Carl had distinctive red frizzy hair, a brilliant mind, a sometimes cynical air, and a wonderfully jaded sense of humor. It took a while to get through that shell to discover how much he really cared about the way policy issues affected real people. I met others in those days who could make great impassioned speeches that were performances without substance. The contrast between Carl's methodical activism and the showboating reformers taught me much—that people who espoused great compassion often had little of that precious commodity and that others hid their passion behind a cool exterior. What this taught me was to be careful not to mistake style for substance—to look beyond the veneer to what lay underneath.

Bill Coats was the other person of great import to my development. Bill supervised much of my work during my early days at the Dangerous Drugs Commission, and I learned much from our contrasting styles. Bill challenged me in two ways. When I would hand him a 10-page report on some issue he had asked me to investigate, he would ask me to present the same report in one page. It was a challenging and, at first, quite frustrating exercise. Bill accurately sensed that I made up for a lack of clarity of thinking by the sheer volume of what I could create on paper. His demands for me to outline and condense my writing sharpened my thinking and writing. The other difference was in how we thought. I thought in words; Bill thought in pictures. When we would meet, I would be taking notes and he would be drawing some kind of map or diagram. He began to ask me to diagram my writing—to portray my thinking graphically. It was and still is difficult for me to do this, but what I discovered was that such an exercise opened whole new ways to look at a problem and its potential solutions.

Carl had a clear image of what treatment organizations needed to look like and viewed policy as a vehicle to actuate that vision. Bill had a clear vision of what service relationships should look like within treatment programs and that vision guided all of his work. I learned much from Carl and Bill's contrasting but complementary visions and different styles of thinking. Carl and Bill are still inside my head, and I consult with them periodically about issues of import. I've created space for them there and know each of their styles well enough to recognize the kind of questions they would raise and the type of comments they would make in response to different problems. They are still a great help to me. Who's in your head? Is it time you invited in some helpful companions?

Planning and Research Adventures

Months after my employment as a training specialist with the Dangerous Drugs Commission (DDC), an event unfolded that altered my professional life. Deputy Director Carl Akins entered my office one morning and without fanfare remarked, "Rumor has it you can write." He went on to explain that the National Institute on Drug Abuse (NIDA) had rejected the state plan for Illinois that DDC had submitted, that all federal treatment dollars for Illinois were held up pending approval of a revised plan, and that the two senior planners had just resigned. He said simply, "Can you help us out?" In the weeks that followed, I worked day and night and finally got a plan crafted that was approved by NIDA. As a reward of sorts, I was permanently transferred to the planning and research division, which allowed me to work on other planning documents, reports to the legislature, and various research projects.

One early event in this transition taught me a great lesson. A few months into my new position, Carl again entered my office, handed me a document and said, "We need to craft a response to this. Can you get me a draft in the next week?" Since "no" was not yet in my professional vocabulary, I assured him that I could. What he had handed me was a resolution from the state legislature noting the shift in heroin distribution in Illinois from the traditional Asian heroin to Mexican brown heroin and calling on the DDC to investigate this trend and report to the legislature how to respond. The report was typically alarmist, with suggestions that DDC establish an addict registry in Illinois and consider a number of equally Draconian responses.

I labored over this report amidst considerable stress sparked primarily by being rebuffed in my attempts to get clarification from agency leaders about what policy directions I should recommend in the report. Once submitted, I eagerly awaited the response and was

135

rewarded with two surprises. The first was an acknowledgment that my response was just fine and that it would be submitted with only minor changes. The second surprise was that in the coming months the agency actually did what I had committed it to do in what I had written.

I had come to DDC in part to understand how policy decisions were made. I learned that sometimes these policies are shaped by someone stepping in to fill a vacuum at a time of critical need. Are there vacuums of unmet needs on the horizon that you can fill?

Pins in a Map (Heroin Deaths in Chicago)

One of my responsibilities within the planning and research division of the Illinois Dangerous Drugs Commission was analyzing drug trends within the state. One study I completed was of drug-related deaths in Chicago. To visually portray my findings, I placed a large city map of Chicago on the wall of my office that demarcated the many Chicago communities. Using death data from the Cook County Coroner's Office for one year, I used colored pins to plot types of drug deaths (by drug or drugs involved), demographic characteristics of those who died, where they lived, and where they died. The latter two categories I visually portrayed by using string to connect the pin for where individuals lived to the pin indicating the location of where they died. (Yes, these were the days just before such analyses would be done in a fraction of a second on computers.)

As hundreds of pins and lengths of string filled the map, several patterns were striking. The first visual message was the sheer number of Chicago communities where drug-related deaths occurred. Drug-related deaths crossed all ethnic and social class boundaries in the city. That said, the majority of deaths occurred in a few communities, indicating epidemic levels of opiate addiction. The color of the pins also conveyed that drug choices differed widely and that those choices tended to be clustered within particular ethnic communities. The strings also told a poignant story of individuals who had left their homes in one neighborhood, drove to another community where they procured and used drugs, and then died before making it back home. As I stared at the strings indicating the last trips of their lives, I wondered if any of those individuals leaving home that fateful morning had any premonition of doom or a sense of that particular day being special. The map served as a continual reminder to me of the deadly seriousness of the work of our

136

field and the enduring pain within the families and friends that surrounded each of the pins on that map.

Riding the Waves: From Ts and Blues to China White

One of my responsibilities at the Dangerous Drugs Commission (DDC) was to monitor drug trends and communicate to the executive staff about new trends warranting their attention. Over a short period of time, I generated reports on everything from PCP to poisoned marijuana (with the pesticide, Paraquat). In 1977, something was shifting in the Chicago drug culture as a result of a disruption in drug trafficking patterns. Chicago was in the transition between Asian heroin and Mexican brown heroin, and in that transition there were days where addicts could not cop dope no matter what kind of financial resources they had. The immediate result was experimentation with any drug or combination of drugs that could stave off withdrawal sickness. Such experiments were the genesis of the "Ts and Blues" epidemic in Chicago.

Talwin (pentazacine) is a non-narcotic analgesic that was long-prescribed for the treatment of pain and that exhibited only moderate addiction potential (mostly among medical personnel). Pyribenzamine is an over-the-counter antihistamine used to treat a wide variety of cold and sinus conditions. The drugs separately revealed no significant propensity for misuse, but in 1977 and 1978, they were mixed together and injected as a heroin substitute under the moniker, "Ts and Blues." To stem the tide, DDC executives quickly moved to legally reclassify Talwin as a Schedule II drug requiring triplicate prescription (a move that generally meant a kiss of death to drugs that had previously enjoyed high sales). Preparing for that process, DDC leaders asked me to compile the data that would support rescheduling. At the scheduling hearings, I faced off against some of the most renowned addiction researchers in the country, each of whom reported that controlled studies had shown that Talwin did not have a high potential for addiction. I countered with evidence of Talwin-related deaths and emergency room admission in Chicago and skyrocketing Talwin-related treatment admissions. The drug was rescheduled, but I left the hearing feeling as if a reputable drug company had been assaulted by conditions over which they had little control. I also knew that the future of drug control was in jeopardy by this new trend toward planned

137

synergism and that the historical practice of studying each drug in isolation would not be enough to protect public safety in the future.

The story of Talwin and its rescheduling in Illinois is included here for another reason. Often, a long time-lag exists between the sudden rise of a new drug pattern and changes in social policies to control that pattern. This disparity results from the time-lag in data collection and reporting systems. By the time such systems fully document a new trend, that trend could be months or even years into its emergence. I had state-of-the-art data reporting systems at DDC but I first heard about "Ts and Blues" long before these data systems triggered an alarm bell. In my part-time job, I worked with ex-addict counselors who were the first to tell me about "Ts and Blues." Those clues led me to check with numerous treatment clinics and hospital emergency rooms that confirmed this new drug trend. My point here is the need for front line clinicians to be close observers of drug consumption patterns and to trigger an alarm to local and state authorities when they see a new pattern that has significant public health implications. When you observe such a pattern, obtain as much information as you can about it and communicate that information to the authorities as quickly as you can. The importance of such action is revealed in another incident that occurred in the late 1970s.

Designer drugs represent efforts by chemists in the illicit drug markets to alter the molecular structure of psychoactive drugs to create *analogues*—chemical cousins—of their originals. These new substances may have effects and risks quite different than the original substances on which they are modeled. In 1976, a bright college student wanted to continue using the narcotic Demerol, but was concerned about possible legal apprehension. In response, he synthesized a drug. Desmethylprodine (MPPP), was similar to Demerol but not legally controlled. He used MPPP for six months without incident, but then made a mistake in the synthesis procedure, producing not MPPP, but the highly potent neurotoxin, 1-methyl-4-phenyl-1,2,3,6-tetrahydropyridine, (MPTP). Following ingestion of MPTP, the young man suffered paralysis, muscle spasms, and a loss of speech. In short, he had developed symptoms that resembled Parkinson's disease. In the summer of 1982, Dr. J. William Langston treated a forty-year-old man and his girlfriend with Parkinson's-like symptoms. Analysis of the drugs they had consumed confirmed the presence of MPTP in a product sold as heroin under the brand name, "China White." By 1985, the Centers for Disease Control had identified 400 MPTP-impaired individuals and 100 deaths related to designer opiates. Because of the accelerated pace of new product synthesis in the illicit drug culture and the heightened use of drug combinations, Randall Webber and I predict a major designer drug disaster in the coming decades. The magnitude of death and debilitation produced by such a disaster will depend on how quickly the disaster is recognized and contained. Containing that disaster quickly could well depend on the observational abilities of someone like yourself on the front lines of addiction treatment and recovery support.

A Judge and a Joint

One of the downsides of working for the Dangerous Drugs Commission (DDC) was that I was cut off from clinical work for the first time in my career. Although I thought a break from the intensity of addiction counseling might be good for me, I missed it greatly and began seeking out options that would continue to sharpen my clinical skills. My Gateway network quickly provided an option. The Cook County State's Attorney sponsored a first offender's program that diverted first time offenders charged with possession of small amounts of marijuana to a series of educational groups run primarily by ex-addicts from two of Chicago's large treatment systems—Gateway House and Safari House. Offenders who successfully completed the group sessions had their charges dropped, avoiding criminal penalties and a record of the arrest. Every Saturday, 400-500 first offenders met in groups of 25-30 to receive drug-related information and to explore, to the extent they were capable and willing, their own drug use. I was invited to become one of the group facilitators and worked within this program for two years. It was an amazing source of education—I suspect more for me than for the many participants who went through my groups.

The first offender's program opened my eyes to a different world of drug use. The job seemed initially impossible. Let me explain why. Most of the offenders came from Chicago's highly segregated Black and Hispanic neighborhoods and equally segregated and often equally poor White ethnic enclaves. The few suburban White kids whose arrest brought them into this mix were usually too terrified to speak and I suspect many never used drugs again for fear that they would have to repeat this experience. This was the late 1970s—a period of surging marijuana use in America and a period of increased tolerance for its use. What that meant was that you had to work to get arrested on a simple possession charge. Such arrests were often a product of innate stupidity and drug-induced impairment in judgment. I instructed each new cycle of group members to begin the first group by introducing themselves by name and briefly describing the circumstances of their arrests. Here's a sample of such circumstances.

> A 22-year-old calls the fire department to report a fire in his kitchen started by a short in the electrical socket used to run the grow light for a scraggly-looking marijuana plant. The firemen put out the fire and then called the police to arrest him and confiscate the marijuana.

> A 15-year-old is in traffic court for driving without a license, resplendent in his black leather jacket and black beret. Told to remove his hat by the judge, the young man reluctantly complies, only to have a joint the size of a cigar fall from his beret onto the floor in front of the judge's bench. He was, of course, arrested in the courtroom.

> A 19-year-old calls the police to report that two armed men ripped him off for all the drugs he had. When the police asked if the men took all the drugs, the young man reported that they took all but two joints. When the police arrive at his home to take the report, they asked to see the two remaining joints that were not stolen. You got it; he was arrested for possession of marijuana.

> A 17-year-old accompanies his 15-year-old brother to the first meeting of the first offender's groups. As the brothers enter the building where the groups are held, the 17-year-old sets off the metal detectors at the doorways of the building. What set off the alarm was a brass smoking pipe filled with—well, you can guess.

It's clear from stories like the above that we were often not working with the brightest of Chicago's citizens. Many who arrived each Saturday morning were barely able to track the group discussions. Some arrived hung over with clothes reeking of stale alcohol and reefer. Others entered with dead eyes, their lives seemingly over before they had begun. Others walked into those rooms openly hostile. Some saw it as a joke. Still others showed up just to slump in their seats and do their time. So the question was: What could you do under such circumstances? The surprising answer is: A lot.

Building rapport under such circumstances was among the greatest challenges of my clinical career. By the time five weeks had passed, the machismo had mellowed, the testing had moved to begrudging respect, even the brooding "slumpers" were posing questions, and many participants expressed genuine interest in the topics we were discussing. Discussions about addiction and the family and the process of recovery seemed to be of particular interest. One of the most openly hostile of these young group members called me a few weeks after he dropped out of the program to ask me how to get his "no-account junkie brother" into treatment.

My point here is a simple one: we can touch lives even in what appear to be the most hopeless, futile, and absurd situations.

Working Wounded

Nineteen-seventy-six was a major turning point in my life—a new city, a new and demanding job, a part-time position that dramatically expanded my clinical frontiers, and the final push to complete my Master's program. In the middle of all of it, my marriage disintegrated. I was devastated. The loss of my wife was a source of great pain, but the forced separation from my daughter was more unbearable than I can yet describe these decades later. Not since my earliest days of recovery had I so desperately needed support. My recovery network and small circle of friends kept me pasted together until my own healing could begin. The question from that period most relevant to the purpose of this professional memoir is, "How does one serve in a helping role with others at a time one is so deeply wounded?" Only a few readers who achieve long service careers will escape personal confrontation with that question.

We all go through experiences of loss, crises in physical and emotional health, and developmental transitions that draw heavily on our energy reserves. I learned many professional lessons during this low point of my life. First, I had to let myself be taken care of—not an easy task for those of us programmed to care for others. I had to totally surrender myself to circumstances over which I had no control. I had to reach out to emotionally purge what I was going through and to fill the suddenly empty space in my life. And I had to get my priorities straight.

I told myself every day that my recovery, my daughter, and my work were most important, and I stayed focused on those priorities. I also told myself that a purpose buried within me was unfolding in my life. Getting through this period required blind faith that a dawn would follow these darkest of nights. That dawn did arrive, but it was a long time in coming.

I'm not sure what it would have been like to have been doing full-time clinical work during this period, but I did learn that with vision and purpose we can rise above our pain or, failing that, use pain as a tool for self-understanding and a bridge of empathy with others who are also suffering.

Tough Feedback in Pierre

While working at the Dangerous Drugs Commission (DDC), I was invited to speak at a conference in Pierre, South Dakota on "sniffing and huffing" (the inhalation of volatile solvents for purposes of intoxication). I had spent considerable time studying this phenomenon, had co-authored a paper with Roger Krohe on the treatment of inhalant dependence, and felt that I could offer something as a presenter. On my way to Pierre, I met Dr. Tom Russell, who operated two regional training centers for the National Institute on Drug Abuse. Tom had been invited to evaluate the conference where I was speaking. The conference was focused on problems related to the use of inhalants by Native American children, adolescents, and adults, and a large portion of the conference audience was from the state's Native American reservations. This was one of my first contacts with Native American tribes, and I looked forward to learning from my experiences there.

I delivered my presentation early in the conference with my usual gusto and was pleased with what seemed like a reasonable level of appreciative applause when I finished. The last days at the conference were spent listening and learning as much as I could about the local tribes and the problems they were encountering. As it happened, I shared a flight out of Pierre with Tom Russell and asked him for his thoughts on the conference in general and my presentation in particular (a shallow effort to fish for praise.) After lukewarm praise of the overall conference, Tom shared the following feedback: 1) my presentation was one of the worst he had ever heard, 2) the content was too clinically-oriented for the audience, 3) my presentation language was far too technical, 4) I had offered no insight into the particular dynamics of

Indian inhalant problems, and 5) my presentation was far too animated for this particular audience. For one accustomed to high praise for my presentations, this was a lot to absorb. But it didn't take much self-reflection to realize that Tom was absolutely correct in his judgment of that presentation. It was my first realization that a great presentation in one setting can be an awful presentation in another setting. It was not the last lesson I would learn from Tom Russell. I had no idea that within a year I would be working for his company, Health Control Systems.

Becoming a Trainer

One of the most remarkable people I met within Chicago's ex-addict community was a woman by the name of Barbara Bedford. When we first met, I had instantly liked her spunky personality, her commanding competence, and her no bullsh** approach to communicating. Barbara had worked her way through multiple positions in the Illinois Drug Abuse Program and had then accepted a position directing the National Institute on Drug Abuse's (NIDA's) regional training center in Chicago where she oversaw delivery of addictions training and technical assistance to 10 states—all under contract with a company, Health Control Systems, owned by Dr. Tom Russell.

In 1978, Barbara scheduled a meeting with me where she said she wanted to bid me in the position of Deputy Director in her application for refunding of the regional training center. In spite of my desire to work with Barbara, I was somewhat ambivalent about the offer because of the stability and my enjoyment of the work I was doing at the Dangerous Drugs Commission (DDC). Barbara overwhelmed that resistance with the argument that it was time I extended myself to understand the addictions field at a higher level. She also promised that she would provide opportunities for projects beyond my imagination. Feeling starry-eyed from the power of her personal charisma, I asked for a day to reflect on the offer.

The next morning I was having coffee before work and one of DDC's long-time state employees stopped to chat with me. He was animated because he had just heard that another DDC employee might be leaving and expressed his outrage at this decision. He then spoke with great passion about the state benefits and the years, months, and days he had left before retiring and what his state pension would be. He reminded me of so many civil service employees who had traded their

143

dreams for security. My reaction was one of instant fear of how easily I could become fixated on money and safety. Ten minutes later, I called Barbara and told her she could bid me in the proposal. A few months later, she called to say the proposal had been successful and to formally offer me the position. I left DDC to begin my movement from a state to a regional and national platform in the addictions field.

We all face different life circumstances and must make such calls not only for ourselves but also in terms of what is best for those we love. What calls have you had to make?

The National Training System

On June 17, 1971 President Richard Nixon declared a "War on Drugs." The problem was he had no trained soldiers to fight that war. The task of recruiting and training that army fell upon the training units of two newly created organizations—the National Institute of Alcohol Abuse and Alcoholism (NIAAA) and the National Institute on Drug Abuse (NIDA). My first position with the Dangerous Drugs Commission (DDC) involved me in NIDA's National Training System (NTS). The NTS was made up of multiple components: A national training center, regional training centers, contracted training officers in each state and territory, and several specialty contracts focused on different aspects of career development for everyone from physicians to ex-addicts. It was an incredible system pioneered by people like Dr. Lonnie Mitchell and George Zeiner.

My role at the bottom rung of this system was to help develop training and credentialing resources for people working in Illinois' addiction treatment programs. To fulfill that job required attending meetings with my counterparts from around the country and collaborating with NIDA's national and regional training center personnel. It was an experience that allowed me to observe some of the country's premier trainers and develop the presentation skills that would put me on the training circuit for much of the next 30 years. There are windows of opportunities in systems just as there are in the lives of individuals. I assumed that this amazing system would last forever, given the brilliant minds that had created it and the skilled people who worked in it, but once a workforce had been recruited and quickly professionalized, this system was dismantled in the early 1980s. It was another of the Camelot periods I was exposed to in the early development of the field. I look back today with deep appreciation for what I gained from that system and also with regret that I did not more fully utilize more of the opportunities that came rushing at me in those days. I mistakenly assumed such opportunities would always be there. I was wrong.

Working within NIDA's national training system was an immense privilege. First, I learned the knowledge and technical skills to become a master trainer and in the process realized just how much I had been flying by the seat of my pants as a self-educated trainer. I felt like a kid in a candy store getting repeated opportunities to work with some of the most skilled trainers in the country. I also was able to observe and directly participate in the transformation of addiction counseling from a "paraprofessional" role with little credibility to a legitimized occupation within the broader arena of health and human services. It took decades to achieve that status, but being present in the earliest days of that professionalization movement was quite exciting.

Working at NIDA's regional training center offered immense opportunities for professional development. I helped develop some national training courses, became known as a skilled trainer in the Midwest and then in other regions of the country, and had numerous opportunities to work on special projects. My work on professional burnout was rapidly gaining national visibility and led to the publication of a 3-part monograph series that constituted the core of my first book and led to work on a national training package on staff burnout. Another special project I led was development of a regional training plan for Native American addiction treatment programs. It was through that project that I first visited numbers of Native reservations and began my education about Native cultures under the tutelage of Wanda Frog, Goldie Johnson, Eunice Larrabee, Al Pooley, and others. I recall this period as one of incredibly hard work but also a period of exhilarating learning that laid the foundation for much that was to come.

Making a difference in the world hinges in part on networks of relationships that allow you to get into positions where you can make a significant difference. The national training system afforded an opportunity to get to observe, meet, and sometimes get to know some of the leading figures in the rise of modern addiction treatment. I didn't know at the time that I would later be contacting many of these individuals to help me reconstruct the history of the modern treatment system.

In retrospect, I wonder how my life would have been different if I had been lured to stay in a career track within the Illinois Dangerous Drugs Commission. I'm sure I would have attained one of the senior manager roles there within a few years, made more money in the short run, and had the bounty of state benefits that I turned my back on. Moving from working inside a state agency to a regional and eventually a national position was the right decision for me. It involved trading predictability and financial security for a tenuous life of working on short-term federal contracts that had no promise of sustained continuity. It was an incredible window of opportunity that I am glad I took. In my early negotiations with Barbara Bedford, I recall thinking that if I didn't take the position now that I could perhaps move to such a position a few years later. What I didn't know was that in a few years President Ronald Reagan would begin dismantling parts of the federal infrastructure and that NIDA's national training system would become a casualty of that process. If I had waited in hopes of later working in that system, no such opportunity would have been available to me. Everything I would later accomplish in the addictions field hinged on that decision.

What crucial or missed opportunities have you experienced in your career to date? The adage, "When the student is ready, the teacher will appear" has much to commend it. I'm not sure about the teacher, but that does seem to be the case with opportunities. They seem to come from nowhere and yet I believe they all flow from a process of preparation. Are you preparing yourself for the arrival of such unexpected opportunities? Who do you need to meet and get to know to expand your sphere of influence? How can you begin that process?

Innocence and Ignorance

After ten years in the field, there were areas where the depth of my knowledge had grown but its width remained narrow to the point of embarrassment. I could traverse drug cultures and recovery cultures of many varieties and was beginning to figure out what it meant to be a local professional in this field, but an incident in 1978 underscored just how little I know about living in the mainstream culture. My new position at the National Institute on Drug Abuse (NIDA) training center required my first extensive national travel. My office had dutifully made

146

my flight reservations and things went fine on my first trip until I arrived at the airport and proceeded to the rental car counter. My rental car had been reserved and I assumed that I would pay cash for it. At the counter I was told to my horror that they did not accept cash and that I would need a major credit card. Temporarily relieved, I presented my Sears credit card that, where I had lived most of my life, constituted not just a major credit care but THE major credit card. I will never forget the look of humored incomprehension at my naiveté on the face of the car rental clerk. Sometimes you just have to laugh at yourself.

In our amazement at our clients' sustained survival in predatory subcultures, we may forget what they do not know and cannot do when taken out of that world. Without guidance into the civilian world, they will return to that world whose geography, ground rules, and activities they can comfortably navigate. As they attempt to leave such a world, we must help them learn to laugh at themselves and keep moving forward through new terrain, just as we sometimes must also do. Shared embarrassment and laughter is an alternative to shame and regressive flight—for the people we serve and for ourselves.

Sprints and Marathons

It was during my days as a trainer that I first became aware of two patterns of contribution to the addictions field. One such pattern is people who bring technical or support skills to the field and greatly contribute to the work of the field, but who will only remain working in the field until better opportunities come along. When such opportunities arise in other fields, they leave the addictions field with little regret. These people are the sprinters that every field needs to conduct its core activities. The second pattern is reflected in people who may work in evolving roles within the field, but whose life commitment is to the addictions field. They are the marathoners who provide continuity for the field. Both groups are needed and contribute in different ways.

The health of the field is influenced by the ratio between these two groups. A field of all sprinters is a field without history, traditions, and core values—and potentially a field without a future. It is a field vulnerable for colonization by more powerful forces within its operating environment. A field of all marathoners is a field at high risk of stagnation—becoming a closed system at risk of eventual implosion or dying of old age. It is the mix and the proper ratio between sprinters and marathoners that keeps the field strong and vibrant. So what is the ideal

147

ratio? I think the field, and organizations within the field, needs a core of at least 40% of the workforce in the marathoner pattern and it needs them in strategic roles across the sectors of the field (e.g., administration, management, addiction medicine, addiction counseling, prevention and early intervention, research, education and training, recovery support, etc.). That core should also not exceed 75 percent of the workforce.

In looking at your own organization, community, and state, what percentage of the workforce are marathoners? Which group are you in?

Stigma: A Premature Victory

Many forces came together in the 1970s to destigmatize alcohol and other drug problems. Alcoholism recovery advocates sent the message for three decades that the alcoholic was a sick (rather than bad) person who can be helped and was worthy of help. Drug-related casualties among white middle and upper class youth brought the reality of addiction within the experience of mainstream America. New educational campaigns defined the alcoholic as a parent, sibling, friend, neighbor, and co-worker and dissipated the image of the alcoholic as a Skid Row wino. Some brave people stepped forward in 1976 to put a human face and voice on alcoholism and alcoholism recovery.

Planned by Walter Murphy and sponsored by the National Council on Alcoholism, Operation Understanding was held on May 8, 1976. At that event, 52 prominent Americans, including noted politicians, business leaders, scientists, sports figures, and movie and television celebrities stepped before the television cameras to announce that they had once suffered from alcoholism, but today stood as living proof that long-term recovery from alcoholism was possible. It was a pivotal moment in the history of alcoholism and alcoholism recovery in America and sparked what came to be known in the late 1970s through the mid-1980s as the recovery movement.

Operation Understanding and the larger movement to destigmatize alcoholism succeeded within this window of time beyond anything its designers could have imagined. For a brief period of time, the stigma attached to alcoholism rapidly melted. The image of the alcoholic shifted from that of the Skid Row wino to mother or father, brother or sister, son or daughter, friend or co-worker—a person worthy of compassion and help. And that help came in large doses—insurance coverage for inpatient and outpatient care in hospitals and freestanding programs, alcoholism-focused employee assistance programs in business and industry, criminal justice diversion programs, and a rapidly expanding network of recovery mutual aid groups.

During these same years, the National Institute on Alcohol Abuse and Alcoholism (NIAAA) launched successful media campaigns aimed at redefining America's conception of the alcoholic. Year-by-year, the image of the alcoholics as Skid Row wino gave way to an understanding that alcoholism crossed all boundaries of geography, gender, ethnicity, social class, and profession. What this meant at the front lines of addiction treatment was that we were seeing people at earlier stages of problem development and people who had greater resources to bring to their recovery initiation and maintenance efforts. All this was a product of changing social perception. Marty Mann's decades-long campaign to convince America that alcoholism was a disease and that the alcoholic was redeemable was bearing fruit across the country. But an event was coming that would pale all others in the movement toward the cultural destigmatization of alcoholism. And what an event it was.

The Transformative Power of Recovery: Testimony of a First Lady

In April 1978, President and First Lady Betty Ford announced to the nation that Mrs. Ford had sought treatment and was recovering from addiction to alcohol and other drugs. Mrs. Ford's daughter, Susan Ford Bales, had initiated a formal family intervention process that resulted in Mrs. Ford's admission to treatment and her later announcement to the nation. Mrs. Ford, President Ford, Susan Ford Bales, and the other Ford children offered themselves as living proof of three propositions: 1) there is hope for families affected by addiction, 2) the family can play a catalytic role in recovery initiation, and 3) individual family members and the family as a whole need a sustained process of recovery and recovery support.

The public reactions to the First Lady's announcement and the sustained evidence of her successful recovery brought women into addiction treatment in unprecedented numbers. The number of individuals and families transformed by the Fords' gift of their story is incalculable. In the years that followed, family-centered addiction treatment and support reached its apex, and intervention as a therapeutic strategy entered the American consciousness. This alone would be a proud legacy, but the Ford family was not finished. At the encouragement of Ambassador Leonard Firestone, Betty Ford brought her support and her name to a new non-profit addiction treatment center on the grounds of the Eisenhower Medical Center in Rancho Mirage, California. Lending her name to this center served as a permanent reminder that addiction could touch any family and that recovery was available for those who sought it. The Betty Ford Center opened its doors October 4, 1982. In the intervening decades, the Ford family remained actively involved, participating in Board meetings, assisting with fund raising, lecturing to patients, and cooking hamburgers for staff at their annual picnic. The Ford family has remained the force at the core of the Betty Ford Center serving as a constant reminder that addiction treatment and recovery are, at their best, family-centered processes.

In the years since the Betty Ford Center first opened its doors, tens of thousands of individuals have been treated at the Center—more than half of whom have been women. Through these years, the Center developed specialized programs for licensed professionals, innovative programs of focused continuing care and state-of-the-art family and children's programs. In 2006, Betty Ford announced the creation of the Betty Ford Institute (BFI), which operated independently from the Betty Ford Center and focused its efforts on recovery-focused research dissemination, public and professional education, and policy advocacy. The Betty Ford Center would later merge with Hazelden—two iconic institutions now one.

Research studies on stigmatized health conditions reveal that contact with people in stable recovery lowers social stigma (rather than recognizing the condition as a medical illness). The alcoholic as Skid Row wino stereotype simply could not withstand the critical mass of disclosures by people in recovery. Nothing does more to break down stigma than increasing personal contact with recovery within one's own family and social network. The second thing that happened was disclosure of major health conditions by warmly regarded celebrities that everyone felt they knew: the "Marlboro Man" with his cancer diagnosis, Rock Hudson and Magic Johnson with their AIDS diagnoses, Michael J. Fox with Parkinson's disease, and Christopher Reeves with his spinal cord injuries. Betty Ford fought against social stigma of alcoholism like no person before.

The hope within the addiction field following First Lady Betty Ford's disclosure of her recovery status was that this event would mark the final, irrevocable tipping point in the movement to destigmatize addiction recovery. What we didn't realize was that new forces, a new president, and a new idea—zero tolerance—was emerging from the nation's capital that within a decade would send recovering people back into hiding. As that new decade was about to open, I was invited to transfer to Washington, DC to work on projects with the National Institute on Drug Abuse's (NIDA's) National Drug Abuse Center.

Chapter Seven
The Washington, DC Years (1979-1982)

Two historic milestones were germinating in the late 1970s that would detonate in the following years. The mysterious deaths of young gay men and injection drug users portended the arrival of HIV/AIDS, and new patterns of cocaine addiction triggered a period of mass hysteria and mass incarceration.

I witnessed these events during my own transition from Chicago to Washington, DC. During my brief three years there, I experienced a disconnection from the front lines of the field, which explains the paucity of this chapter, and I faced a medical diagnosis that prompted my retreat to family in Illinois and my return to deep engagement in the front lines of addiction treatment and recovery in America.

A Different Kind of City

My employer at the central region's training center of the National Institute on Drug Abuse (NIDA) was Health Control Systems, Inc. (HCS)—one of innumerable management consulting firms (known locally in Washington, DC as "Beltway Bandits") doing contractual work for the federal government. HCS, in addition to operating two NIDA regional training centers, also had the contract to operate the National Drug Abuse Center, the National Center for Alcohol Education, and the Minority Internship Project. They operated out of HCS offices in the Washington, DC area. In the late summer of 1979, I accepted an offer to move from Chicago to the corporate offices of HCS in DC to work on multiple addiction-related contracts and provide training and consulting services requested of me from state and local addiction agencies. My goal in moving to Washington was to get close to the center of American drug policy. I wanted to study the policymakers, the policy development processes, and how policies evolve over time. My years in Washington offered a laboratory for such study.

What most struck me about Washington, DC was the dichotomy between this city and the rest of the country. Life inside the "beltway" was dominated by politics—it was the sole business of the city. Inside this bubble, everyone seemed linked to the government in some way.

152

This situation created an unreality that made it difficult to stay grounded on any issue. Staying attuned to life outside the bubble was hard in this world of power, prestige, and perpetual manipulation. It was like a virtual world whose rhetoric was completely disconnected from the realities it feigned to represent and address.

Washington, DC brought my first substantial national visibility in the field and also the temptation to leave the field. Washington is a beautiful city filled with an interesting mix of museums, ethnicities, and restaurants, and I loved exploring it. My fondest memories of Washington, DC are of Saturday mornings with my young daughter sharing our beignets, orange juice, and coffee at a New Orleans Café at 18th and Columbia before heading for our regular visits to the zoo, shopping in the neighborhood, and lunch at one of innumerable ethnic restaurants.

A Premature Eulogy

While I was working in Washington, DC, I continued to get calls to do presentations at what was then an annual addictions conference sponsored by the Illinois Dangerous Drugs Commission (DDC). When Bob Stachura from DDC made his annual call to invite me to present, we discussed what to talk about and, without thinking, I offered one of my workshop titles on managing what was then called professional and organizational burnout—a subject I had presented before at the conference and what I was most known for at that time around the country. Bob called back a few days later to reaffirm DDC's desire for me to present at the conference but wanted another topic. I agreed to the shift in topics but asked about the need for the switch. Based on our long friendship, Bob responded quite candidly that his supervisor had reacted to my proposed topic by suggesting that I was a "one-note Johnny" whose career would die if I continued to build it around a single narrow topic of interest. Her comments upset me for several days until I realized that she was absolutely right. I was experiencing the euphoric flush of riding the wave of a popular topic and had not realized that getting so linked to a faddish, ephemeral subject could result in my reputation declining in tandem with that topic. Once again, one of my critics had served as a benefactor.

In the years that would follow, I would caution up-and-coming clinicians and trainers against becoming exclusively identified with a single topic, theory, technique, or client group. While specialization is often the way we make contributions to the field, we must be cautious that such specialization does not become a prison we become entrapped within. If we can only sing one song, people will tire of it, no matter how well-composed and how passionately we deliver it. Do you have one song? Is it time to learn new songs or learn to sing your favorite song in a new way?

Stigma and a Silenced Story

The 1970s was a great decade to be in recovery. Stigma was diminishing from this status and the "recovery chic" period was opening up. The image of alcoholics and addicts had shifted from Skid Row winos and deranged predators to one's family members, friends, neighbors, and co-workers. In those days, someone bumping into me was an excuse to tell my recovery story. That destigmatization process and the resulting cultural coming-out peaked in the late 1970s, and were followed by the chilling winds of "zero tolerance" and "Just say no." Those shifting attitudes drew recovering people back into positions of silence and also impacted those who worked in addiction treatment. Telling other professionals or people not in recovery that one worked in the trenches of addiction treatment always sparked the question, "How did you get into that field?" which was code for "Were you (or are you) an alcoholic or addict?" As stigma grew through the decade of the 1980s, persons in recovery hid deeper within subterranean subcultures and the only images filling the television screens were celebrities marching off to rehab to escape the consequences of their latest public indiscretions.

By the early 1980s, I was tired of being an ex-addict, tired of telling my story to people who didn't care about it, couldn't understand it, or professionally or socially devalued me because of it. Like a lot of others, I became vague in response to questions in social settings about what I did for a living and became more discrete when answering questions in professional settings about how I got into the addictions field. I disclosed my recovery status less and less in tandem with increased social stigma and my own increasing credentials. As alcoholics and addicts were re-demonized in this culture, I joined millions of other people in recovery who "passed" as "normals" by rigorously hiding my recovery status. Such silence was rationalized by misguided notions of the "anonymity" tradition of Twelve-Step fellowships and escalating preoccupations with professional "boundary management" and discouragement of self-disclosure in therapist-client and professional relationships. What it was really about was STIGMA and the shame that it induced, even inside the professional world of addiction treatment.

When stigma attached to severe alcohol and drug problems decreases, those of us working with these problems are viewed as making positive contributions to our society. We are valued and people engage us in conversation and solicit our advice about such problems experienced within their worlds. What we experience during such times is respect, evident in the way people listen to us and express their value for what we do. When stigma increases, we encounter discomfort and distrust from people when we disclose our occupations. Secondary stigma is the extension of negative feelings and attitudes toward alcoholics and addicts to persons who work professionally with alcoholics and addicts. Comments such as, "That must be very difficult work" and "It must take a very special person to do that kind of work" mask what people are really thinking: "You must be insane to choose to spend your life working with alcoholics and addicts!"

Secondary stigma is having one's value and sanity questioned the second you disclose that you work in addiction treatment. Secondary stigma is having other helping professionals look down on your career choice. Secondary stigma is withholding one's own recovery status out of a sense of embarrassment and shame or, for some professionals, emphasizing that they've never been addicted in response to the question, "How did you happen to get in that kind of work?" Secondary stigma is feeling you have no right to assert your value regardless of whether you are in recovery or not.

Can you recall times you have experienced secondary stigma? How do you feel inside when people ask how you chose to work in this field? (See later discussion of Courtesy Stigma.)

Production Writing (Life as a Beltway Bandit)

The experiences working on multiple contracts and simultaneously generating proposals to government agencies for new projects was exhilarating but enormously demanding. The image of being chained to a desk and not being able to come out until a legal pad was filled with writing that secretaries would eagerly type is not far

155

from the truth. (This was before all writers composed on computers.) But the experience did two things for me. First it taught me to be a fast study. I remember Tom Russell telling me that we were going to write a proposal to write a curriculum to train hospice nurses. I responded "But I don't know anything about hospice care." Tom's reply was always the same, "But you will." And then he would hand me stacks of books and research materials I was expected to digest at a speed that seemed impossible. The second thing I learned was to write on command. There was no such thing as writer's block. My two cohorts (Randy Adams and Cynthia Kunz) and I were expected to crank out proposal sections or training curricula on a timeline that was not negotiable. And we did. What kept Randy, Cynthia, and I sane—or relatively sane—was our mutual respect and our support of one another.

Rumors of a Coming Plague

Part of my responsibilities during 1979-1981 was working on the development of a Hospice Training Program for Nurses curriculum—yes, we actually won that contract. I had drifted into a few projects like this as HCS had lost funding of some of its major addiction-related training projects. My task with the hospice training project was to work with experts on death and dying to write this training curriculum. It was during informal dinners with these experts that discussions first turned to accounts of a new, extremely infectious and lethal disease that was striking young gay men. As this disease spread and acquired a name, Acquired Immunodeficiency Syndrome (AIDS), discussions turned to how this disease was being transmitted. While there were many early theories on the source of AIDS transmission, there was uniformity on the potential import if this disease turned out to be bloodborne. It was at that moment that I realized that this professional sojourn outside of the addictions field was potentially revealing an event of momentous impact to that field. If AIDS was transmitted in the same manner that Hepatitis B was transmitted, then it was clear that this new disease would ravage addicts enmeshed within drug-injecting, needle-sharing subcultures across the country and also ravage their sexual partners. Within a matter of months, I was hearing reports of the mysterious "wasting" deaths of addicts in New York City and Chicago. I was not aware at that time that I would be called in just a few years to help respond to this new disease among addicts.

This story is included to again underscore the importance of the frontline clinician in identifying new trends that have enormous import to the future of addiction treatment and the broader public health of the country. The trend data from the nation's major reporting systems are notoriously time-delayed. The data in the research study released today is often months, if not years, old. That means that those working on the frontlines of addiction treatment may see an event or trend long before it is announced in the journals they read or the conferences they attend. Therefore, it's important to monitor and talk about what you are seeing clinically. The outreach workers, the detox nurses and technicians, frontline addiction counselors, and recovery coaches may be the first to hear reports of, or observe the effects of, some newly synthesized substance, the horribly toxic effects of some new drug combination, or the emergence of a new drug-related disease. We have a responsibility to listen, observe, investigate, and collect what evidence we can and get this information to the proper authorities as quickly as possible. That ability and assertiveness could save thousands of lives. Our voiced observations are extremely important and constitute one of the earliest public health warning systems. Pardon the repetition on this point, but I cannot emphasize enough how important this may be. Are you seeing anything right now that might turn out to be of great national import?

International Work and the Peace Corps

It had taken years to stretch beyond my parochial Midwestern roots to develop something of a national perspective on addiction/treatment policies and practices. It would take much longer to realize that this broadened perspective was itself limited to the American cultural context. Two career-expanding opportunities presented themselves during my tenure in Washington, DC. The first was an HCS-operated international training project sponsored by the National Institute of Drug Abuse (NIDA). My prolonged conversations with Jerry Harrison-Burns, director of that project, and the opportunity to work with Jerry mark the first awakening to the different alcohol and other drug (AOD) problems that exist around the world and variable ways countries respond to such problems. I also had opportunities to conduct training with the Peace Corps unit responsible for managing personal and health problems experienced by volunteers. The cases of AOD-related problems that I became aware of in this context pushed me to think about various etiological factors in the development of AOD problems and how such problems could be resolved in cultural contexts lacking the treatment and recovery resources then available in most American communities.

What range of experiences limit how you perceive AOD problems and their solutions? Do you feel a need to have those perspectives stretched? How might you do that?

Basic Training with the Marines

If there was ever an unlikely match, it was Bill White and the United States Marine Corps. Everything about my past politics and lifestyle and even my appearance suggested this was not a good match. And yet I found myself directing the United States Marine Corps (USMC) Alcohol and Drug Abuse Training Project in 1981-1982. That experience opened up opportunities to train for other military organizations, including the Canadian Department of Defense. It was something of an adjustment, but I came to enjoy and excel in this work. But before that could happen, I had to give up the delusion that my past knowledge, and even my previous experience with the other military branches, prepared me for this role. Working for the USMC required nothing short of a complete immersion in USMC culture. I had not served in any branch of the military, let along the testosterone-fueled milieu of the USMC. My politics, notions of manhood, and lack of physicality (by USMC standards) were light years away from those I trained. And yet these rough and tumble Marines and I somehow forged a partnership where we learned from each other. My effectiveness grew in tandem with my understanding of the USMC culture and as my need to justify myself in this environment diminished. What I had to do first was shut up and listen and observe—the language, the traditions, the etiquette, the personalities, and the rank-defined power. It took a while. It should not have worked, but somehow it did. My work with the USMC was one of the bright spots in my Washington tenure.

I gained several lessons from this unexpected chapter in my career, but one of the more important was not to prejudge a potential assignment. To have refused this project based on my stereotypes of USMC officers and my fears of how they would perceive me would have deprived me of a rewarding professional opportunity. What we refuse to say no to can be as important as what we say yes to.

158

A Lost Connection with the Field

In spite of bright spots of intense learning, I came to view my move to DC as a mistake—a major diversion in my career, and yet I learned things during that period that helped me in the years to follow. My writing skills improved considerably during those years, and my work on projects outside the field brought me closer to the decision that I had to get back to my roots, back to what I was destined to do. Today I view this period differently. Mistakes can be an important source of information that may have been otherwise unavailable to us. Mistakes can be an important source of feedback and an impetus for action. I didn't know how much I was committed to this field until I went through a period that pushed me further and further from its core. If you are living a mistake as you read this, what can you draw positively from it? What do you need to do? In my own case, events beyond my control propelled changes in my life that drew me back to the center of the addiction treatment field.

Chapter Eight
Back to Treatment (1982-1985)

The early 1980s were in some ways a Camelot period for addiction treatment in the United States. AIDS and social panic over cocaine had not yet transformed national social policy towards addiction, substantial progress had been made in destigmatizing alcoholism (if not addiction to other drugs), insurance companies were paying for the medical treatment of addiction, and addiction treatment programs were rapidly expanding in the US. The growing legions of addiction counselors had redefined themselves as a new profession, and recovery support resources, traditional and new alternatives, were expanding.

It was in this context, that life circumstances led me back to the clinical world of addiction treatment. Below are some stories from this period that I hope you will find relevant to your own experience or which will prepare you for future journeys.

A Health Crisis and a Panicked Decision

As 1982 opened, I experienced a rapid deterioration in my health. My physician said I had a condition—ankylosing spondylitis—that would lead to progressive skeletal-muscular degeneration and a significantly shortened life expectancy. Facing this bleak long-term prognosis and a daily confrontation with pain, it dawned on me that I was living half a country away from my family with virtually no one in the DC area to assist with my care when I would need it. So, I made the decision to leave Washington, DC and return to Decatur, Illinois where I could be close to my parents and siblings. I also decided that if my work time was to be limited, I wanted to spend it working again in addiction treatment. I didn't expect to get a job close to Decatur and assumed that I would probably return to Chicago. To facilitate this transition, I called my recovery network and shared with these friends my condition and my need to return to Illinois as soon as possible. I asked that they keep their eyes open for work opportunities that might be of interest to me.

Within a week, Diane Schwartz, one of my close Gateway friends, called to tell me that there was an advertisement in the *Chicago*

Tribune for the director of an alcoholism treatment unit at St. Mary's Hospital in, guess where?, Decatur, Illinois. I flew home, and interviewed with the hospital administrators and unit staff. Shortly after, I was offered the position, and made my plans to return to the Decatur area after being away for seventeen years. But one more surprise awaited me before leaving DC. With all my belongings packed and on their way to Illinois, I was staying with a friend (Dr. Carl Akins) and struggling to finish a final week of training US Marine Corps alcohol and drug control officers. With only a few days left before my drive to Illinois, I awoke and collapsed in pain as I tried to step out of bed. Carl somehow reached my doctor who decided I needed an emergency orthopedic consult. The orthopedic surgeon, after running innumerable tests, reported to me that I was not suffering from a degenerative disease, but a ruptured disk in my back. His team of specialists was able to get me pasted together enough to make the trip to Decatur where I faced a year of continued physical therapy and slowly—ever so slowly—diminishing pain.

Again, a strange set of circumstances conspired to change my life. Sometimes when your life gets off kilter and you drift off the path you were meant to walk, fate thrusts itself into your life to get you redirected. My precipitous decision to move back home to have a support network not only placed me back in the center of addiction treatment, but set the stage for subsequent service opportunities to the field. As a reward for getting my life refocused, the gods expressed their pleasure by introducing me to Rita Chaney, the woman who would become the great love of my life. The lesson here is a simple one: when we align ourselves with the direction that reflects what we are truly destined to do, unexpected assistance and rewards often follow. Do you have the sense that you are on such a destined path? If not, from what direction is your path calling?

Lost Language of the Heart

There was something of a crisis awaiting my arrival at St. Mary's Hospital. No one had told me of an impending accreditation site visit scheduled a few weeks after my arrival. While the program I inherited was well-organized, there was no formal policy and procedure manual. That meant I spent much of the first weeks not directing anything, but writing around the clock to prepare for the Joint Commission on

Accreditation of Healthcare Organizations (JCAHO) site visit. In spite of my fears, we survived the site visit just fine and received the accreditation status so critical to the Unit's immediate future. What this initial exercise provided was an opportunity to reflect on the changes in the milieu of addiction treatment since my last full-time role as a clinical director six years earlier. At that time, JCAHO accreditation was the gold standard—a promise that insurance companies would pay for addiction treatment as they paid for the treatment of other disorders. JCAHO accreditation was also symbolic of our professional and cultural credibility.

Having chased that dream for close to a decade, I can recall reflecting on words that did not appear in the policy and procedural manual I drafted in adherence to JCAHO standards—words like empathy, compassion, love, hope, God, honesty, humility, and recovery community. I realized that the "language of the heart" (the sharing of experience, strength, and hope from one addict to another) was being rapidly replaced within the addiction treatment milieu by the language of regulatory compliance and the clinical argot of the ascending fields of addiction counseling and addiction medicine.

The latter were greatly influenced by the fields of psychiatry, psychology, and social work—ironically, fields that had failed disastrously in their historical attempts to treat addiction and whose practitioners had often held addicts in thinly-veiled contempt. I found it strange that my awareness of these influences emerged while I worked in a hospital (St. Mary's) with a long history of value-focused care. St. Mary's actually opened their Twelve-Step-oriented treatment program before addiction units in hospitals had become popular or profitable.

This new language was not something to co-exist with the language of old; it was a replacement language. Colleagues at that time said, "We just have to use this language in order to get funded." But the words seemed more ominous to me in ways I could not yet articulate. Being replaced was not just language, but core messages about recovery and the milieu and relationships in which newly birthed recovery could be nurtured until it was strong enough to seek its own destiny. What was being drained out of treatment in retrospect was in fact recovery itself. More than 15 years later, I called for the reconnection of treatment and recovery, but in 1982 I did not have the clarity of perception or the words to signal an alarm. Words are so important—the ones imposed on us, the words of our own heart that have yet to be born. To speak out, we must first see and understand. Are you feeling things that need to

162

be spoken? Push to find the clarity. Push to find the words. The words have the power to suffocate or liberate ourselves and those we serve.

Recovery as a Cultural Phenomenon

I returned to Illinois at a time addiction treatment and recovery blossomed all over the country. The number of programs in the Decatur area seemed to double and triple overnight. When I arrived at St. Mary's Hospital in 1982, the hospital's addiction treatment unit was one of the few private programs between Chicago and St. Louis. When I left four years later, eight such programs existed within a 90-minute drive of Decatur. Addiction treatment programs were popping up everywhere. As I mentioned earlier, recovery was emerging as something of a cultural phenomenon. New recovery mutual aid groups were forming—Women for Sobriety, Secular Organizations for Sobriety, and Rational Recovery, to name just a few. Recovering celebrities were coming out publicly with their recovery stories. Hazelden and others were selling recovery books, tapes, and other paraphernalia in unprecedented quantities. Recovery sections of local bookstores steadily expanded. AA's Twelve-Step program was being adapted for every conceivable problem. Everyone seemed to be getting into recovery.

If you want to kill anything in America, make it a super success and the inevitable backlash will damage if not kill it. Such was the case with the recovery phenomenon. The over-selling of recovery also contributed to the excessive proliferation of treatment programs and the subsequent rise in unethical service and business practices. These practices, in turn, triggered a backlash of managed behavioral health care in the late 1980s and early 1990s that led to the closing of a large number of inpatient addiction treatment programs. The fleeting recovery movement of the 1980s was hijacked by the public and private treatment industries, celebrity speakers and authors, and the recovery publishers and paraphernalia peddlers. It was a movement without substance—one more intended to generate profit than to change public opinion or public policy. Recovery teddy bears and other obscenities collectively symbolized this commercialization of recovery. And yet this recovery as a fad period sowed the seeds for a grassroots recovery advocacy movement that rose in the closing years of the 20th century.

Even false starts can be historically significant in cultivating the soil where future movements will thrive. By the turn of the new

163

millennium, a new recovery advocacy movement rose with a more authentic foundation and a vision of forming a more substantive and sustainable movement. Individuals, like social movements, often benefit from false starts. Can you think of a false start in your own life that laid the groundwork for a later success? If you are experiencing what feels like such a false start at the moment, mine its lessons. This process may be a key to future successes.

Pseudo-addiction, Real Recovery

Recovery was hot—the latest American super phenomenon. This made visible something that existed before and that has continued to exist since: people without significant alcohol and other drug problems who embrace an addiction and recovery identity and use the Twelve Steps or other recovery programs as an organizing framework for personal healing and health.

In my years as a streetworker, I had recognized the phenomena of pseudo-addiction—persons who feigned drug use or exaggerated the extent of their drug use and its consequences to achieve social membership in a social network of drug users. Their addiction was not to a drug, but to an identity and a social group where needs could be met that had remained unfulfilled outside that setting. They looked like, talked like, walked like an addict, but had never really experienced addiction. In the 1980s, this group grew due to their attraction to the culture of recovery.

During this time, some people whose alcohol and other drug problems, if they existed at all, did not meet diagnostic criteria for a substance use disorder entered AA, NA, and other recovery support groups. These people were swept up in the recovery culture. Two trajectories typified their course of participation in treatment and/or recovery communities. The first was intense involvement followed by disillusionment and movement to the next fad and its emerging gurus. The second was sustained and meaningful involvement. By happenstance, people in the latter group drifted into a community of recovering addicts and discovered something of great value—a philosophy and style of living and a community of mutual support where they felt a sense of acceptance and belonging. Little attention has been given to this group of individuals who used *addiction* as a metaphor for their own personal wounds and imperfections and used

164

recovery as a catalytic metaphor for personal transformation. I discovered from this group in the 1980s that people can reap the gifts of recovery even without a history of addiction. It was in this context that years later I would suggest that all people were in need of recovery.

Recovery of a Woman of Distinction

During the late 1970s and early 1980s, the National Council on Alcoholism and Drug Dependence (NCADD) and the National Institute of Alcohol Abuse and Alcoholism (NIAAA) made significant strides in countering the social stigma attached to alcoholism. The stereotype of the alcoholic as a Skid Row wino faded in the midst of media campaigns that portrayed the alcoholic as our mothers and fathers, sisters and brothers, sons and daughters, friends, neighbors, and co-workers. The earlier noted "Operation Understanding," in which 52 celebrities from all walks of life publicly announced their sustained recovery from alcoholism, marked a watershed in changing attitudes toward alcoholism. But for women, that event paled in comparison to the effect of First Lady Betty Ford announcing her recovery from addiction to alcohol and other drugs. Betty Ford's announcement had a particularly dramatic impact on addicted women of influence. Changing public attitudes about women and alcohol problems and the availability of hospital-based alcoholism programs brought many women into treatment whose alcoholism would have in earlier years remained hidden within their families. Here is one example of such an unveiling.

I have vivid images of Jane's entry onto the alcoholism unit at St. Mary's Hospital. She entered with an entourage of family members flanking her on both sides—an obviously affluent family, physically and emotionally supporting the matriarch's entry into alcoholism treatment. She was dressed to kill, hair and make-up perfect, and a long dress with flowing sleeves—all masking her physical emaciation. She quickly settled into the routines of her physical, lab work, psychosocial assessment, and the daily treatment activities. When her lab results returned two days later, we were shocked at what we saw. She had the highest liver scores seen in the fifteen-year history of the unit. The numbers painted a picture of extensive alcohol-related liver disease and the probability that Jane was dying. The doctors agreed that she would not live more than a year.

Jane's story is unique only in its severity. What she shared with other women who were treated in the 1970s and 1980s was that her alcoholism was far more advanced at the time she first sought treatment than her male peers initially entering treatment. The intense social and moral stigma attached to alcoholism and women had long-delayed the day when Jane and her family would seek help. The effects of such stigma on women were and continue to be quite deadly in America, particularly for women whose alcoholism is cloistered behind the walls of wealth. But this is more than a story about stigma and its deadly consequences.

Jane and her family faced news of her medical condition with more courage than one could have expected. There was a question of whether Jane should continue the three- to four-week treatment regimen within our unit, but she boldly announced that she wanted to finish what she had started. She worked hard in treatment. Her impending death accelerated this process of reviewing her life, her alcoholism, and its consequences. Through this process, she seemed to discover a previously hidden core within herself, a discovery physically evident by shedding an expensively clothed and painted veneer for casual clothes and a minimum of makeup. The week her family spent in the formal family week program was also marked by intense work on family relationships and the anticipatory grief that all were experiencing. Jane completed treatment and became actively involved in AA in the months preceding her death. I was amazed as she and her family described changes that I usually associated with much longer periods of sobriety.

At the end of Jane's life, her physical pain was unrelenting and only partially ameliorated by medication. On a day when her pain was almost intolerable, her husband, in desperation, asked if she thought a drink would help. She smiled at his offer and responded that getting sober was the hardest achievement of her life and that she wanted to "face the devil sober." She died a few days later—sober since the day she entered treatment. The quality of her sobriety defied measurement by time. Her recovery was only an inch wide if measured in time, but it was a mile deep. She is one of the most courageous women I have ever met.

Her story is embedded in a larger context. Through what circumstances did this woman and her family seek help only months from her death? The answer is a simple formula. When the stigma attached to addiction increases, people seek help at later and later stages of problem severity. This relationship is intensified in women, for whom such stigma has long been magnified. The woman of distinction

166

whose story we have shared died as much from stigma and shame as she did from alcohol dependence.

The "Species" of Addiction

When I entered the treatment field, alcoholism was viewed like a bacterial infection. You either had it or you didn't. And if you had it, as the theory went, it flowed from a specific but unknown etiological agent; (we called it "Factor X"), followed a predictable progression ending in sobriety, insanity, or death; and responded to a narrow approach to treatment and recovery support. Treatment program philosophies varied, but each program adhered to a single pathway model of addiction and recovery. It was in conducting clinical supervision and leading clinical staff meetings at St. Mary's that I further questioned this single pathway approach. The sheer volume of initial case presentations, the opportunity to observe the course of treatment and post-treatment outcomes for hundreds and hundreds of patients brought home to me quite different conclusions. Put simply, I began to argue that: 1) addiction flows from multiple etiological pathways, 2) these pathways are reflected in highly diverse patterns of onset and problem progression, 3) each pattern responds to quite varied approaches to treatment, and 4) there are multiple pathways and styles of long-term addiction recovery.

Borrowing from the work of E. M. Jellinek, I referred to these subgroups as the "species" of addiction, and identified nine such species based on their respective etiological pathways. The sometimes overlapping etiological subtypes I described included: 1) biological (primarily genetic) vulnerability, 2) self-medication of a diagnosed or undiagnosed medical disorder, 3) self-medication of emotional pain related to developmental trauma or acute or cumulative distress, 4) masking, manifestation, or self-medication of a primary psychiatric illness, 5) family-oriented patterns of addiction, 6) peer-oriented patterns of addiction, 7) culture-oriented patterns of addiction, and 8) addiction linked to spiritual anomie. This species theory garnered considerable attention and resistance in the early 1980s when I first promoted it to frontline addiction counselors and clinical supervisors.

I began to use the metaphor of hardware and software to describe client responses to treatment. I suggested that when the client's hardware (age, gender, ethnicity, culture, developmental experience, drug choice, addiction career) matched treatment software designed for

167

such hardware, the result could be a process of transformational change and sustained recovery. I also posited that when the treatment software was not compatible with a client's hardware, the results included premature disengagement, administrative discharge, non-responsiveness to treatment, or an adverse response to treatment.

Think of the prevailing philosophy that guides how you view and intervene with clients and their families. And consider the characteristics of the people now entering treatment with you. Which clients are ideally suited for the particular software you offer? Where are mismatches most likely to occur? How can you rewrite your treatment software to make it compatible with these latter groups of clients?

Family Week

One of the distinctive features of St. Mary's addiction treatment unit was its strong emphasis on family involvement. Those admitted to the unit generally stayed four weeks—the standard length of treatment in the early 1980s, and intense family education and therapy was provided throughout the third week. Recruitment of families was as intense as was the emotional experience of the week itself. Patients, families, and professional visitors lauded the family program, which was a source of great pride to the hospital. I shared that pride, but I had some unnamed reservation about the program that remained on the periphery of my consciousness. It was not concern about staff who ran the program; Mary Jo Comerford and Mary Ann Holsapple were among the most skilled counselors with whom I had ever worked, and they had that special indefinable touch needed to work with families and children. It was not about any portion of the program activities. In fact, it took years to define the nature of what I was feeling in those years.

A predictable family dance took place within family week—the building tension and emotional catharsis of the first days, the mid-week inclusion of the primary patient and the intensity of those first honest communications, and, quite often, a breakthrough of reconciliation and hope—all within five days. Yes, families were encouraged to go to Al-Anon and many were referred to family therapy, but there was an unstated assumption within most family programs of that era. The critical assumption was this: Bring the alcoholic or addict into stable recovery and most of the family problems will naturally dissipate on their own without sustained peer or professional support. (That assumption was evident in the fact that families were not offered sustained post-treatment monitoring, stage-appropriate recovery education, or recovery coaching as an integral part of their treatment experience.) Of course, we as a field erred in that assumption—as research in the following decades would reveal.

It turns out from subsequent research that recovery is destabilizing to family roles and family relationships. Families that have withstood every insult of addiction often break apart in early recovery when critically needed outside supports are lacking. It was only decades later when I began to read the research of Stephanie Brown and others about the developmental stages of family recovery that I realized that gnawing discomfort I had about early family programs. That discomfort was not with what we did, but with what we failed to do—provide a family-focused framework for sustained monitoring and support. I still have hopes that a day will come when not providing such support to families will be unthinkable.

Theodor Reik wrote a classic therapy text, *Listening with the Third Ear,* suggesting the need for psychoanalysts to listen to their own unconscious to better understand and treat their patients. Listening with that same ear to our vaguest discomforts related to clinical practices may provide clues to new clinical breakthroughs of great import. Can you recall a recent time of such discomfort? Is it time to further probe the source of that discomfort?

"How's the census?"

The alcoholism unit at St. Mary's was atypical in that it was started a decade before alcoholism became popular and profitable for general hospitals in the United States. St. Mary's was one of the hospitals operated by the Third Order of the Sisters of Saint Francis whose early involvement in alcoholism treatment grew out of their service mission. St. Mary's was joined by a larger number of hospitals in the 1980s who discovered that addiction treatment units could charge higher rates, generate extended lengths of stay, and, as a result, could be highly profitable. By the mid-1980s, hospitals were experiencing the first aggressive wave of managed care that produced plummeting lengths of stay, low hospital census, and dramatically heightened competition between hospitals.

169

The alcoholism unit at St. Mary's operated at close to 100% occupancy (partially attributable to our practice of adding a bed or two to the unit when it was full with pressure for admission coming from those on the waiting list). Thus my surprise when I saw the first financial reports on the unit noting that the unit was losing money. Upon closer scrutiny, I realized that the source of the deficit of costs over income was an inordinately high overhead rate charged to the unit by the hospital. It took months to sort out an accounting method that I came to learn was common in hospitals of this period. The high profits of the addiction treatment units were used to subsidize units that lost money every year (e.g., the maternity wards and pediatric units) by charging an excessively high rate of administrative overhead to the former. It was ironic that alcoholics and addicts, who still bore the brunt of considerable community stigma, were subsidizing the delivery of babies and the care of children in many communities.

The place of affection that addiction units had earned in the hearts of hospital administrators began to slip as those units became subjected to decreased lengths of stay by managed care and increased competition from the growing number of hospital-based treatment programs. As daily census on such units began to vacillate, the pressure to fill beds became intense. During this period, I recognized the veneer-thin commitment most hospitals had to the treatment of addiction. Although I considered St. Mary's Hospital to be an excellent institution, I was never asked by my administrators about the recovery rate for the unit I led. But the question "How's the census?" was an unrelenting refrain. I recognized at that point that the then-popular addiction treatment units were a loosely attached appendage to most hospitals and that these units could disappear overnight the second that income-generating function ceased to exist. That day came sooner than I predicted. The definitive history of this period has yet to be written, but such a history will have to address the fact that the motivations for launching addiction treatment units by many hospitals was more one of financial exploitation than a deep commitment to serve this population. But hospitals were not the only institutions making money from the treatment of addiction.

Treatment Profiteering

The trend of private insurance companies paying for the treatment of alcoholism and subsequently other addictions unleashed an unprecedented wave of institutional profiteering. In addition to the proliferation of addiction treatment units in hospitals, private, free-standing treatment programs grew at record pace in the 1980s. It was a predator's ball. People with little knowledge of addiction recovery entered the business of addiction treatment as an investment to make money and sucked every dollar possible out of these new businesses. The operational assessment philosophy was, "If you have the insurance, you have the disease." The admonition to staff was, "If you can't find it (substance use disorder diagnosis), you haven't looked hard enough." Inappropriate admissions and re-admissions, inappropriate lengths of stay, inadequate treatment, and insufficient post-treatment monitoring and support (the latter not reimbursed by insurance companies) were pervasive. It was only a question of time before it would all collapse. And when it did, it was once again those suffering from alcohol and other drug problems, their families, and local communities who were most injured.

In a touch of tragic irony, some of the individuals who had profiteered by filling beds of treatment institutions migrated to the managed behavioral health care industry where they made additional profits by keeping people out of those same beds. If all this seems a bit cynical, it is. Part of the price of stigma is that you can be as victimized as much by those who pledge their love to you as those who do little to conceal their hate. Those of the highest social status and social untouchables were vulnerable to such exploitation. It is sometimes hard to separate the healers from the hustlers. Such conditions often continue until disempowered people begin to take control of their own life circumstances and gain voice and control over the institutions allegedly designed to serve them.

So what does this mean for us at a personal level? It means that, to those we serve, we must give back a level of resources commensurate to the resources that come to us through this service process. It means that we must hold our institutions accountable to a higher service ethic. It means that we cannot talk about the size of our annual budgets and the numbers of our employees without talking about the rate of recovery of those we serve. Ultimately, only the latter has meaning. Healer versus hustler is not a fixed dichotomy. Innumerable forces push us from the former to the latter. People who want to remain healers must fight to do so—must fight forces outside and within themselves to sustain that status.

171

An Early Meditation on the Media

Two of the pressures I faced as an addiction treatment administrator were keeping the beds full (generating profit for the hospital) and helping cultivate a positive image of the hospital in the larger community. That brought me back into direct work with local media channels—something I had not been involved in since leaving Lighthouse in 1976. One of the local television news figures at that time in Decatur was Mike Cheever of WAND TV. Mike ran a weekday news and interview program and, after positive responses to my first appearances, arranged to have me do a regular program every three to four weeks. I served as the local "Dr. Drew"—providing a regular stream of information about addiction and recovery and answering personal questions from callers to the program.

My regular television appearances did help achieve the goals of generating admissions to the treatment unit and generating positive PR for the hospital, but it also had an unintended effect. My regular contacts brought me closer to understanding the underlying dynamics and politics of the media as a business and a cultural institution. It took some time for me to figure out that no one at the station had much concern for the accuracy or helpfulness of the content of what I shared as long as the subjects and my delivery of them created drama and attention—the more the better. And with drama often came subtle and blatant forms of stereotyping and misinformation. In presenting only dozens of the most depraved accounts of addiction and a few of the most miraculous recoveries (the primary media interest was in the former), what the public was denied was the thousands of stories that existed between these poles. And I found that isolated moments of good information were often sandwiched between alcohol and prescription drug advertisements and reports that demonized and stigmatized people with alcohol and other drug problems.

Media virgins may assume that journalists and reporters are interested in serving the public good, and I suspect many start out with precisely that intent, but sustaining that desire within a corporate media structure is difficult. As a whole, the media is a predatory industry. So when reporters and journalists call with questions, don't assume they are looking for objective information from which to draw conclusions. Someone unseen to you has already drawn a conclusion and you are being called to confirm it. What I learned from my early local media contact—later confirmed at a national level—is that the media can be used as it uses you, but rarely does anyone come out of the transaction without feeling the need for a shower and a confessional.

Devil at the Table

Moving from a national focus back to work in a local community provided a great learning laboratory in which I could apply many new perspectives developed over the six years since I had worked full time in direct clinical services. That local work brought me into contact with all manner of community agencies, civic clubs, task forces, and planning groups concerned with alcohol and other drug problems. One of the most central of these was the local alcoholism council. As director of the local treatment center, I had a seat on the board along with a mix of people concerned with alcohol problems—a lawyer, a physician, an educator, AA and Al-Anon members, and a mix of local political leaders and business representatives, including the owner of a beer distributor. Having representatives of the alcohol industry sitting on local alcoholism boards was not unusual in those years. On the surface, they were good board members. They attended regularly, visibly represented these councils in the community, contributed financially on a routine basis, and could be counted on when their councils were in financial crisis. Our local industry representative did all that and was one of the nicest people I had ever met.

As a member and later president of the local council, I initially saw nothing insidious about this representative of the brewing industry's activities on the board. But I began to change that view over time. What I began to notice were not signs of some deep conspiracy but an assertion of interests that were in conflict with the founding mission of the council. Here's what I began to notice. Mr. Beer, as we shall call him, kept our attention focused on alcoholism and, in particular, the growing "drug abuse" problem. He loved the new biological models of alcoholism positing that a small subpopulation of individuals becomes "alcoholic" because of a unique biological/genetic vulnerability. This model placed the source of alcoholism inside the individual, not within the products Mr. Beer distributed or the marketing strategies he and his industry employed to promote them.

What quickly silenced Mr. Beer were discussions about binge drinking or references to alcohol products that seemed to be designed for 16-year-old taste buds, or new alcoholic products aggressively marketed to women or communities of color. I also began to reflect on his request to have his donations for printed educational materials acknowledged by an expression of appreciation on the back of what was being distributed. He also made sure (behind the scenes) that discussions of such issues as alcohol taxation, the mandatory labeling of alcohol products, and advertising restriction for alcohol products never appeared on the council's agenda. I also noted that while his company regularly donated money to the alcoholism council, it always did so in amounts large enough to create gratitude but small enough as to avoid contributing to the council's maturation as an organization. This was the budding of my consciousness that serious discussions needed to occur about the prevention and treatment fields' relationships with the alcohol, tobacco, and pharmaceutical industries. The echoes of those early debates can still be heard and will continue to reverberate through the coming pages.

The alcohol industry is not unique in having interests that sometimes conflict with the broader health of the community. The next time you are at a meeting, look around the room and ask yourself what institutional interests lie behind the discussions that are occurring. Then ask yourself what interests you may unconsciously represent. Given two competing proposals, do we advocate for the proposal that responds to the community's most current critical need, or do we advocate for the other proposal on the table that would bring funds to our organization? (See further discussion in Chapter Fifteen.)

The World of Employee Assistance

St Mary's Hospital, like hospitals everywhere in the early 1980s, was looking for innovative ways to extend their services into the communities they served and to launch programs that positioned them, even briefly, ahead of their competitors. I convinced the hospital leaders that one way it could extend its expertise in psychiatric and addiction treatment into the community was to develop employee assistance services for local business and industry. After weeks of briefing them on the evolution of occupational alcoholism programs into "broad-brush" employee assistance programs and the growing trend for companies to externally contract for such services, they agreed to launch such services at our hospital. I was involved in designing the program, recruiting Kevin McAvoy as its Director, and, in the weeks before Kevin arrived, visiting the major local employers with the

174

hospital CEO Sister Ann Pitsenberger to market the program. I knew the program would succeed, as it did for many years. With Sister Ann meeting with those executives, it just felt like we had God on our side. What I could not have anticipated was that this program would far outlast the hospital's addiction treatment unit, partially as a result of external forces that would radically alter the viability of inpatient addiction treatment and also as a result of Kevin's skilled leadership of St. Mary's employee assistance program.

The World of Student Assistance

In 1985, I was asked to serve as an evaluator of a student assistance program provided contractually to a rural high school by R.B. King, a private counseling center. This provided my first in-depth look into the growing student assistance movement—a movement that integrated prevention and early intervention activities in the nation's high schools and later in middle and elementary schools. Originally modeled on employee assistance programs in the workplace, student assistance programs provided a framework for intervening with children and adolescents at the earliest stages in the development of alcohol, other drug, and related problems. This early involvement revealed to me how the most serendipitous event can shape our lives. I had no inkling at that time that I would play an important role supporting this movement, later serving on the editorial board of the *Student Assistance Journal* and on the Scientific Advisory Board of the Student Assistance Association. I had no inkling as well that my personal life would be forever changed by this first consultation. (It was at that consultation that I met Rita Chaney with whom I would forge a lasting life partnership.) The smallest decisions can set in motion chains of events that exert ever-growing influence on our lives. The opportunity for such a decision may be moving toward you. Are you open and ready?

Sacred Space

I had always experienced treatment environments as emotionally demanding and recognized early on the need for replenishment rituals of some kind. While at St. Mary's, I made another inadvertent discovery about creating sacred space in our lives so that

175

replenishment can occur. When I relocated to Decatur from Washington, DC, I was also looking for an escape from the intensity of the urban environments I had lived in the past six years. I found that escape when I bought an isolated, aging cottage on Lake Decatur. I gutted and rebuilt the cottage and spent much of my time away from St. Mary's creating these wonderful gardens filled with wooden paths, bridges, pergolas, fire pits, and sculptures—all surrounded with exotic plants. Each day, I could leave the intensity of the hospital and enter what I came to think of as my sacred space and be daily renewed. My first books were written sitting on the patio surrounded by this wondrous landscape. I would later replicate this experience building a bamboo garden when Rita and I relocated to Florida. Each of us needs replenishing activities to sustain our work and personal health, but we can also benefit from sacred space. Do you have sacred space? Where might you find or create it?

A Temptation to Leave the Field

During my tenure at St. Mary's Hospital, I became involved in the larger world of the hospital, serving on many committees and volunteering to lead numerous community projects. In what turned out to be my last year at the hospital, the assistant administrator who supervised the treatment unit, the social work department, and several other departments, resigned his position. I received word through the grapevine that the hospital administration would be pleased if I applied for the position. Here was another potential pathway out of addiction treatment into a position that paid very well, was a high-status job within the community where I lived, and would groom me for a variety of roles within the larger hospital system. It was an attractive position, but one I gracefully declined to pursue. Every instinct I had told me this was not the path for me.

When I later witnessed what hospitals went through in the late 1980s and 1990s, I couldn't imagine the misery I would have gone through if I had pursued and obtained that position. I believe everything in my life prepared me to live on the frontier of the field of addiction treatment, and crossing the boundary of that field into other professional arenas has always been an abandonment of who I am at a most fundamental level. So what happens when someone dangles money or prestige in front of you with an offer to leave the field? Listen to your heart. We're not all supposed to be in this field. If you figure out you are not, then leave. But if you feel your heart pulling you back, then listen to it. The same is true for what we do in the field. Each of us has to center and continually re-center ourselves as we change, as the field changes, and as the world changes.

The fact that I was being pulled so far into administrative and management roles in the field suggested the need to re-evaluate my directions. Once again, I decided that if I was to remain in this field, I had to get even deeper into the heart of the field. For me, that heart rested not in the management of ever-complex organizational systems, but rather the frontlines of clinical work and research that would help unravel the mysterious transformation processes that marked the journey from addiction to recovery. What plane of space do you currently occupy in the field? Is it time for you to move deeper into the heart of the field? For you, what would that next step be?

Chapter Nine
Lessons from the
Training/Consulting/Research Life
(1986-2005)

T
he year 1986 marked my full-time plunge into the worlds of addiction-related training, consulting, and research. I say "addiction-related" because my shift to recovery-focused activities in these areas had not yet arrived. The stories and brief reflections in this chapter illuminate some of what I learned over the span of the next two decades within Chestnut Health Systems' newly created Lighthouse Institute.

Mutual Trust, Mutual Risk, and a Leap of Faith

In 1974, a bright, young seminarian and pastor named Russell Hagen became involved in Lighthouse in an effort to assist one of his parishioners. His initial contact led to an internship in pastoral counseling at Lighthouse and a later decision on my part to hire Russ as a Lighthouse counselor. Russ was incredibly committed to the field and, like the rest of us, worked ungodly hours doing whatever was necessary—from crisis on-call and detox work to his later clinical duties as a counselor. We enjoyed working together and became good friends through that process. After I left Lighthouse, went to Chicago, Washington, DC, and then back to Illinois, Russ and I occasionally visited to keep up with each other's lives. I took considerable pride in the fact that Russ had gone on to serve as the clinical director of Lighthouse and then the CEO of what became known as Chestnut Health Systems (CHS).

In the fall of 1985, Russ and I saw each other at a conference, and he asked me what I was up to. I told him that I was trying to convince my hospital to organize a Department of Behavioral Medicine with a research and training institute. I shared with him that the hospital executives couldn't see the potential of such a unit and were not sure such a unit could financially support itself, let alone make a profit. It was a brief conversation, and I left the conference not suspecting what would follow.

Days later, Russ called me and said that he had given considerable thought to our discussion and that he would like to talk to me about possibly pursuing this idea of a research and training institute at CHS. After further conversations in November 1985, he went to the CHS board and, in essence said, "I have this project I want us to pursue, there is no precedent for it, and we have not one penny of funding, but I have a guy who I think could make it work." Because of Russ's past track record with such instincts, the board approved his proposal, and on January 1, 1986, I became the first full-time employee of the newly created research and training division of CHS—a division that at the time of this writing employs some 100 staff with an annual operating budget of more than $13 million. I take no credit for anything other than helping lay the foundation for CHS and its research and training division. Others far more capable than I—Mark and Susan Godley, Mike Dennis, Christy Scott, and others—came behind me to build something beyond anything I could have envisioned or created.

My re-entry into the world of training, consulting, and research contains several points worthy of consideration. First and foremost, opportunities that will or will not open up for you are often a function of your past relationships. Establishing relationships where you can consistently demonstrate your commitment and competence opens doorways of opportunity. The adventure that Russ and I started was based on a well-timed idea, Russ's evaluation of my level of commitment and skills, and a relationship between Russ and I that was based on mutual trust (a track record with each other) and mutual risk (including my understanding that I would have no job if the new division did not financially support itself within one year). Some of you are in, or will be in, similar positions of authority where your capacity for calculated risk will be tested. I don't think you can beat the combination that has been the key to Lighthouse Institute's (LI) success for more than twenty years: bring together people who share mutual respect, trust, and risk around well-timed ideas and services. Set clear standards of accountability and then get out of their way and let them do what they love doing.

An opposite lesson is that Lighthouse Institute might never have existed if the administrators at St. Mary's Hospital could have grasped the vision of what became LI. Today, there is no alcoholism treatment unit at St. Mary's Hospital and no behavioral health research and

179

training unit. It is as if that thriving unit of the early 1980s never existed. The Bible is right, "Where there is no vision, the people perish."

Getting Fired on My First Day

I brought one small contract with me to the newly founded Lighthouse Institute—a contract to provide consultation on the development of an addiction treatment unit in a small Northern Illinois community hospital. The hospital had just hired a unit coordinator and on my first day at the Lighthouse Institute (January 2, 1986), another consultant (Janet Harper) and I met with the hospital CEO and the newly hired unit coordinator. I felt the day went pretty well, and was surprised when my co-consultant called later to tell me that the CEO had called her and wanted her to continue the consultation without me. It seems the new unit director did not feel he could work well with me. I had just been fired from the only income-generating job that I had brought to the new CHS division. I hoped this was not an omen about the fate of this new adventure.

My firing may have been a product of some personality mismatch, but I suspect the problem was even more basic. In my excitement of launching the new division, I injected too much of myself into the consultation process. I worked too hard to impress the CEO and the unit director with my technical knowledge and my own philosophy of treatment. I treated the visit as a training assignment, rather than a consultation process. I failed to adequately listen, failed to ask the right questions, failed to affirm their own expertise, and failed to build a relationship before the technical aspects of the consultation began. I deserved to be fired.

So what can we take from this incident? Perhaps several key points. First, it's all about the relationships. Second, helping others is not about making them feel good about you; it's about helping them feel good about themselves and their capabilities. And third, when you think you're looking good, you're probably not (an old therapeutic community mantra). Unfortunately, these lessons are learned, inevitably forgotten, and must be relearned until the self-reminders become a part of who we are.

There is another lesson that followed on the heels of this incident. Russ Hagen and I made one two-day marketing trip to Chicago in the early months of launching the Lighthouse Institute—one of the few conscious marketing efforts in the Institute's history. During that visit, we met with Gateway House, TASC, and Lutheran Social Services—they all contracted with us for training services that helped provide a financial foundation for LI's early years. The Gateway training was particularly significant to me as my personal and professional life had continued to weave in and out of the Gateway network for two decades. Sustained relationships between people evolve into sustained relationships between institutions. Once again, Gateway played an important role in my life. Such debts are hard to pay, but I've tried. Do you have such debts? Have they been paid?

From Pain to Publication

After the near implosion of Lighthouse treatment program in the mid-1970s and my drift into the role of an organizational consultant (See next chapter), I wrote a number of papers on staff burnout in human service organizations and the broader issue of organizational health and decay. The focus of my work was the conceptualization of organizations as dynamic systems that operated in much the same way as families. This creative approach shifted the focus of burnout from the individual to the relationship between the individual and the organization and the organization's relationship with its external environment. The model I developed grew out of hundreds of consultations and discussions within the addictions field. The energy I brought to this subject suggested the need to draw something positive from my earlier distress to Lighthouse.

I began pulling all of these experiences into a book, and it was ironic that I finished this draft only weeks before being invited to go back to work for Lighthouse. When I described the book to Chestnut CEO, Russ Hagen, he suggested we publish it through CHS and use it to seed publishing activities within the new training and research division. That's precisely what happened. The book—my first—was entitled *Incest in the Organizational Family: The Ecology of Burnout in Closed Systems.* It was published in 1986 and went through multiple printings. A second edition was prepared and published by Hazelden in 1997 under the title, *The Incestuous Workplace: Stress and Distress in the Organizational Family* and remained in print there until 2007. Its complete text is available for free download from my website.

Many people have been wounded by experiences they encountered in their personal and professional lives. *The Incestuous Workplace* is an example of how the healing of such wounds can be transformed into an instrument of service and a catalyst for social change. Why do we spend years trying to make sense of a distressing episode in our lives and not pass on to others what we learned from that experience? Are there distressing experiences in your personal or professional life that can be used as a platform for positive contributions to the individuals, families, and communities you serve? How can you accomplish this?

An Addicted Judge Finds Recovery

I sought out numerous opportunities in my career to provide addiction-related training within the criminal justice system, but was long frustrated about the inability to reach judges, who seemed to exist in their own closed world. In the late 1980s, I collaborated with the Illinois Department of Transportation, the Administrative Office of the Illinois Courts, and the University of Illinois in designing and implementing one of the most successful judicial training programs in the country. Over the next two decades, this program trained hundreds of judges from across Illinois and was also adapted for delivery to probation officers, states attorneys, and DUI (driving under the influence) evaluators. The key to this success was a judges-only admission requirement, the use of a faculty made up primarily of judges, training content that focused on judicial decision-making, and training that afforded opportunities to refine decision-making skills in peer discussions of real judicial cases. Attractive training locations and really good food also helped!

While I was mostly unsuccessful in recruiting judges to other training venues, I was enthralled with how hungry judges were in this new program for information to enhance the quality of the decisions they made from the bench. My role in the training was to outline the various clinical subpopulations of DUI offenders and talk about the role of addiction treatment as a sentencing option. The information I provided was the most detailed orientation on substance use disorders that many of the judges had ever heard. While not designed for that purpose, many judges applied this information to those they had known with alcohol or drug problems and sometimes to themselves. The following is an example of the power of objective information when provided in a venue where the listener's defense structure is not activated.

Some of the judges I trained had heard a brief overview of alcoholism somewhere in their legal training, but few had been exposed to the detailed profiles I presented within the judicial training program. In my presentation, I reviewed several of the earlier-noted "species" of alcohol-related problems, but spent considerable time on the dominant pattern of alcoholism in the United States. One particular day, I was training about 50 judges and began describing the following profile. I depicted the intergenerational transmission of this pattern of alcohol problems via typical family histories they occurred in, described the frequent early pattern of alcohol exposure (euphoric recall of the first exposure to alcohol, atypical alcohol tolerance, etc.), and the lack of early drinking-related consequences. I then proceeded to describe the slow and subtle stages of alcohol dependence with particular attention to key indicators such as an increase in frequency and intensity of drinking-related memory loss, loss of volitional control over alcohol intake, failed resolutions to control the timing and quantity of alcohol consumption, radical personality change while drinking, and an increase in drinking-related guilt and remorse.

As I went through my usual presentation, I noticed one judge who seemed to have a "deer caught in the headlights" look on his face. I proceeded with my lecture and there was a point toward the end of the talk that my eyes again locked on those of this particular judge. At that moment, I knew beyond a shadow of a doubt that this judge was suffering from the same pattern I had just described and that he had also arrived at the same realization. He and I never exchanged a word during the two and a half days of training, but we made eye contact a few more times—the kind that might be experienced among people with a shared secret.

I received a call from the judge shortly afterwards. He opened the conversation by saying that he suspected I would not be surprised by his call. He acknowledged that I had "told his life story" in the training and that he had returned home emotionally shaken. After some painful, soul-searching discussions with his wife, he had decided that he needed to enter treatment for his alcoholism. His question was straightforward: "How do I start this process?" I helped get him admitted to a treatment center and helped him work through how he could get involved in a recovery support group that would not conflict with his role as a judge. He is now all these years later still in stable recovery, and I continue to get an email of thanks from him each year around the time of his sobriety birthday.

Those still suffering from alcohol and other drug addictions wear many guises. As addiction professionals, we never know when our words to the public or other professionals will penetrate that guise and ignite the process of recovery. Following many experiences as the one I just told, I vowed to describe the various patterns of how alcohol and other drug problems manifest themselves with as much detail and objectivity as possible and to combine that description with a clear message of hope for permanent recovery. Such words can and do make a difference in people's lives—including those we encounter outside the clinical setting. As professionals, we can serve as what I would later come to describe as *recovery carriers*.

Fads, Phenomena, and Bullsh** Detectors

Early in my training career I discovered the existence of sprint topics and marathon topics. Sprint topics emerge quickly, become red hot, and then burn themselves out, often leaving nothing of substance behind. Sprint topics tempt all trainers, particularly trainers with elegant delivery styles but only a shallow depth of knowledge. In contrast, marathon topics provide knowledge and skill on areas so close to the center of the addiction, treatment, and recovery experiences that they will never be out of date, only subtly refined through accumulated knowledge and wisdom. Within every trainer is a deep desire for acceptance, affection, and acknowledgement. That core of vulnerability, along with financial necessity, tempts one from the stamina of the marathoner into the world of the sprint runner.

It would be a lie to say I felt no such temptations in my training career, as would a declaration that I never drifted toward the sprint territory. But I had good warning bells that sharpened my level of consciousness when I approached this territory. Those bells sounded loudly in the height of the recovery craze of the 1980s. I watched trainers become as hot as their topics and briefly become rich, pandering subjects that were little more than junk science and emotional manipulation. Were there days I felt envy and jealousy toward those achieving such rewards? Of course! But as requests came to me to present on these topics, I declined them, even when my refusals and referrals to others were followed by pleas "but we want to know what YOU think about these subjects." I declined these pleas, even though I was not always able to articulate my aversion to these subjects even to myself. As I today witness the tattered reputations of once celebrated speakers in the addictions field, I am grateful to have avoided the siren calls to join them.

The question here is "How does one distinguish the frontier that points to the future of our field from faddish topics that masquerade as that frontier?" Every addiction counselor should cultivate a shell of skepticism about those who position themselves as experts. The challenge is to separate your reactions to the person from your reactions to the ideas and approaches being promoted. There are many charming, entertaining, and nurturing trainers who promote ideas that have no scientific credibility or clinical utility. Their charm, their capacity to entertain, and their ability to affirm the value of our work masks the fact that there is little substance to what they have to offer. We know this when we enjoy a training event but realize a few hours or days later that we took nothing of substance from that quite enjoyable experience. We can also get caught up in a trainer's passionate advocacy for a particular position. The problem is that passion is not a good measure of what is factually true or clinically effective across diverse populations. Don't ever be afraid to challenge any authority by simply asking, "Says who?" or perhaps less confrontationally, "Can you provide a scientific source to help me better understand this?" Trainers who can't answer that question don't deserve the title.

"Crack Babies" and the Anatomy of a Drug Panic

Cocaine has been a part of the American drug culture since the 1870s, but its role before the 1960s was relatively obscure. Although cocaine had been targeted in various anti-drug propaganda campaigns, it had never constituted a major drug problem in America. The lack of visible cocaine-related casualties led some such as Richard Ashley, author of *Cocaine: Its History, Uses and Effects* (1975), to characterize cocaine as a non-addicting drug whose dangers had been grossly exaggerated. Historically, this benign view of cocaine grew out of several circumstances. First, the high unit price ($80-100 a gram) and low availability of cocaine limited first time use of cocaine and the quantities of cocaine that most drug users could consume. Second, the low purity of cocaine and a preferred and inefficient method of administration (intranasal ingestion) masked the addiction potential of the drug. These circumstances changed in the early 1980s—first with the process of freebasing and then with the introduction of a new product—crack. The increased purity of ingested cocaine, a remarkably efficient method of administration (smoking), and the low unit cost of crack ($5-10) all coalesced to increase the addictive properties and social costs of cocaine.

The early social alarm over crack cocaine contained many central propositions: 1) cocaine use results in instant addiction, 2) addiction to cocaine is so intense that few recover from it, 3) cocaine addiction is fueling new patterns of crime and violence, 4) prenatal cocaine exposure is devastating to fetal and childhood development, and 5) prenatally exposed infants and children constitute a biological underclass that will demand unprecedented resources from schools and communities in the coming years. The cocaine epidemic of the 1980s helped fuel the restigmatization, demedicalization, and recriminalization of alcohol and other drug problems.

The cocaine drug panic generated, as drug panics always do, a new generation of moral entrepreneurs whose careers are built on their purported expertise on the new drug. Such entrepreneurs fan public fear for their own personal and institutional aggrandizement. They expound a folk science that almost always proves to be ill-conceived and simply wrong. Nearly every early declaration on the effects of prenatal cocaine exposure had to be retracted, but the shadow of many cocaine policies remain in place as does the explosive growth in the American prison. Child welfare systems rode the wake of the cocaine panic. Several lessons from this period should guide us in the face of new drug panics:

1. Initial reports on any alleged drug epidemic are notoriously unreliable.
2. Hysteria surrounding a drug epidemic and the social forces unleashed by such hysteria can produce as much damage or even greater damage than the real or imagined epidemic.
3. Many organizations and individuals reap financial and other benefits from this period of moral panic—the child welfare system, the criminal justice system, the addiction treatment system, and new self-proclaimed national and local experts. In the 1980s and 1990s, young Black men and women and their infants constituted the primary raw materials from which such gains were harvested.
4. Reports that emphasized the potential devastation of infants and children prenatally-exposed to cocaine emphasized the potential

186

pathology of such exposure, grossly underestimating the resilience of these infants and children.

Addiction professionals have important roles in calming drug panics, challenging claims of the drug warriors, and providing assistance to those affected by new drug patterns. In January 2009, the *New York Times* published an article entitled, "The Epidemic that Wasn't"—a review of the research on the now grown up cocaine-exposed infants of the 1980s. The article reported subtle enduring effects, but an overall resiliency in functioning of these children. The headlines about "Crack Babies" raged through all the media outlets in the mid-1980s into the 1990s. The retraction of these claims arrived 15-20 years later—far too late and infrequent for the kids wounded by such labels and the parents who had lost their children to an oft-abusive foster care system, and an ever-expanding prison system, all fueled by junk science and institutional greed. Unfortunately, some junk science has a long life expectancy. The *Times* exposé was a quiet post-mortem on a drug panic that did far more harm to young children than the drug they had been exposed to.

Project SAFE

In the spring of 1986, I received a request to serve as the evaluator of a demonstration project that integrated the resources of the child welfare system and the addiction treatment system. Eventually christened Project SAFE, it focused on intervening in the lives of women with histories of alcohol- or other drug-related neglect or abuse of their children. The intervention model involved assertive outreach, case management (including transportation and child care), joint service planning between local child welfare agencies and local treatment programs, gender-specific addiction treatment, and culturally-nuanced parenting training. The federal financial resources that came to Illinois for Project SAFE were part of the national response to the hysteria surrounding crack cocaine addiction.

I almost turned down the opportunity to evaluate this project on the grounds that a female evaluator would better reflect the gender-specific focus of Project SAFE. After encouragement from multiple parties, I agreed to take on this project, not knowing that I would serve as the evaluator of this program over the next sixteen years, go on to evaluate numerous other women's treatment initiatives, and that my

187

involvement in these projects would change almost everything I believed about addiction and recovery. Today I shudder at the thought of how close I came to declining involvement in Project SAFE simply based on my gender.

One of the lessons I took from having made this decision was to not let anyone—including myself—dictate what I can or can't do based on my gender, my ethnicity, my age, or any other arbitrary characteristic that reveals nothing about my knowledge, skill, or level of motivation. The refusal to accept such limitations has constituted the foundation of some of the most profound learning experiences of my life. Have others imposed such limitations on you? Have you imposed such limitations on yourself? Is it time to break out of the cell to which you and others have restricted your possibilities?

A Lesson about Safety and Women

In 1987, I received an unusual letter from Maya Hennessey, who was then directing Grateful House, one of the oldest halfway houses for alcoholic women in the United States. In her letter, Maya said she was tired of repeatedly hearing my name in relationship to the treatment of addicted women. (I was doing a lot of research, writing, and training on this issue.) In essence, she said, "Come help us, or get out of my life!" Her letter and my agreement to visit Grateful House marked the beginning of an enduring friendship and professional collaboration. One of the most important of the many lessons I would learn from Maya occurred during my first visit to Grateful House.

I was struck by the elaborate preparations that had surrounded my visit. Female clients had been told days ahead and regularly reminded of my coming visit. Clients were given the option of being absent during my visit or could remain in parts of the House that I was not shown. I was physically supervised the entire time of my visit. When I commented on this, Maya explained to me that everything she did at Grateful House was with an eye toward assuring physical and psychological safety. She went on to explain.

When I first came to Grateful House, I would sometimes stay overnight to cover the house if the women who usually worked nights could not do so. When working nights, I began to notice a pattern. Late in the evening, each of the women in the house

188

would come downstairs and wander around for a few moments. At first, I thought it was because they wanted to talk about something, but it was something else that drew them there. Each would wander through the downstairs rooms, briefly speak to me, and then go upstairs to sleep for the night. It took me a while to figure out what they were doing. They were walking perimeter! These women, who had experienced all manner of brutality in their lives were checking who was on duty, were checking doors and windows, were checking if anything visible outside posed a threat to them. When they confirmed their relative safety, they would then go to bed. It was the beginning of my understanding of how crucial physical and psychological safety was to the treatment of addicted women.

Here's why Maya's story haunted me. In my tenure at Lighthouse, I had also covered for my night managers and had noted this unusual ritual among women. But in my case, these women were a small minority in a house filled with men! I had never figured out what those women were doing with this late night ritual until I heard Maya's story. Many of these women did not stay in residential treatment long, and when they left, our post-mortem of their stays focused on their psychological deficits, e.g., the assertion that they weren't ready for recovery yet. The truth is that it was we who were not yet ready to treat them. Not ready, because we had taken so little effort in assuring their physical and psychological safety. What Maya so eloquently conveyed to me during my visit to Grateful House was that effective services to women are predicated upon safety. In the following years, that lesson would be confirmed again and again in my evaluation of women's treatment programs.

A Rendezvous with Hope (Lessons from an Outreach Worker)

Through my tenure in the addictions field, the question of readiness for treatment and recovery was thought of as a pain quotient. In the earliest years, we believed that people didn't enter recovery until they had truly "hit bottom." If a client didn't fit that criterion of pain-induced readiness, they were often refused admission to treatment (and if we did admit them, we often threw them out shortly afterward). Then we recognized that the reason it took people so long to hit bottom was that they were protected from the painful consequences of their alcohol

189

and other drug use by a class of people we christened "enablers." So we then set about teaching enablers to stop rescuing and protecting their beloved alcoholics/addicts. Vern Johnson then came along and convinced us we could raise the bottom through a process he called *intervention*. Intervention removed the safety net of protection and confronted the alcoholic/addict with the consequences of his or her drug use and promised additional consequences if this behavior continued. Staging such interventions within families and the workplace was something of a revolution—and later an industry—that brought large numbers of culturally empowered people into treatment. But all these philosophies and technologies were about the use of pain as a catalyst of addiction recovery. So, I brought this view to my work as an evaluator of Project SAFE.

Client engagement in Project SAFE relied on an extremely assertive approach to community outreach that often involved many visits before a woman entered formal treatment services. I was interviewing one of the outreach workers and could tell she was becoming frustrated with my questions about how clients entered treatment and particularly my attempts to isolate the painful crisis that had propelled the decision to enter treatment. The outreach worker finally turned to me and said the following:

> Bill, you're not getting it! My clients don't hit bottom; my clients live on the bottom. Their capacities for physical and emotional pain are beyond your comprehension. If we wait for them to hit bottom, they will die! The issue of engaging them is not an absence of pain, it is an absence of HOPE!

The outreach worker went on to describe how the treatment system needed to shift from a pain-based to a hope-based approach to engage the kind of women she was working with. Let's now explore that approach through the eyes of those who were on the receiving end of these assertive outreach services.

"She followed me into Hell and brought me back."

As the evaluator of Project SAFE, I had the opportunity to interview women many months and years after they had completed addiction treatment. More specifically, I interviewed women in stable recovery who, at the point of initial contact with Project SAFE, had a poor prognosis for recovery. Initially, they presented with a massive number of severe and complex problems, involvement in toxic relationships, and innumerable other personal and environmental obstacles to recovery. As I faced these amazingly resilient women, I asked each of them to tell me about the sparks that had ignited their recovery journey. Each of them talked about the role their outreach worker had played in their lives. The following comments were typical.

> *I couldn't get rid of that woman! She came and just kept coming back—even tried talking to me through the locked door of a crack house. She wore me down. She followed me into Hell and brought me back.*

> (This woman is describing the first day she went to treatment—after eight weeks of outreach contacts.) *It was like a thousand other days. My babies had been taken and I was out there in the life. I'd stopped by my place to pick up some clothes and there was a knock on the door. And here was this crazy lady one more time, looking like she was happy to see me. I looked at her and said, "Don't say a word; let's go"* (for an assessment at the treatment cente*r). She saw something in me that I didn't see in myself, so I finally just took her word for it and gave this thing* (recovery) *a try.*

> *And she kept sending me those mushy notes—you know the kind I'm talking about.* (Actually, I had no idea what she was talking about.) *You know, the kind that say, "Hope you're having a good day, I'm thinking about you, hope you are doing well" and all that stuff. I treated her pretty bad the first time she came, but she hung in there and wouldn't give up on me. I can't imagine where I would be today if she hadn't kept coming back. She hung in with me through all the ups and downs of treatment and getting my kids back.*

These remarkable women taught me that, for the disempowered, the spark of recovery is a synergy of pain and hope experienced in the context of a catalytic relationship. Life and their addictions had delivered to these women more than enough pain; what was needed was an unrelenting source of hope. That hope was delivered by a cadre of recovering women who lacked much by way of professional credentials and polish, but who brought an inextinguishable and contagious faith in the transformative power of recovery. These outreach workers knew recovery was possible. They were the living proof of that proposition. What these outreach workers were able to achieve stands as testimony that the addiction treatment system needs to move beyond treating those who are ready for treatment to priming recovery motivation in those who are not yet ready. As the outreach worker so eloquently scolded me, "If we wait for them to hit bottom, they will die."

The Engagement Dance

The outreach workers of Project SAFE had a remarkable ability to engage women who were initially hostile or ambivalent about participating in professional treatment, but the outreach worker's ability to eventually get these women to a treatment center did not necessarily mean that the clients then lived happily ever after. The on-going engagement process was turbulent, to say the least. Within this intensive outpatient model (4-5 hours per day five days a week wrapped in day-care services, transportation, and home visits), clients would willingly come to treatment most days but also used cocaine or other drugs at night. Clients would come to treatment, get mad at their therapist or other clients, storm out shouting obscenities, and then call back later to make sure it was okay to come back to treatment the next day. Extreme attitudinal and behavioral ambivalence was the norm. On every dimension of change, the positive and the negative co-existed and battled for dominance. Here is a vivid example of such an observed co-occurrence.

A woman in treatment at a site that provided onsite day care enters the large day care room to pick up her small child at the end of the treatment day. (She has been in treatment about two weeks and has just come out of her third parenting training class.) Seeing his mother, the youngster, obviously enjoying himself, runs the opposite direction as fast as he can. The mother, with anger-etched face and hands on her hips, screams, "Jeremy, if you don't get back here right now, I'm gonna whip your ass!" Then with a strange look on her face, she adds, "But I'm gonna talk to you first."

Here we have the automatic pilot ("I'm gonna to whip your ass") and next to it this brand new fragile behavior ("But I'm gonna talk to you first"). The central task in treatment is to build a relationship through which the former can weaken each day and the latter strengthen. Clients with chaos-filled lives must be engaged in a process of change that often involves two steps forward and one back. This dance of engagement we do is a fine clinical art and tips the scales positively toward recovery and pre-recovery behaviors. It also requires a milieu focused more on care than control and more on the recovery process than rules. If we, as addiction professionals and recovery support specialists, are not willing to involve ourselves in this dance of engagement, we are not worthy of the titles. If we, as addiction treatment programs, are not willing to manage this dance of engagement, we should not admit such clients because of the resulting disservice that would likely ensue.

Women and men with histories of traumatic victimization may be as addicted to chaos and drama as they are the drugs they're using. Such chaos externalizes their pain and distracts them from painful experiences. Such clients must be detoxified from such chaos and drama in the same way the drugs in their bodies must be detoxified. They need healing sanctuaries.

Traumagenic Factors

The clinical management of trauma was an enduring theme within Project SAFE's evaluation debriefings and training conferences. The exact role of trauma in the etiology of addiction was something of a mystery. Little doubt prevailed about the over-representation of developmental victimization in the lives of Project SAFE clients. Rates of reported victimization ranged from 45-65% at intake and such reported rates increased through the treatment process. Consistent reports of a relationship between addiction severity and childhood sexual abuse were present. Those with more severe substance use disorders reported higher rates of childhood victimization. It was tempting to simply theorize a causative link between childhood sexual abuse and the development of substance-related problems in adolescence and adulthood. Even a cursory review of the research literature challenged this supposition by documenting many women in community populations who reported such victimization who never subsequently developed a substance use or psychiatric disorder. The question was: What distinguishes the women we were seeing in Project SAFE from resilient women in the larger community?

As Project SAFE evolved over the years, an answer to—or at least a theory about—that question emerged. Clinical staff, as they absorbed more details about victimization histories, theorized that it was not the fact of victimization that predicted future substance-related problems but the nature and duration of such victimization. Most of us who had worked on this project knew resilient and high functioning women who had been sexually abused as children. When we compared these women with our Project SAFE clients, we found significant differences. While both groups could answer to the affirmative that they had been abused, women in Project Safe were distinguished by an early age of onset of victimization, longer duration of victimization, victimization by more than one perpetrator, victimization by perpetrators drawn primarily from the family or kinship network, more invasive forms of sexual abuse, and were more likely to have experienced broader forms of physical violence or threat of such violence as a dimension of the victimization experience. While a significant number of women in both groups broke silence as a child about the victimization to an adult, those in Project SAFE were not believed or they were believed and they were blamed—the result of these occurrences was often an actual increase in abuse events. Project SAFE did not have the research dollars to formally test this theory, but our observations were subsequently confirmed via trauma research in the 1990s.

One thing we came to understand that has yet to be fully tested was the relationship between traumagenic factors and resiliency factors. We suspect that many women (and men) have experienced childhood sexual abuse with the above traumagenic factors, but did not go on to develop a broad spectrum of possible disorders. We suspect that some resiliency factors can neutralize the traumagenic factors, but it is unclear at this time what those factors are. We suspected they could include sources of family support, a long-term healing intimate relationship, personal assets that bring confidence and esteem, religious faith, and other as yet unknown factors. What we liked about this theory was that it seemed to apply to all of us. We all bring areas of vulnerability and offsetting assets. Personal recovery and effective clinical work hinge on the skilled management of both conditions. The therapeutic hour is about client and therapist managing their assets and vulnerabilities.

What is your perception of the role of trauma and traumagenic factors in the etiology of addiction and the processes of recovery?

Addiction to Chaos and Crisis

One of the things that most struck me about women in Project SAFE was the amount of drama and chaos that characterized their lives. At first, I saw this propensity for perpetual crisis as a function of the chaos in their environment (a function of poverty and community disorganization) or as an enduring trait of personality (a reflection of what clinicians had long described as histrionic personality or borderline personality), but those interpretations changed as I interviewed greater numbers of women over the course of their recoveries. I came to see chaos and crises, not as a trait of community or character, but as a strategy. I came to see chaos in the lives of traumatized addicted women akin to psychological cutting—a means of deflecting and diverting attention from deep and overwhelming emotional pain. The resulting crises serve to create focus and sparked a mobilization of internal resources. It serves as an external alarm bell that attracts new sources of support. Chaos is more than part of the problem, it is a strategy of resolution that works in the short run, but fails in the long run.

The function of chaos and crisis became most evident when it was temporarily brought under control. Their absence, via effective case management and a safe and nurturing environment, triggered a process of emotional thawing and release of deep pent-up emotions among Project SAFE women that was far scarier than the routine chaos and crises of their daily lives. These feelings often triggered flight back into chaos or behavior that sparked a new crisis, again shifting attention away from these emotions. The challenge in Project SAFE was not how to get women to open up emotionally, but how to get them to open up in ways that did not trigger panic, regression, and acting out. The lesson that I took from these observations was that all behavior—no matter how incomprehensible—is purposeful. Our challenge is to ask and answer two simple questions: 1) What needs are being met by this seemingly inexplicable behavior? 2) How can new behaviors be introduced that meet these needs in less destructive ways?

Have you experienced clients whose lives reflect this "addiction to crisis" pattern? What is your own experience trying to serve these men and women?

On Lovers and Losers

In Project SAFE, this pattern of addiction to crisis was nowhere more evident than in the arena of intimate relationships. Consider the following story. While visiting a treatment program to conduct training, the director approached me with the question, "Do you remember Marla? She stopped in today to say hello to everyone and thought she recognized you as that research guy. She said she would be happy to talk to you again if you wanted to interview her." I did remember Marla as one of the first Project SAFE clients. I first interviewed her in 1987 and then interviewed her again in 1988.

I remember Marla from her responses to the following question I asked her on both occasions. "Of all the things you have been through since the first day you were admitted to treatment, what have you found most difficult?" The first time I interviewed her, Marla was five months into her recovery and she answered, "Cocaine! Not using cocaine for five months is the hardest thing I have ever done in my life."

Over a year later, I was looking forward to interviewing Marla because she was one of the most remarkable early success stories in Project SAFE, having completed her GED and enrolled in a local community college. In this second interview, Marla's response had changed. She said, "Everyone thinks I am doing so well, and in many ways I guess I am. I haven't picked up since the day I came to treatment. I have my babies back and they are doing great. I have a great sponsor." She then teared up and said, "But most days I feel like I'm losing my mind." I was witnessing a client whose sustained trauma was catching up with her. Lacking the chemical anesthesia and the diversion of daily crises, this brave woman was beginning to thaw out and experience the rawness of long-suppressed emotion. I responded as best I could to her comments but left feeling that her continued recovery, if sustained, would be something of a miracle.

So here I was more than ten years later. The miracle had occurred, and I had an opportunity to hear about it. I told the director I would be delighted to talk to Marla. She remembered our first interview but had no recollection of the second interview I found so poignant. I couldn't help asking her once again, "Of all the things you've experienced since you first came to treatment, what has been most difficult for you?" She reflected on this question and responded as follows: "Losers! This thing about losers." She proceeded to describe a litany of destructive relationships during her active addiction and early recovery years. Perhaps the only good news was that each bad choice during the recovery phase was a little less toxic than the one that preceded it.

I then asked her, "When you look back over all of this, what do you think was going on? How do you make sense out of this today?" I will never forget her response. She said, "What I understand today is: if I'm attracted to them, they're high-risk!" There it was. She wasn't attracted to these seriously disturbed men in spite of their problems and characterological excesses. She was drawn to them because of such problems. If in her earlier life she entered a room with 50 fully actualized men and one psychopath, she and the psychopath would find each other with uncanny precision. I actually had the impulsive thought that we should hire women with Marla's history to help us assess other clients. Any person who they were attracted to could be placed in treatment or jail on the grounds that they needed either or both.

What is remarkable in this story is that Marla somehow worked her way through this tragic pattern. Many do not. Different aspects of this pattern have been described in the research literature under such terms as *scripts*, *codependency*, *non-random mating*, *compulsive re-enactment*, *victimization cycles*, and *assortative mating*. Collectively, these terms depict a process of people selecting intimate partners whose problems mirror or complement their own. Breaking these patterns can be far harder than severing a drug relationship. Have you witnessed such relationship patterns? Did such patterns accelerate or decelerate over time? What factors tipped the scales to help people break such patterns?

Model Corruption

I learned many lessons from Project SAFE, but one of the most painful was the potential corruption of successful models of intervention. After Project SAFE had established itself as a successful treatment model, a number of circumstances occurred that undermined the effectiveness of this network of programs. Staff turnover bled knowledge of the core model out of several sites, leaving the model present in name only. The lack of a mechanism to consistently train new staff created a situation where many sites drifted from the original model toward philosophies and techniques that were far less effective. As money tightened, crucial parts of the model were altered or dropped. The scope and assertiveness of outreach services declined. Service duration was shortened. Post-treatment monitoring and support diminished. Interagency case conferences lessened in frequency or stopped altogether. Mechanisms of support for staff dissipated.

As a result, Project SAFE in many sites became only a shadow of its former self. As clinical outcomes deteriorated in tandem with these changes, people who had heard of my earlier positive evaluation of this model approached me to share their experience that this model was no longer achieving such a level of success. Such reports broke my heart and taught me an important lesson. Building a successful model of treatment does not assure the future of that model. Such models must be actively protected to maintain their fidelity and to shelter them from numerous corrupting influences.

The sites where Project SAFE remained strong revealed how such protection can occur, they defined the essential elements of the model and were adamant in their insistence that the model would no longer be Project SAFE if any of those critical ingredients were compromised. Such model codification protected Project SAFE as its oversight and frontline execution passed from hands to hands over time. Second, the knowledgeable involvement of administrators allowed them to assure project continuity and to fight for model integrity with funding and regulatory authorities. Lessons from this experience are clear. It is not enough to create a successful model of treatment. You must help that model evolve over time in ways that enhance rather than undermine its clinical integrity.

Have you had experience with a program that experienced such corruption? If you could go back in time, what actions might have served to better protect that program from subsequent violations? What are you doing today to enhance the future integrity of what you are creating?

Personal Failures: A Trainee's Intervention

In 1987, I celebrated 20 years working in the addictions field. During those years, I perceived myself as a laborer rather than a "leader," but an incident occurred in fall of 1987 that forced me to confront the role that was emerging for me. The incident in question involved the issue of smoking.

Like most of my professional peers and my clients, I had continued to smoke heavily throughout my career. I brushed off comments about my need to quit with the bluster that addicts have long made into an art form. Here's the incident that changed that.

A training participant—a spunky, young woman who looked like she was in high school—marched up to me as I was smoking during break at a workshop that I was presenting for a hundred addiction counselors. She said the following:

> *As much as you apparently know about addiction, I can't believe that you smoke. Do you know that every smoker here loves to see you smoke? Seeing you smoke is a powerful affirmation of their addiction. Whether you smoke or not is more than a personal issue. To smoke as a role model, given what you do, is to enable addiction among hundreds of professionals in this field. You should think about that.*

Not waiting for a response, she turned and walked away. I wanted to write her off as one more overly rabid anti-smoker, but her words wouldn't go away. They haunted me!

I had been able to justify my own potentially self-destructive smoking behavior, but was haunted by the thought that my behavior could so profoundly and negatively influence the lives of people I professed great respect and affection for. Within days, I no longer smoked publicly. I snuck off into bathrooms and back corners like a true *dope fiend*! Within a month I had made a covenant with myself to quit and within three months smoked what I hope was the last cigarette of my life. During the weeks between this trainee's intervention and my last cigarette, I gave serious thought to how the addictions field had failed to confront the devastating issue of smoking. At this time I was writing my book, *Pathways from the Culture of Addiction to the Culture of Recovery*, and wrote these words in the weeks BEFORE I quit smoking:

199

Treatment professionals must boldly recognize nicotine as an addictive and highly lethal drug. It is time the field stopped burying its leaders, frontline service practitioners and its clients, who achieving abstinence from alcohol and traditionally defined drugs, have their lives cut short as a result of drug-related (nicotine) disease. Day-by-day, month-by-month, the field must stigmatize and sever its continued relationship with this drug.

I knew when I wrote those words with a cigarette burning in front of me that I could not be a smoker when those words were published. After repeated attempts, I smoked my last cigarette a few months later. I owe a debt of gratitude to this unknown trainee who taught me a lot about what it means to be a role model in this field. And the point is: we are all role models.

Are there toxic habits or other behaviors that stand as gross incongruities between your aspirational values and the life you are living? Work in this field doesn't require perfection, but it does eventually demand congruity between our words and the lives we are living. Living your life as a role model doesn't mean you have to lose your true self in the process. Our field has long been filled, not just with personalities, but with true characters.

A Family Tradition

What credentials can be drawn upon to face the many challenges one faces in the addictions field? My experience is that you draw upon anything and everything you can. On a visit with my parents, I mentioned that I was going to be doing my first training with an audience made up exclusively of judges. I also shared that I was a bit intimidated by this assignment. My mother, as she has all my life, assured me that I would do well. My father, with his usual mischievous smile, told me that I shouldn't be worried—that men in my family had been standing before judges for several generations. (Unfortunately, this is true and their defiant disregard for those judges likely played a role in their complex careers in the Texas criminal justice system.)

Sitting in the room a few days later where the judicial training was about to occur, I couldn't help recall my father's efforts to boost my credentials for standing before such an audience. As I stood up to begin my presentation, the one thing I knew was that I was going to walk out of that room a free man—no matter what the judges thought of me and what I had to say. I stood that day with confidence, wishing that my coming exit from that room might be the beginning of a new tradition for the men in my family.

We face many challenges working in this field, and we must find our courage where we can. What source of such courage can you find in your family history?

The Case of the Helpful Seamstress

A variety of situations can test the character and competence of the professional trainer, and I have had more than my fair share of them. One of the strangest of these misadventures occurred as part of a series of workshops I provided for two agencies with service sites in central and southern Illinois. The regular routine was for the central Illinois staff contingents to meet early in the morning and drive to a southern Illinois site where others joined us for the day of training. On this day, we met as usual for our trek south and arrived at the training site about five minutes before the training was set to begin. As I slid out of the seat of the van, the rear of my pants ripped from seam to seam. To complicate matters, I happened to be wearing fire-red underwear. My now red-flapping fanny was exposed with each and every step I took. The question was what to do, and I had little time to consider my options.

I entered the training room, openly confessing embarrassment at my predicament but vowing to try to do the training without offending anyone present. I wrapped a jacket around my waist to cover my rear end, and tried as best I could to keep my composure under the circumstances. I got through the morning without much further distress for the trainees, most of whom seemed to be taking impish delight in my predicament. When we broke for lunch, my rescuer suddenly appeared. An older trainee announced that she was a seamstress, lived only a few blocks away, and that she would be happy to drive me to her home and quickly repair my pants. I graciously accepted her offer and we proceeded to her home where she asked me to step into a curtained room, remove my pants and hand them through the curtain to her, and I quickly did. It was after my pants were gone that I realized I was standing in the bedroom of a woman I did not know and I was dressed only in a shirt and tie and my damned fancy red drawers. It further dawned on me that her husband could arrive home unexpectedly and never believe any explanation I could offer for my presence in his bedroom or my attire. My ears became finely tuned to the sounds of car engines and car doors as I awaited the husband's arrival and my impending demise. My misery ended as my angel of mercy finally returned my pants. I was never so happy to leave a woman's bedroom in my life. I recall little else of this experience (trauma does that!), but I do recall arriving home that evening to my wife's usual question, "How did the training go?"

Seasoned trainers have many such training horror stories (e.g., stories of trainers forgetting to turn their lapel microphones off when they enter bathrooms during breaks). But such stories collectively reveal something important about many roles and experiences within the addictions field. Each of us will encounter embarrassing, humiliating, or mortifying situations (hopefully few) over the course of our career, and each of us will have to draw on resources within our character to respond to them. Sometimes, as in the curious case of the helpful seamstress, you just have to accept the absolute ludicrousness of the situation and have a good laugh at yourself. I survived that experience and other days of greater infamy. You will too.

A Meditation on Violence

I had been called on many times over the course of my clinical career to evaluate and testify on the potential relationship between substance use and acts of violence. In the late 1980s and early 1990s, I received innumerable requests to present workshops on this subject. I think my major contribution to the field on this subject was to clearly illustrate the potential complexity of the relationship between substance use and interpersonal violence. I used the formula P (person) + D (drug) + E (environment) =V (violence) to depict the multiple factors that can interact to influence the risk of violence. My clinical experience led me to identify multiple potential interactions in this relationship. In focusing on the P and the D interaction, I noted that a drug could have an independent effect (no influence on an act of violence), an additive effect (increasing pre-existing risk for violence), a rationalizing effect ("the drug made me do it"), a causative effect (eliciting violence in someone without a pre-existing risk for aggression), a synergistic effect (eliciting extreme violence in a person already at high risk of violence), and a neutralizing effect (reducing the risk of violence in someone at high risk for violence). In discussing the E effect, I noted the potential for a contextual effect where an act of violence was shaped more by a social environment (such as an illicit drug market) where violence is a learned way to achieve status and power and to resolve problems.

One motivation for my training and writing on this subject was to alter the traditional assumption in the treatment field that aggression was a product of the radical personality change commonly occurring in later stages of addiction and that such violence would spontaneously remit with sustained sobriety. I wanted to challenge this assumption and portray a much more complex relationship between violence and substance use—one requiring independent evaluation and, potentially, concurrent treatment. Are there clinical issues you have given considerable thought to? How might you share the insights you have developed on these issues with the larger field?

A Waste of Money

There is nothing in federal or state government that has less chance of survival than the pet project of a lame duck agency director. In the late 1980s, one such agency director contracted with the Lighthouse Institute to conduct an evaluation of the state's addiction treatment workforce and to recommend an ideal system of workforce development. The effort that went into this project at one level was a complete waste of time—with the director leaving his position within days following submission of our study. The question was whether anything could be salvaged from it.

It was clear to me by the midpoint of this project that nothing—absolutely nothing—was going to materialize as a result of our work. Given that reality, I changed the purpose of the project in my own mind. The purpose became educating myself. I used this opportunity as a rehearsal for a time when greater opportunities would arise to influence workforce development initiatives. One of the important discoveries within that project was an invisible demographic time-bomb set to explode within the near future of the addiction treatment field. A core of age-homogenous leaders who entered key leadership positions and who were now solidifying their leadership achievements, were poised to leave together in mass in the future. I knew there was a coming leadership crisis—a subject that would later absorb a considerable amount of my attention.

The process described here is one of reframing. How do we take the proverbial lemons and make lemonade? How do we take the worst of a situation and redefine our role in it? How do we transform something of minimal or no value into something of potentially great value? That shift must often come from within us rather than from external changes in our working environment. Think of the least satisfying aspect of your current role. Is there a way to reframe your approach to this task to deepen and heighten its meaning and value to you, your organization, the community, and the field?

Carrying Light

I have always viewed training events that I conducted as an opportunity to receive as well as give. I think such learning tends to decline in tandem with the popularity of a trainer and the size of the training venue. For this reason, I tried to continue training in small venues, even as demands for large conference keynotes increased. One of the organizations I trained for using this small group (less than 30 people) format was Prevention First in Illinois. One of the workshops I gave was on managing personal and organizational stress. As part of this workshop, I often talk about the need for balancing one's professional and personal lives and the value of caring for oneself and one's closest family and personal relationships. It was in this discussion that one of the trainees shared an adage that his father had shared with him. The adage is, "One must be careful in carrying light to the community to not leave one's own home in darkness." It is perhaps one of the most profound statements I have heard in my life—and one that professional helpers and social activists would be well-served in heeding. How many of us have entered our personal lives so drained that we had little light to offer those we most loved? On a day I was expected to offer great wisdom to my students, one of my students imparted instead a wonderful gift to me. I have tried to heed his father's admonition. Do those closest to you need some of your light today?

The Mystery of the Missing Chapter

I was pleased with my first book. I knew some ideas and experiences captured in *Incest in the Organizational Family* existed nowhere else in print. I meticulously described toxic organizational

204

systems and potential strategies to prevent and correct such conditions. But there was a chapter missing in the book that was revealed at nearly every workshop where I presented this material. Inevitably, someone would ask, "Bill, what do you do if you're trapped in such a system and can't get out?" This experience of being trapped is not uncommon. Such entrapment can come from golden handcuffs, approaching retirement, and limited job options, as well as an inability to geographically relocate. When this first book was published in 1986, I didn't know how to answer that question. My cumulative experience had not provided enough living case studies of people who had lived through such a situation to truly know what their choices were. But slowly those experiences came and the positive options became clearer.

By 1993, I could describe three broad strategies of responding internally to toxic systems: 1) activism, 2) self-containment and self-protection, and 3) creative disengagement. As these options became clearer, I felt even deeper regret about the missing chapter that I was now finally ready to write. This missing piece had finally fallen into place, allowing me to come full circle on this particular issue and move on to other challenges. But how would I fill in this missing chapter? After some months of reflecting on this question, I received a call from Steve Lehman, an editor at Hazelden Publishing, who informed me that Hazelden wanted to publish a new edition of *Incest in the Organizational Family*. I quickly agreed to their offer on the condition that I could add the missing chapter. The work had indeed come full circle and was now complete.

Do you recognize how the missing chapter is a metaphor about how we learn within and contribute to the addictions field? Many unanswered questions arise out of our experience in this field. Many will never be answered, and answers that do come arrive in slowly delivered pieces that require considerable assembly and often reveal still missing pieces. As we learn within this field, we have a responsibility to announce our progress and join with other kindred spirits who are working on the same questions. Through this synergy of collaboration, many of these questions and problems finally reveal their secrets to us. A corps of long-committed workers is critical to pass on historical knowledge to a new generation of workers. For me, the missing chapter is a story about the value of enduring, the value of reflecting, and the importance of passing it on—as I have tried to do in these pages.

Rituals of Renewal

One of the benefits of working on multiple projects is that seemingly unconnected areas of study can create amazing synergies when they cross the same space. One such breakthrough in my career occurred in the 1990s. My organizational work had kindled an interest in how individuals sustained exemplary performance and health in high stress human service environments. At the same time, I was studying activities of daily life that marked the most durable and enriching styles of long-term recovery from addiction. I found four core activities to be the key to both questions.

Centering rituals are activities usually performed alone that allow one to re-assert important life values, clarify personal priorities, and maintain congruence between the internal self and the social self. Prayer, meditation, reading inspirational literature, positive self-talk, daily goal-setting, and an end-of-the-day review are examples of centering practices. Such rituals draw upon resources deep within us that help focus our decisions and actions. I have used two centering rituals throughout my professional life. The first involves taking a few moments before each significant activity to clear my mind of everything but the impending event, whether that be a client interview or a presentation I am about to give. I ask myself what is needed in this situation and then try to find that missing ingredient inside myself and focus on it. The second centering ritual I use is to focus my mind each morning on what I want to be and do that day and then to review each day at its close to evaluate how well I performed. I tick off the things I'm pleased with, the areas in which I fell short, and rehearse in my mind how I could have done things differently. I then let go of the day with the closing thought, "I will do better tomorrow."

Mirroring rituals involve the act of relating to people who share our aspirational values and who lift us up and draw the best from within us. I have spent a lifetime collecting such people, and I've used regular contact with these individuals to elevate my character and spirit. I have people who stir my energy, people who stir my mind, people who console pain and disappointment, and people who tell me to slow down and take care of myself. If centering rituals reveal to me what I need to do, mirroring rituals deliver the people into my life that will help me do those things. Email has dramatically enhanced the accessibility and presence of such people in my life and became increasingly important as my travel limitations increased.

Acts of self-care and acts of responsibility are activities that support one's physical and emotional health, acts of caretaking toward one's family and intimate social circle and acts of responsible citizenship. While self-care has long-been recognized as a crucial foundation for sustained service to others, less attention has been given to the importance of taking care of our most important relationships. Acts of responsible citizenship flow from the realization that we must balance our acts of individual healing with efforts to shape a world where wounds can be prevented and the health of the healed can be sustained.

Unpaid acts of service outside the professional helping role constitute the fourth ritual of renewal. This is quite counterintuitive and when I first began to talk about it in the late 1980s, I feared someone would throw a blanket over me and cart me off to Minnesota for co-dependency treatment. But when we ask exemplary performers what they do outside the human service environment to sustain their health and professional vitality, large numbers of them report volunteering for this or that. When asked what those activities do for them professionally, they often respond that such acts help remind them of who they are and why they originally chose to enter the helping professions. I have tried to consistently maintain involvement in "service work" that I am not paid for and that I gain no professional recognition from. I do service work to make amends, give back, and shape my character.

I am frequently asked how to sustain oneself and one's performance over a long career. I've never found anything that improved on these four rituals of renewal: centering rituals, mirroring rituals, acts of self-care, and unpaid acts of service.

Tithing: Time, Energy, and Money

One of the side-effects of achieving success as a trainer and consultant is the inevitable escalation of fees for these services. Such fee escalation has the unintended effect of narrowing one's world. With success comes decreased contact with the poorest communities, poorest organizations, and poorest clients. While prominent speakers on the lecture circuit speak of changing the world, the fact is they are in touch with an ever-shrinking and unrepresentative portion of it. My

207

understanding of this proposition is not theoretical; it is autobiographical.

By the early 1990s, I was in increasing demand on the speaking circuit of national and state addiction conferences and couldn't respond to all of the requests coming to me for training and consultation. Increasing the daily rate that Chestnut charged for my services at that time helped support the growth of the research and training division. It didn't take long, however, before I realized that any further increase in such fees would sever relationships with organizations and individuals to whom I was deeply committed.

Three strategies helped prevent this eventuality. First, I advocated within Chestnut to keep fees for our services and products as reasonable as possible so that most organizations within the field could afford our services. Second, I decided to allocate 10% of my available days to organizations that could not afford to pay my normal daily rate. I came to view this as a process of professional tithing that served as a reminder of the service ethic that had brought me into this field. Third, I tried to find ways to combine donated and reimbursed training and consultation services. For example, I often donated evening presentations to recovery advocacy organizations located in communities where I was being paid to speak on the days following these evening presentations. Doing so allowed me to serve communities and organizations with the least and the most resources.

Stewardship is the issue here. Who has access to your time and talents? Which parts of the world are you touching or failing to touch? How could you ration yourself to expand the number or nature of those you touch? The rule of 10% (or any more or less percentage of committed time) is testimony to how much can be accomplished without formal public or private funding. Committing to unpaid time is testimony to the power of what an individual can do when they think in terms of community need and personal service—outside the arena of one's profession and organizational role and without regard to financial remuneration.

Your work and its recognition will build professional currency. The question is how you will spend such currency. Nothing is wrong with hard-earned currency being used to gain positions of greater responsibility and greater personal financial reward, but we also need to consider how we might invest that currency in changing the world in some specific ways. Professional currency has the power to be spent in service, and professional currency that has not been spent by the time we disengage from active work in the field is currency wasted. The goal is to return the professional currency we gained from the field back to the field. The goal is a zero balance—a career of service completed.

AIDS Case Management in Chicago

One of the most deserving organizations in the 1980s and 1990s I donated services to was the AIDS Foundation of Chicago (AFC). As HIV infection and AIDS rose among IV drug users, their sexual partners, and their children, AFC increasingly called upon me to help provide addiction-related training to AIDS case managers working in Chicago and surrounding communities. Terrie Matthes and other AFC staff members were straightforward in their appeal to me: Help us now and if and when we receive adequate funding, we will not forget that you were there to help us before the funding arrived.

The AIDS epidemic was such an important issue that I was compelled to find a way to positively participate in this crisis. The training I volunteered to AFC was my way of becoming part of the AIDS activist movement. It was also a way to educate myself so that I could help send a wake-up call about what AIDS would mean to the future of addiction treatment and recovery in America. My work with AFC took a new turn when they called me in 1992 with exciting news: "We have just received a small grant to develop a book about AIDS case management in Chicago, and we want you to write it." This request was an incredible privilege for me and a way I could honor the lives of the AIDS case managers who I held in such high regard. For eighteen months, I interviewed those who were part of the service delivery network of the AFC, individuals and families served by AFC, and those allied agencies who worked with AFC. The resulting product, *Voices of Survival, Voices of Service: AIDS Case Management in Chicago*, was published in 1994 and helped spread the co-op model of AIDS case management that was pioneered in Chicago.

Critical problems facing our country and our world will sometimes impinge on the addictions field. When they do, we must find a way to play our part, no matter how small, in the solutions to these problems. I think we are each held accountable for what we do or fail to do in the face of such crises. My work with the AIDS Foundation of Chicago was my small way of stepping out of the role of passive bystander of the AIDS epidemic. I brought the expertise I had gained in the addictions field to bear on helping forge solutions to that epidemic.

What critical issues do you see today that alarm or inspire you? What positive role might you play in these issues?

Beauty and AIDS

Authoring *Voices of Survival, Voices of Service* required extensive interviews with individuals and families living with HIV and AIDS, as well as interviews with case managers who worked with the AIDS Foundation of Chicago. My tenure as a trainer with the agency and my desire to make a positive contribution to the problem of AIDS led me to lots of AIDS-related trainings as well as contact with people who were living with AIDS. But at this early stage of the epidemic, most people identified with AIDS were already quite sick. In spite of all the education we were trying to convey to the public at that time that anyone could be HIV positive or have AIDS, many people still believed that they could somehow tell if a person had AIDS. Such potentially lethal misconceptions were rooted in the images of AIDS-related emaciation and bodies marked with Kaposi's sarcoma that filled television screens of that period. Intellectually, I knew that scores of those who were HIV positive or living with AIDS were physically indistinguishable from those not infected. But deep inside, I believed I could instinctively distinguish the healthy from the sick—that I would somehow "know"— the same notion that had led to multiple HIV infections.

During my interviews for the book, I met dozens of people who confirmed the power of my radar. I sensed that many people I interviewed were sick the second they entered the interview room, and some clearly did not have long to live. (These were the days before AIDS had been transformed from an imminently fatal disease to a chronic illness.) But one afternoon in Chicago, two interviews forever altered my perception of AIDS at an emotional level. On that afternoon, I interviewed two of the most beautiful human beings (one female, one male) I had ever seen in my life. It was hard not to simply stare at them—difficult to concentrate on the content of their words. Their physical beauty was so profound that it was unnerving. They didn't just look healthy; their faces and bodies were radiant sculptures of perfection—the kind of perfection that leaves one in awe and bumbling in its presence. And these most beautiful human beings were living with AIDS. I left Chicago that afternoon with an emotional understanding of AIDS more profound than anything my training and earlier work had provided. And in something of a panic, I called my daughter that night and told her repeatedly, "You really can't tell!" I'm sure she thought I was suffering from some form of temporary insanity.

Each of us likes to see ourselves as personally and professionally enlightened. It's hard to confront and let go of the stereotypes, blind spots, and biases buried deep within us. We often need the help of those we serve to root them out. On a sunny day in Chicago, two beautiful human beings taught me how little I knew about the face of AIDS.

Getting Ethical

I didn't set out to be an ethicist in the addictions field and still do not see myself as such, but a number of circumstances came together in the early 1990s that pulled me into this role. My tenure in the field granted me elder status and I began receiving a growing number of phone calls from around the country from directors, supervisors, and line staff wanting to discretely sort out complex ethical and legal issues that had arisen within their programs. I kept notes of these consultations and found myself possessing case studies of some especially difficult ethical issues in the field. Such issues were almost never discussed beyond whispered conversations within the walls of a particular program. These consultations revealed cases of financial mismanagement, the relapse of recovering counselors, the sexual exploitation of clients, conflicts of interest related to secondary employment, and the misrepresentation of credentials, to name a few.

The range of these ethical dilemmas was remarkable and encompassed issued related to personal conduct of staff outside the work environment, business practices, professional conduct, conduct in relationships with clients and families, conduct in professional peer relationships, conduct involving threats to public safety, and ethical issues within specialized roles such as prevention, outreach, early intervention, research, and training. I realized I was in possession of hundreds of ethical dilemmas and discussions of them that could create the field's first book of ethical case studies. I felt a compulsion to get this book into the field and break the "no talk" rule on many of these issues. (The only ethics book in the addictions field at this time was the excellent but brief primer, *Ethics for Addiction Professionals,* by Father James Royce and Dr. LeClair Bissell.)

I was convinced during the late 1980s and early 1990s that ethical breaches in the field (particularly unethical business practices) were reaching a detonation point that could mortally wound the field via public exposés and a cultural backlash against addiction treatment. My history research had revealed a scary precedent: such exposés of ethical abuses by 19th century inebriate homes, inebriate asylums, private addiction cure institutes, and bottled home cures had damaged the public reputation of these institutions and contributed to the collapse of America's first network of addiction treatment programs. I was afraid the same thing could happen again and felt time was of the essence if such a fate was to be avoided.

As word spread that I was working on an ethical casebook for the field, numerous people called and asked if I was going to include this situation or that situation. Everyone had stories, and they all helped extend or sharpen the issues included in the book. I started with a number of assumptions as work on the book began. First, I knew most addiction counselors thought the subject of ethics was boring, so I had to make the book very engaging by maximizing the power of stories and minimizing theory. Second, I knew that many counselors were afraid of what delving into this subject might reveal about their own past or present conduct, so I had to create a safe, non-shaming environment within the book for people to honestly examine their own behavior. Third, I knew, if I was going to impact practices in the field, I had to write the book for multiple audiences—CEOs, managers, frontline clinicians, non-clinical personnel, and the growing specialty roles in the field.

Critical Incidents: Ethical Issues in the Prevention and Treatment of Addiction was published in 1994 (a second co-authored edition in 2001) and became widely used as an ethics training text in the field. For the next five years, I delivered training based on the book throughout North America, doing what I could to heighten ethical sensitivities and sharpen ethical decision-making in the field. Work on the book was not completed in time to stem the backlash against profiteering in the treatment industry—a backlash that led to a dramatic reduction in addiction treatment benefits and the closing of a large number of inpatient and residential programs by the mid-1990s. But, by all accounts, the book did stake out the ethical territory within the field and cultivate discussion of many issues that in the past had only been talked about in hushed tones. To this day, I regret that I didn't complete the book five years earlier. I think the field was ready for the book then, but I could not have written it at that point, and no one else stepped forward to do it. Could the release of this book five years earlier have made a difference in the modern history of the field? I don't know.

The work on *Critical Incidents* has some implications that transcend special concerns about ethical conduct in the field. The first lesson I would like to mention involves how I came to be involved in this project. We must be open to projects we would not choose. To accept a calling to fill a void in the field, we must transcend our own sense of inadequacy. I knew this work needed to be done, but I had a hundred reasons why I was not the person to do it. But I believed in my heart that circumstances had conspired to place me in a position to take on this task and that I had a responsibility to step forward and do it. But I had to get past the squeamish preoccupation that others would question my authority to take on this subject (e.g., "Who does he think he is to define ethics for the field?"). In response, I sought ways to diminish, rather than increase, my authority. I tried to consciously become a servant of the field, rather than its conscience. I tried to fill a void by using my own imperfect professional life as a tool to advance the field. My hope was not to write the last word on ethics for the field, but to offer words to stimulate discussion and consensus-building on key issues facing the field.

Always, Sometimes, Never

My first book, *Incest in the Organizational Family* included a discussion of abuses of power inside closed institutional systems. I'd heard of cases involving staff crossing ethical boundaries with service consumers within such systems, and I noticed a growing movement of the late 1980s and early 1990s to confront professional helpers' sexual exploitation of their clients. This movement produced national conferences at which I was invited to speak and contributions within edited books, such as *Breach of Trust.* Through that process, I was introduced to the work of the Walk-In Counseling Center in Minneapolis, Minnesota. Under the leadership of Dr. Gary Schoener, the Center counseled clients who had been sexually exploited by professional helpers and provided international training and consultation services to assist organizations in preventing and responding to incidents of sexual exploitation. Gary's and his staff members' contributions to this area have been widely recognized.

213

Through Gary, I met Jeanette Hofstee Milgrom, who for years provided a good deal of the training offered by the Walk-In Counseling Center. During this same period, I was researching the book, *Critical Incidents: Ethical Issues in the Prevention and Treatment of Addiction,* and delivering training on ethical and boundary issues in addiction treatment. During both of these activities, I struggled to find a way to teach ethical decision-making related to the management of relationship boundaries between professional helpers and their clients. Jeanette provided a wonderful answer to this dilemma. Her method was to create a safe way for professional helpers to discuss boundary appropriateness in small groups using a simple but remarkably effective framework.

Jeanette offered a long list of possible actions of a helper and asked trainees to make a judgment of whether each action would be always okay, never okay, or sometimes okay and sometimes not okay. If the judgment was for the latter category, trainees were asked to elaborate on when it is and is not appropriate to take that action. The list of behaviors spanned a wide range of verbal statements (e.g., "You are a very special person," "You are special to me," "You are a beautiful person," or "You are beautiful"), communication issues (e.g., using profanity with or directed at a client, using drug culture argot, or using terms of endearment), physical touch (e.g., touching a client's face, holding a client's hand, multiple variations of hugging, having a sexual relationship with a former client, or having a sexual relationship with a client's family member), plus innumerable other boundary decisions (e.g., friendship with a current or former client, visiting a client in their home, giving a client one's personal phone number, transporting a client in one's own vehicle, employing a client to do work at one's home, or purchasing something from a client). The discussions within my training events triggered by these exercises probably did more to sharpen the ethical decision-making of trainees than anything else I did through the 1980s and 1990s.

Jeanette's contribution illustrates the importance of teaching aids that are engaging, simple, concrete, challenging, and safe. I used Jeanette's "Always, Never, Sometimes" training framework on boundary issues for more than 20 years and adapted her teaching aid on later training that I designed. Thanks Jeanette. You made a difference and helped me make a difference as well.

Personal/Professional Nexus

One of the most difficult ethical terrains to navigate is the boundary between personal and professional conduct. When, for example, does behavior outside the workplace constitute personal and as such, private behavior, and when, if ever, does such behavior cross a boundary that involves professional duties and obligations? The concept of nexus suggests that what one does outside the workplace is indeed private until an inextricable link develops between private behavior and professional performance. The potential for such linkage requires each of us to carefully measure the potential ripple of private behavior into our professional life. A good filter is to ask: How will my participation in this activity potentially harm my clients, my organization, my community, and the larger professional field?

Considering that question provided a shield of safety that served me well over a long career. As I crisscrossed the country in my training activities, I solicited stories from addiction professionals about incidents they had directly experienced or witnessed that inflicted such injury. Those stories heightened my own ethical sensitivities and shaped a strategy that I used in my training and writing activities. The success of the strategy lay in its simplicity: Convey ethical principles in the form of stories. The use of unfinished stories, posing key questions (e.g., "What are the ethical issues here?" and "What would you do in such a situation?"), and revealing what really happened in this incident provided an engaging means of exploring many ethical issues, including the nexus between personal conduct and professional integrity. This training and the eventual incorporation of these stories into the book, *Critical Incidents,* was more an expression of the will of the field than an act of individual achievement. I think that is true of the best contributions to the field.

Crisis in New Brunswick

My training and consultation activities increased through the late 1980s and early 1990s. Traveling up to 150 days a year exerts a unique physical and emotional strain. Traveling at that level of intensity requires a high degree of self-encapsulation and a high degree of family stability. Most of the time my family and I handled the rigors of this work well, but I didn't realize just how perfectly everything had to go to support such a lifestyle. That lesson was brought home to me in a most distressing way.

In October of 1993, I traveled to the province of New Brunswick, Canada to present a keynote address at one of the early Canadian conferences on sexual exploitation of clients by professional helpers. On the plane, I was excited to see Dr. Gary Schoener, a good friend and colleague, who was also scheduled to present at the conference. Gary and I had a delightful time talking on the long flight. As I stepped off the plane, I was greeted with a message that there was an emergency and that I needed to call my office immediately. When I called, my assistant told me that Rita, the woman I lived with and would later marry, had started hemorrhaging and that she was now in surgery. The only flight I could get to return home was early the next morning. I spent one of the worst nights of my life trying to monitor the aftermath of the surgery from more than 2,000 miles away.

That night brought a whole new definition of powerlessness into my life. Gary was a source of great support and also agreed to deliver my talk, which he had heard many times. We all get by with a little help from our friends. Rita was quite understanding about my absence, but that did little to assuage my guilt and regret for not being with her through such a crisis. It also revealed to me in ways previously unacknowledged to her or myself just how much I loved this woman.

This story is not about the need to forsake our dreams. It is about not taking for granted the stability and support that make fulfilling those dreams possible. We all owe a debt of gratitude for those whose sacrifices make our contributions possible. To whom do you owe such a debt? Perhaps it is time to remind them of your gratitude. Are there people to whom you have not adequately expressed your love? Perhaps it's time to do so.

Touching the Future

In 1995, Sid Farrar from Hazelden Publishing called to tell me he had just finished reading my book, *Culture of Addiction, Culture of Recovery*, and wanted to visit me in Bloomington to discuss the possibility of Hazelden publishing a new edition of the book. The visit went well and in the months that followed I had the pleasure of working with Judy Delaney who served as Hazelden's editor for the new edition entitled, *Pathways from the Culture of Addiction to the Culture of Recovery*. But this is not a story about writing and publishing a book; it is a story about organizational instability. In the months following publication of the book, nearly everyone I had worked with on this project lost their jobs in what would be a series of shake-ups within Hazelden Publishing—shake-ups intended to help Hazelden recapture the glory days of recovery publishing it had experienced in the 1980s.

Change is a constant in our lives, but change in the addictions field is accelerated by our precarious position within the culture, our organizational instability, and the high rates of staff turnover within the field. Policies and programs created today may be gone tomorrow. So, we must find ways to develop legacies that transcend such transience. We must leave our legacies in the hearts of the individuals and families we serve. We must leave our imprint in the lives of others who have chosen to work in this field. We must survive the day so that greater service is possible in future days. We must find a way to capture what this field has taught us so we can pass it on to future generations of addiction professionals. Permanence of the structures of our field is not possible, but we can live our professional lives in ways that the lives of others are forever altered. We can leave an imprint if we recognize what is transient and what is enduring. Whether we serve as an administrator, clinician, recovery coach, researcher, educator, or one of the other numerous roles in this field, we can touch the future.

On a day many years from now, a counselor browsing in a used book store reaches for a tattered book entitled, *Pathways from the Culture of Addiction to the Culture of Recovery*. On a page of that book, she finds words that bring something new to her work with one client whose recovery in turn touches everyone in his or her life, including a newborn child whose life could have taken a different course without a father or mother's new capacity to love. In that process, I will have touched and influenced the future. How can you extend your reach into that future?

Common Factors

In 1997, Chestnut Health Systems was awarded a contract from the Center for Substance Abuse Treatment to coordinate the largest multi-site clinical trial of adolescent treatment that had ever been conducted—the Cannabis Youth Treatment study. For the next three years, I served as the Cross-site Clinical Coordinator of this study. The study compared different manualized interventions across four research-based and community-based treatment sites. The resulting evaluation of a combination of motivational interviewing and cognitive behavioral therapy (using different doses and formats), a community reinforcement approach, multidimensional family therapy, and a family support network approach concluded that all five interventions had positive effects and only a few differences in outcome across the interventions. This lack of differential effectiveness was also the major finding in Project MATCH and the National Institute on Drug Abuse's (NIDA's) Collaborative Cocaine Study. These findings cast a shadow on the dream of finding the singular most effective treatment for addiction and the dream of matching particular types of clients to particular treatment interventions. The good news in all of this was that the treatments being investigated did demonstrate positive effects even though none showed technical superiority over the others.

This replicated finding does not mean that ALL treatment is the same. It does mean that the most promising treatments being studied, though reflecting diverse theoretical models and service practices, generate similar positive outcomes. This finding sparked interest in common factors across these theoretical models that generate their therapeutic effects. While such common factors have not been isolated in addiction treatment, the common factors research in psychotherapy may give us clues to likely findings. I suspect when all is said and done, those common factors will include therapeutic alliance (empathy, warmth, positive regard, safety, and trust), therapist belief in the intervention (optimism and hope), explanatory metaphors for problem development and resolution (e.g., personally and culturally meaningful rationales for altering one's relationship with alcohol and other drugs), opportunities for self-reflection and emotional self-disclosure, focus on identity reconstruction and reconstruction of intimate and social relationships, acquisition of new problem-solving skills, and adequacy of service dose. What do you currently bring to each service relationship? Are the above ingredients reflected in those relationships?

Talking It without Walking It

One incident during the early start-up of the Cannabis Youth Treatment study left an enduring mark on my understanding of addiction counseling. To assure model fidelity with each of the five treatments we were evaluating, all therapy sessions were videotaped and reviewed by independent evaluators to provide feedback and to prevent "therapist drift" from the respective models. Such fidelity monitoring complemented traditional clinical supervision in which cases were presented and discussed by the therapist with a clinical supervisor.

At the start-up of one of the sites, I had the opportunity to participate in the clinical supervision session with one of the therapists and to then view the first videotape of the therapist's counseling session. During the clinical supervision session, the therapist presented the case with ease and clarity, describing the client with what seemed a great deal of empathy and clinical sophistication, and she demonstrated a clear mastery over theoretical and practical aspects of the particular treatment she was delivering. The clinical supervision session went well and I was looking forward with great anticipation to reviewing the videotape of the first counseling sessions between this therapist and her client. You will then understand my surprise when, a few hours later, the tape began and I witnessed the therapist's complete inability to establish rapport with this young client and perhaps the worst counseling skills I had ever witnessed. The counselor made extended speeches, interrupted, argued, confronted, and used little of the key ingredients of the protocol she was expected to implement in each session. It was as if the woman in clinical supervision and the woman in the counseling session were two completely different people.

This incident shook me. I thought of all my years of supervising counselors assuming I could gauge the quality of clinical work based on how a counselor talked about his or her clients and their sessions together. The incident above confirmed for me how little we really know about what goes on behind closed doors in the name of addiction counseling. I will never again work as a clinical supervisor without auditing (via taped reviews) or directly observing the work of those I supervise. I hope you won't either.

Training Physicians in Grenada

I had met Dr. Peter Bourne, President Carter's Drug Czar, at a number of professional conferences. I later received a call from him in 1998 in his role as Vice Chancellor of St. George's University Medical School in Grenada, West Indies. He asked if I would consider serving as a visiting professor of behavioral science and deliver a series of lectures on the assessment and treatment of substance use disorders. It turned out to be an opportunity beyond my imagining as I stood before scores of medical students from countries across the world. I visited the campus over the next several years, absorbing a great deal about medical school education and even more about alcohol and drug problems around the world. Once again, I felt a teaching opportunity had been transformed into a wonderful learning experience for me. Since then, I have always viewed each new invitation to teach as an opportunity for unexpected learning.

My experiences at St. George's also brought another lesson. My first experience standing before a few hundred international medical students was a bit intimidating, but their responses were informative and unexpected. They were hungry to learn about addiction and recovery in their role as aspiring physicians, but they also sought me out repeatedly for quiet conversations about family members or concerns about their own alcohol and drug use. Having such personal conversations with students from so many countries conveyed to me like no other experience the truly universal phenomenon of alcohol and other drug problems. If we get too preoccupied with ourselves and our limitations, we may miss some remarkable opportunities for service. I could easily have turned down Dr. Bourne's invitation out of fear I did not have enough to offer medical students.

Finding a Voice

Finding a voice means little without platforms from which that voice can be heard. After years of working on the front lines of addiction counseling, I chose two new platforms—speaking and writing—and had to find how I could best be heard in each arena. In the former, I began cultivating opportunities to speak to large groups of frontline addiction professionals and to state and federal policymakers. For the writing platform, I set a goal of developing relationships with editors of key journals and over time was able to submit articles allowing me to regularly reach the audiences I hoped to influence and serve. These columns provided venues to access the scientific community (via my photo-essay series in *Addiction*, regular articles in *Alcoholism Treatment Quarterly*, and my articles in other peer-reviewed journals), the service community (via my regular column in *Counselor* and articles in the *Addiction Professional*), and the recovery community (via columns in *Recover Magazine, Recovery Rising: The Journal of the Recovery Advocacy Movement*, and numerous recovery advocacy newsletters).

Reaching beyond the demands of one's role responsibilities to serve a higher purpose requires vision and voice. How would you like to change the world? What unmet need captures your passion? Who must you reach to exert an influence on this need? What platforms would allow you to reach this audience?

A Flashbulb Memory

As a professional trainer, I faced my share of unexpected challenges—from freezing and overheated rooms through equipment disasters to trainees from Hell, but none of this prepared me for September 11, 2001. On that morning, I was walking through the halls of a hotel to enter the ballroom where I was scheduled to give a three-hour keynote address for Michigan's annual statewide addictions conference. Like most of America, I was horrified to see the images coming from a television screen off the lobby. The images of two airplanes crashing into the World Trade Center Towers and everything else we witnessed as a country that day will be forever imprinted in our minds.

The question the conference organizers faced that morning was what to do with the conference. They asked me to bring the several hundred participants together to make a group decision on how and whether to proceed. We assembled the participants and gave people the option of canceling the conference. They decided to take a break so people could call home and check on their families and let them know they were safe but that airlines had cancelled all flights. They also were adamant that they wanted to continue the conference. They felt that to cancel the conference was to capitulate to terrorists. With that decision made, I proceeded through my toughest day as a trainer.

My preoccupation that day was with my own need to get through my responsibilities and offer what comfort I could to those present. There would be other national disasters (e.g., Hurricane Katrina) that would let me know that buried within such a disaster are special needs that the treatment system must respond to. Disasters of great magnitude leave in their wake critical needs of addicted people and those in recovery and their families. Whether that need is for detoxification, alternative arrangements for those in medication-assisted recovery, sober housing, or new meeting locations for recovery mutual aid societies, we must assess those needs and respond as best we can. If a natural disaster occurred in your community today that left your facilities uninhabitable, how would you maintain continuity of service to your clients? I had never asked that question until I witnessed the disruption of treatment and recovery support services in New York City in the aftermath of September 11, 2001.

I didn't realize how much I was affected by that day until I was invited back four years later to keynote that same conference. There was a sense of panic in the moments the invitation arrived—signaling to me that this was probably something I needed to do. So in September 2005, I went back to greet many of the people who had shared the horror of September 11, 2001 with me. There was something healing about that day for me and perhaps for others as well. We as individuals and a culture had found a way to absorb this wound and go on, each in our own way.

The Rutgers' Experience

The Yale Summer School of Alcohol Studies was founded in 1943 and in its early years trained the recovery advocates that became leaders in what historians call the Modern Alcoholism Movement—leaders from AA, the Yale Center of Alcohol Studies, the Research Council on Problems of Alcohol, and the National Committee for Education on Alcoholism. These leaders changed public attitudes toward alcoholism and laid the foundation of modern alcoholism treatment. It is hard to imagine that alcoholism specialists from around the United States and Canada would come to Connecticut each summer to learn from the likes of AA co-founder, Bill Wilson, Marty Mann, E. M. Jellinek, Mark Keller, Dr. Selden Bacon, and other notables. This summer school tradition continued after the Yale Center of Alcohol Studies moved to Rutgers University in 1962.

In 2004, I was contacted by Dr. Gail Milgram, head of the Rutgers Summer Schools, and invited for the first time to present to the 200+ participants within this intense learning experience. It was a great honor for me and one I continued for many years as my schedule and health allowed. On my first visit to Rutgers, the aging of the field's leadership was most poignantly apparent. I was at the evening dinner with all the summer school faculty and participants. The faculty sitting around me—most of whom had taught at the summer school for decades—and newcomers (myself included) were all in our late fifties or sixties. It was visibly apparent that the field's long-time leaders— represented by the faculty at Rutgers—were aging and our successors were not yet identified among the Rutgers participants—many of whom were only slightly younger than the faculty. It was another confirmation of the coming leadership crisis within the field.

Consultations with Civilians

It was like a thousand other airline flights. I was writing an article on my laptop at 35,000 feet between one speaking engagement and the next when the person next to me says, "I couldn't help noticing what you were writing about. May I ask you a question?" I always know what is coming. It is a question about the out-of-control drinking or drug use of a partner, son or daughter, mother or father, brother or sister, friend or co-worker. I have always shut off my computer in response to such questions on the assumption that there are no words I can write that have greater potential import than the words that I will respond with to this question. I have been fielding such informal questions for decades and have learned as much as I have given in response to them.

Civilians (those without experience in the worlds of addiction, addiction treatment, and addiction recovery) can learn much from us in these casual encounters, and we can learn much from such encounters as well. As much as we might cherish our privacy, we have a responsibility to extend ourselves to people whom the forces of stigma and shame prevent from entering our offices. Every situation where someone asks you what you do for a living is an opportunity to deliver information and hope. We are all outreach workers.

Retiring from the Road in Rhinelander

I had traveled more than 100 days per year for almost twenty years—moving from treatment program to treatment program and addictions conference to addictions conference. The date I had set to end my role as a full-time trainer and consultant was July 1, 2005. (I had vowed to do only one presentation a month after that date.) So, by late 2003 and throughout 2004, I turned down invitations for speaking engagements for events after June 2005. I had great difficulty declining such requests and a few came in that forced me to make an exception to my own rule about future travel. One such invitation came from Rhinelander, Wisconsin. I had been invited to Rhinelander so many summers that my training there had become something of a ritual for myself and addictions counselors from all over Northern Wisconsin. When Tony Albright called to invite me once again to the summer gathering of addiction counselors at Nicolet College, it seemed a great place to end my full-time road career. So I spent the last days in June 2005 with frontline addiction counselors for whom I had developed great affection.

The affection that they expressed to me at the end of that training I shall always remember. When I was presented a beaded ceremonial medicine pouch as a gift from one of the local Indian tribes in appreciation of my work, I found myself at a complete loss for words. After speaking millions of words all across America, I had no words to express my emotion at that moment. Sometimes we are most eloquent when we are silent.

When I returned home, I looked at the gift I had been given and thought back to the day so long ago that my ego had been bruised with the quite accurate charge that I lacked knowledge of and sensitivity toward Indian People (See Chapter Twelve). As I looked at the beauty of the beaded pouch in my hands, it seemed at that moment that my earlier ignorance and insensitivity had been forgiven. At least that was my hope. That beaded medicine bag has hung over my writing desk for all of the years since.

"I'm getting too old for this S***"

My career in the addictions field has been marked by a series of specialty roles. My early work as a streetworker and my specialty work with young people capitalized on my own youth and high energy level. My mid-career roles as a planner, researcher, and trainer required more maturity and greater technical skills. The concentrated training and consulting activity of the late 1980s and 1990s required a deepening of my technical knowledge, but it also required the ability to survive the physical and emotional rigor of spending more than 100+ days per years crisscrossing North America and beyond. What surprises me at this point in my life is the ease with which I performed this latter role so long, and the ways in which my family and I adapted to the strain of that lifestyle. But just as I had re-invented myself many times within this field, I found in the opening years of the 21st century that I could no longer physically or emotionally sustain the pace that had been my norm for more than 15 years. Getting up in the middle of the night to get to an airport, getting home late at night from airports, and physically being on my feet all day training became simply too much for me. It was a difficult truth to grasp: my heart was still willing to move forward, but my body could no longer keep up.

The realization that I was getting too old to continue within my central role in the field might have been a painful experience. What made it bearable was that I had planned my transition to get off the road over a number of years. As I slowly cut my travel down (reducing my presentations by about 15-20 per year), I increased my research responsibilities and my writing activities. So late in my career, I morphed one more time into another identity within the field. And perhaps that is part of the key for each of us. How do we redefine ourselves personally and professionally over the span of our lives? The key to such redefinition, at least for me, seems to be to continue to find that zone of creativity that best matches the needs of the field and determine, within that range of needs, the activities that I can and want to do. Are you currently in such a zone? Do you feel a new stage emerging?

Role Evolution

If you look back over the years we have reviewed, it is evident that my life in the addictions field has been marked by several overlapping and recurring roles: streetworker, community organizer, therapist, clinical supervisor, researcher and planner, trainer, historian, recovery advocate, and author. Each of the transitions in these roles was marked by predictable stages: a sense that my work in one area was nearing completion, a crisis of dissatisfaction (a sense that I was not doing my best work or that I had exhausted what I had to contribute in this area), a powerful pull in a new direction, and a leap of faith into an unexpected opportunity. That process is illustrated by my transition from full-time trainer to full-time writer in 2005-2006.

My plan to reduce my travel was planned and phased over about five years, but I assumed I would need to continue some level of training to generate the income I needed to support my role within the research institute at Chestnut Health Systems. The irony is that even as my travel reduced, the remaining travel became less tolerable. I found myself constantly wondering how I handled (and thrived amidst) the travel for all those years. Although I was prepared to take a substantial salary cut to reduce my travel time, something quite remarkable occurred in 2005 and 2006. With no effort on my part, a series of offers came to me that generated full-time support for my research and writing activities, including work on various Chestnut studies and collaborations with such researchers as Drs. David Best, Larry Davidson, Mike Dennis, Robert DuPont, Mike Flaherty, Mark Godley, Susan Godley, John Kelly, Alexandre Laudet, William Miller, Maria Pagano, and Christy Scott. Seen as a whole, these opportunities had a sense of destiny about them. The gods were trying to signal what was planned next for me.

This experience reconfirmed several lessons for me. First, we must allow our life's work to evolve dynamically through multiple roles or welcome serial shifts in focus within a particular role. That evolution is the essence of a renewal process that allows us to reignite our own passion and continue to bring our best to those we serve. Second, periods of dissatisfaction are our own spirit's means of calling us to make changes in our lives. Such acute discomfort is as crucial to our long-term health and contributions as are peak periods of satisfaction. The challenge is to listen and respond to both discomfort and deep satisfaction. Third, preparing ourselves and opening ourselves to new possibilities creates those very opportunities. Even during times I felt those opportunities didn't come quickly enough, I later came to understand that a purpose existed within that waiting time. I needed to understand certain things more fully. I needed to further refine some skills to prepare me for that next step. I have learned to trust this process. Does your professional life confirm such lessons? Are other lessons apparent as you look back over your own experience?

226

Peak Experiences and Writing Rituals

I am often asked the key to generating so much written work—a quality that can be a virtue or vice depending on the quality of the writing. Writing productivity requires observing internal and external circumstances that accompany "being in the zone" and then trying to consciously replicate those circumstances. The three keys to my writing productivity are: first, I write nearly every day—yes, including a few hours most weekends. This keeps the writing process well-greased and moving forward. Second, I have created a physical space to write that others would find horribly distracting but which inspires me—walls of books, visual reminders of the diversity of my audiences, and finished products that indicate there really is light at the end of the writing projects currently under way. Third, during my peak years, I always had multiple projects going simultaneously—always more than five and often more than ten in some stage of development. I don't believe in writer's block, only a project that is not fully incubated. I regularly move back and forth between various projects, deciding which one is ready to take its next step forward. That, of course, requires planning ahead, starting early, and making sure each project has enough time to properly ferment.

Each of us must find those strategies that elicit the best from us. Such discoveries require disciplined self-observation. The trick is not to find what works for other people, but to find out that unique combination of things that will work for you. When someone asks me what he or she should do first, I always say, "Wait and watch." The trick is to catch yourself when you are in that zone of super-creativity or super-productivity, observe its key ingredients and then experiment with how to replicate them. As a start, think of a recent period of creative output you feel really good about. What were the physical and social contexts for that work? What attitudes and feelings did you bring to those moments? Who did you interact with before, during, and after this experience? What did the subject of that moment bring to your excitement? Did those moments offer any clues about who you are as a person and what you should be doing with your life?

A Special Torch Passing

Between 1990 and 2005, I became something of a fixture in the multiple systems in Illinois dealing with the alcohol/drug-impaired driver. Every year, I trained traffic court judges, prosecutors, specialized probation officers, evaluators and treatment personnel, and the Secretary of State hearing officers who approved or denied reinstatement of driving privileges. Nearly everyone in the system completed training I provided and most of them finished multiple levels of such training. I enjoyed the training role and participating in the major public safety advisory bodies during these years. I felt good about some of the achievements we had made. In addition to the widespread training, we made substantial changes in DUI laws, elevated the sophistication of the evaluation process and its role in sentencing, and developed aggressive systems of case management for those offenders at highest risk of recidivism. But such achievements sometimes hinge on the continued presence of key people and can be swept away with great speed when those individuals leave their positions. So the challenge I faced was how to institutionalize the work I had invested 15 years of my life in to achieve.

In consort with the Administrative Office of the Illinois Courts and the Center for Legal and Policy Studies at the University of Illinois-Springfield, a team of eight potential replacements was recruited. In April 2006, we met for two days to train team members to adapt and deliver the material I had presented. The training team consisted of four judges, two probation officer supervisors, and two addiction professionals. All had significant past training experience. They were all excited if a bit nervous about taking over my role responsibilities in this area, and we negotiated a number of ways I would continue to service as a shadow consultant to support their first trainings and to help them regularly incorporate new research into their presentations. I thought letting go of an area that had been so much a part of my professional identity was going to be difficult, but that is not what I experienced. As I watched these incredibly talented individuals absorb and personalize this information and refine the designs they would use to deliver this material, I was struck by the fact that none of us is irreplaceable, but that we do have a responsibility to identify and prepare our replacements. I also realized that we have a responsibility to then get out of their way so they have room to grow personally and professionally.

As I traveled from Illinois back to my home in Florida, I had a sense of completeness and a sense of hope that those who had accepted my passed torch would far transcend my own achievements. Rather than be threatened by that possibility, I felt pleased that those final days of preparing my replacements had helped make that achievement possible and likely. The challenge of leadership succession is not to clone ourselves, but to nurture people who will use the foundation of our own work and their unique talents to eclipse what we were able to achieve. The goal of torch passing is not to perpetuate the present but to assure evolutionary advancement. Flying out of Chicago on an early spring morning in 2006, I had the sweet feeling that such advancement in at least one area of my professional life was assured.

Dream Lesson

Dreams have never been of much use to me. I have rarely remembered them and even more rarely made much sense out of them. I tend to live at two speeds, high and off (collapse), and have always suspected you need to live in the twain to extract anything of meaning from dreams into waking reality. So when all of my peers in the 1970s would bring their rich dream material into group Gestalt therapy sessions, I would have to twiddle my thumbs. It was, therefore, a rare event to wake near my 60th birthday with remarkably clear memories of a prolonged dream.

The dream on its surface was ridiculous. The images were of a training workshop I was conducting where I was violating every training rule and not using any of the well-honed training techniques I had mastered over 35+ years as a trainer. The scenes were chaotic— images of me holding side conversations with trainees in the front while trainees in the back finally disengaged and talked to each other or got up and left. When I tried to move from one PowerPoint slide to another, each click brought another television channel. Then, crowds of people from outside entered saying that we were in their room. These training atrocities continued to unfold one after another for what seemed an unending period of time. Importantly, they elicited feelings of embarrassment, humiliation, sadness, and loss. I woke from this experience confused, but also relieved that I was dreaming and that the scene I had experienced so intensely was not real. Or was it? I wish I could say this was a single dream, but it was one that was repeated

229

within minor variations over months preceding and following the end of my training career.

The dream was about the stages of learning and a warning confirmation of my decision to reduce my training activities before the scenes in my dreams did become reality. When I reflect back over my professional life, I see a coming of age stage in which my task was to build and refine my knowledge and skills, a stage of maturation in which the challenge was to sustain and refine those knowledge and skills over time, and finally the emergence of an elder status in which the challenge was to extract wisdom from this cumulative experience while, at the same time, actively managing the decline in some of those skills. The dream was an omen of what could happen if I tried to sustain my training activity beyond the point that I could physically, emotionally, and intellectually maintain my peak performance.

A few years ago, Ernie Kurtz chastised me with the suggestion that I was acting like I was going to live forever (given the number of days I was spending on the road training) and that I needed to consider the possibility that my permanent legacy to the field, if there was to be one, might lie in another area. I think that day marked the beginning of my entrance into elder status in the field. My dream a few years later was confirmation that I made the right decision. Are you approaching or resisting such a transition? Is it time to step forward to embrace a new life stage or to begin disengaging from one stage and preparing for the next? Your dreams may guide you.

A Retirement (Of Sorts)

As I write this (in 2008), I am approaching 40 years of full-time employment in the addictions field and approaching an age that people have started asking me how long I plan to continue working. Those milestones prompt reflection on how I will bring my formal career to some kind of closure. I have always thought of my work in this field more an act of service than employment, more an avocation than a vocation, so this question is not as simple as it seems. I have also spent a good portion of my career witnessing people end their careers badly— bad for them, bad for their organizations, and bad for the field. I have seen my share of people who, after making great contributions, left the field in a fit of self-destruction. As a result, I have decided that one of my last contributions to the field will be an attempt to create a model for healthy, phased disengagement from my organization and the field that others can emulate.

I have a wonderful role model for this. Mel Schulstad, one of the pioneers of modern addiction counseling, remained active in the field into his early eighties and then told me he needed to disengage before he embarrassed himself and the field. He did that quite gracefully, but, after convincing me he was getting too old to contribute professionally, he announced that he was getting remarried and heading off to Hawaii for his honeymoon. And then he continued contributing to the field. (He just celebrated his 92nd birthday at the time of this writing.) Yes, some incredible people have worked in this field.

Floyd Dell once reflected that idleness was not doing nothing; it was being free to do anything. That's how I view my coming disengagement from certain activities in the field. It's not that I want to get to the point of not doing anything in the field; it is getting to a point that I can do anything without the consideration of needed income to support my family or worrying that what I say or do will affect Chestnut Health Systems and other organizations with whom I am closely associated. One of the problems of most professions is that there is no equivalent role of the relief pitcher. We must finish what we start no matter how badly we perform in the later innings. However, with careful planning we can dictate when the game is over for us, or when we need to move from a central to a peripheral role.

My vision is to phase down my employment and then use two resources—my elder status and available time—to continue to contribute to the field within the limits of my health and abilities. I have suggested earlier that work in this field was more analogous to a marathon than a sprint. Extending that analogy, it is as important to end the race strong as it is to pace its beginning and middle. My plan is to continue to find pleasurable niches of activity so that the marathon phases into a peaceful stroll that has no end in sight. I will leave it to others reading this in the years ahead to judge the success of that strategy. How did I do?

Chapter Ten
A Meditation on Closed Systems (1978-1990)

I have tried to consciously direct my work in the addictions field, but my entry into some important areas of work lacked conscious forethought. My drift into organizational consultation work was just such a process. That drift began as a process of personal sense-making when I witnessed my own and other programs destructively imploding after achieving remarkable levels of organizational achievement. Staff burnout was something of a fad topic in the addictions world in the late 1970s, but my interest went beyond how individuals experienced deteriorations in health and performance as a result of sustained contact with high-stress work environments. I was interested in how organizational systems could themselves become sick over time and how systems dysfunction affected the health of organizational members. Also of interest was the rise and fall of organizations—human service agencies that became so sick that they experienced organizational death.

For 12 years, I devoted a portion of my time to the subject of professional and organizational distress and how it could be ameliorating to the benefit of those helped and the helpers and their organizations. Below are some of the experiences and reflections from this phase of my career that I hope will be a form of inoculation that can guide you through these risk-filled waters.

Drift into Organizational Consultation

My interest in this subject was not academic; it was highly personal. As a clinical supervisor at Lighthouse in 1973, I helped lead that organization to an exemplary level of service quality for this period, primarily through the work of a deeply committed and competent team of people. And yet within three years, I watched the dynamics within that team deteriorate in tandem with the physical, emotional, and relational health of team members. The program was heading toward an implosion that would leave many professional and personal lives in shambles. As clinical director of this program, I could neither understand nor intervene to stop what was unfolding. As this process began to wound my own life, I did the only thing that seemed open to me. I resigned and, in a state of disorientation, left Lighthouse and central Illinois. My flight to Chicago was an important career decision, but I know in my heart that it was in great part flight from a sense of impending doom. The source of that foreboding was a mystery to me. I knew only that the lives of many people who started this incredible program were a few years later unraveling (e.g., relapses, affairs between staff, marriage break-ups, and emotional casualties) and that I was impotent to understand it or do anything to prevent it.

When I met with Dr. Alan Walker from Goddard College to plan the course of study for my Master's degree, I told him I wanted to understand and help others understand a destructive organizational process. Thus, I began a prolonged meditation on the dynamics of closed organizational systems. I wrote an initial paper (*Incest in the Organizational Family: An Initial Inquiry*) while at Goddard in 1977 and published a series of three monographs in 1979 on personal and organizational burnout that elaborated the concepts I was developing.

These papers turned out to be quite a catalyst. The first paper had a life of its own—moving from person to person across the country—duplicated so many times that some copies were barely legible. As it spread, the phone calls started. "We are experiencing in our program exactly what you describe in your paper. Will you come help us?" And it was in part my inability to say no to these requests that led to mixing organizational consultation work within my evolving training and clinical consultation career.

Sometimes we choose and sometimes we are chosen. In this case, I was recruited by the field to address a shadow side of the organizational life of addiction treatment programs. As I responded to these calls, it became quickly apparent that something far more universal was afoot than the aberration of organizational dynamics in a small treatment program in central Illinois. Again, my personal and local experiences opened clues to a larger universal process.

This story serves as another example of mining a small local incident to reveal larger dynamics afoot within a field or a culture. What do you see going on at this moment in your organization and your community? What clues do these happenings afford on what is emerging as the "big picture" within the field or the larger culture?

233

Organizational Shadow

A shadow side to each organization is present just as a shadow side to each individual exists. We achieve wholeness and the ability to contain potentially destructive decisions and processes when we acknowledge this shadow. The question is whether we can muster the courage to face this part of ourselves and our collective life together. As I began my consultation work to improve the health of addiction treatment programs, the first revelation was the power of organizations to wound people. It struck me as a tragic irony that people who had entered work in human service agencies with the express purpose of helping others could themselves become casualties inside these agencies.

In the 1970s and 1980s, I witnessed the rise and fall of many early addiction leaders—individuals who achieved considerable acclaim within the field only to leave with their professional career ended ignobly and their personal lives and health in shambles. I witnessed groups of people who had been great friends become bitter enemies. I watched marriages and other sustained relationships collapse as a ripple effect of organizational processes. I entered organizations in the aftermath of the relapse, the arrest, or suicide of a staff member. I experienced organizational ghosts—individuals who had been viciously extruded from an organization but whose haunting presence remained. All of this illuminated an underbelly of organizational life—a beast within—that called for recognition and assertive management. The conclusion that I drew was that our ability to help others is only as good as the health of the organizational setting through which such help is offered. It didn't take long in my consulting career to discover processes that could wound clients as well as their professional helpers.

Have you experienced this shadow side of organizations? How did this experience influence you? In retrospect, what was the influence of that period on the future of the organization and its leaders?

Closed Incestuous Systems Revisited

A lot of staff casualties occurred in the early history of addiction treatment. We tended to define the source of this casualty process as

234

residing inside the character of the fallen staff members. But it began to dawn on me that something more insidious was happening—some indefinable process that threatened to make casualties of all of us who ventured in this work. Family systems theory helped define a process of incestuous closure that seemed to plague early addiction treatment programs. That closure was marked by a progressive isolation from outside professional and social worlds, charismatic leadership, ideological dogma, over-compensation for lack of competence with excessive commitment, the erosion of pre-existing intimate relationships, the scapegoating of the most differentiated members, and the propensity of members to meet all of their professional, social, and sexual needs inside the boundary of the organization.

These processes unfolded over a period of years, with the earliest stages of such closure experienced more as extreme euphoria than distress. But such progressive isolation transformed the organization into an organism that could feed only on itself, with inevitable implosions that turned the organization milieu into a soap opera and often ended in excessive behaviors of numerous varieties: abuses of power, breaches of ethical and legal standards, the fall of the high priest, and, in some cases, the complete implosion of the organization. Like ex-cult members, board members, staff members, volunteers, and clients wandered around for years trying to make sense of what had happened. Explanations often focused on the character of the charismatic leader, but such leaders were often as much a victim of this process as other organizational members.

The descriptions of this process opened up opportunities for consultations with organizations that had undergone or recognized they were going through such a process. Contacts with these organizations afforded opportunities to open these systems, alter leadership styles, and increase the self-care activities of organizational members. All of this work came through word-of-mouth referrals that resulted as much from my tenure in the field and my willingness to listen as it did any competence as an organizational consultant. Sometimes we are called into a role for which we are unprepared. What things should you consider in deciding whether to step forward and embrace this calling or deciding that you are unsuited for this role?

Treating Sick Systems

Much in my clinical work was applicable to my work as an organizational consultant. For example, in counseling and psychotherapy, the concepts of "transference" and "countertransference" describe the irrational forces the client and therapist bring to the helping relationship that can potentially undermine the integrity and work of this relationship. The exact same process occurs in the relationship between the organizational consultant and the individuals they work with during the consultation. Such feelings have to be acknowledged and actively managed. I also found the stages of organizational consultation similar to the stages of clinical work: screening, engagement, assessment, diagnosis, treatment, post-treatment monitoring, and service termination. What might the role of therapist for an organization or a whole community look like? What have you learned about the change process in individuals and families that could be applied to these larger systems? Years later, I would explore these questions as I sought to elucidate the concept of community recovery.

On Gatekeeping

In my work with distressed organizations, I observed a relationship between such distress and the frequency and intensity of contacts outside the organization. Most human systems are "open" via a high level of interaction between the system and the outside world. People, products, services, ideas, information, and feelings are exchanged back and forth across the boundary separating the organization from its environment. Regulating the frequency and intensity of such interactions are gatekeepers who increase or decrease boundary flow based on organizational beliefs and the dictates of system leadership. Gatekeepers act as a filter, screening out influences that could threaten system stability. Gatekeepers control immigration and emigration. They determine who and what will enter the organization and who and what will be screened out. Interactions that are likely to be ego-syntonic are facilitated; interactions that are likely to be ego-dystonic are blocked. As boundary flow increases, systems move toward openness; as boundary transactions decrease, systems move toward closure.

In early stages of closure, gatekeepers are primarily concerned with controlling what influences enter the system. In later stages, concern grows about who and what are leaving the system. Efforts then intensify to keep people, ideas, and information from escaping the system. People must be contained if the system's secrets are to be protected. Who are the gatekeepers in the system within which you currently work? Does the intensity of gatekeeping encourage or discourage relationships with those outside the organization?

Organizational Dogma

I also noticed within many distressed organizations that the organizational mission was transformed into a holy cause. Over time, a shift from substance to form occurs within closed systems. Philosophy becomes gospel, key ideas become canonized into dogma and doctrine, and these articles of faith are concretized in fixed maxims and slogans. The core ideas that emerged early in the history of closed systems, because they were a means to achieve organizational survival and status, later become ends in themselves. These ideas become divorced from the mission and elevated to the status of religious commandments. Ideologies within closed systems are not just defined as true; they are defined as THE TRUTH and truth that is fully evolved and complete. Any suggested refinements or revisions are seen as a violation of its perfection. One's relationship to this truth is not one of further investigation or interpretation but one of accepting, honoring, and defending. The suggestion that this truth may need modification or refinement is viewed as heresy. Conversion is an integral part of one's entrance into a closed system. This conversion is not final and irrevocable. It can be a forerunner of other even more jolting conversions—some in bold and unpredictable directions. Belief systems of the converted are surprisingly unstable. De-conversion and conversion to other even diametrically opposed ideologies are not uncommon.

Ideas are used to test loyalty in closed systems. They become litmus tests of inclusion and exclusion—instruments of coercion used to induce conformity. Ideas once used to liberate and empower are later called forth to silence and control. The dogma generally includes at least two dimensions. The first is an articulated stance or approach to one's products or services. This dogma defines system uniqueness and is the basis for individual identification. The second dimension is a definition of the systems relationship with the outside world. This relationship may be defined as collaborative, competitive, defensive, or offensive.

237

In the end, dogma is often sacrificed to ego. The holy idea, the visionary goal, eventually is sacrificed for the ego's (usually the leader's) appetite for power, recognition, money, or sensory gratification. The demand for commitment to an idea shifts to commitment to the institution in which such ideas are embedded and, finally, to institutional leaders. Thus, Emerson's essay on self-reliance could be found as part of the literature and rhetoric of an organization (Synanon) that produced obedient followers willing to sacrifice personal autonomy for the rewards of belonging to a cohesive community. This self-perceived possession of truth I came to think of as a Cassandra's Curse: the curse of always having the right answer. How can anyone communicate, discuss, or negotiate with people who have sole possession of the truth? This curse doesn't produce dialogue; it produces speeches. What is the most closed system in which you have participated?

High Priests and the Curse of Icarus

The closed systems with which I consulted also were often marked by a distinct style of centralized, charismatic leadership. Peter Drucker, in his delightful book *Adventures of a Bystander,* describes how Henry Luce ran his magazines. Drucker's description captures some of the flavor of the management style of the high priest in the closed system. According to Drucker, Henry Luce managed by splitting those who worked for him. He did this by cultivating and then exploiting factions and feuds. Drucker tells another story that reveals how one can avoid the insulation from feedback characteristic of the high priest role. Studying General Motors as an external consultant, Drucker found himself surprised that Alfred Sloan, the then-President of GM was consistent in his solicitation of Drucker's feedback. According to Drucker, Sloan responded as follows: "I have been the top man for fifty years and I'm used to having my own way. I'd better find out whether I'm an Emperor without clothes, and no one inside GM is likely to tell me." These two stories capture the essence of the high priest role and its antithesis.

The deification of the high priest comes from the strength projected from each individual onto the leader. The greater the strength projected into the leader, the greater the self-perceived weakness (and subsequent dependence) of the members. In the face of such unworthiness, member value is achieved through identification with the leader and the group. The role and personality of the leader and the organizational

238

ideology get fused in the deification of the high priest. The person becomes an icon—a subject of worship, a target of corporate idolatry. Synanon members often referred to Chuck Dederich as their savior, and Dederich himself made similar comparisons. When asked about the need to tape all of his musings and exhortations to the community, he responded that the history of Christianity would have been quite different if Jesus had owned a tape recorder. Dederich saw Synanon on par with Christianity and himself a messiah. I recall a funny story told by an ex-Synanon member. One day Dederich asked a procurement (hustling) crew to see if they could get a donated or discounted burial plot for Dederich. At the end of his instructions, he added, "And tell them I will only need it for three days." Such stories drew great laughs inside the Synanon community, but they also revealed truths that would darken over time.

Dederich was something of a messiah. Who else but a potential megalomaniac would take on such a challenge? Imagine a job description for someone to found Synanon:

> Wanted: A visionary man or woman who can organize a thousand drug addicts, prostitutes, felons, and former asylum patients into a self-managed therapeutic community. The job will require 24 hours a day for ten years. The position pays no salary or benefits.

The same characteristics needed to successfully launch a project like that have within them the seeds for the person's and the system's future self-destruction. I have come to think of this vulnerability as the curse of Icarus. In Greek mythology, Icarus was the figure who forged wings from feathers and wax to escape his imprisonment in a labyrinth, but was doomed when his intoxication with his powers of flight led him too close to the sun. The same thing can happen to individuals and organizations. Are there individuals you know who have experienced the curse of Icarus? Do you know anyone who is now at risk for such a fall?

I think a number of leaders move close to this point of self-destruction, experience a breakthrough of self-awareness, and then move back to a position of humility, health, and effectiveness. It is the leadership equivalent of a near-death experience. And some leaders who've come close to self-destruction or who have fallen from grace use the experience as a point of positive transformation. The mythological antidote to the

239

fall of Icarus is the Phoenix rising from the funeral pyre. These kinds of rebirths and resurrections do occur. Have you experienced or observed any such falls or near-falls from grace?

Case Study of a Fall from Grace

I knew Ron Hunsicker for years as the long-tenured leader of the National Association of Addiction Treatment Providers (NAATP). We communicated many times over the years regarding requests for me to speak at the annual NAATP membership gathering and we collaborated on the research I used to write the history of NAATP. I saw him as hardworking and a very capable voice to represent the nation's private treatment sector. I also viewed him as having his head in the right place, someone who could rise above the fray and do what was right rather than what was politically expedient. And, of course, I liked and respected him, which made the news I received in May of 2010 all the more shocking. The news was that Ron had been suspended (and later terminated) by the NAATP board amidst reports of financial irregularities in the use of NAATP funds. I knew nothing of the details of these allegations, but I knew lessons existed somewhere in this tragic story. In the weeks that followed, I asked many of the NAATP Board members how this could have happened. The answer from everyone is the same, "We were all busy CEOs who came together three times a year, and we trusted [him]."

And that is part of the moral of this tale: trust without validation is not an environment conducive to the health of leaders or their organizations. We are all vulnerable for moral drift, and mechanisms of accountability are needed to inhibit and check such drift. In the days following news of Ron's departure from NAATP, I reflected on the many leaders in this field I had worked with who had also experienced a fall from grace. I know that such falls are not unique to addiction treatment, but I could not help but wonder if we as a field had somehow failed these lost leaders. I wondered if the end of their professional stories might have been different if we had prepared them better, monitored them more closely, and supported them more consistently and effectively. I suspect some of these falls from grace represented the inevitable consequence of deep and enduring character defects, but I suspect others could have been avoided. Reflecting on the latter led me to question the circumstances under which corners could be cut, rules bent, ethical values ignored, and instincts for self-preservation abandoned. When I talked with individuals who had experienced such falls, I found a common cluster of themes: long tenure, minimal accountability, over-extension, and a creeping sense of entitlement. If there is a warning sign to heed, it is the self-declaration "I deserve it" while in a state of sustained exhaustion.

Image is Everything

One of the things I began to observe about closed systems was their preoccupation with pageantry in interacting with outsiders. The outer veneer of the closed system is carefully crafted and polished. Image is everything. Like the dysfunctional family, the worse things get inside, the greater the effort to project an image of perfection to the outside world. Outside relationships are elevated to the status of highly sophisticated propaganda. To visit a closed system is to serve as audience to a perfectly executed play—perhaps too perfect. One is treated to the mythology of the organization's creation, its canonical history, its unparalleled science and technology, its religious values, and its financial acumen. Impressive? Yes, but too impressive. In late stages of closure, the pageant breaks down due to the system's disconnection from the outside world. When Congressman Leo Ryan arrived in Jonestown, Guyana in November 1978, perhaps Jim Jones thought the pageant would work one more time. And it seemed at first that it would, but then the pageant began to unravel with an outcome more tragic than any could have conceived.

I am reminded of Eric Hoffer's observation that the less justified a person feels in claiming value for self, the more willing he or she is to embrace a holy cause and a charismatic leader. The preoccupation with image is for organizations what grandiosity is for the alcoholic. The trick is to balance legitimate pride in organizational accomplishment with a good dose of organizational humility. How might such humility be demonstrated and maintained?

Euphoria as a Warning Sign

When I interviewed staff members within distressed organizations, their current depleted state was in marked contrast to their descriptions of their early experiences within the organization. The early

241

euphoria in closed systems is an intoxicating mixture of challenge, clarity of purpose, intellectual and spiritual fulfillment, and unconditional acceptance and love. People feel like they are on fire with the intensity of it; nothing can compete with it. It is epiphany, ecstasy, defining moment, and flow—all experienced simultaneously. At the heart of this euphoria are a sense of passion, the experience of commitment, the incredible camaraderie, and a readiness for self-sacrifice. It is wonderfully exhilarating.

Some of the most fulfilling periods of my life have been within these early stages of organizational closure. People become dependent upon this intensity, yet can simultaneously be worn out by it. Such intensity is maintained by a constant crisis orientation within the organization and, by extension, within the lives of organizational members. Even the healthiest of organizations need periods of such coming together. There are dangers, however, when this passion is married to a fundamental misconstruction of reality. Passion must be tempered with 20/20 vision and a willingness to closely examine yourself and your environment every day. Emotion must be tempered by reason and sustained reality testing. Can you recall such a period of professional euphoria in your career?

Addiction to Crisis Revisited

In working within and consulting with closed systems, I came to recognize how addiction to crisis is central to the experiential life of these organizations. And this addiction metaphor applies quite literally. The phenomenon of tolerance is the idea that over time it takes crises of greater frequency and magnitude to satiate the need. This phenomenon has a predictable withdrawal period when things have been too quiet or when one leaves the system for a short time. The crisis-seeking behavior has a compulsive quality—as if one or more key persons are addicted to the adrenalin and endorphins the crises bring. These systems seem to consistently be living on the edge financially and emotionally. They seem to always respond to internal or external threats that demand a new mobilization of energy with the promise that things will slow down when we get over this latest hump. Such crisis orientation is used to evoke ever-greater levels of loyalty and commitment. The climate is one of great emotional intensity and this is one of the payoffs for participation. Closed systems provide us with a sense of participating in an intense drama for high stakes—a sense that we are fighting valiantly for the big issues.

Many closed systems take on an essentially psychopathic character. In their elitist view of the world, they exist as a sovereign entity where external rules do not apply. Leaders of closed systems often espouse support of the rules for others, but believe special circumstances exist that suspend the application of these rules to themselves. These beliefs contribute to how they can propose or defend a principle at the exact time they are violating it. Leaders of closed systems often operate under the principle that the ends justify the means. Given devotion to the holy cause, any means becomes justifiable. It begins with what might be considered minor indiscretions—disregard for zoning and licensing regulations or a failure to adequately document financial transactions or the fabrication of some piece of documentation. Organizational leaders and members always see themselves cutting corners in the name of some higher good. When exposed for such indiscretions, they portray themselves as passionately committed humanitarians caught in the red tape of incompetent and non-caring bureaucrats. In later stages of closure, grosser breaches of ethical and legal conduct occur as a result of the deterioration of the physical and emotional health of organizational leaders and members.

Many closed systems display patterns of exorbitant salaries, big bonuses, large pensions, personal loans, and perks of inconceivable proportions, such as cars, airplanes, homes, clothing, servants, chauffeurs, and bodyguards. Many closed systems have used a service veneer to exploit their not-for-profit tax structure to subsidize an extravagant lifestyle for the high priest and his or her inner circle. Secret slush funds, fund diversion, and creative accounting channel funds destined for clients to those at the center of power in the organization. While cycles of expansion (mostly to increase human labor and financial resources) and compression occur, the long-term history of closed systems is always one of ever tightening circles that drive out all but the most committed members. Each purge involves loyalty tests involving ever-greater surrender of individual will. Charles Dederich's tests of faith for Synanon members included shaved heads, mandatory vasectomies, coerced abortions for pregnant members, and, at one point, a forced switching of intimate partners within the Synanon community. Purges may also follow unsuccessful attempts to overthrow organizational leadership or may follow simple acts of heresy related to the core beliefs of the system. What began as isolated scapegoating and extrusion of a few heretics often shows up later as wholesale purges. Have you ever been part of, or observed, such a purge? If so, what lessons did you draw from that experience?

Professional Closure

What I saw time and time again in my organizational consulting work were predictable stages in the professional closure of organizations. The most frequent of these stages involved:

- emergence of organizational dogma—a rigid, and unchallengeable belief system,
- centralization of power and preference for charismatic styles of leadership,
- progressive isolation of the organization and its members from the outside professional and social world,
- the homogenization of the workforce by age, race, sex, religion, or values via a tendency to isolate and expel those who were different,
- excessive demands for time and emotional energy of workers,
- the development of a work-dominated social network by organizational members,
- the intense focusing on the personal and interpersonal problems of staff,
- the disruption of team functioning from problems arising in worker-worker social and sexual relationships,
- the projection of organizational problems on an outside enemy or scapegoating and extrusion of individual workers,
- the escalation of interpersonal and inter-group conflict to include staff plots, conspiracies, or coups against organizational leadership,
- the emergence of a punitive, abusive organizational culture, and
- the fall of the "high priest"/"priestess" and the implosion or renewal of the organization.

While closed systems need to increase their interaction with the outside world, diffused systems need to decrease such contact and define themselves internally. In closed systems, you are trying to weaken connectedness between organizational members, but in diffused systems, you are attempting to increase relationship-building activities between workers. Closed systems need to soften and update their ideology, diffused systems need to develop a clear sense of mission, a guiding vision, and a set of core values. Not only are the strategies different, but the processes to implement these strategies vary. Have you witnessed the process through which a wounded organization recaptured its health? How did changes in boundary transactions affect this return to health?

Renegade Subcultures

I often found renegade subcultures existing within the distressed organizations who sought my assistance. Renegade subcultures usually emerge from an inadequate definition of system norms, inadequate methods for inculcating system norms, or the failure to enforce system norms. All three of these elements are often present when organizational members are isolated from those persons who develop, transmit, and enforce system norms, e.g., night shift, satellite offices, part-time staff. At the height of my organizational consulting activities, a large human service system called to schedule several days of consultation. At the time of the initial call, one of the items on the agenda was a request to provide consultation to a number of supervisors on various "problem employees" with whom they were encountering difficulty. In a later call to finalize the agenda, the Director noted that this item had been deleted as it seemed these problems "had solved themselves." I told the Director that I was interested in how these problems had been resolved, as it was my experience that "problem employees" rarely experienced a spontaneous surge in attitude and productivity.

He called me back a few days later to tell me what he had discovered. While the problems seem to have individually solved themselves, a look at the whole system revealed a potentially new problem. Over a number of months, a variety of problem employees had transferred into a particular program and were all working under the direction of one night supervisor, who had himself been moved to nights because of conflict with other workers. Needless to say, we spent considerable time exploring how to intervene in what was

245

quickly becoming a renegade subculture. A cursory investigation revealed a number of abuses that were already beginning to unfold on this shift.

This story illustrates an important principle. Any reports of abuse or exploitation should trigger environmental scanning for broader patterns of abuse. A single event may be the one opportunity to uncover hidden, more systemic abuses. The micro-response to a report of exploitation focuses on the alleged incident/relationship. The macro-response asks what this event can tell us about the broader picture of organizational health and the potential for other hidden patterns of exploitation.

Leaving Closed Systems

The closed systems with which I worked became so all-consuming, so socially isolating, and so identity-defining to organizational members, that they became disoriented and emotionally overwhelmed when they, if ever, left the system. The often predictable response to such distress was to return to the fold—a common phenomenon within cults. Each time an individual leaves and returns, the price of readmission is a greater piece of the individual self. At the extreme, the individual self finally disappears leaving only a collective self. While interviewing people, I have noticed a predictable pattern in persons who have left and returned to closed systems, some many times. After describing horrible personal experiences in the organization, they are finally speechless in their efforts to explain their decisions to return. "I know, given everything I've said, the decision to go back sounds crazy. But I did, and I can't explain it." What they can't explain is their erosion of selfhood, their professional and social isolation, and the powerful call to return to the closed system particularly during times of emotional vulnerability.

Getting past the disorientation of leaving a closed system is so hard that some people are pulled back in an effort to get some closure on the experience. It is like a toxic family or intimate relationship. If we don't leave the way we'd like, we have to keep going back and trying it all over again. Attempting to leave a closed organization is similar to trying to leave a closed family: no healthy, guilt-free pathways of exit are possible. We go back to closed systems for the same reasons we go back to toxic intimate relationships—to understand, to expiate our fantasy that it can be different this time,

246

and to get a degree of emotional closure that allows us finally to move forward with our lives.

If we don't have emotional closure, we can even be emotionally involved in the system after we leave. Persons who have left the same closed system are intensely drawn to one another. I have heard story after story of survivors banding together for some process of collective decompression. I know former employees (survivors) of one particularly toxic system that continued to meet regularly for lunch years after they left the organization. It became a well-organized network that helped decompress each new generation of workers being extruded from the system. As paradoxical as it might sound, some of these groups take on some of the same qualities as the system they left. Groups of cult survivors banding together are themselves prone to take on cult-like qualities. Have you ever left a particularly closed system? How did you manage the process of disengagement?

Darwin's Legacy

I was recently re-reading Darwin's *Origin of Species* and it renewed my thinking about the process of natural selection governing the survival of social systems. The variation in the character of organizations bestows advantages and disadvantages related to their survival. In some ways, my occupational stress studies have always been about the ecology of organizations—the ways in which organizations relate to and adapt to their environment. My studies of closed systems have in some ways been studies about the extinction of social systems that failed to adapt to a rapidly changing environment. Evolution teaches us that in rapidly changing environments, species that mutate the fastest have the greatest chance of survival. We need to learn how to help our organizations consciously mutate at a higher rate of speed.

I am fascinated by the structures and processes that either enhance or impede organizational survival. The goal is not to get rid of all the day-to-day problems; it is to listen to what these problems are trying to tell us about the strained health of the organization. The consultant who helps quiet the day-to-day problems without addressing secondary and primary problems silences the warning system that could save the organization. This behavior is like the doctor's who, missing the diagnosis of cancer, prescribes drugs that mask the growing signs of cancer—to the patient and the doctor. This isn't help; this is malpractice.

People are attracted to closed systems because they promise emotional fulfillment and emotional intensity and for a period of time they provide these benefits. But physical and emotional depletion eventually lead to numbness and a lost sense of self. Closed systems can be incredibly seductive. All of us crave family, fraternity, and something meaningful we can devote our energy to. That's what the closed system holds out to us. All it asks in return is our commitment which sometimes is a euphemism for our freedom and our soul.

Mission, Time, and Money

Organizations have a process of inversion where products and services designed to be projected outward shift inward to serve the personal and professional interests of key organizational members. One indication of such inversion is perks that have gone mad! Such inversion is evident in the exploitation of corporate resources for personal gain, attitudes of entitlement, or the loss or corruption of organizational vision. As a consultant, I tried to sense where the majority of organizational time, energy, and resources were being directed. Two things within an organization never lie: time and money. I don't care what kind of rhetoric one hears, the heart of an organization is revealed by looking at how time and money are allocated. How are these two commodities allocated within your organization?

An Appropriate Death

I encountered a concept in my work with hospice programs many years ago that is worth noting. Many hospice programs have as their goal helping the persons they serve achieve an "appropriate death." An appropriate death is how a person would choose to die for themselves if they had control over such circumstances. I think we can help a dying organization achieve an appropriate death. What I mean is that the history of the organization can be brought to a close with as much dignity as possible, and the health of individuals who have been and are part of the organization can be supported during and after this process. I have assisted with this process a few times and attempted to build in rituals that allowed individuals to achieve some level of emotional closure on their experience

248

within these organizations. Rigor mortis has already begun to set into some organizations. These organizations are dying; they just don't know it yet. By helping weak organizations achieve an appropriate death, we create the conditions in which new and more vital organizations can serve the community. Sometimes organizations have to die to create the space for more vibrant and effective organizations to rise. Have you witnessed this in your own community?

What am I doing here?

As noted, my career as an organizational consultant was more a product of drift than choice. It evolved first from responding to requests from addiction agencies and then slowly expanded to consulting with other human service agencies, governmental agencies, and then to private businesses. While that work provided needed income in the early years of Lighthouse Institute, it was, in retrospect, a diversion from what I and the Institute needed to be doing. Rather than an issue of competence; it was an issue of personal heart and organizational mission. I eventually found myself with people who did not share my values and interests and doing work that mattered little to me. I needed to get myself re-centered.

Every calling has a heart—a zone of peak experience produced by the intersection of what we can do well, what we love doing, and the needs of our chosen field at a particular point in time. When these three forces align (and it takes ALL three), it creates a zone of deep satisfaction and intense productivity. When we drift out of that zone, there is a loss of joy, then discomfort, and then pain. The path that centers us within this zone is often not well-marked and only our feelings (and that voice) can keep us moving towards our destiny. Sometimes the external noise makes it hard to hear the voice of our own heart, but in the early 1990s I was listening and that voice was telling me it was time to shed distractions and get back to my roots. But it wasn't just that simple. That voice was telling me I needed to redefine those roots. It wasn't just a need to get back to more focused work in the addictions field or back to more clinically-oriented work. Something more fundamental was required. I had stretched the range of my expertise to the point it was a mile wide, but an inch deep. It was time to shrink that focus until it was an inch wide and a mile deep. It would take a few years to find that deepest center, but I was starting a process

249

of re-evaluation that would bring me to dedicate the rest of my life to the study of recovery.

Are you currently within such a zone of productivity and satisfaction or have you drifted from or have yet to find this zone? What do you need to do to keep, regain, or attain it?

Chapter Eleven
The Historian as Healer (1994-2016)

My role as an addiction treatment and recovery historian began with a shocking surprise, turned into a hobby that then morphed into an impassioned avocation. When I entered the field in the 1960s, I had a sense that alcohol and drug problems had a long history but virtually no awareness that treatment had an equally long history. The same lack of knowledge pervaded the subject of recovery. Knowledge of AA's birth in the 1930s existed and a few AA history buffs knew of one earlier group (the Washingtonians), but no one was aware of the dozens of other pre-AA recovery mutual support societies. Instead, we believed we were pioneering an addiction treatment system for the first time in history. I had worked in the field five years and that belief had gone unchallenged until I was walking by a table at a flea market one Saturday morning and noticed lying on a table of antiques a yellowed promotional flyer on something called an "inebriate asylum" that promised cure of the "alcohol, tobacco and drug habits." The date on the flyer was 1887. I was stunned to see evidence of such early treatment and vowed to see if I could find out what exactly such treatment entailed.

I started collecting material on the history of addiction, addiction treatment, and addiction recovery in 1974 and have continued collecting and organizing this information as of this writing. As I traveled from city to city, I built a large collection of historical materials from my meandering through the nation's used bookstores and antique shops. I also found some wonderful archives of original documents, such as the library of the Woman's Christian Temperance Union in Evanston, Illinois. These explorations helped me fill in many missing chapters of the history I was slowly constructing. I was becoming a collector, but had no intimations yet of my coming emergence as a historian.

What follows are stories from my work reconstructing the history of addiction treatment and recovery in the United States, particularly how that role emerged within my larger contributions to the field. I've included some of what I learned about the challenges of historical research and writing and a few of the lessons buried within these historical investigations.

Slaying the Dragon

Several steps culminated in my decision to write the book that became *Slaying the Dragon: The History of Addiction Treatment and Recovery in America*. First, I produced several history-themed papers as part of my Master's work at Goddard College in the late 1970s. With my appetite for history whetted, I intensified my search in antiquarian bookstores and flea markets for books and artifacts related to the history of treatment and recovery. By the time I returned to Chestnut Health Systems (CHS) in 1986, I had assembled quite a collection that I hoped I could one day turn into a permanent addiction studies archive. Russ Hagen and Mark Godley shared my interest in history and, in 1988, I began formally transferring my collection to CHS to what became the Illinois Addiction Studies Archives. It was about that same time that I began to think seriously about writing what I hoped would be the definitive history of addiction treatment and recovery in the United States. I knew people who were smarter and better writers, but I also knew that this project would take years of meticulous research and writing and I didn't know anyone else in the field willing to start and sustain such a feat. Whatever skills were lacking (and these deficits were considerable when I began), I knew I could compensate for those deficits with discipline, endurance, and a willingness to learn. So the story of *Slaying the Dragon* is a story of small steps that led to a big decision and a story of the power of personal commitment. The overall project was overwhelming to think about, but the project was manageable by asking each day over the course of two decades what I could do to move it forward. I took thousands of such steps before the first edition of the book rolled off the presses in 1998. Have you dreamed of such a project? What first steps could you take to set that dream in motion?

Guidance from a Revered Historian

I knew of Ernie Kurtz through his first book (*Not-God: A History of Alcoholics Anonymous*) and through references to him from many people who had attended his lectures over the years. I had not met him, but I reached a point in the early 1990s during my research on *Slaying the Dragon* in which I was in desperate need of his assistance in researching the book's four AA-related chapters. After six months of working up the courage to introduce myself to him and solicit his help, I finally got the first letter off to Ernie. I did not know at that moment that it would be among the most important letters of my life.

Ernie responded graciously and that began a string of letters, then emails, and then face-to-face visits that altered my life. We quickly branched out from discussion of the AA chapters to the whole book and my larger interest in historical research. I brought no historical training and Ernie brought a PhD in history from Harvard. I obviously had a lot to learn within this relationship. And learn I did—learning that transformed me from a clinician turned amateur historian to someone whose historical research and writings would later receive praise from many quarters. That praise belongs not to me but to Ernie, whose guidance empowered me to document (in books and scores of articles) the history of addiction treatment and recovery in a way that had never before existed.

As shy as I am and as hard as it was (and still is) to contact people of significant reputation in the field, I have learned that the difference between a stagnant and fulfilled professional life is the difference between waiting for something to happen and making something happen. Mentors do not fall out of the sky; they are usually too busy to come find you. If you are bemoaning their absence, go get them.

One other dimension of my mentorship with Ernie Kurtz is noteworthy. When I asked Ernie how I could pay him for all of his guidance and support (including offers of financial compensation for his time), he always responded with words close to the following, long before *Pay It Forward* became a popular catchphrase:

> *Days will come when others will come to you seeking your knowledge and advice. They will not come at the most convenient times and some may not seem initially to merit your time and energy. When those requests come, say yes to them. The way you can pay me back for my time and attentions is to pass on what I have given you. When they later ask how they can best express their gratitude to you, tell them the same thing.*

In the years since I first began working with Ernie Kurtz, many people have sought my advice and assistance. I have tried to remain faithful to my pledge to Ernie to keep passing it on. In 2007, I found a way to further extend Ernie's legacy when I interviewed him for a documentary video on his life and work. Later I would create a repository of his collected papers and interviews on my website. Is there someone to whom you are similarly indebted? How could you extend the reach of what he or she has given you?

A Chance Meeting in West Virginia

Shortly after I began working with Ernie Kurtz, he informed me that I had to make a "pilgrimage" to meet Charlie Bishop, Jr. in West Virginia. Ernie didn't provide a lot of detail about what to expect other than to tell me that my research on *Slaying the Dragon* would be incomplete without visiting Charlie. So a few months later, I contacted Charlie and made the trip to Wheeling, West Virginia. Charlie's house was non-descript from the outside, but all that changed when you walked in the front door. Every wall of Charlie's house was filled with bookcases and piles of books. Manuscripts, pamphlets, and tapes were stacked on furniture and the floor of every room. I mean THOUSANDS of books and artifacts! And they were all on the subject of alcohol or alcoholism. Charlie welcomed me like a long-lost brother, and I spent several days moving from bookcase to bookcase taking notes that would be invaluable for my *Dragon* project. As I worked, Charlie entertained me with stories about where he had found this book or that rare manuscript. My favorite was a strange tale of how he came to purchase a semi-truck load of temperance literature from the Anti-Saloon League.

Charlie's collection was eventually transferred to Brown University as the heart of the Chester B. Kirk Collection on Alcoholism and Alcoholics Anonymous, but Charlie continued his collecting activities. Charlie and I have continued our friendship over all these intervening years. I have met thousands of people during my tenure in the addictions field, including some real characters. A character I will never forget for his graciousness, grace, humility, spunk, and continued friendship is Charlie Bishop, Jr., AKA "The Bishop of Books." Thanks Charlie.

At the Feet of "Amateurs"

I would be remiss in these musings to omit another group of people who exerted a significant influence on my work. Through my research on *Slaying the Dragon*, I discovered early on a network of amateur collectors, AA and NA historians, and others who had stumbled for reasons of their own into collecting books, artifacts, and ephemera on alcohol- or drug-related subjects, such as the Keeley Institute or the early bottled and boxed home cures for addiction.

Some of these individuals were organized into formal groups such as AAHistoryLovers while others were lone researchers or collectors, but all proved invaluable to my history-related projects. Such individuals were rarely if ever invited to professional/academic conferences on the history of addiction/treatment/recovery and were often viewed with some condescension as amateurs. I came to have enormous respect for the tenacious and creative ways they ferreted out answers to important historical questions. Some of the most important new discoveries about the history of AA and NA, for example, have come from these so-called amateurs.

The professionalization of addiction counseling has led to the worship of education and credentialed teachers, but it is important we not discount the larger lay community to which this field owes its existence and whose continued contributions should be gratefully recognized. What sources of knowledge close to you have you not fully tapped to aid your work and your own development?

The Joy of Historical Discovery

The penultimate of historical research is working with primary source documents that have not been mined for their historical value. Moments of such research are quite special. While working on reconstructing the early history of addiction treatment in America, I was fortunate that the archives of the Keeley Institute, the largest network of addiction cure institutes in the late 19th and early 20th century, were housed at the Illinois State Historical Society in Springfield, Illinois—then an hour's drive from my home. I was also blessed with Dr. Leslie Keeley's obsession with record-keeping. Much of the Keeley records were bound in leather volumes, but many materials also remained wrapped in the original papers in which they had been first shipped to the Historical Society. My access to these closed records was facilitated by James Oughton, Jr.,—then the sole survivor of the founding families of Keeley Institute, who not only granted me permission to view the Keeley collection but also gifted me with several Keeley-related photographs, one of which would later grace the cover of *Slaying the Dragon*.

On a day in 1993, I was randomly exploring the large volume of Keeley documents and I unwrapped a ledger marked, "Keeley Physician Log." As I scanned its contents, I found a half-page biography of each physician who had worked at the more than 120 Keeley Institutes from the 1880s to the 1950s. Each bio listed the name of the physician, where they were trained, and their Keeley employment history. This log also contained a category noting whether the physician had ever been addicted, the drug to which he or she was addicted, and the dates they were treated at a Keeley Institute. I ended up finding the record of more than 100 recovering physicians who had been hired to work at one of the Keeley Institute facilities. At that moment, I experienced the thrill of knowing a unique chapter in the history of addiction treatment and recovery that no one else knew and that had never been published. It was an amazing day among many hundreds of amazing discoveries that went into what became *Slaying the Dragon*.

Disappointment and Hidden Opportunity

Throughout the mid-1990s, I was working daily on chapter drafts of *Slaying the Dragon: The History of Addiction Treatment and Recovery in America* and considering various publishing options. Bill Pittman, who worked at Hazelden and who had founded Hazelden's addiction archives, aggressively courted me to publish *Slaying the Dragon* through Hazelden Publishing. I eventually agreed, and we negotiated various contract details and stayed in close communication throughout the drafting and editing process. Bill promised a contract as soon as the manuscript was completed.

As time approached to send the book to press, I suddenly encountered delays regarding the promised contract. After months of delays, Bill conveyed (accurately or inaccurately) that the leaders of Hazelden's publishing division had decided not to publish *Slaying the Dragon*. Those months set the publishing back a year and prompted the decision at Chestnut Health Systems to publish the book rather than risk a similar fiasco with another publisher. After an agonizing process of final editing that was far beyond our technical capacities, the first edition of *Slaying the Dragon* was finally released in the spring of 1998.

We were able to create the book I had envisioned, price it at a level that anyone in the field could afford, and sell it at a marked discount to recovery advocacy organizations who could in turn sell it at full price to raise funds to support their activities. The book went on to go through printing after printing in the next decade and generated enough royalties, even at its low price, to help support my daughter's undergraduate and graduate education. Ironically, the book was later sold through Hazelden's catalog, and Hazelden would again court me to consider publishing a new edition of the book with them—an offer I consistently declined. My policy has always been to trust people rather than institutions, but sometimes the people can disappoint as well. And yet, as this case illustrates, today's bitter disappointment may be an opportunity in disguise.

Are there bitter disappointments you have experienced that bore unexpected fruit? If you have recently experienced such a disappointment, keep your eyes open for newly opening doors. As a popular country song proclaims, God's greatest gifts may arrive in the form of unanswered prayers.

Flirtation with Fame

In early 1997, I received a call from Karen O'Brien, a producer working with Bill Moyers on the development of a Public Broadcasting Service (PBS) special on addiction in America. She was soliciting ideas, stories, and potential people that should be interviewed for their special. Over the following several months, I forwarded suggestions in response to her requests. Karen and the other producers used me as a sounding board for various ideas that were being presented to them. I liked this shadow consultant role and never expected to actually be a part of the show. That happened quite by accident. Karen called one day, mentioning they wanted to produce a program in which they could depict the treatment and recovery of women. I gave her several possibilities, including a couple of programs I had evaluated.

The Moyers team contacted all of the programs and ended up doing a piece of their larger story on Project SAFE. After filming a Project SAFE graduation and interviewing clients, outreach workers, and counselors who worked in the project, they decided they wanted to interview me in my role as the evaluator of the program. So, I took the trip to New York City and took part in a long interview with Bill Moyers. Bill and his wife, Judith Davidson Moyers, were very gracious during my visit, as were all of the producers I had worked with over the months preceding the interview. When I arrived at the site of the shooting, I was invited upstairs to relax until they were ready for my interview. In the room where I waited, I couldn't help but notice one of my books with what looked like a hundred sticky notes protruding from its pages. It was obvious that a great deal of homework had been done in preparation for my interview. That homework was evident a short time later as I was asked some of the most probing questions about addiction, treatment, and recovery that I had ever faced in my career. I left feeling I'd just had the most positive experience with the media in my professional life and believing that this was a show that might make a difference.

The five-part series, *Moyers on Addiction: Close to Home*, premiered on PBS March 27, 1998. The show, at that time, met my expectations and did much to stir public discussion of everything from alcohol and other drug social policies to the biology of addiction and the processes of treatment and recovery. In the years that followed, I met scores of people whose lives had been touched by the show and who recognized me from my appearance in it. What I didn't know at the time was that I would have the opportunity a few years later to work with their son, William Cope Moyers, within an emerging new recovery advocacy movement.

The Showtime project that followed the PBS special also came out of nowhere. I received a call from Susan Emerling, a producer, who told me that Showtime was backing a number of prominent movie directors to each do a documentary on some aspect of life in the 20th century. She said she was working as a writer on a project that director Robert Zemekis—of *Back to the Future* and *Forest Gump* fame—was doing on the history of drug use in the 20th century. Several people had suggested that I might be a resource for her. That conversation began a several month process for me of sending information and photographs to her that finally culminated in her, Zemekis, and a film crew coming to Bloomington to interview me. The show, *The Pursuit of Happiness: Smoking, Drinking and Drugging in the 20th Century,* aired for the first time on September 13, 1999. The show was a ribald view of the history of America's ambivalent infatuation with and suppression of intoxicants. Interspersed with comedians and vivid television and film images were a few historians who provided the historical connecting tissue to this story. I hope my contributions earned me recognition in the latter rather than former group.

On May 31, 2006, I received two unexpected calls. The first was from Janet Klein, a producer for *60 Minutes*, who explained that she was exploring the possibility of doing a show on "private rehab centers" and asked to be briefed on the history of treatment and the status of private treatment centers in the United States. The second was a call from Susan Gray of Northern Light Productions in Boston who was preparing a proposal for a PBS documentary on the history of AA. In August, Susan Gray called to confirm the project was moving forward and confirmed my willingness to assist with it. Both of these proposed projects fizzled out over the coming months as would many more that would follow, but other media projects moved forward and were completed.

Noting my involvement in such projects here is to explore both the potential benefits and the hazards of contact with the media. The potential to reach an unfathomable number of people through the media of newspapers, magazines, television, and film is enormous and a rare opportunity. At the same time, the risks should not be ignored. Some of the risks are: being misunderstood or misquoted, or having an excerpted comment taken out of context and placed within an agenda unknown to you and that you would not support. In short, you can be used by the media in your efforts to do something positive. The risks and fallout that can accrue to you and your organization warrant a degree of caution anytime someone calls from the media to solicit your opinion.

Another risk with the media is actually a risk to yourself. The need for recognition and a sense of distinction must surely rank close to the human needs for food, water, and sex. Media attention is a potentially intoxicating and dangerous form of recognition. It can be a self-altering experience—one marked by acute self-consciousness and self-inflation. Strive to keep grounded through your fifteen minutes of fame—no matter how large or small the stage—so that such fleeting visibility doesn't alter who you are as a person. I was honored to have my work recognized through invitations to serve in these expert roles, but sometimes, it was tempting to make this more about me than the issues I discussed. The antidote for such self-infatuation is the unrelenting mantra: "Rise Above! This is not about you; stay focused on the message!" This is about service, not self. The dustbin of history is filled with fallen gurus who thought otherwise.

Finding a Community

Accolades for professional accomplishment accrue to individuals, but such accomplishments are often the product of a network of creativity and achievement. I had always been blessed with a rich network of professional supports, but meeting Ernie Kurtz brought me into a relationship with a community of historians and historical sources. To my endless questions, Ernie would often say that I needed to call this or that person, and, just as often, he was linking someone else to me as a resource on some obscure question on the history of treatment or recovery.

This growing network constituted a potential community that later came to life for me when Dr. David Musto from Yale and Dr. David Lewis from Brown University each hosted conferences that brought many of the alcohol and drug historians together for the first time. My work changed as a result of my membership in this fledgling but growing community. It opened up resources that I could draw upon and created opportunities for collaboration and co-authorship. My sense of accountability to this community heightened the quality of my work, and my ability to draw upon that community increased the depth of my work. Some of us are fortunate enough to be drawn into an existing community while others may need to forge such a community.

Do you have such a connection to a community of shared experience and aspirations? If not, who might serve as a guide to lead you into a relationship with such a community? If no person comes to mind, you may be the person to lead development of such a community.

Telling Stories with Pictures

One of my unexpected surprises in researching *Slaying the Dragon* was the discovery of photographs that told the story of addiction treatment and recovery far more eloquently than I could in words. Of the hundreds of such images, only a few dozen could be included when *Slaying the Dragon* was first published. To feed my fascination with such images, I continued collecting them. Then in 2001, I received an invitation from Griffith Edwards, the long-esteemed Editor of the international journal, *Addiction*. He had found the photos in *Slaying the Dragon* fascinating and invited me to initiate a photo history series in *Addiction* that would attempt to tell the story of addiction treatment and recovery through such historical images. I readily accepted and continued for some time to periodically submit these photographic essays for publication in this series.

I mention this now as a way to ask you to reflect on the variety of media that can be used to educate individuals and families seeking help, our professional peers, policymakers, and the public. Change can come through multiple media: a photo, a poster, a painting, a sculpture, a song, a poem, a piece of literature, a speech, or a slogan. The next time you enter your office, look at it with fresh eyes. What evokes, inspires, challenges, and teaches? Do the objects reflect the diversity of those you serve? Is it time you found fresh media to convey your most essential messages? What is the story you are trying to convey through the cultural trappings of your office? What new ways could you use to tell that story? My primary tools for years had been the spoken and written word. My work on the photo essays forced me outside that framework. I found it quite liberating to explore communicating in a new medium. Perhaps you will also.

Academia: Stranger in a Strange Land

My historical writings brought invitations to lecture in several academic settings in the early 2000s, including Yale, the Philadelphia College of Physicians, Brown University, and St. George's University Medical School. In these settings, I first met some of the pioneer scholars who were unveiling the history of alcohol and drug use in America. I was intimidated to finally meet David Musto, David Courtwright, Jim Baumohl, Robin Room, Ron Roizen, Jerry Levine, John Burnham, and other noted drug historians, as well as some of the modern policy and treatment pioneers—Jerome Jaffe, Herb Kleber, Robert DuPont, Peter Bourne, and David Lewis, to name just a few. I would later have the opportunity to collaborate with many of these leaders on various projects.

It was in the academic settings that I was most self-conscious. "What am I doing here?" was a constant refrain in my head as I moved through these events. I vacillated between near-silence and defensive (almost aggressive) challenges to other speakers about the relevance of this or that to the real world of addiction, treatment, and recovery. I

261

often left swearing I would never return to these settings, only months later to find myself back again. At one level, I wanted the recognition and credibility my presence there would represent. On the other, each encounter left me in awe of the gap between the worlds of academic research, clinical practice in addiction treatment, and the lived experience of long-term recovery. They really are three quite different worlds—each with its own peculiar language, rituals, and etiquette. It took me a long time to figure out that my greatest value might not be in my acceptance within these worlds, but my acceptance as an ambassador linking these three worlds. On that basis, I became more comfortable entering academic institutions. I came to realize I was not there seeking acceptance as a member of those institutions but was instead there as a "bridge person."

What worlds might you help bridge?

Writing Wrongs: Historian as Healer

As my interest in the history of addiction intensified and my network of mentors and peers who shared this interest grew, I realized that I was approaching this subject from a different angle. My interest in history was not simply to discover and convey new historical information as an end in itself. I was interested in history as a medium for personal transformation and social change. I was, in short, a historian with an agenda. I must confess some discomfort with this realization, as it seemed to violate standards of scholarly detachment and objectivity.

And then I ran across an essay by Aurora Levins Morales entitled "The Historian as Curandera." Morales' essay is about the role history plays as a weapon of colonization and a tool of personal and cultural liberation. In her view, controlling elites rob the colonized of their own history and implant a new history that legitimizes the inequality of power as "natural, inevitable, and permanent." The role of the activist historian is thus to rediscover the lost stories of the oppressed and use these stories to help the oppressed redefine their past, redefine themselves, and re-envision their future. The goal of the historian activist is to use one's resurrected history to create a "culture of resistance." Morales suggests several strategies for the activist historian: tell untold, lost or rarely told stories; identify misinformation and expose and contradict it; expose the stories that have been lost in

262

culturally dominant history; ask provocative questions; explore non-traditional sources of historical evidence; personalize and portray stories that reveal people as actors rather than victims; reveal complexities and ambiguities; and make history accessible to real people.

Morales' essay conveyed more articulately than I ever could the role I was seeking through my historical research and writing. My goal was to use history to change people's lives and to change the professional field to which I committed my life. The stories I was uncovering were informative and entertaining, but my interest in them was primarily in the lessons that could be conveyed through them—lessons that could influence individual and institutional decision-making.

As I began presenting my research on the history of resistance to and recovery from alcohol problems among Native American tribes, I was struck by the power of these stories to Native American audiences. Their responses revealed the healing power of restored history. Based on this experience, I focused on historical research that was marked by personal meaning and cultural potency as well as scholarly accuracy. I also committed myself to making the history I was revealing relevant to the people whose lives were affected by it. This freed me to escape my preoccupation with scholarly journals and to communicate history through presentations, posted essays, and books that were written and priced for accessibility. Thank you Aurora Levins Morales for your message and for teaching me a lesson about the medium in which such messages can be communicated. Is there a teacher you need to thank?

Rise and Fall of an Inebriate Asylum

I first met John Crowley in 1997 at a Brown University meeting of scholars who were involved in historical research on alcoholism and Alcoholics Anonymous. I had greatly admired his writing, particularly an essay he had written on the recovery narratives of Frederick Douglass and John Gough, and looked forward to exploring our mutual interest in the early history of alcoholism treatment in America. John was particularly interested in the history of the New York State Inebriate Asylum and had discovered some previously unknown documents about the Asylum. John asked me to co-author a book about the New York State Inebriate Asylum and its charismatic founder, Dr. Joseph

263

Turner. After negotiating a contract with the University of Massachusetts Press, we began our collaboration. I learned two lessons from this project, one from the collaboration process and the other from the story revealed by our research.

John and I brought contrasting backgrounds to this project. At the time, he was head of the English Department at Syracuse University, was one of the leading experts on the portrayal of alcoholism in American literature, and possessed writing skills beyond anything I could ever aspire to. We also wrote for different audiences—John for literary scholars and I for frontline treatment professionals and people in recovery. And yet, somehow, our work on this project came together. In my earlier collaborations, I recruited co-authors whose views mirrored my own and whose knowledge and skills were similar. By the time *Drunkard's Refuge: The Lessons of the New York State Inebriate Asylum* was released in 2004, I had decided to open myself to a wider variety of collaborations.

In the two years that followed, I co-authored articles with innumerable individuals and began collaborations on two other books. I learned a great deal from each of these collaborations, and I set goals for other people with whom I hoped to collaborate before the end of my writing career. When I looked at the list of those potential collaborations, I realized they fell into two groups. One group consisted of people I considered elders within the field—people from whom I wanted to draw knowledge and personally engage. The other group was filled with some of the rising stars of the field whose emerging leadership I wanted to acknowledge and who would offer me fresh perspectives on old issues.

In this process I had done two things of great professional importance: asked for what I needed from those who could best provide it and passed on what I had acquired to those who could best use it. These activities were not sequential; I am still doing both. Each of us has a responsibility to keep this generational cycle unbroken by remaining a student and not shying away from our own teaching opportunities. Are you doing both?

Reading Historical Cycles

We can read, interpret, and respond to predictable cycles that occur in the history of alcohol and other drug (AOD) problems. We can

264

anticipate what is coming with some degree of certainty, as long as we remain open to unknown phenomena that have no historical precedent.

My involvement in trying to read these cycles grew out of a shared interest with one of my colleagues. Randy Webber and I had spent countless hours discussing various drug trends since first meeting in the mid-1970s, and those discussions had intensified when Randy joined the Lighthouse Institute. Randy and I were being asked to do workshops on drug trends in the late 1980s, and, in preparation for those workshops, we generated a number of predictions of what we thought would be coming in the next decade. At the time we made those predictions, overall experimentation with illicit drugs (other than cocaine) was shrinking by every available survey among young people, opiate addiction was on the decline, and cannabis use was being restigmatized and recriminalized. In that context, we made the following three predictions for the 1990s: 1) a new wave of illicit polydrug experimentation will rise among young people, 2) new patterns of stimulant use will supplant cocaine use, and 3) cycles of widespread cocaine and methamphetamine use will be followed by rising patterns of alcoholism, sedativism, and narcotic addiction. When those predictions came to pass, we were asked, "How did you do that?"

Before I brag about how we did it, let me confess what we missed. We failed to predict heroin purity of 40%+ that, in combination with fear of disease transmission through needle-sharing, shifted the method of heroin ingestion for many new users from injection to intranasal ingestion or smoking. We also failed to predict that our anticipated rise of opiate use would include a dramatic increase in the misuse of prescription opioids and that this trend would penetrate many rural areas without historical problems of opiate addiction. (I later analyzed this pattern in the co-authored book, *When Painkillers Become Dangerous*.)

The way Randy and I formulated our predictions was by identifying certain principles that seemed to underlie seemingly unfathomable drug trends. We first noted that drugs often remained dormant for long periods before awakening as the center of drug epidemics. (This dormancy principle should have allowed us to anticipate new patterns of prescription opioid dependence.) We noted that the emergence of the illicit drug epidemic of the 1960s was heavily influenced by the collision of demographics (the largest population of adolescents in the history of the country) and cultural anomie (the re-evaluation of the values that had dominated the years following World

War II). We noted that once they emerged, drug epidemics often went into hibernation, only to emerge later in more virulent forms. We noted that many drug epidemics really didn't go away, but cycled into other patterns of drug use in a predictable and sequenced pattern. Based on the coming increase of adolescents in the 1990s (as a percentage of the total population), growing cultural clashes of values in the late 1980s and youthful infatuation with the 1960s, we predicted increases in youthful polydrug experimentation. Because earlier cycles of stimulant dependence had often involved shifts from short-acting stimulants to long-acting stimulants and were then followed by increases in alcoholism and narcotic addiction, we predicted that the cocaine binges of the 1980s would be followed by increases in methamphetamine use and then opiate use in the 1990s.

Such cyclical patterns can also be seen in other areas of the field. There are, for example, alternating patterns to organize specialized addiction treatment services, gradual integration of those services into broader health and human service systems, progressive disillusionment with the lack of responsiveness of these larger systems, and then a resurging movement to organize specialized services for those addicted to alcohol and other drugs. I have tracked these cycles of specialization and generalization and the parallel efforts to centralize and then decentralize the organization of prevention and treatment services throughout American history and over the course of my own career.

Cycles also occur where we stigmatize and criminalize AOD problems in one era; destigmatize, medicalize, and decriminalize these problems in the next era; only to again regress toward restigmatization, demedicalization, and recriminalization.

Vacillating cycles of emphasis on secular, spiritual, and religious approaches to the resolution of AOD problems take place as well as alternating cycles in the prevailing belief of who is best suited to help resolve these problems, from persons credentialed by education to persons credentialed by direct experience.

Understanding historical cycles has several lessons and also reminds us of the power to observe, predict, and influence the larger patterns within which we perform our service work. We must ride these historical waves at the same time we try to understand and influence these cycles of history.

I would add one final note of caution here: Announcements about new discoveries related to the sources and solutions to alcohol and other drug problems are notoriously unreliable. My advice in this area is simple: cultivate an informed skepticism about such claims and test early scientific reports against your own direct experience. History will share her secrets with you if you listen, but such lessons from the past are no substitute for careful and sustained observation of the present. If we only view the present through our knowledge of repeating cycles of the past, we will be ill-prepared for that which is fundamentally new.

Methamphetamine: Here we go again!

Through my many years in the addictions field, I had avoided focusing on the subject of methamphetamine. Such avoidance came from some misguided notion that distance from methamphetamine, both as a substance and a subject, was a safeguard for my own recovery. During the 1970s and 1980s, that avoidance was pretty easy to arrange since methamphetamine as a drug trend had gone into hibernation. But the 1990s witnessed a resurrection from such dormancy, and I was able to witness—this time from a detached distance, a renewed methamphetamine epidemic. In 2006, Dr. Ralph Weisheit, a professor within the criminal justice department at Illinois State University, invited me to co-author a book on methamphetamine. It seemed time to plumb my own experience and lend my professional skills to a subject so close to the core of my entrance into the field. The book, *Methamphetamine: Its History, Pharmacology and Treatment*, was released in April 2009 by Hazelden.

Research on the methamphetamine book was personally well-timed. The academic research and writing allowed me to finally achieve a degree of distance from the more disastrous personal research I had done on this subject so many years earlier. Through this process, I drew a deeper appreciation of the power of bibliotherapy—the power of the mind to help heal wounds of the heart. We each must become students of our deepest injuries and then become healers and teachers.

Connecting the Dots (Big Picture Thinking)

A major shift in our position in the field of addiction treatment occurs when we rise above the parochial demands of our present role to see the field and the needs of its service constituents as a whole. When

I attempted to make that shift, I found something particularly helpful. As I went through the evolving demands of my professional life, I tried to ask what each small event was telling me about the larger picture of what was going on with addiction, treatment, and recovery in America. I was connecting the small dots of my daily life together to form a larger picture of what was beginning to unfold. Here's one example.

In the late 1980s, I was asked to speak at a conference in which I addressed addiction treatment administrators in the morning and addiction counselors in the afternoon. Just before I stood up to speak in the morning, I looked out at the audience—really looked—and asked myself who these people were. Yes, the audience was predominately white and male—less white and less male than it would have been even a few years earlier—but the striking image was one of age. I tried to find the youngest and oldest faces in the room and what was surprising was the small gap between these categories. Less than a five to seven year age difference separated the youngest and the oldest. All were late middle-aged and had already assumed leadership positions in the field—some for quite some time while others had come to leadership positions after years of service in the field. But as I asked what the larger picture was, I was immediately struck by the coming leadership crisis in the field. Most of these people would mature within the field and then leave in mass between 2005 and 2015, and their mass exodus in such a short window of time would mark a period of enormous vulnerability (and opportunity) for the field. As I reflected on this later that day, I decided that this was an issue I should write and speak about.

The afternoon of that same day, I stared out at 100+ addiction counselors and again asked myself the question I had raised that morning. What I saw was a room that was overwhelmingly white and 70% women. I was witnessing the growing feminization of the frontlines of addiction treatment, but I was also witnessing a growing mismatch between the characteristics of clients (still predominately male but increasingly men and women of color) and the frontline service providers (increasingly white women).

Look around you. Read the details of your professional world as if it were a map holding clues as to the larger picture of trends that have yet to be recognized and explored. What do you see?

Predicting the Future

Most people who make predictions about the future end up making fools of themselves. In 2003, Dr. Tom McGovern and I risked just such a fate by trying to suggest what we as a field could expect in the coming decades. Here are the predictions we made.

1. The federal/state/local partnership created by the Comprehensive Alcoholism Prevention and Treatment Act of 1970 (known as the Hughes Act) will be challenged by the growing restigmatization, demedicalization, and recriminalization of severe alcohol and other drug problems.
2. The federal investment in an alcohol problems research infrastructure will reap significant rewards in the coming decades, including fundamentally new pharmacological adjuncts to treatment.
3. The integration of the treatment of alcohol and other drug problems will encompass the treatment of nicotine addiction alongside the treatment of other drug addictions, but the over-extension of the concept of addiction to other problem areas will spur a redefinition of the boundaries of the field, e.g., distinguishing the use of *addiction* as a medical concept versus the personal use of the concept of *addiction* as an organizing metaphor for behavioral change.
4. The categorical segregation of the treatment of substance use disorders will be severely challenged in the next two decades as addiction treatment programs are absorbed into larger umbrellas of "behavioral health" and "human services."
5. Multi-pathway models of understanding and intervening in alcohol problems will replace more traditional, single-pathway models.
6. The next two decades will witness attempts to integrate the emerging public health and medical/clinical models of understanding and responding to alcohol and other drug (AOD) problems.
7. Differences between community and clinical populations will widen with the multiple problem client/family (greater problem severity and psychiatric co-morbidity and fewer recovery assets)

becoming the norm within publicly funded treatment programs, creating a dichotomy between individuals who can resolve alcohol problems with recovery self-management tools (e.g., manuals and online recovery support services) or brief professional intervention versus those who will require multi-agency models of sustained recovery management.

8. Escalating life expectancies and the demographic aging of the "war babies" will spark growing concern about the problem of late-onset AOD problems, which will emerge as a major specialty within the addiction treatment field.

9. The recognition of addiction medicine as a recognized specialty will continue, but will be offset by greater involvement of primary physicians, physician assistants, and nurse practitioners in the treatment of AOD problems.

10. The continued professionalization of the role of the addiction counselor (e.g., the licensure movement) will be balanced by new roles (recovery coaches and recovery support specialists) that will bring greater numbers of recovering people back into the field.

11. Professional roles in the field, dominated by men in the early history of the field, will be increasingly filled by women, sparking special efforts to recruit men to fill direct service roles.

12. The organizing mantra of the next decade will be the call to bridge the gap between clinical research and clinical practice in the resolution of AOD problems.

13. The next decade will witness the widespread application of disease (recovery) management technologies from primary medicine to the treatment of severe and persistent alcohol problems.

14. Research findings will compare and contrast explicitly religious and spiritual frameworks of recovery from explicitly secular frameworks.

15. A movement to push the breakthroughs in knowledge about clients with common needs from the enclave of the demonstration project to the mainstream of the field will occur.

16. A significant movement in the next decade to get the treatment field ethically re-centered will take place, e.g., new ethical decision-making models, upgrading organization codes of professional practice, and advanced training to enhance ethical sensitivities and ethical decision-making skills.

17. New roles that focus on harm reduction, pre-treatment/engagement, and sustained recovery support will call for a re-evaluation of traditional definitions of appropriateness related to ethical conduct, particularly those governing relationship boundaries.

18. The treatment field will face in the next decade what it has never faced in its history: a strong consumer/constituency movement.

19. The locus of treatment will expand beyond the institutional/office environment to the natural environment of each client.

20. Demands for the field to shift its research focus from one of pathology to one of resilience and recovery will increase.

21. The growing "varieties of recovery experience" will continue to manifest themselves within the growing diversification of mutual aid structures, confirming in local communities across the country AA cofounder Bill Wilson's 1944 observation that "the roads to recovery are many."

22. The rapidly approaching loss of long-tenured clinical and administrative leaders will constitute one of the most significant challenges to the future integrity and existence of the field.

For those of you reading this in the future, how did we do with these predictions? De we deserve the title of prophets or fools? From where you sit today, what predictions would you make about the future of the addiction treatment field? What might you do to influence that future?

Institutional Histories

As my reputation as the field's historian grew, I had opportunities to research and write both brief and extensive histories of some of the field's major professional and advocacy organizations, including the National Council on Alcoholism and Drug Dependence (NCADD), NAADAC: The Association of Addiction Professionals, the National Association of Addiction Treatment Providers (NAATP), and the Smithers Foundation. Other needed histories include those of the American Society of Addiction Medicine (ASAM), Faces and Voices of Recovery, the American Association for the Treatment of Opioid

Dependence (AATOD), and the Therapeutic Communities Association of America (TCAA).

Each of the organizational profiles I researched and composed added to my understanding of the field by providing access to internal documents and each organization's elders. The history of each of these organizations was influenced by the history of their organizational members and affiliates. The history of each organization also told a piece of the larger story of the field. In writing the larger history of the field, I saw myself constructing a giant jigsaw puzzle, the final image was unknown until the major pieces were in place. Each person who works in the field contributes to the field's history by shaping the character of the organization within which he or she works. What have you done to make history today? Has the history of your own organization been written and updated? How might you help with such a contribution?

Organizational Recovery

The term parallel process was first used to suggest that the processes unfolding between a therapist and his or her client are often replicated within the process of clinical supervision. In 2007-2008, I took on a project that revealed to me a larger meaning of this term—the potential for organizations in the addictions field to replicate within their own histories the processes of addiction and recovery. The project was to author a history of the National Association of Addiction Treatment Providers (NAATP) to honor the 30-year anniversary of the organization.

As alcoholism treatment expanded dramatically in the 1970s through the infusion of government funding and expansion of insurance coverage for alcoholism treatment, a small number of treatment program leaders in California began talking about the need for an association that could represent the interests of private treatment agencies supported primarily by insurance reimbursement and client self-pay. These discussions led to the founding of the organization that evolved into the National Association of Addiction Treatment Providers (NAATP). In my interviews with early NAATP Board Members, they described the 1970s as a period of innocence and exhilaration. The field of private treatment grew in a medium of passion for recovery within organizations that had little sense of themselves as businesses.

272

These same leaders described such innocence being corrupted through the explosive growth of private treatment and the subsequent industrialization, commercialization, and intense competition within the field. NAATP grew in tandem with the burgeoning field under the leadership of its first director, Michael Q. Ford. At its peak in the 1980s, NAATP represented more than 600 private treatment programs and became one of the leading organizations in the addictions field.

But something was happening within the addiction treatment field—something insidious and pervasive. NAATP Board members described the field as becoming addicted to money, regulatory compliance, and organizational prestige. And the field itself began to take on the characteristics of its most challenging clients. Grandiosity, narcissism, black-white thinking, isolation, denial of reality, refusal to accept personal responsibility (e.g., acknowledge excesses within the treatment industry that had spawned the managed care era), and projection of blame, to name just a few, seemed to dominate the institutional character of the field.

The early warning signs threatening NAATP and the larger field began in the late 1980s with reports of decreased profits by hospital-based addiction treatment units amidst the emergence of an aggressive system of managed care. Denials of admissions and shortened lengths of stays led to precipitous drops in daily patient census within treatment units and by 1990 Michael Ford was penning articles about the war on addiction treatment. Between 1989 and 1993, the field lost about 40% of inpatient addiction treatment capacity in the US as program after program closed. Two events were particularly significant. First was the dismantling of CompCare, one of the largest providers of addiction treatment in the US, and the collapse of Parkside in 1993, the largest provider of such services. The field seemed to be under siege. If there was a "bottom experience" for the NAATP, it was the 1997 annual NAATP meeting at which less than 50 members participated. Those attending described it as feeling like a funeral wake. NAATP membership and dues collection collapsed and a real question arose of whether NAATP could revive itself as an organization.

A core of board members rallied NAATP, moved the NAATP office from California to the East Coast, and hired a new full-time Executive Director. The new director and the board began a sustained process of organizational renewal that elevated NAATP again to a leadership position in the treatment field. When I stood to deliver a keynote at the 2008 NAATP conference, I looked out on more than 500 people in attendance from all over the United States, and, more than the numbers, at faces once again imbued with animated energy about the future of the field. What I was looking at that morning was the face of organizational recovery.

NAATP and the field it represented had survived its near-death experience and undergone a process of institutional renewal. The question was whether NAATP and the field could move beyond the elimination of problems and the transcendence of unexpected crises (which soon arrived) to the achievement of an exceptional and sustainable level of health and community service. That question could not be answered that day, but instead would be contingent upon a new generation of leaders willing to pick up the mantle of leadership and write the future of addiction treatment and recovery in America.

Has your organizations taken on the character excesses of the addict? Is it in need of recovery? What role might you play in initiating such a recovery process?

Why Addiction Treatment?

I was asked to give a short lecture as part of the luncheon awards ceremony of the 2007 meeting of the American Society of Addiction Medicine. I obsessed a great deal over what to present in the 30 minutes I had been allocated and finally settled on trying to answer the question of why there was a distinct field of addiction medicine and a larger arena of specialized addiction treatment. I tried to answer the question by examining addiction specialists' contributions historically that distinguished them from other fields of health and human service professionals who addressed those with severe alcohol and other drug problems. I suggested that such distinction historically rests upon the following nine propositions and that these core ideas provided the rationale for a specialized field of addiction treatment.

1. Substance use disorders spring from multiple etiological roots and vary in their severity, complexity, duration, and outcome. Such variability calls for specialized and sustained training, skilled differential diagnosis, and highly individualized approaches to service planning and delivery.
2. Addiction is a primary disorder and primarily a disorder of the brain. A central rationale for our field's existence is that

addiction recovery is best facilitated by practitioners who can distinguish addiction disease from the biopsychosocial consequences of alcohol and other drug use and who can offer their patients tools to reclaim their health and powers of personal decision-making.

3. Well-intentioned but uninformed attempts to treat substance use disorders can result, and have resulted, in significant harm to individuals and families. So, humility and caution and the need for specialized training for those charged with treating addiction are paramount.

4. Addiction recovery is a reality in the lives of millions of individuals and families. Addiction medicine is founded on a deep belief in this reality, the importance of vividly conveying hope for full recovery to individuals and families, and the willingness to offer sustained guidance through that process.

5. Multiple pathways and styles of long-term recovery exist. What we offer at our best are practitioners who possess a deep knowledge of and a deep respect for these diverse pathways and styles of recovery.

6. Addiction recovery is more than the removal of alcohol and drugs from an otherwise unchanged life. Facilitating the attainment of global health within the recovery process requires knowledge of the far-reaching influences of addiction, the stages of recovery, and the zones of action and experience within which recovery unfolds. That core knowledge and those core skills exist in no other professional field.

7. Recovery maintenance is a distinctly different process than recovery initiation. The understanding of recovery as an enduring process underscores the importance of sustained monitoring and support, stage-appropriate recovery education, and, when needed, early re-intervention—all provided by practitioners with an intimate knowledge of the long-term recovery process.

8. Addiction recovery is not durable until it is nested in the community—within the physical and cultural environment of each patient/family. Addiction specialists are distinguished by their knowledge of addiction, but even more so by their knowledge of the physical and social ecology of recovery.

9. Addiction treatment is founded on an empowering service relationship that is free of contempt and moral censure,

characterized by emotional authenticity and candor, and focused on the strengths and resiliencies of each individual and family.

Excerpts from this speech were later published in the *Journal of Addictive Diseases,* and I was able to later (2014) publish the responses of many addiction professionals to the question of the distinctiveness of the addictions field in the book, *The History of Addiction Counseling in the United States.* Would you offer different answers regarding the distinguishing characteristics of addiction medicine and the larger field of addiction treatment?

Japanese Dragon

I first met Dr. Katsuro Aso at a NAADAC: The Association of Addiction Professionals conference in June of 2000. Dr. Aso approached me to say that he had read many of my publications and that some of the pieces I had written had gained some visibility among Japanese psychiatrists and addiction specialists. He presented me with a beautifully carved gold bookmark and asked if he could continue to correspond with me. In 2002, Dr. Aso asked if he could translate a chapter of *Slaying the Dragon* into Japanese. One of the great thrills of my career was receiving this first Japanese-translated chapter. This event was followed by an introduction to other Japanese addiction specialists and an invitation to visit and lecture in Japan. This occurrence led to a request by Minowa MAC—a community-based alcoholism treatment program in Tokyo, to translate my entire book, *Slaying the Dragon*, into Japanese. Over the next five years, four translators worked on this task, peppering me with periodic questions about the meaning of particular terms from the historical lexicon of addiction treatment. The day I was handed the published copy of the Japanese translation of *Slaying the Dragon* was one of the most personally gratifying moments of my professional life.

In the years I was writing *Slaying the Dragon*, I hoped that a modest number of addiction counselors would be exposed to the stories in the book. I could never have dreamed that these stories would travel around the world and inspire people from different cultures. The lesson from this for us all is that the potential extent of our reach and influence can never be fully known, but the potential for such influence is ever-present. If we think, speak, and write clearly about our experience and our own truths, our words may unexpectedly convey universal truths. Ideas inside you could reach cultures you have never seen. Is it time you gave them an opportunity to escape and to seek their destiny in the world? Don't underestimate the potential range of your influence.

Land of the Rising Sun

The lecture trip to Japan took five years to plan. Those years were spent trying to coordinate schedules and give me time to heal unexpected health challenges. The dates were finally set: October 30-November 11, 2007. The plan was to lecture and/or visit hospitals and recovery support groups in Tokyo, Kyoto, and Osaka. The trip was a whirlwind from the moment my wife and I stepped off the plane. I could spend pages and pages talking about the kindness and graciousness of the Japanese people. I could spend pages talking about what I learned and what I hoped to contribute to the Japanese recovery movement. But in sustaining the established style of this professional memoir, I will offer three stories from this first visit to Japan that I think hold great meaning for those working in addiction treatment.

The major alcoholism recovery mutual aid group in Japan with more than 12,000 members at the time of my visit was Danshukai. The national association of local Danshukai groups is known as the All Nippon Abstinence Association. During my visit to Japan, I met with Danshukai leaders and attended a Danshukai meeting in Kyoto. I was fascinated by the way in which Danshukai drew from Japanese culture to forge a viable alcoholism recovery framework. While Danshukai contains elements that parallel AA, such as a process of amends and service work, its program makes no reference to a personal God and its meeting structure is built around the family rather than the individual. The meetings are also much more structured than AA meetings with everyone signing in upon their entry to the meeting and then being called on to speak by one of the meeting co-leaders. There was no counterpart to AA anonymity. Danshukai members used their full names and many wore pins on their clothing signaling their Danshukai membership.

English speaking AA meetings began in Japan following the Second World War, but the first Japanese AA meetings did not begin until 1975. At the time of my visit to the Japan AA General Service Office, there were 480 AA meetings in Japan and more than 500 members. More than 50,000 copies of AA's Big Book had been sold in the years prior to my visit to Japan. AA has required special adaptations to Japanese culture. Initially evident is the names AA members use for themselves. The Japanese rarely use first names in their communications so the traditional use of first name and last initial in AA was resisted. To resolve this dilemma, AA members each take a nickname (and often an English nickname at that) by which they are known in the fellowship. So two of my Japanese AA mentors were known in the meetings as "Bob" and "Smiley." Because Danshukai had established itself as a couples-oriented program, AA carved out a niche in many communities as a recovery sanctuary for those without such family ties. Due to the Shinto and Buddhist influence in Japan, Japanese understanding of steps one and two are quite different than in a predominately Christian context such as the United States. Variations exist—some subtle and some dramatic—in meeting rituals, sponsorship, interpretation, and degrees of adherence with AA traditions. In total, I was left with one overwhelming conclusion as I witnessed all the cultural permutations: when men and women who are suffering reach out to one another to find escape from their suffering, RECOVERY WILL FIND A WAY.

S.Y. was one of the most physically, emotionally, and spiritually vibrant people I had ever met in my life. He had physical stamina that I envied. He had a contagious smile that cast light all around him. And S.Y.'s life was filled with service to others. We had a powerful connection during my time in Tokyo that transcended our inability to speak each other's language. We found a way to transcend boundaries of language, culture, and personal legacies (we both had family members in the Pacific battles of World War II, and he had himself been injured as a child from the American bombing of Japan). When I asked S.Y. the source of his vitality at 68 years of age, he responded through our interpreter, "Alcoholism shrinks your body and soul; the program fills you back up." I guess that just about says it all. I went to Japan as a teacher and became a student. I feel like S.Y is still with me.

While in Japan, I spoke of the rising recovery advocacy movement in the US and shared photos of people in recovery and their families hosting public recovery celebration events. Two years after returning from Japan I received news from Mototugu and Yasuko Aria of the first public recovery march in Tokyo. Needless to say, I was deeply moved that my visit may have contributed even in a small way to the rise of a recovery advocacy movement in Japan. Sowing seeds is

278

what it is all about, even when it is unclear if and when such seeds will sprout.

The Life and Work of Ernie Kurtz

In late 2008, I received a memorable request from Dr. Ollie Morgan, Professor at the University of Scranton. I knew of Ollie's interest in the history of AA and through his articles calling on the addictions field to get refocused on the vision of long-term recovery. Ollie reported that he had obtained a contract to edit a book entitled, *Recovery through Catholic Eyes: Catholic Figures in the History of the Recovery Movement*. He explained that the book would contain chapters on the lives of such people as Father Ed Dowling, Sister Ignatia Gavin, Father John Ford, Father Ralph Pfau, Dr. Austin Ripley, Father Joe Martin, and Sister Therese Golden. The book would be dedicated to Ernie Kurtz, and Ollie asked me if I would write the closing chapter on Ernie's life and work. This opportunity was a great honor and impossible to decline.

Through the early months of 2009, I obsessed over how to do this chapter justice and made all kinds of notes regarding my own personal views about Ernie's contributions to the recovery movement. As I got past my own self-consciousness of having been chosen to write this chapter, it dawned on me that this chapter was not about my ideas; it was about Ernie's. The key to this chapter was to make myself invisible within it and to let Ernie's own voice prevail through excerpts from his writings. Ernie had also been enthralled his whole life with the power of storytelling and it seemed to me that I needed to find a way for Ernie to tell his own story and for others to tell the story of Ernie's influence on their lives.

Storing my notes away for future reference, I proceeded to do a series of interviews with Ernie and to interview a dozen others who had worked with Ernie over the past decades. The finished chapter was, in retrospect, one of the most enjoyable writing projects of my career. It was an act of gratitude for all Ernie had done for me and a collective tribute from many whose lives Ernie had profoundly influenced. It was also a biography that in decades to come would stand as a declaration that here was a man whose life made a difference. That's all any of us could ask. (A footnote to this story is that the book Ollie was working on failed to materialize so this chapter was published in an abridged

279

form in the journal, *Alcoholism Treatment Quarterly,* 2014, 32(4), 458-484, and posted in full on my website.)

Bookstore Anthropology

Over the course of my career, I have tried to find creative ways to monitor the pulse of the addiction treatment field and the field's evolving status within the larger culture. Doing so required looking beyond such obvious things as media coverage of the field, policy shifts, and funding levels to far more subtle indicators. I noted earlier the value of monitoring responses of people in social encounters to our disclosure of what we do for a living. A second is to monitor bookstore shelf space.

When I entered the field in the late '60s, there was no designated shelf space for addiction or recovery. There was a new genre of "drug abuse" books arriving but treatment and recovery books were hard to find and a shelf or bookcase marked "Recovery" would have been unthinkable. Then came the recovery publishing boom of the 1980s. For a moment, it seemed everyone was in recovery from something as Twelve-Step programs became the latest fad and a corrupted mix of pop psychology and new age spirituality. In the large bookstores, the "recovery section" often filled 3-5 bookcases. Then the number of bookcases dropped and shelf space diminished during the backlash movements of the 1990s into the new century. By turning recovery into a highly commercialized commodity and overselling treatment and a growing industry of recovery paraphernalia, the field went from a brief zone of super success to one of declining credibility.

How important are alcohol and other drug problems and their resolution in the culture at this moment? Check the shelf space in your local bookstores. Who has or is vying for cultural ownership of alcohol and other drug problems? Do we have our own territory marked out? If not, where can we be found? In self-help? In health and medicine? In psychology, sociology, or religion? In crime? Are we there at all? You can find out a lot at a bookstore without ever opening a book.

Offering Tribute: The Pioneer Series

As I aged within the field, I became acutely aware of how much history would soon be lost via the disengagement or death of long-tenured leaders in policy, clinical practice, recovery support, research, and education/training. With that awareness came the idea to collect an oral history of modern addiction treatment and recovery by interviewing key leaders so their stories could be preserved for posterity and shared with the field. The interviews began in 2006, and more than 100 interviews have been completed and posted to date. I have been deeply touched by the graciousness of those I have asked to discuss their life and work.

The project was also a way to quiet my own voice and return to the student role that I had always cherished. The interviews affirmed for me what remarkable people had built and sustained this national network of recovery support. My hope was to interview as many leaders as possible whose collective voices outlined the modern history of addiction treatment and recovery. Are there important voices in your organization or community whose stories have not been told? Perhaps you could help find a way to capture some of these stories.

Dragon Revisited

The first edition of *Slaying the Dragon* went to press in early 1998. By 2010, I was regularly getting questions on if and when I was going to publish a new updated edition of the book. I made a decision late that year to take on this project. As I reviewed the first edition, I was struck by two things. First, new historical discoveries that occurred since its original publication would need to be included in the second edition. This fact revealed to me again that history, like science, is never complete. It is always on probation pending new discoveries about the past and the unfolding present and future. Second, I was struck by how much had transpired of historical importance in the past decade. This realization posed the challenge of trying to sort and convey what was most significant—all while events and their outcomes were still furiously unfolding. And yet, there was much that had not changed in the field—things that needed to be carefully preserved as well as things that should be shed, but which were being maintained by active resistance or the weight of inertia.

281

Most of us think of history in passive terms—as something to be retrospectively observed, but history is a living thing, and we are all players in this unfolding drama. We can be unknowing actors shaping history by our obliviousness of what is unfolding around us, or we can conduct our lives with a consciousness that we are actors on the stage of history. The challenge I gave to myself in updating the past and modern history of the field was to convey this potential power to my readers.

Another perspective I brought to renewed work on *Dragon* was a sense of my own limitations as a historian within the field. What I felt best about the book that I had created was the history of the field that existed before any of us arrived to be part of it. By the time I got to the modern era of treatment, I was exhausted and probably too enmeshed myself in this period to do it justice as a thorough and objective history. As I approach the task now, I worry that I will not have the physical/emotional energy or the intellectual power to meet my own expectations for capturing this modern period. And yet, I must go on with the full expectation and hope that others will come behind me who will take on this history with greater skill and depth. No one will be more delighted if this happens than I will. History progresses by imperfect increment. If we are lucky, we have the privilege of adding the smallest of steps in this process. Are you ready to take such a step?

From Year of the Dragon to a NAADAC Invitation

Work on the new edition of *Slaying the Dragon* proceeded in 2012 and 2013, and, in June 2014, the new edition rolled off the presses. I had often experienced a kind of disorientation (post-partum depression?) following completion of some of my other books, but I did not experience this with the second edition of *Slaying the Dragon,* perhaps because I was thrust into another project before the ink was dry on the new *Dragon* copies.

In early 2014, Cynthia Moreno-Tuohy, the Executive Director of NAADAC: The Association of Addiction Professionals, contacted me with an enticing proposal. She proposed that I research and write a book on the history of addiction counseling and of NAADAC. She shared that she had raised funds to support such an effort which had long been dreamed of by Mel Shulstad and other early pioneers of addiction counseling. Archival documents had been collected since the mid-1990s and oral history interviews had been taped at various NAADAC events over the years. Now was the time to weave these raw materials into a singular historical narrative. Cynthia's goal was to have the book completed for distribution at the 40th anniversary NAADAC conference in Seattle, Washington at the end of September.

Given the promise I had made to Mel before his death in 2012 that I would find some way to get this long-envisioned book written, I readily agreed to Cynthia's proposal, even though I was unsure the book could be written in that short a time period. The months April-August of 2014 were consumed with this project. I enlisted the aid of my wife, Rita Chaney, to help with the literature search and to transcribe the large volume of interviews.

An interesting quirk of fate occurred in the creation of the NAADAC book. The planned book was to be approximately 225 pages, but as I worked on the manuscript I completely forgot that its planned size of 6" X 9" would expand the number of pages from the 9" X 12" manuscript pages on my computer. As a result, when I turned in the 225-page manuscript to the printer, it grew to 521 pages when reformatted for printing. I was deeply embarrassed though NAADAC graciously covered the added printing cost of the longer book. The printed version contained far more information than would have been possible if our original plan had been followed. Accident? I don't know. I still wonder if Mel Schulstad was smiling down on this whole process.

The History of Addiction Counseling in the United States: Promoting Personal, Family, and Community Recovery rolled off the presses in September 2014 and was placed in the hands of more than 700 NAADAC members attending the 40th anniversary conference. The promise to Mel had been fulfilled, as had been my own goal of writing the histories of addiction treatment, addiction counseling, and addiction recovery in the United States. I experienced a deep sense of personal satisfaction in the knowledge that whatever other personal goals fell short of completion, this work was done. And it was done with full knowledge that others more capable of doing this work existed, but none during these years who could muster the sustained discipline to achieve it. If projects such as these waited for the perfect person, most would remain unfulfilled. The best person for any task is the person who can get it done in spite of their own limitations and the obstacles the world chooses to thrust in their path. Is there an unmet need that calls to you? Have you hesitated out of your own insecurities about talent and time? Maybe it is time to take the leap.

The Siren Call of History

History is a ritual of remembrance, reflection, and celebration, but it can also serve as a ritual of renewal and recommitment to the future. History is imbedded in each of us in ways that are unseen until we develop a degree of historical consciousness. Cultivating such consciousness requires the courage to face the fact that the seeds of history's greatest accomplishments and greatest brutalities exist in the present—in our own world, country, community, family, and yes, in our own heart. The study of history can be a magnifying lens on the present, or it can be a seductive escape from the present and our own accountabilities.

Every historian's lament is the darkness of unanswered questions that no existing sources can illuminate. The pull of such mysteries can be so great that some of us find we have left the present and live in that past. The desire to answer these questions can be so great that we sometimes wonder, "Would I give up my life as I know it for the opportunity to go back for a period to discover firsthand the answers to these mysteries?" If that opportunity truly existed, the things that would keep us in this world reveal our greatest treasures. What would keep you here?

Chapter Twelve
The Varieties of Recovery Experience
(1990-2015)

One of the sustained meditations in my life has been on what Ernie Kurtz and I christened *the varieties of recovery experience*. In the early 1980s, I began thinking about what E. M. Jellinek (See his *Disease Concept of Alcoholism*) had called the "species" of alcoholism and the divergent pathways and styles of recovery that could unfold from these species. Building on Jellinek's work, I began to suggest that alcohol and other drug-related problems spring from multiple etiological roots, unfold in diverse profiles and patterns, respond to quite different methods of treatment, and are marked by highly varied pathways and styles of long-term recovery. I brought that same deep belief in multiple pathways of recovery into my later recovery advocacy work.

In this chapter, we will explore incidents that contributed to my understanding of these "varieties" and reflect on your own experiences with such recovery diversity.

"Dual Diagnosis is a lie!"

In the late 1980s, I arrived early at a conference center where I was scheduled to present a full day workshop on what was then commonly called "dual diagnosis"—the assessment and treatment of individuals presenting to treatment with co-occurring substance use and psychiatric disorders. As I was getting organized at the front of the ballroom, one of the attendees scheduled to be at the workshop approached me and, without even introducing herself, announced, "Dual diagnosis is a lie!" I considered this a pretty provocative statement in light of the fact that I was about to talk about this subject for the next seven hours. When I asked her to explain what she meant, she responded with the following retort: "I would challenge you to come to my office and look at my caseload and find any client who ONLY has two problems!"

I smiled at her observation and went on to conduct my usual workshop, but her words haunted me in the hours following the workshop. She had named something that few of us were seeing at that time: The emergence of multiple-problem clients and families as the norm within human service caseloads across the United States. Something was shifting. Clients were presenting with problems of a greater number, severity, and complexity than had ever been seen before, and they also were bringing less personal and social resources to cope with such problems. Most importantly, they were not faring well in the categorically segregated service system into which human service agencies had been divided. In the years that followed, I devoted a great deal of attention to this changing profile of service recipients, but my moment of awakening began on the day of that conference. On that day, my trainee was the teacher.

How are the characteristics of those you work with today different than when you first entered the field? What are you learning from those who seem most ill-suited for the services you are offering?

Signing in Minneapolis

The purpose of one of the human service units within Hennepin County was to serve individuals living with hearing impairments. When the head of that unit contacted me in the late 1980s and asked me to provide training to their unit, I hesitated. My concern was that I had not worked with signers as a trainer before and was afraid I would make embarrassing miscues that would decrease the effectiveness of the training. After some assurance, I agreed to conduct a workshop that turned out to be one of the most humbling but rewarding of my career. In the years that followed, I worked many times with people who were signing for one or two hearing impaired participants, but what I encountered that first time was something quite different. I had always viewed hearing impairment as a personal disability. What I was not aware of was the existence of an elaborate deaf culture with its own language, values, and rituals. Everyone in the workshop that day was immersed in that culture. I was an outsider graciously offered a brief glimpse into their world. Experiences that heighten our sense of vulnerability are often great opportunities. At every opportunity, stretch yourself. How might you do that in the coming year?

Cultural Incompetence (Critics as Benefactors)

When Alcoholics Anonymous was first publicly criticized in a 1963 magazine article, AA cofounder Bill Wilson responded in the *AA Grapevine*. Rather than attacking the author critical of AA or offering a point-by-point defense of AA, Wilson took the position that AA members should view critics as benefactors, and that AA should use criticism lodged against it to self-assess and improve AA. Wilson's response was a remarkable act of personal and institutional humility. I have tried to emulate that stance over the course of my career, even when I thought criticism of my work was unfounded. But sometimes the criticism was/is well-deserved. Such was the case during a workshop I delivered in 1988 in Minnesota.

I was conducting a workshop on promoting personal and organizational health for the human service departments of Hennepin County. My presentation of the basic material to the 150+ participants went as expected except for the following incident. At the morning break, a participant approached me and said that she was offended by my use of the phrase "circling the wagons" in reference to organizational members rallying together at a time of crisis. She said the phrase demeaned Indian people and that I should not use it in my presentations. I acknowledged that this was the first time I had ever heard any concern about this phrase and thanked her for calling this to my attention. As the training proceeded in the late morning, I unthinkingly used the phrase "too many chiefs and not enough Indians" in some point I was trying to make. At the lunch break, the same participant came up and angrily expressed her objection to that phrase and said that she could not remain in any training with a presenter so insensitive to Indian culture. She later wrote a letter to me expressing again her distress and disappointment with my insensitivity. A similar letter was sent to the head of training at Hennepin County requesting that I not be used as a trainer again.

My first response to these events was one of defensiveness. I ranted about the growing political correctness in which people attended training not to learn but to wait for their opportunity to pounce on the speakers for what they said or failed to say. I ranted, and then I tried to listen to what was being said to me. In the end, I admitted to myself and others that this lone critic was right—that my audiences were getting more and more diverse and that I had a responsibility to learn about the cultures from whence they came and how best to communicate across these cultural boundaries. The criticism I received that day wounded my ego, but it was an invitation to learning that set the stage for later chapters of my career, chapters that would not have been possible if this woman had not had the courage to approach me face-to-face. I owe her a debt of gratitude.

Learning across cultures is not without its continuing gaffs. Years later, after considerable work educating myself about Native American tribal cultures, I was invited to speak to a large, primarily Indian audience on the history of recovery among Native tribes. When I finished speaking, I was greeted by sounds of chirps, whistles, and cries that were impossible for me to interpret. I realized at that moment that I had a lot of facts in my head about Native American tribal history and cultures, but that I had yet to immerse myself experientially in the nuances of cultures that could never be conveyed on paper or through one-to-one interactions with members of those cultures. What I learned was that you have to give yourself permission to make mistakes (they are unavoidable) and to put yourself in contact with cultures where those mistakes can be made, forgiven, and used as opportunities for learning. The alternative of isolated ignorance is not a viable option for those of us working in the addictions field. Is it time to extend your cultural knowledge of addiction and recovery? Is there a resource near you that could facilitate that process?

Metaphors of Transformation

In the early 1990s, I invited Rita Chaney to explore with me how transformative words, phrases, and metaphors could be used to change peoples' lives and how such metaphors differed for men and women. We opened our discussion of metaphors with the following introduction.

> *Metaphors are terms or phrases—crystallizations of ideas or constructs—that through analogy and comparison label and elucidate complex experience. Metaphors can enhance understanding of one's experience and open up a vision of the course of action one must take. There are many such examples in the chemical dependency field. The construct of "allergy" has been an important notion around which many persons within AA have cognitively framed their sobriety decision. The more dominant*

"disease concept" is a construct whose utility far transcends its eventual disposition in scientific debate. Such constructs are "true" in the sense that they validate and make sense of otherwise incomprehensible and sanity-challenging experiences for many persons. They are metaphorically true to the extent that they provide a cognitive cornerstone through which untold numbers of addicts organize their movement from addiction to recovery....It is our belief that there are contrasting metaphors for men and women that can serve as the catalysts for personal transformation. Words, symbols, and constructs which men may use to free themselves may provide no such liberating influence on women and may inadvertently drive them into the darker shadows of their chemical and social imprisonment.

We then proceeded to compare metaphors that had been originally developed out of male experience with metaphors that had been drawn exclusively from women's experience. We used a comparison of the Steps of Alcoholics Anonymous and the Statements of Acceptance for Women for Sobriety for this exercise. What we found was quite striking. Women's metaphors of change emphasize: 1) empowerment (discovery of hidden power within) and self-mastery rather than acceptance of powerlessness (and reliance on power outside the self) and surrender, 2) hope (seeing the top) rather than pain (hitting bottom), 3) achievement of personal identity rather than connectedness (pronouns of I, my, myself rather than we, our, ourselves), 4) divided attention (fitting sobriety into multiple role responsibilities) rather than focused attention (sobriety as a singular obsession), 5) the resolution of shame versus the resolution of guilt, 6) self-affirmation rather than self-effacement (humility), 7) acts of self-care rather than acts of service to others, 8) the importance of physical and psychological safety, 9) self-acceptance of one's body, and 10) the metaphors of *uncovery* (exposing aspects of self that have been hidden) and *discovery* (acquiring that which one never had) as opposed to *recovery* (retrieving what has been lost). After constructing this dualistic comparison of women and men's styles of recovery, we proceeded to take the model apart by noting the existence of men who used feminist styles of recovery and women for whom the masculine style of recovery worked just fine.

No matter how beautifully constructed and no matter the degree of scientific evidence, we must remember that we treat individuals, not normative groups. And yet our exploration of metaphors of personal transformation opened new ways for us to see the recovery process and new ways of guiding women through this process. I felt our work told part but not all of an important story. What was missing was an explanation of research findings that women affiliate with and benefit from AA at equal or higher levels than men. What was missing was an explanation of how the women who make up 38% of AA worldwide membership have adapted AA's central constructs to fit their experience. Years later, Dr. Jolene Sanders and other researchers would conduct landmark studies of women in Twelve-Step programs to provide such explanations.

How have women you have worked with adapted AA, NA, and other Twelve-Step program concepts and practices to meet their recovery support needs?

Psychosurgery Revisited

I learned a great deal in my travels around the country lecturing on the history of addiction treatment and recovery. Someone at every stop had a story to tell me, and the stories helped give depth to what I had learned and opened new chapters in this history of which I was unaware. Some told me stories of addicted relatives treated with exotic methods—from accounts of the "Keeley Cure" to LSD treatments in state psychiatric hospitals. My audiences were always amazed at the harmful things done in the name of treatment, but some of their personal stories confirmed that periods of such harm extended much further into modern history than I had assumed was the case.

One of the periods I found most shocking was the era when psychosurgery was extolled as a treatment for chronic alcoholism and other addictions. Following a lecture I gave in 2000, a woman in the audience shared her own near-close encounter with this procedure. In 1971, she was hospitalized for acute alcohol poisoning at a prominent hospital in Philadelphia. After her acute condition was resolved, her quite prominent psychiatrist outlined two treatment choices that she and her family should consider. She could be committed for one year for treatment at the state psychiatric hospital, or she could undergo what he described as a "new brain surgery" (a lobotomy) that he claimed would permanently remove her cravings for alcohol. The woman thought the surgery a better alternative than being locked up for a year, but a chance conversation between her father and a coworker in recovery brought a woman from Alcoholics Anonymous to her bedside and the beginning of what has now been more than four decades of sanity, sobriety, and service. Today she is one of the leading recovery advocates in the United States. Her story reveals that we are little more than a generation away from these infamous days. We should never forget the potential to recapitulate "harm in the name of help" within our own era.

Styles of Secular Recovery

I guess it all started when Marty Nicolaus reviewed my book, *Slaying the Dragon,* on the website of LifeRing Secular Recovery—a non-religious, non-spiritual alternative to AA. Marty and I exchanged periodic emails. Soon after, I received the request to keynote the LifeRing Annual Congress in San Francisco in 2004. That meeting provided an opportunity to listen to LifeRing group leaders from across North America share their experiences leading secular-based recovery support groups. A few years later, I wrote a three-part series for *Counselor Magazine* on religious, secular, and spiritual frameworks of recovery. Again, I called Marty to ask him to collaborate with me on describing the different styles of secular recovery.

These activities provided an opportunity to reflect on what distinguished secular frameworks of recovery from explicitly religious frameworks, such as Alcoholics Victorious and Celebrate Recovery from spiritual frameworks, such as AA and NA. Many similarities across these recovery support structures were evident, but the ultimate distinction was in the source of recovery initiation and recovery maintenance. That conclusion was reinforced years later in my interviews with Dr. Joe Gerstein, Dr. Tom Horvath, and other leaders of SMART Recovery.

Religious pathways involved a connection to a resource beyond the self as the catalyst for recovery initiation. They involved a deep surrender of self and a sense of having been rescued and redeemed by this external force. Recovery maintenance within these pathways involves disengagement from the culture of addiction and enmeshment of oneself in a shared community of faith. Spiritual pathways involve a similar sense of transcendence (though with a less defined source), a similar sense of having been rescued, and a revolution in character. In contrast, secular frameworks of recovery draw upon hidden resources within the self and define recovery as an assertion of self. Secular metaphors of change are about asserting power and control rather than on admission of powerlessness and the experience of surrendering.

What I found interesting was the variety of ways an altered sense of self was at the center of the recovery experience across these pathways. Whether the self changes through connection to an external source of power or a conscious process of reconstructing one's identity, social network, and life meaning from the inside out, transformation of self is clearly at the center of the recovery process.

I now see these variations in style as legitimate alternatives within a wide variety of recovery pathways. It seemed to me that the best addiction counselors identify dimensions of these variations in their own experience. Doing so provides a foundation of empathic identification through which the counselor can listen and support these varied recovery styles. Can you recall times you encountered life-shaping sources of strength outside your own self that exerted a profound influence on your identity and character? Can you recall times when you drew upon sources of strength inside yourself that you were previously unaware of?

Faith and Recovery in Atlanta

David Whiters was one of the many rising stars in the new recovery advocacy movement. He founded Recovery Consultants of Atlanta and directed a faith-based recovery initiative funded by the Center for Substance Abuse Treatment. David is one of those people in recovery whose light shines incredibly bright. His passion and joy are so contagious that they bring the recovery message to people who never saw recovery as an option until they caught it from him.

On a warm afternoon in Atlanta, I stood with David watching a young man putting finishing touches on a mural celebrating recovery. The mural covered the lower wall of a building sandwiched between a pawn shop and a police station. Perfect location! And perfect message! But David shared that the mural was only part of what was planned for this invitation to recovery. On each individual brick above the mural, people in recovery would sign their first name and sobriety/clean date. David's idea was that as the names on the wall grew, everyone walking by would know that a community of recovering people was waiting for their arrival. I later witnessed many murals of invitation for cultural and spiritual connection in my work in the City of Philadelphia, but on that day in Atlanta, I was deeply touched by this celebration of and invitation to recovery. How visible is addiction in your community? Is it time recovery achieved a high level of visibility?

The Rev and Brother Mickey

One of my favorite verses in the Bible is, "Where there is no vision, the people perish" (Proverbs, 29:18). In the mid-1980s, Henry T. Wells served a community that had lost its way, and many of its people were perishing from addiction and a host of related problems. Wells himself could easily have been one of those casualties. Escaping a long history of addiction through the support of his wife, Margaret, and treatment at Geoffrey Hospital, he began inviting people into his home who needed support through their early recoveries. That effort led to his founding One Day at A Time (ODAAT) in 1983—an organization committed to providing recovery support services to low income people and their families who are impacted by addiction, homelessness, and HIV/AIDS. Today, ODAAT is a program of the Greater Philadelphia Urban Affairs Coalition and serves thousands of men and women and their families each year. Known in his community as "Rev" and the "Grandfather of Recovery," Henry Wells was the consummate activist. He organized "casket marches" to protest the deaths of young people from drug-related violence in Philadelphia and organized awareness marches that brought increased financial aid to community-based programs providing recovery support services. He passed on in 2013.

Reverend Wells was one of those people whose life is a daily testimony. I was blessed to have had the opportunity to meet with Reverend Wells, his son, Mel, who is carrying on his father's work, and many other faith-based recovery leaders across the country. Addiction treatment professionals have a tendency to look down on such grassroots recovery organizations, but I have come to have deep respect for their work and the recoveries these programs have helped initiate and sustain. One can argue whether these faith-based programs constitute "treatment"; most of them do not define themselves in this way. But they reach people long before they are seen in addiction treatment and they support people long after "graduation" from addiction treatment. Faith-based organizations constitute an invisible network of recovery support throughout the United States, from the urban missions and community organizations, like ODAAT, to rural recovery colonies.

In 1962, Mickey and Laura Evans had a vision and a calling to build a camp in the South Florida wilderness for men recovering from alcoholism. That vision turned into Dunklin Memorial Camp and, for more than 50 years, has served individuals and families whose lives have been wounded by alcohol and other drugs. I began hearing about the camp when I moved to Florida in 2003. A few years later, Tom Sledd drove me into a wilderness that Florida tourists never see for my first visit to Dunklin. My interest was twofold. First, I was interested in learning more about faith-based pathways of addiction recovery. Second, I was fascinated in the recent growth of recovery homes and recovery colonies—a trend I saw as a historically important development within the American culture of recovery. My first visit to interview Mickey was followed by others and I soon found myself both drawing strength from this community and expanding my own service work to include this community. Let me share a visit to Dunklin through my eyes.

The first striking characteristic of Dunklin is its remoteness. The question, "Are we lost?" is common on first and subsequent visits. Entering Dunklin, you'll find, not a facility, but a self-contained, self-sufficient community. You'll see the dormitories, homes for staff, homes for families to stay for weekend visits, mess hall, tabernacle, school, computer lab, library, lumber mill and furniture workshop, hog and cattle pens, fruit groves and sugar cane fields, health clinic, rodeo grounds, and a cemetery. Then there is the effusive love that connects the members of this community. Work crews circle in prayer before beginning work in the various industries; hugs abound as the community enters the mess hall for lunch and prayers that precede each meal—real prayers, not those memorized and delivered in rote. This is not a treatment center; it is a healing community—a community of shared experience, strength, and hope.

From its humble beginnings in 1962, the Dunklin vision expanded to encompass a larger vision of residential recovery, family recovery, ministry training, and development of new cities of refuge (Dunklin-type communities around the world), outreach through jail and prison ministries, and Overcomers Groups in local communities. That vision has already extended Dunklin's work across Southeastern United States, Costa Rica, Brazil, and beyond.

Mickey Evans and I lived very different lives and walked a different pathway of recovery, but few people I have ever met are more deeply committed to suffering addicts and their families and communities. Mickey Evans died in 2014. Everyone at Dunklin called Mickey Evans "Brother Mickey." So did I. Reverend Mel and Brother Mickey are examples of "recovery carriers" that can be found outside the walls of professional addiction treatment centers. If you haven't yet journeyed into this territory, perhaps it is time to explore the hinterlands of addiction recovery in the US.

Jewish Journeys in Recovery

In 2002, I received a gracious invitation to speak at a meeting in New York City of Jewish Alcoholics, Chemically Dependent People and Significant Others, commonly known as JACS. JACS was founded in 1978 to provide mutual support for Jewish people in recovery—a unique blend of Jewish tradition and Alcoholics Anonymous—and to advocate for effective responses to alcoholism within local Jewish communities. I offered a short presentation on early Jewish influences on AA, e.g., Henry Z., who founded the Forest Hills Group in NY; Bob M., who entered AA in Chicago in 1941, Irv M., a business partner of Clarence S., who entered AA in Cleveland in 1940, Eddie G., who entered AA in Cleveland in the 1940s, and Bernard Smith, who served as AA's lawyer in 1940 and went on to become Chairman of AA's Board of Trustees. I also talked about Jewish contributions to modern addiction treatment, particularly the contributions of Rabbi Abraham Twerski.

It was a delightful exchange with those present. What I most distinctly remember from my first meeting with JACS was the personal stories of what it meant to be Jewish and alcoholic. Historically, the rate of alcoholism among Jews has been so low that members of the Jewish community who succumbed to alcoholism were seen by that very fact as less Jewish. Stigma related to alcoholism crosses cultural boundaries, but I discovered from JACS the particularly heavy weight of such stigma within the Jewish culture—a weight that made it difficult for individuals and families to confront the reality of alcoholism and to fully embrace recovery.

Addiction and recovery both occur within particular cultural contexts that can exert great influence on addiction and recovery careers. What differences in such contexts exist in the lives of the individuals and families you serve?

Yelling "Stop!"

In January 2000, Dr. Alex DeLuca, then the long-tenured Director of the Smithers Addiction Treatment and Research Center, provided permission for the local Moderation Management (MM) group to hold weekly MM meetings at the Smithers facility. Following the publication of newspaper articles in July that conveyed the impression that the Smithers Center had abandoned its abstinence philosophy, Dr. DeLuca resigned amidst growing public controversy, including a Smithers Foundation advertisement in the Sunday *New York Times* and *New York Post* that christened MM "an abomination." This report stirred broad criticism of Dr. DeLuca from the professional field until two addiction medicine pioneers issued a joint statement confronting the entire field's response to this incident. The following is an excerpt from the statement issued by Anne Geller, M.D. and LeClair Bissell, M.D.

How many of you were prepared to accept what was said in the Post, a biased report of a brutally edited article, without doing any further research? Is that how you normally get your medical information? This seems to have turned into a religious war without the use of any medical, scientific or even collegial common sense. We are ashamed of all of you who rushed into comment without checking your sources and hope that you will remember this episode when it's your turn to be the recipients of media distortion....It is enormously depressing to us, both now in retirement to witness the same mindless zealotry that so beset our field 30 years ago again raise its head to make us a laughing stock in the medical scientific community. We have repeatedly stated that we wish to be in the medical mainstream, to have addictions treated as any other medical illness, to base our treatments on the science and to examine the data carefully. In your attacks on DeLuca you did none of this. You behaved like a bunch of religious fanatics with Satan in sight. Shame on you.

On January 20, 2000, Audrey Kishline, the founder of Moderation Management, announced to MM members that she had decided to seek an abstinence goal and would be attending AA, Women for Sobriety, and SMART Recovery meetings to achieve this goal. On March 25, 2000, Kishline was involved in a head-on collision that killed a 38-year-old father and his 12-year-old daughter. At the time, Kishline had a blood-alcohol level three times the legal limit.

These events reheated the debate about "controlled drinking"— a debate that quickly reached a level of frenzied acrimony in the popular and professional media. Editorial and Internet posts blamed MM for the deaths resulting from Kishline's intoxication. Anti-AA forces noted that Kishline had left MM at the time and that responsibility of this incident lay at AA's doorway, not MM's. And on and on it went. It was in the middle of all this heat that Ernie Kurtz and I discussed the idea of a joint statement by addiction scholars that could dampen the acrimony and add some objective truth to this growing cultural war. Following invitations for collaboration and many drafts, a statement was released that included the following words:

> [The fact] *That Ms. Kishline was intoxicated at the time of the crash has been claimed to indicate the failure of the approach of one or another of the mutual-aid groups Ms. Kishline attended. Such claims are not in accord with everyday experience in the field, in which relapse is common, whichever approach the drinker adopts. Recovery from serious alcohol problems is a difficult goal, and there are different paths to it. We believe that the approach represented by Alcoholics Anonymous and that represented by Moderation Management are both needed.*

Thirty-four prominent professionals in the field signed the document. They represented diverse ideological poles and many points in between. I consider that moment a historically important footnote in the American debate about moderation versus abstinence in the resolution of alcohol problems.

Sometimes we contribute by refusing to participate in frenzied debate when everyone is yelling and no one is listening. Sometimes we serve by refusing to participate in inflammatory debates. At other times we contribute by mustering all the dignity we can to declare, "This must stop!" Sometimes, what we prevent from happening is as important as what we make happen.

Moderation in New York City

In 2002 and 2003, I conducted a series of interviews with key figures in Moderation Management (MM). These interviews included Audrey Kishline, the founder of MM, key figures in the early evolution of MM, the current leaders of MM in New York City, and interviews with several current and former MM members. I drew several conclusions from this experience. First, I realized that both addiction treatment and mainstream recovery mutual aid societies had historically focused on people with high levels of severity of alcohol dependence with little attention to persons with less severe alcohol problems. MM leaders were quite explicit that their purpose was to offer support to the non-dependent problem drinker. I interviewed people in the latter category for whom MM seemed to be a good alternative for them. Second, I was struck by the concern of MM leaders about people with severe alcohol dependence who might use MM as a way to avoid the need for an abstinence strategy. I also was able to interview individuals in this category who had hoped for a moderated solution but migrated toward abstinence as a result of their failure to achieve the initial 30-day period of abstinence recommended by MM or who could not continue to adhere to MM moderation guidelines. Some of the latter were in AA or other abstinence support groups at the time I interviewed them and expressed appreciation for MM speeding up the time it took them to make a decision to stop drinking completely.

Does your community have people with mild to moderate alcohol problems of relatively short duration? What resources are available for such persons?

The Kishline Legacy

Audrey Kishline was a most singular figure in the modern history of addiction. She was the founder of Moderation Management (MM), left MM to seek abstinence in AA and SMART Recovery, killed a father and daughter in a vehicular crash while intoxicated, went to prison, and upon her release continued to vacillate between resuming drinking and efforts to achieve stable sobriety. That story ended when she committed suicide on December 19, 2014. I had communicated with

Audrey over a period of 15 years both to interview her about the history of MM and to offer what support I could to her recovery efforts. I remember saying to my wife on multiple occasions that I feared Audrey's story would end tragically.

Audrey Kishline deserves a footnote in the modern history of alcohol problems. She promoted moderation as an alternative for people with less severe alcohol problems even though ultimately that solution did not work for her. Several messages can be drawn from Audrey's life, but one that stands out for me is that of professional humility. Audrey had access to many resources—specialized addiction treatments, Twelve-Step recovery groups via AA, and secular alternatives to AA. And she regularly communicated with some of the top addiction experts in the world. None of these resources ultimately altered the devastating trajectory of her life. The same could be said for untold numbers of other people whose families are devastated by deaths that followed all manner of efforts to achieve and sustain recovery. No one can claim moral or professional superiority in the face of such losses. While we celebrate recovery for many, the loss of many others demands a posture of humility and renewed commitment to reach those whose lives are not transformed by our best efforts. Each loss should be pause for reflection on what alternatives might have made a difference in that person's life. What have you learned from such losses?

Audrey also presented me with a unique ethical issue related to historical research. I interviewed her multiple times and in the two years prior to her death we had communicated about merging those interviews together into a single interview about the history of MM that would be posted on my website. We had passed drafts back and forth and all that was needed was final approval from Audrey to post the interview. We put that project on hold at Audrey's request so she could focus on some of the things going on in her personal life. With her subsequent death, the question is what should become of the interview that never received Audrey's final approval? I am still wrestling with this question, but going on three years after her death, the final draft of the merged interviews remains held in confidence.

Mistaking a Part for the Whole

In my early career, I was adamant about abstinence as the only viable solution to alcohol and other drug (AOD) problems—problems that I then universally framed as "addiction." At that time, declaring that moderated use was a legitimate, potentially effective strategy for some people with AOD problems would have been tantamount to waving the proverbial red flag in front of a bull. Thirty years later, I was writing articles advocating precisely that position. This dramatic transition in views is worthy of explanation.

When I began clinical work in the addictions field, I assumed that what I was seeing in the treatment setting was simply the "tip of the iceberg" of the larger pool of such problems in the community. I further assumed that what I was learning about the nature of AOD problems in the clinical setting gave me authority to speak about such problems in the larger community. Thus, when the subject of moderated use arose, I could unequivocally declare that such a proposition was nonsense because such a strategy had so consistently failed among hundreds of clients whose life stories I had followed so closely. In retrospect, I was right, but I was also wrong.

I was right in the sense that I was accurately representing my professional experience and the personal experience of those I saw in treatment. But I was wrong in over-extending this narrow band of experience far beyond the world to which it was applicable. One of the most important lessons I would learn in my professional career was that alcohol and drug problems in the community look different than such problems in clinical settings. In community studies (e.g., epidemiological surveys), the majority of alcohol and drug problems are mild to moderate in severity and resolve themselves without professional intervention or involvement in formal recovery support groups. The scientific verification that mild to moderate alcohol and even some severe AOD problems were resolvable through what researchers christened *maturing out*, *spontaneous recovery*, or *natural recovery* raised some provocative questions.

Why can't everyone just rein in their alcohol or drug use when it gets to be a problem? Why do we even need this thing called addiction treatment? The answer was that those in clinical settings shared characteristics that reduced the likelihood of such natural recovery. Compared to those with AOD problems in community studies, those entering clinical settings present with greater personal vulnerability (family histories of addiction, early age of onset of use, developmental trauma), greater problem severity (severe dependence) and complexity (co-occurring medical, psychiatric, social and/or legal problems), greater personal and environmental obstacles to recovery, and lower

300

recovery capital (assets that can aid recovery initiation and maintenance). It turns out that comparing those who succeed and those who fail at the moderated resolution of AOD problems is indeed a comparison of apples and oranges.

One of the ethical mandates of addiction professionals is to practice within and only within the boundaries of our education, training, and experience. An addendum to that mandate is to recognize that our education, training, and experience represent a limited part of what is known about addiction, treatment, and recovery. Such a recognition calls for professional humility and holding all of our opinions on probation pending new discoveries in the field and new learning experiences. Many parties can be harmed when we mistake a part of the truth for the whole truth.

Transformative Change

Throughout my career, I have been fascinated with what has come to be called *transformative change* (TC)—change that is unplanned, profound, positive, and permanent. Much of this no doubt stemmed from the TC experience that had launched my own recovery. I had written about such change in two of my books, but continued to be enthralled by TC accounts in my historical studies and in my travels across North America. In 2003, I was given an opportunity to explore this subject in great depth when William Miller invited me to write an article for a special issue on TC that he was editing for *In Session: The Journal of Clinical Psychology*. My requested focus was the role of TC in the history of addiction recovery in America.

I explored the histories of six individuals whose respective recoveries were sparked by a TC experience and who went on to lead major abstinence-based recovery or recovery advocacy movements. The individuals I selected were Handsome Lake, John Gough, Jerry McAuley, Bill Wilson, Marty Mann, and Malcolm X. I was able to confirm four things through the lives of these historic figures:

1. TC is a historically legitimate method of recovery initiation and consolidation.
2. The TC experience has many shared elements (preparatory anguish, isolation, the collapse of one's defense structure, a wrenching breakthrough of self-perception or insight; a new or

301

renewed connection to strength outside the self; and discovery of hidden resources inside the self).

3. The TC experience must be respected and allowed to emerge under its own momentum.
4. The role of the professional helper is one of being with someone through this process, validating the legitimacy of the experience, and making the transition between recovery initiation and recovery maintenance.

Most individuals recover from addiction through a process of incremental change, but recovery for some is more akin to a lightning strike that is so profoundly disorienting that it forever cleaves one's life into the categories of *before* and *after*. Whether one sees the source of such transformation as coming from outside or deep within the self, it is important for each addiction counselor to have faith in the power of such forces.

Bill Wilson and Malcolm X, two men whose backgrounds and lives could not have been more different, experienced something so profound in a moment of desperate isolation—one in a hospital room and one in a jail cell—that it forever altered their lives and altered history. Their experiences confirm the existence of brief developmental windows of opportunity—breakthroughs of perception and understanding of oneself and one's relationship with the world—so profound that they can forever alter the trajectory of one's life. Psychological death (disintegration of the old self) and resurrection (birth of a new self) are common ingredients of the TC-based recovery experience. To witness and be present in the face of such transformations is one of the most sacred experiences one can have as an addictions counselor or recovery coach. Though rare, these experiences are to be cherished in their own right for their ability, when witnessed, to serve as a source of our own renewal. Have you personally encountered individuals whose recovery was sparked by a TC experience? What have you learned from such individuals?

Treating the Rich and Famous

The proliferation of hospital-based and private treatment programs in the 1980s opened the doors of treatment to working class people with insurance and to the middle and lower classes as well. It also generated a market for treating the rich and famous in treatment facilities that resembled spas and vacation retreats, including golf courses, privately catered meals, and other such indulgences. When the hospital units and many of the private programs closed in the wake of aggressive managed care, the market for the treatment of those with great wealth and fame continued and seemed to grow in the late 1990s into the new century. Small communities such as Malibu, California were noted for the number and extravagance of addiction treatment centers. Many of these facilities charged in excess of $50,000 for a month of treatment. The high post-treatment addiction recurrence rates following discharge from these facilities led to new industries—expensive extended care facilities and private recovery coaches who, for exorbitant fees, would provide 24-hour supervision to get one through the early days of recovery outside of a treatment center.

I've spent my career helping build and enhance the quality of the public treatment system in the United States, but my publications and speaking engagements have brought me periodic contact with this hidden world of addiction treatment and those who are served and sometimes financially exploited within this world. I've also had periodic contact with the family members of those who have been recycled through such exclusive centers multiple times without achieving enduring recovery. Those contacts have provided some insight into the relationship between wealth, celebrity status, and recovery.

First let me acknowledge that there are no ennobling qualities of poverty that make it easier to enter the kingdom of recovery. The severity and multiplicity of problems in which addiction are nested among the poor and the lack of resources or inadequate quality of resources available to the poor have quite the opposite effect. But wealth and cultural stardom bring their own curses. While they open an enormous range of resources, they bring unique handicaps to recovery. Those handicaps are illustrated historically in the life of Willie Seabrook.

Willie Seabrook was a noted early 20th century author, known for such works as *The Magic Island and The White Monk of Timbuctoo*. Seabrook drank heavily like many of his generation of writers until his drinking quashed his writing. On December 5, 1933, his literary friends sent him from Paris back to the United States for hospitalization at the Bloomingdale Asylum for the Insane—an exclusive psychiatric hospital. Seabrook was admitted for treatment of his alcoholism at a time when most treatment programs had disappeared following the passage of Prohibition.

Willie Seabrook was detoxified with the aid of sedatives, bromides, and hydrotherapy packs and then entered the ward life of the asylum where his days were filled with crafts, exercise, books, movies, nutritious meals, and periodic visits with his psychiatrists. After spending six months in the asylum, Willie was discharged with the understanding that he should abstain from drinking for at least another six months. Keeping his doctor's orders, Willie didn't begin drinking until after a year of self-imposed sobriety.

During the months of sobriety and the early months of resumed drinking, Willie wrote a book in which he expressed great confidence that the emotional difficulties that caused his alcoholism were now successfully resolved. The evidence of this cure was that he was writing again and had not returned to his pattern of binge drinking. In the closing paragraph, he noted his new capacity to drink without his past difficulties. He proclaimed, "I seem to be cured of drunkenness." The book, *Asylum*, was published and widely read, offering many alcoholics who could afford such treatment hope for a similar "cure." After its publication, Willie Seabrook's drinking reverted to its former pattern and he continued to be admitted to many other private asylums. He was never able to achieve sustained sobriety and in 1945, at the age of 59, he committed suicide.

Willie Seabrook's life is a testament that financial and social access to the most expensive treatment in America is not a ticket of admission to recovery. In fact, Willie's life suggests many things that make such recovery more difficult for the cultural celebrity, whether of local, national, or international variety. These include unlimited access to alcohol and other drugs, a sense of invulnerability and entitlement, a social network protective of one's addiction, and the mistaken notion that coddled detoxification and physical convalescence constitute a cure for addiction. Perhaps the greatest irony is that after all the expenditure of dollars, the rich and famous finally find recovery in fellowships whose support is not for sale and whose principles (e.g., anonymity) and core values (humility, gratitude, service) are not ones usually associated with wealth and fame.

Finding Frederick Douglass and Malcolm X

Each of us must find people whose lives can help elevate our own. I have been blessed to know such people, but I have also found such individuals in my study of history. As the 21st century opened, I became quite interested in identifying people whose lives exemplified what I had come to think of as transcendent recovery—a style of recovery in which people use the experience of recovery from addiction as a catalyst for personal transformation and social change. It seemed to me that identifying and celebrating the lives of such individuals within particular ethnic cultures could exert a profound effect on those seeking recovery. Don Coyhis and I found many Native Americans who exemplified this style of recovery during research for *Alcohol Problems in Native America: The Untold Story of Resistance and Recovery*. The lives of Handsome Lake, the Shawnee and Kickapoo Prophets, William Apess, George Copway, and Quanah Parker, to name just a few, touched us deeply.

As the research and writing on that project came to an end, I turned my attention to African Americans who had recovered from addiction and went on to live heroic lives of service. In 2006, I collaborated with Mark and Tanya Sanders on a profile of two such figures—Frederick Douglass and Malcolm X. This project illustrates a particular point about the virtue of tenaciousness within historical research.

Our research on Malcolm X had been in progress for a long time and his disclosures of his addiction and incarceration in his speeches and published autobiography made documentation of his recovery status fairly easy, although subsequent biographies questioned the severity of his addiction. Douglass, however, was another story. John Crowley had first suggested to me Douglass' possible recovery status, and he had written a wonderful essay to this effect. But my early reading of Douglass' writings left me unconvinced. Yes, there were hints, and his declarations of the role of alcohol as part of the machinery of slavery were incredibly eloquent, but there simply was not enough evidence in Douglass' own words to extol him as the earliest and most prominent African American in recovery. Years passed and I continued to read and reread Douglass' autobiographies, speeches, and letters. Then I discovered two speeches delivered in Scotland in 1846, and they contained the words I had been looking for:

> *I used to love drink—That's a fact. I found in me all those characteristics leading to drunkenness.* (February 18, 1846 Speech in Glasgow, Scotland)

> *I have had some experience with intemperance.... I knew once what it was like to drink with all the ardour of an old soaker [drunkard].... Some of the slaves were not able to drink their share [portions of alcohol provided by the slave master], but I was able to drink my own and theirs too. I took it because it made me feel I was a great man.* (March 40, 1846 Speech in Paisley, Scotland)

Here in Douglass' own words was the unequivocal confirmation I had been seeking. Here was one of the greatest African Americans—and greatest human beings—who ever lived, and here was the evidence that his achievements rested on a foundation of personal recovery. There would be other milestones Mark, Tanya, and I shared in reconstructing the history of addiction recovery within the African American community, but none more important or more exhilarating.

Plotting the Varieties of Recovery Experience

In 2005, Ernie Kurtz and I collaborated on a paper illuminating what we had come to think of as "the varieties of recovery experience." This paper provided a wonderful opportunity to synthesize scientific research on recovery, biographical accounts of recovery, and decades of listening to the stories of people in recovery. I consider this paper one of the most important of my career and still recommend it as a mind-stretching experience for any addictions counselor, recovery support specialist, or recovery advocate. In that 2005 paper, we plotted variations in the scope of recovery (variations in primary and secondary chemical and global health), the depth of recovery (partial, full, and amplified), the context of recovery initiation (solo, peer-assisted, professionally-assisted), frameworks of recovery initiation (religious, spiritual, secular), temporal styles of recovery initiation (transformative change, incremental change, and drift), recovery identity (recovery

306

positive, recovery neutral, recovery negative), and recovery relationship styles (acultural, bicultural, and enmeshed). We also addressed the questions of recovery stability/durability (When does the risk of future relapse dramatically decline?) and recovery termination (Is recovery ever completed?).

The essay was included in a monograph entitled *Recovery Management* distributed by the Great Lakes Addiction Technology Transfer Center and was subsequently published in 2006 in the *International Journal of Self Help and Self Care*. As I reviewed the proofs of the latter publication, I felt that this was one of the most solid contributions of my professional career. Our goal in this exercise was to familiarize addictions counselors with the multiple pathways and styles of recovery as a means of replacing the countertransference ("my way is the best way") and power struggles ("my way or the highway") that had long plagued addiction treatment with a position of tolerance and respect ("recovery by any means necessary"). Time will tell if we were able to achieve that. A good omen is the rise in studies of such varieties and the recent appearance of multiple pathways of recovery conferences around the US.

To what extent are such "varieties" understood and respected within your current work setting?

Relapse of an Old Friend

Sally and David Brown published a biography of Marty Mann in 2001 that contained a bombshell. The bombshell was not the public revelation of Marty's sexual orientation and long-term relationship with Priscilla Peck—a fact long known in AA and recovery advocacy circles. No, the real bombshell was that Marty Mann, the founder of the nation's premier alcoholism-focused public policy organization and who for decades was the face and voice of alcoholism recovery in America, experienced a recurrence of drinking after more than 20 years of recovery during the time she served as the country's leading recovery advocate. That revelation stirred my interest in the phenomenon of addiction recurrence after prolonged recovery—a subject that had haunted me as a result of the tragic outcomes of such cases I had witnessed over a lifetime in the worlds of addiction treatment and recovery. The problem of addiction recurrence after prolonged recovery—a subject that was virtually missing from the scientific literature—confirmed anew just how little we as a professional field and culture knew about the processes and pitfalls of long-term recovery.

In early 2006, this became a personal issue through episodes of friends in long-term recovery experiencing such a recurrence (of varying durations and levels of intensity). As family members and others in recovery rallied around those who had experienced a reactivation of addiction, it struck me just how hard it is to sustain recovery over a lifetime. And the problem is that it really doesn't seem to be hard much of the time. There are periods of incredible stability when recovery is, like the mechanics of breathing, taken for granted. Periods of truly peak experience occur. Recovery is an amazing gift—a doorway of entry into another level of consciousness. And minor bumps are present along the way. But overall, viewing recovery as a task completed is very easy—something to check off from one's ultimate "to do" list. None of this prepares us for the need to redefine recovery over the course of the life cycle.

We tritely state in treatment that recovery is a process rather than an event, but we still treat it like it is a one-hundred-yard dash. In reality, recovery remains a work in progress throughout one's life. Recovery defined in the context of an intimate relationship must be redefined if that relationship is lost. Recovery defined in the context of retrieved health and occupational stability must be redefined if that personal health and professional stability are lost. Recovery must evolve in tandem with the purpose and meaning one finds in living. When that purpose and meaning diminish or are lost completely, recovery has no foundation upon which it can sustain itself. AA, NA, and other Twelve-Step programs have served as that continuity of support for many people, and its Steps are framed vaguely enough to allow for constant reinterpretation as one's life's circumstances change.

In 2009, I collaborated with Mel Schulstad on an article that openly acknowledged this evolving interpretation of Twelve-Step programs and raised critical questions that remain unanswered about this phenomenon and the best responses to it. The addictions research community has failed the recovery community in this area through its utter silence on a life and death issue. When Mel and I finished that article, we were both unclear whether our anger, our frustrating sense of powerlessness, or our need to protect our own vulnerabilities had been our primary motivation for writing the article. Sometimes you have to write to keep from screaming.

308

"Methadonia" 2005

I've conveyed earlier that attitudes toward addiction and recovery can be monitored by stepping outside our cloistered professional lives and observing people's reactions to the disclosure of our occupations or monitoring something as simple as the shelf space in bookstores devoted to addiction and recovery. Sometimes these attitudes are so blatant that they slap us in the face. Such was the case in 2005 when HBO presented its special, *Methadonia*. The special portrayed the lives of a small group of individuals involved in one methadone clinic in New York City. The HBO special portrayed methadone as an alternative intoxicant, and it portrayed patients in methadone maintenance treatment as profane, morally depraved individuals with little aptitude for responsible citizenship. Patients were portrayed as stoned—slurring their speech and nodding out in group therapy. The sole addiction counselor in the special represented the art of counseling as yelling at clients to "be quiet" while she tried to verbally batter them into superficial compliance with her views of what it took to get off heroin.

What was lacking in the HBO film was four decades of scientific findings about the effectiveness of methadone as a treatment for narcotic addiction, acknowledgement of all the prestigious scientific bodies that had previously endorsed methadone maintenance treatment, an accurate portrayal of professional addiction counseling, and, most importantly, the portrayal of the lives of people in stable long-term, medication-assisted recovery. The absence of the faces and voices of such patients and the missing science on opiate addiction left *Methadonia* an embodiment of stereotypes and social stigma. It was the grown-up child of a policy of "zero tolerance" birthed a quarter century earlier.

On the night *Methadonia* premiered, HBO became part of America's drug problem. By confirming the worst prevailing stereotypes of addicts and showing no voices of recovery, HBO made it even harder for those in medication-assisted recovery to reveal publicly what too often remains a shameful secret. History will judge our culture and our professional field harshly for the ignorance and bigotry that have cast those in medication-assisted recovery into a pariah status.

A few weeks after viewing *Methadonia*, I received a call from an HBO producer requesting my participation in another documentary on addiction. I ranted on and on about *Methadonia* to someone who had

309

nothing to do with it and declined to be part of the next HBO addiction documentary. At that moment, I had become convinced that the media and its representatives were more a part of the problem than the solution, and I wished to punish them by withdrawing my participation in their illusion of objective reporting. My response was childish, probably counterproductive, and yet wonderfully cathartic. Sometimes you have to spit in the wind even if you know the consequence.

A certain class of media representatives are essentially stigma pimps—people who exploit stereotypes and fear to advance their own careers. The only way to counter their influence is to refuse to collaborate with them in any way and find instead journalists of integrity who are willing to tell a more balanced and complete story. Some of the media pimps promise fame and fortune or manipulate good intentions to elicit our cooperation. Recognize them by their focus on the most sensational and lurid aspects of the problem and their lack of interest in the far less dramatic lived solutions. Refuse to be an accomplice in such exploitation.

Family Recovery: A President's Probing Question

In the fall of 2005, I was invited to make a presentation to the Betty Ford Center's Board and Chairman's Council on the history of addiction treatment and recovery among American women. It was a very special moment for me as those attending included President Gerald Ford, Mrs. Betty Ford, and Susan Bales Ford, President and Mrs. Ford's daughter and just-elected Chair of the Board of the Betty Ford Center. Speaking on the history of treatment and recovery in the presence of key figures within that history was a unique, if somewhat intimidating, honor. After my presentation and responses to questions, President Ford, then 92, asked me the following question: "What percentage of men and women come to treatment with strong support from their families for their recovery?" That same support had played a central role in the recovery of First Lady Betty Ford and countless others, and yet, from the standpoint of history and science, I was forced to acknowledge that there was no available answer to his question. It seems one of the most basic questions related to the context of recovery initiation had not been a subject of scientific interest. I knew of no study in which such data had been systematically collected and analyzed. That failure underscored how our biopsychological models of intervention into alcohol and other drug (AOD) problems had woefully ignored the

310

family and community context in which recovery either succeeded or failed. I left my encounters with these distinguished figures resolving that, in my continued focus on the study of recovery, I would be ever mindful of the family and community context in which that recovery process was nested.

When I began my training career, my greatest fear was that I would face a question that I could not answer. Today, I consider such questions a gift. The questions we can't answer are the really important ones. These are the ones that push us deep into the essence of the field or push us through the doorway of its future. President Ford opened such a doorway for me by posing a singular question that neither I nor the field could answer. When President Ford died on December 27, 2006, I thought of my gratitude for his life and for his question.

Transcending Privilege

Whatever success I have experienced in my life is tempered by the realization that many opportunities in my life came to me unearned as a birthright. Doors opened for me that were closed to others. That card of privilege was filled with cultural assets I had not earned or even sought, including my whiteness, my maleness, my heterosexuality. Although there was no money within my humble background, I was assured by this culture that I was still the master of my fate and could achieve anything I could envision and work toward. And my experience confirmed that truth. I didn't recognize this privilege as something special; it was part of the air I and other culturally empowered males breathed during our coming of age. But something happened to me as a teenager. I developed an awareness whose acuity increased throughout my life. It was the awareness that my privilege came at a price exacted from others and, in the end, exacted from my own soul.

The awareness of privilege triggered strange responses. First, I wanted to hide my privileged status by diluting the characteristics that were the grounds of that privilege. Then, I wanted to reject it completely (a kind of personal strike) by escaping my own culture and becoming something other than what I was. These stages were marked by racial guilt and a need to atone for the sins of those who had created and sustained this system of privilege that inflated or deflated all touched by it. Finally, I decided that there was no escape from my whiteness, my maleness, and my heterosexuality and that if I was really concerned with

311

the issue of justice, then I had to embrace a paradox. I had to use the benefits granted me by a system of unearned entitlement to undermine that very system—to widen the doorways to status, safety, and security for those for whom those doors had been historically closed. I did that by becoming a student of the historical and cultural experience of disempowered communities and by entering into sustained collaborative relationships with these communities and their leaders.

Without setting out to do it, I found myself crossing boundaries into cultural terrain in which white, heterosexual men were not always welcomed. I knew this was dangerous professional territory. I had witnessed White men and women denying their own cultural identities and turning themselves into "Wannabe" parodies by taking on mannerisms of speech, dress, and cultural tastes of a particular community of color. Such absorption into another culture often had more to do with flight from one's own history and self than a legitimate honoring of another culture. I knew I wanted to avoid becoming such a parody, but I wasn't sure what steps to take. It took years of experiments in moving beyond my maleness, whiteness, and other defining dimensions.

Whiteness (and the racism and privilege buried deeply within it) is heavy and loud—it bestows the right to walk with confidence and visibility, as well as the rights to speak, speak frequently, and speak loudly. Those seeking to break outside White socialization must learn to walk softly, shut up, and listen—really listen with one's whole being. We must dilute our whiteness without rejecting it. We dilute our whiteness by doing our homework on our own and other cultures, learning the etiquette of other cultures, learning the processes through which cultural revitalization movements rise and evolve, and figuring out what roles, if any, are available to offer assistance to such movements. For me, these continuing experiments required two things: 1) a refusal to let my maleness or my whiteness or my heterosexuality limit the issues that I address in my presentations and writing, and 2) a willingness to let myself make mistakes and learn from them as I move into new cultural territory and move past the boundaries others have defined for me. What cultural barriers have been set up to define what roles you should and should not play? Is it time to step beyond those boundaries?

312

Super Recovery: The PHP Story

In 2006, I received a request from Dr. Bob DuPont, Dr. Greg Skipper, and Dr. Tom McLellan to provide a historical introduction to a presentation on physician health programs (PHPs) they were doing at the American Society of Addiction Medicine Conference in San Diego, California. Preparing that presentation opened a window into the phenomenon of super recovery—patients treated within programs that achieved inordinately high long-term recovery rates. This was a most interesting exercise in no great part due to the fact that most of my career had been spent focused on those whose extreme problem severity and complexity had made such achievement difficult. I had always attributed high and low recovery rates primarily to individual differences as opposed to program characteristics, but my study of physician health programs challenged that view. The exceptionally high success rates (70-95% long-term recovery rates across a number of rigorous studies) could easily be explained by the high recovery capital that physicians possess, but one could also argue that physicians as a group share characteristics that should compromise recovery outcomes, e.g., high addiction severity, elaborate system of personal and professional enabling, and ready access to powerful psychoactive drugs. This balance of vulnerability and recovery capital led me to ask what program characteristics were typical of PHPs that were not part of mainstream addiction treatment in the United States. In 2007, Drs. DuPont, Skipper, and I examined this question and concluded that the key to the PHP success rate could be found in the following program characteristics: 1) use of a motivational fulcrum, 2) comprehensive assessment and abstinence-based treatment, 3) peer-based recovery coaching, 4) lifestyle modifications, 5) assertive linkage to communities of recovery, 6) sustained (5-year) monitoring, support, and early re-intervention, and 7) service integration.

How many of these characteristics typify the program in which you are currently working? What actions could you take to incorporate these key elements within your own clinical practice?

LGBT: Feeding Stigma with Silence

One of the ethical mantras for clinicians and trainers is to accurately represent and practice within the boundaries of one's education, training, and experience. That mandate had dictated the kinds of issues I trained on and the kinds of illustrations and stories I used within those selected topics. I tried to consciously avoid moving into territory beyond the boundaries of my knowledge and expertise. I later came to understand that what I thought was an enlightened position was actually a failure on my part—a failure of courage and a failure of knowledge.

One of the issues I had avoided addressing was the common needs of lesbian, gay, bisexual, and transgendered (LGBT) people entering addiction treatment. I felt avoiding such a position was necessary given my lack of knowledge in this area. This veil of enlightened ignorance was punctured when a trainee wrote extensive comments in the evaluation of one of my workshops. The trainee noted that they had been to many of my workshops and never heard me say a word about the LGBT community, their patterns of alcohol and other drug (AOD) use, their needs in treatment, or their challenges in achieving long-term recovery. The trainee noted that if people only went to my workshops, they would not even know that LGBT people existed. I asked myself, "How I can I speak about these issues as a trainer if I don't know about them? Wouldn't I be violating the mandate to only practice within the boundaries of my education, training, and experience?"

When I spoke to prominent LGBT leaders in the addictions field about this, they provided a clear message of their expectations. "We're not asking you to speak for our movement; we're asking you to acknowledge our existence. We're asking you to filter the broader work you do through what such work means to us." We do have a responsibility to practice within the boundaries of our education, training, and experience, but we also have a responsibility to extend those boundaries. With the most righteous of rationales, I had avoided that responsibility. It has taken several years to fill in some of those missing pieces of my personal and professional education.

In 2007, I was asked to review a wonderful book by Audrey Borden entitled, *The History of Gay People in Alcoholics Anonymous.* The quality of the book was such that I was delighted to offer words of praise and help promote the book. Other articles, speeches, and blogs followed that addressed LGBT concerns—perhaps a form of amends. The lesson here is a clear one: Guilt can be useful if you do something about it. Are there any such amends you need to make?

314

This is not to suggest that we must become involved in or become experts on everything. I was invited to take on some projects over my career that I was, quite simply, unsuited for. When I agreed to involve myself in such projects, my life was subsequently filled with regret and dread. I counted the days until I was free of such projects. It was not that some of these were not important projects; it was simply that I was unsuited to work on them. As time passed, I became better at figuring out such mismatches before they occurred and became better at gracefully declining involvement in such projects. What I know today is that what we say no to is as important to our long-term contributions to a field as what we say yes to. What have you said yes to against your better instincts? Is there anything on the horizon moving toward you that deserves a graceful refusal?

Methadone Revisited: The Price of Principle

My evolving views about methadone maintenance treatment (MMT) were noted earlier in these pages, but in 2009 the subject of MMT engaged me in a way that I could not avoid. Here was the dilemma. I was sure the conclusions I was drawing from my historical research, review of scientific studies, and interviews with people in MMT-assisted recovery would elicit great disagreement from many in the addictions field. Yet I felt withholding my advocacy on this issue would be an act of professional cowardice and that I would later inflict harsh judgment on myself for acts of hesitance and silence. The advocacy I embarked on with many collaborators was twofold. First, it involved using my credibility with frontline addiction professionals and members of varied mutual aid groups to reexamine their positions about the legitimacy and value of medication-assisted treatment in general and methadone maintenance in particular. That work challenged deeply ingrained prejudices. Second, it involved challenging the providers of MMT to elevate clinical practices and to develop a recovery-focused approach to MMT. That work challenged prevailing practices and vested financial interests of many MMT providers.

The advocacy work itself involved several critical steps: 1) publishing interviews with prominent methadone advocates (e.g., Lisa Mojer-Torres, Walter Ginter, Joycelyn Woods, and Mark Parrino), 2) addressing the 2009 American Association for the Treatment of Opioid

Dependence annual conference on the subject of MMT and recovery, 3) writing a widely posted monograph on stigma related to medication-assisted treatment and recovery, and 4) writing a series of articles on the role of medication-assisted treatment in recovery-oriented systems of care. No one can take on and resolve a major professional controversy individually. So the question becomes what one can uniquely bring to such a controversy that will move the field forward and, more importantly, help the individuals and families whose quality of life hinges on the outcome of the debate. In my case, I asked what my recovery status, my knowledge of addiction treatment and recovery history, my ability to synthesize scientific studies, and my abilities to speak and write could bring to the status of MMT in the United States. The activities above were my answers to those questions.

My purpose for including my dilemma about MMT is not to influence your views about MMT but to stir your reflections about how to personally respond to some of the field's great debates and to matters of conscience that arise over the course of your career. Such responses require both increasing your knowledge of particular subjects and increasing knowledge of yourself. The latter is a more challenging task than the former.

How could one go from rejecting methadone maintenance as a self-defined matter of conscience only to later offer support for MMT—also as a matter of conscience? Our views on some issues reflect our distance from them. The closer we get the more our views change. What issues of great import to those you serve have you judged from a great distance? Is it time to see and experience these issues from closer proximity? How might you do that?

Those I have engaged in discussions about MMT have bantered back and forth on the science of MMT, but it became clear to me that at heart our viewpoints boiled down to differences in our experiences—and, in fact, differences in my own experiences at different points in time over the course of my career. My "before" and "after" position on methadone was influenced by my review of scientific research but was far more influenced by two specific experiences. The first was contact with people in long-term medication-assisted recovery who shared their stories and their lives with me. They, in short, offered living proof about the role of methadone in recovery from heroin addiction. The second experience was direct contact with MMT programs that reflected a high level of recovery orientation, clinical sophistication, and a rich menu of recovery support services. When I looked back on my own inherited hostility towards methadone, it was grounded in no knowledge of the scientific studies on methadone treatment, no connections to people in successful medication-assisted recovery, and negative experiences with only a few under-resourced MMT programs that were little more than cash-generating methadone filling stations.

So the next time you are in a debate on a polarized issue, ask yourself what differences in experience are reflected in the respective positions. Ask yourself how you might extend your experience on this issue to gain a broadened perspective. Ideological purity can be maintained only in isolation; the real world exists outside that cocoon. Is it time for you to emerge?

NA History Adventures

As work continued on the new edition of *Slaying the Dragon* in 2009, I knew I faced several major challenges. One of those challenges was researching and writing a more complete history of Narcotics Anonymous for inclusion in the new edition. As my research proceeded, I met a new generation of scholars doing research on the early history of the NA fellowship, including Chris Budnick and Boyd Pickard. I began email and telephone exchanges with Chris and Boyd and first met them face-to-face at a conference I was speaking at in Myrtle Beach, South Carolina in January 2010. Their enthusiasm and rapidly developing skills prompted me to invite them to collaborate on researching the expanded NA history in *Slaying the Dragon* and to work on related NA history papers. Their endless enthusiasm for the subject and their willingness to go to any lengths to ferret out rare documents and interview key informants made this one of the most enjoyable collaborations of my career. Chris and Boyd also began a demanding schedule of presenting this information across the United States and in other countries. What I liked best about this collaboration was that we engaged in it not as experts, but as fellow students. As we proceeded, we created something of a collective of people interested in NA history.

My best work has always occurred in the context of a learning community. Is it time you reached out to create or extend such a community?

317

Colliding Worlds: NA and Medication

In 2011, two of my projects collided. While research and writing papers on the history of NA were proceeding, responses to a monograph I had co-authored with Lisa Mojer-Torres on *Recovery-oriented Methadone Maintenance* poured in from many quarters. One of the most frequent responses involved a barrier to the development of peer recovery support within and linked to opioid treatment programs (OTPs). Leaders of OTPs from across and beyond the US reported that attitudes toward medication in general and methadone and buprenorphine in particular constituted a major obstacle to recovery and community re-integration for people in medication-assisted recovery. The resounding question was, "What should we do?" That question led to a follow-up monograph, *Narcotics Anonymous and the Pharmacotherapeutic Treatment of Opioid Addiction.*

Researching and writing this monograph involved issues so intellectually deep and emotionally raw that they made my head and heart hurt day after day. It felt like I had physically entered a project only to discover that there was no exit. I thought about possible escape routes on a number of occasions, but it became clear to me that the only way out of this project was to think and write my way through it—which I eventually did. And yet in retrospect, I cannot recall a project in which I so questioned my courage to keep moving forward. The difficulties included knowing that people I deeply respected would be distressed with my taking on this subject and equally distressed with my tentative conclusions. A regular diet of such projects would be unhealthy, but a few of these over our careers can test and build character. Such episodes are a form of payment to the field for what the field has given us—even when such projects elicit criticisms from friend and foe alike.

The Prevalence of Remission and Recovery

The year 2011 marked another project of note. As recovery emerged as an organizing construct at policy and treatment levels, the question arose regarding the estimated number of people in addiction recovery in the United States. Two of the organizations for whom I worked asked me if I would do a review of existing studies and see if I could provide a science-grounded answer to this question. So for much of 2011, I identified and reviewed two different kinds of studies—more

318

than 400 in total. The first were studies evaluating remission of substance use disorders in community populations—with remission usually defined as having met lifetime criteria for a substance use disorder (SUD) but not meeting such criteria during the past year. These studies revealed a high SUD remission rate (well over 50%) with the majority achieving remission without professional treatment and doing so by decelerating alcohol and other drug (AOD) use rather than through complete and enduring abstinence from AOD use. The second set of studies consisted of addiction treatment outcome studies. Average SUD remission rates in these studies were somewhat lower than in community populations and the primary mode of remission was through abstinence—reflecting the higher degree of problem severity and complexity in clinical populations than in community populations.

Now what is interesting about my review is that we have two different experts on alcohol and drug problems—epidemiologists and clinicians—each describing the truth about such problems as they know it with each reaching radically different conclusions. This is, of course, analogous to the proverbial blind men describing the elephant. The conclusions drawn from each of these populations are "true," but not the whole truth. The message I drew from this is that one must be aware of what part of the elephant one is holding before claiming a truth that we wish to foist on others. How has what you know to be true about addiction and recovery been limited by the narrowness of your exposure to the diverse styles of addiction and recovery and the types of cultural, community, and organizational settings in which you have worked?

Secular, Spiritual, Religious

In 2011, Ernie Kurtz and I began a sustained meditation on the role of self in recovery. This was an extension of our earlier work on the "varieties of recovery experience" and was stimulated by a recovery research project led by Dr. Mike Flaherty. The project involved using in-depth interviews to compare and contrast people in widely divergent pathways of recovery, including Twelve-Step recovery, faith-based recovery, secular recovery, medication-assisted recovery, and natural recovery. One of many things we found within this study was quite different conceptions of the role of self in addiction and addiction recovery. In fact, we discovered two quite distinctive styles—one involving the assertion of self, the other involving transcendence of self.

Some individuals in recovery (particularly those in secular and natural pathways of recovery) tend to emphasize the positive value of self in the recovery process. When interviewed, these persons reference the value of self-knowledge, self-esteem, self-confidence, self-assertion, self-reliance, self-sufficiency, self-discipline, and self-respect. In marked contrast, most people in spiritual and religious pathways of recovery define self as the source of the problem, not the solution. Their stories are filled with negative references to self-seeking, self-centeredness, selfishness, self-will, self-pride, self-deception, self-delusion, and self-pity. In their view, recovery is a process of surrender—emptying the self and relying on resources and relationships beyond the self. Their interviews are filled with references to self-sacrifice and service to others.

So we have two quite different styles of relationship to self in recovery. Plus, the potential exists for these styles to switch at different key moments in recovery. Because addiction counseling is historically rooted in the clinical fields of psychiatry, psychology, and social work, we have tended to view self-exploration, self-assertion, and self-esteem as both integral processes and desired outcomes of our counseling work. And yet these contrasting styles raise interesting questions within each counseling encounter we have: Does this person need to get into themselves or get out of themselves? Or might they need both experiences at different points in the recovery process? What do you think?

Aging, Addiction, and Recovery

Older persons have always been present in addiction treatment and recovery support settings so it wasn't like I had not seen them before, but relocating to Florida in the early 2000s offered a living laboratory on aging, addiction, and recovery. No place on earth has such a concentration of aging people. I observed, listened, and drew several conclusions. First, some older persons with alcohol or drug-related problems (AOD) are simply survivors of a long history of such problems. For them, these problems did not arise in the context of the aging process but extended from earlier stages in the life cycle.

For others, alcohol and other drug-related problems can arise out of the process of aging in persons who have lived full, productive lives without a trace of such problems. The context for developing AOD problems in late life are numerous and rooted in the aging experience: changes in physiological responses to alcohol and other drugs; physical pain and discomfort related to illness or injury; loss of professional identity via job loss or retirement (particularly when forced); loss of significant relationships via death, divorce, or relocation; the onset or exacerbation of psychiatric illness; or involvement in new drinking-focused peer groups. What has been most striking to me is the wide variety of circumstances from which AOD problems can arise in older adults.

Finally, regardless of their catalytic roots or duration, recovery for older adults must be nested within the experience of aging and within a renewed sense of life meaning and purpose. The former means that the older person must have an answer to why they do not drink or use drugs that makes sense in the context of their present life circumstances. A stable life of recovery is possible only if there is meaning and value within that life. Where addiction among older adults is often rooted in loss; recovery is often rooted in connection (or re-connection). As I watch my aging peers enter the worlds of addiction treatment and recovery, I think the most important things those milieus have to offer at their best is a renewed sense of family and community—a world to recover in.

Further NA Adventures

In early 2016, the media was raging about rising opioid addiction and opioid-related deaths. As with earlier moral panics, the coverage, at public and professional levels, was quite skewed. Within a span of two months, three major television specials were produced on the opioid epidemic (CNN, ABC, and CBS). What struck me as I watched these programs was not just the usual preoccupation with the problem with little reference to the long-term recovery solution, but that none of the specials even mentioned Narcotics Anonymous as a potential local community resource for recovery support. This struck me as historically incongruous given that most early NA members were recovering from opioid addiction and that NA had continued to be a major recovery support framework from opioid addiction. In addition to the omission of references to NA at the media level, similar silence was present regarding NA within presentations at professional conferences and within articles on opioid addiction in professional journals. If mentioned at all, NA was most often briefly castigated for its alleged anti-medication bias.

My concern about this neglect led me to invite three prominent recovery researchers—Drs. Marc Galanter from New York University, John Kelly from Harvard, and Keith Humphreys from Stanford—to join me in reviewing the breach between popular and professional perceptions of NA and what was known about NA from the standpoint of scientific studies. The resulting paper, which was published in a prominent addictions journal, received positive reviews within the field and was widely distributed via blogs on social media. I was subsequently invited by Ron H. and Dave F. to present the major findings from this paper in a podcast on one of the major NA social media sites. That show helped disseminate much of NA science to mainstream NA members—findings not appropriate for sharing within the traditions and etiquette governing NA meetings. These episodes—the article and dissemination of knowledge through social media—reflect the art of constructing untold stories and sharing previously untold stories. Such stories are an essential way the research activist, clinical activist, history activist, and recovery activist use knowledge drawn from the past to reshape the future. Are there untold or under-told stories that you could help share and in doing so bring light into places of darkness?

Varieties Collected

As my fascination with the varieties of recovery experience continued to grow, I began to think about how to best convey this information beyond my articles and books. It occurred to me that perhaps I could create a repository of such varieties. That led to adding a section on my website devoted to the history of recovery mutual aid groups (http://www.williamwhitepapers.com/recovery_mutual_aid_history/). Collecting materials for this section of the website with the able assistance of Rita Chaney, provided opportunities to review again the expanding landscape of addiction recovery mutual aid societies in the United States. Once again, I found myself in awe of the varieties of recovery experience. I found myself wishing I had another lifetime to explore varieties of recovery experience that I had yet to discover.

How might you pass on what you have learned about such varieties to others?

Chapter Thirteen
Renewed Activism: The New Recovery Advocacy Movement (1998-2016)

A number of circumstances led to the rise of a new recovery advocacy movement in the United States in the late 1990s. In this chapter, we will explore some of these circumstances and my own evolving role in what could yet be the most influential social movement, in terms of both drug policy in the United States and the expansion of national and local recovery support resources.

Criminalizing Addicted People of Color

I have been often asked how the United States first embarked on an experiment of mass incarceration as a strategy to manage rising drug-related problems. It began in its most recent iteration with a new drug policy of "zero tolerance" introduced by President Ronald Reagan and popularized by his wife's "Just say no" campaign, but it soon crossed the boundaries of both major political parties in the United States. Something seemed quite noble about these campaigns—a claim of high moral ground that struck emotional chords among the American people. But the feel good slogans masked policy outcomes that would not be visible for some time. First was a process of restigmatization through which the idea of "bad drugs" was extended to encompass the idea of "bad people." Addiction was rendered a "bad choice" by bad people who needed to be held accountable—a euphemism for punishment—for their bad choices. People addicted to drugs became monsters to be feared and from which good people needed to be protected. Addicts became "the other"—a category of outsiders who had no moral claim on the country's sympathies.

Restigmatization led to the demedicalization of alcohol and other drug problems and an emerging view that institutional ownership of these problems and those experiencing them should rest with the churches and the courts—not hospitals and doctors. It wasn't just the view that addiction was not a "real disease"; it was the view that drug addicts (no longer "people with drug-related problems") were not as morally worthy of medical care as other citizens.

Restigmatization and demedicalization set the stage for the recriminalization of these problems through a process sociologists call transinstitutionalization—the transfer of problem ownership from one cultural institution to another. During the late 1980s and early 1990s, massive numbers of alcohol and other drug dependent people were transferred from institutions of compassion and care to institutions of control and punishment. And those leaving their communities for sequestration within the nation's increasingly obese prison system were inordinately drawn from poor communities of color. Young Black men became the primary raw materials fueling the new prisons that rescued the deteriorating economies of predominately white, rural communities—all in the name of a holy war on drugs.

The criminal justice and child welfare systems became occupying institutions within poor communities of color. The speed and monolithic intensity of this shift left one spellbound and yet feeling a desperate need to speak out. Addiction scientists, addiction counselors, and addiction trainers and educators all have an ethical duty to remain professionally objective and not use their professional platforms as political soapboxes, but defining moral issues are present in every generation and era. The import of such issues are often only clear in retrospect, issues to which we can all be later held accountable for our voice or our silence, for what we did or failed to do. I joined many to speak out on what was happening and did so in every forum I could find, but activist voices were drowned out by cultural noise that rendered us as unimportant as the fate of poor men and women for whom we were advocating. I still believe that what occurred in poor communities of color in the name of "Just say no" will be later viewed on par with the cultural decimation that accompanied the Indian boarding school era.

What is going on right now that commands your attention? Are there issues of injustice that are not yet culturally visible? The issue is not just one of "Can you make a difference by speaking up?" The issue is "Will you be able to look at yourself later as someone who tried to right a wrong or someone whose silence rendered you an accomplice to injustice?" Speak up. The world needs to hear your voice, and you need to be able to remember that you spoke up in the face of injustice.

Moyers and Moyers

In 1997, I received a phone call informing me that journalist Bill Moyers was developing a new PBS documentary (entitled *Moyers on Addiction: Close to Home*) and that he would like to interview me about my work in general and in particular my work with Project SAFE in Illinois. I had no way of knowing at the time that this documentary would help set the cultural stage for a new recovery advocacy movement in the US or that I would have the pleasure of working in this movement alongside Bill Moyers' son, William Cope Moyers. In fact, at the time I was interviewed, Bill Moyers and his wife and professional partner, Judith Davidson Moyers, were still trying to decide whether their own family experience with addiction and recovery would be acknowledged and discussed within the documentary.

The earlier noted interview with Bill Moyers for his PBS special *Moyers on Addiction: Close to Home* was an exhilarating experience. Moyers and his producers were gracious hosts and Moyers was more prepared, skilled, and personable than any interviewer I had ever encountered. It was a great honor to be included in the documentary, and the whole thing was a positive experience for me—something rare in my history of encounters with the media. One aspect of the interview stands out for me now as an important historical footnote. After a wide ranging discussion about the history of treatment and recovery in the United States, Bill Moyers noted the cycles within this history and asked me what we could expect in the immediate future. Noting the demedicalization, recriminalization, and restigmatization of addiction in the 1980s and early 1990s, I suggested the potential for new advocacy efforts organized by people in recovery and their allies to challenge these policy trends. I had no idea that at the moment *Moyers on Addiction* premiered in March of 1998 that such a process was already quietly rising in the US, nor did I have any inkling of the important role this movement would come to play in my life.

One of the fascinating things about the media is that it can both record history and influence history. That was definitely the case with the Moyers documentary.

The Life and Death of Terry McGovern

In early 1998, I received a call from Jeff Jay inviting me to Washington, DC to receive an award from the McGovern Family Foundation for my book, *Slaying the Dragon*. I was enormously honored to receive such acknowledgment, but the event brought an experience that far surpassed my personal sense of accomplishment.

Following years of struggle with alcoholism, 44-year-old Teresa McGovern froze to death on December 12, 1994, passed out in a snow bank in Madison, Wisconsin. What elevated her story to public consciousness was the fact that her father was a prominent United States Senator and Presidential Candidate. The McGovern family created a foundation to honor Terry's memory by acknowledging contributions to the field of alcoholism treatment.

My conversations with George and Eleanor McGovern at the awards dinner touched me deeply. I never knew Terry McGovern, but I got to know something of her through the love and memories of her parents. I still think about Terry McGovern and still silently dedicate a paper or a particular project to her memory.

How do you make sense out of and extract value and meaning from people who have lost their lives to addiction? I find such losses an opportunity for learning, a call to professional humility, and a source of personal gratitude mixed with a bit of survivor's guilt for having been spared such a fate. Recognizing that the potential life and contributions of each person we serve can be erased in a moment adds a sacred burden to the work we do.

When a new recovery advocacy movement rose on the American landscape in the months following my encounters with the McGoverns, I was reminded how important it was to assure the inclusion of family members in this movement—family members like the McGoverns who would not be able to witness their daughter marching with thousands of others in the recovery celebration events that would soon begin. As that movement gained momentum and maturity, I tried at every opportunity to argue for the full inclusion of affected family members in leadership roles within local and national recovery advocacy organizations. I did that in memory of Terry McGovern and her family.

A Celebration of Government Heroes

Public employees, including those working in municipal, state, and federal agencies responsible for planning and funding of alcohol and other drug (AOD) prevention and treatment services, receive more than their fair share of criticism from multiple quarters, and work within these bureaucracies can be extremely frustrating at times. But, in these organizations, windows of opportunity are present to do things that are truly revolutionary. If a single act set the stage for the rise of a recovery advocacy movement in the United States, it was the creation of the Recovery Community Support Program (RCSP) by the Center for Substance Abuse Treatment (CSAT). That program provided grant money to state, regional, and local grassroots recovery community organizations to mobilize people in recovery as a force for public education and policy advocacy. What emerged as the new recovery advocacy movement was broader than those programs funded through the RCSP, but the RCSP sites were among the strongest and most effective of the newly formed recovery community organizations.

But this story is not about a program, it is about the power of individuals. Two quite remarkable people were instrumental in crafting and implementing CSAT's RCSP: Dr. H. Westley Clark, who at the time was Director of CSAT, and Catherine Nugent, who served as the first RCSP Project Officer. Their vision and boundless enthusiasm for the RCSP and their personal encouragement of so many of the new recovery advocacy leaders were critical to the early launch of a national recovery advocacy movement. In spite of all the political and administrative constraints on them, these two individuals deserve the title of hero for what they contributed. I cannot think of better examples of public employees who made a difference in the lives of individuals and families in recovery than Dr. Westley Clark and Catherine Nugent.

We tend to think of heroes in this field in terms of those working on the frontlines of addiction treatment and recovery support, and that work can indeed be heroic. But we should not forget that heroism also exists within the government entities that plan, fund, regulate, monitor, and evaluate those frontline services. Should an opportunity arise in your future to serve in such a role, consider it. When you encounter a public employee who is making such a difference, thank them.

The Native American Wellbriety Movement

Like most addiction professionals, I remained ill-informed about Native American tribal histories and cultures through most of my early career. While conducting training in Minneapolis, Minnesota on organizational stress, the reader will recall that I had a participant come up and inform me during the day that I had used a colloquialism that was offensive to Native Americans. As a result of that feedback, I resolved to further my education about Native America and to consciously attempt to filter Native perspectives through my future projects.

Ten years later, as I was deep into research on the history of addiction treatment and recovery in America, I ran into hints of early Native American recovery circles that existed more than 200 years before AA and a century before the Washingtonian revival of the 1840s. I became convinced that this was a powerful, untold story, but I was also convinced that I did not have the depth of cultural knowledge or the platform to research and tell this story.

In the 1990s, a vibrant recovery advocacy movement arose within Native communities across North America. It was a great awakening of consciousness about alcohol and drug problems and the healing power of recovery. At the center of what became known as the "Wellbriety Movement" was an organization (White Bison, Inc.) and a man (Don Coyhis). I knew of Don through my national recovery advocacy activities and approached him at a meeting of recovery advocates and briefed him on what I had found in my historical research and the untold story that I suspected might be revealed through additional research. Don became excited about what I shared with him and its potential importance to Native peoples. He offered to collaborate with me on the reconstruction of the history of recovery in Native American tribes. Our plan was to reconstruct that history drawing upon two ways of knowing and transmitting history: the written records within the nation's historical archives and the oral histories of Native tribes in America.

As the project proceeded, White Bison completed a Native adaptation of the Big Book of Alcoholics Anonymous. It was entitled, *The Red Road to Wellbriety*, and I was honored beyond words when Don asked me to write the forward to it. In that introductory piece, I conveyed what we were finding in our research: Recovery from alcohol problems was alive and well in Indian country and had been for more than 250 years. I also conveyed my growing understanding of the relationship between community and personal recovery that had come to me through my work with the Native Wellbriety movement.

The voices that fill these pages reveal how the wounds the individual and community have inflicted on each other can be healed. These voices call for a new relationship between self and community. The Wellbriety of the community creates a healing sanctuary—a culture of recovery—for the wounded individual, just as the growing Wellbriety of the individual feeds the strength of the community. In the Red Road to Wellbriety, the individual, family and community are not separate; they are one. To injure one is to injure all; to heal one is to heal all.

Work on the book, *Alcohol Problems in Native America: The Untold Story of Resistance and Recovery (The Truth about the Lie)*, spanned five years and went to press with the sense that much about this incredible history was yet to be revealed. The book exposed what we called 12 truths—truths challenging the "firewater myths" that had long dominated perceptions of Indian alcohol problems and shaped how Indian peoples viewed their own relationship with alcohol. The book had three compelling achievements. It documented how Native alcohol problems rose in tandem with the use of alcohol as a tool of economic, political, and sexual exploitation and the larger physical and cultural assault on Native communities. It documented how Native communities actively resisted the rise of alcohol problems and organized the earliest recovery mutual aid societies in the world. And it reviewed the scientific evidence that debunked the popular notion that the source of Native American alcohol problems lies in their innate, biological vulnerability to alcohol.

I don't think anything I have authored or co-authored served more as an instrument of healing than *Alcohol Problems in Native America*. The influence of the book was extended far and wide when the Christopher D. Smithers Foundation agreed to sponsor distribution of copies of the book to Native communities and to tribal colleges all across North America. Many expressions of gratitude from Native People came to me for my work on this book, but none more meaningful than a medicine pouch that was passed on to me through Patrick Haggerson of Betty Ford Center from Freddie Johnson and Arthur Dick of the Shuswap Band of Alkali Lake, British Columbia. Alkali Lake had been the subject of the movie, *The Honour of All*, a deeply moving story of how one Native community healed and transformed itself in the face of widespread alcoholism. The medicine pouch from Freddie and Arthur hangs today above my writing desk as a source of blessing and inspiration. It also hangs as a reminder that personal, family, and community resurrection are possible.

Recovery Rising

In April of 2000, I was asked to speak to representatives from the Center for Substance Abuse Treatment's (CSAT's) Recovery Community Support Program (RCSP) sites. For two years, I responded to requests to speak at events hosted by local recovery community organizations (RCOs) and to consult with these organizations on issues related to organization and tactics. As I prepared for the RCSP conference, it seemed a fitting time to step back and describe what I saw happening across all of these sites. I entitled my presentation, "Toward a New Recovery Movement: Historical Reflections on Recovery, Treatment, and Advocacy" and distributed the paper to attendees. What that paper did was help those present and other RCOs see themselves, not just as a local project, but part of a larger MOVEMENT. The paper had far more impact than I could have anticipated and that effect was in part related to the power of naming. This was the first paper acknowledging the existing of a "new recovery advocacy movement" in the United States, and that phrase gave people a chance to recognize themselves as a movement and to elevate their work with a larger sense of historical purpose. My thought at that time was that we had to act like a movement until we became a movement. Naming ourselves was a critical step in that process. As I would discover again and again, never underestimate the power of words.

Marching in Connecticut

One of the most dynamic of the new recovery advocacy organizations at the turn of the century was the Connecticut Community of Addiction Recovery (CCAR). CCAR leaders developed the idea of an annual "Recovery Walks" event that would put a positive face and voice on recovery. The original hope was that they could find 75 people in recovery to publicly identify themselves as persons in recovery via their participation in this event. The first Recovery Walks event held in Bushnell Park in 2000 drew 700 participants and has grown each year, surpassing at the time of this writing (2007) more than 4,000 participants. CCAR's recovery celebration walk inspired similar events across the country, with more than 200,000 people in recovery and their allies participating in such events in 2016.

Many stories have emerged from these events but one episode is particularly striking. One of those attending an early CCAR march had just been visited by a person in recovery that morning who invited him to the march. It would turn out to be the newcomer's first day of recovery. As they crested a hill during the march, the newcomer halted and stared in disbelief at what he was seeing: recovering people and their families marching as far as the eyes could see. Imagine the power of such an experience to someone testing the recovery waters who has never known anyone in recovery. In recovery, as in writing, it is often better to show than to tell.

Losing It

All of us have a moment (or too many moments) in our lives and careers we would like to retrieve and rewrite. Here's one of my worst moments that, as often happens, started out as something I had been looking forward to. I was invited in September 2001 to present a public lecture on recovery advocacy by the Chicago-based Recovery Communities United (RCU)—an organization that I had been deeply involved with. It was one of the events RCU had planned to celebrate National Recovery Month.

What was ill-fated about this presentation was that I had spent the weeks before seeing the American prison system close up. I had encountered private and public addiction treatment program leaders more obsessed with profits and prestige than with the recovery outcomes of their patients. I entered this lecture with a reservoir of raw emotion at the way people experiencing addiction were becoming the raw materials exploited by industrial economies.

My presentation on the new recovery advocacy movement proceeded well until I reached the section about the importance of this movement. It was then I drifted into an emotional diatribe about prisons as the "new plantations"—a reference to the role of the criminal justice system as an occupying institution within poor communities of color— and of treatment institutions more concerned with financial income than recovery outcomes. I had touched on such issues before in public presentations, but never with the emotional intensity expressed that night. At the height of this intensity, I stepped on the third rail of public speaking by (without thinking) dropping an obscenity (even worse—the unforgivable F word) into my talk. As I looked out at the more than 100 people in attendance, the first face my eyes landed on was a young man about 12 years of age who had come to the lecture with his mother. Needless to say, I wanted to die.

I apologized as best I could and went on to finish the talk hoping that this misspoken word would not be the sole impression from my talk. I'm including this story to note that even those who pride ourselves in extreme emotional control can at times be at risk of losing it. If I had continued to be in clinical work, the emotional baggage from my recent weeks' activities would have been grist for the mill for supervision and, as a result, would not have likely spilled into my counseling sessions, but spending my life as a full-time consultant and trainer did not afford the luxury of such supervision.

My response in the following weeks was to withdraw and seek debriefing of this incident with several of my trusted mentors. In this field, we encounter ugliness inside and outside the clinical consulting room. You have to do something with the cumulative poison absorbed in this process. If we don't, it spills out in unexpected places—unleashed on innocents or upon ourselves. In my early clinical work, I thought of myself as a sponge absorbing poison from my clients and community, and to extend the analogy, thought of supervision as a way to squeeze the sponge—a way to empty and refresh myself. If my self-mantra to "squeeze the sponge" had been effectively applied to my continued non-clinical work, I would still not feel so sheepish about a September night in Chicago in 2001.

The Minnesota Recovery Summit

In October 2001, a meeting was hosted by the Recovery Alliance (a new organization funded by the Johnson Institute) that brought recovery advocates together for two days to plan the future of the recovery advocacy movement in America. I was asked to give the closing address at that first recovery advocacy summit and ended my speech with the following thoughts.

We have selected the seeds for this campaign; it is time that we went home and planted them. When you get home and ask others to join us in this campaign, some will say they can't help with this movement because they are too old. Remind them that Handsome Lake was 65 years of age in 1799 when he launched a sobriety-based revitalization movement among the Six Nations Iroquois Confederacy. Tell them how this man who was near death used his own sustained recovery as a springboard to bring sobriety to thousands of Native Americans.

Some will say they are too young. Remind them of the Reverend Alvin Foltz who entered recovery as a teenager and became known as the "saved drunkard boy" and one of the 19th century's most articulate and effective temperance organizers. Remind them that, at the ignition point of the civil rights movement, it was the youngest, not the oldest, minister asked to lead this movement. Remind them that the young King called to lead this movement changed a nation.

Some women will say that the multiple role demands of their lives leave little room to support such a movement. Remind them of the crucial roles women have played in the history of social movements. Remind them that the name of Martin Luther King, Jr., would be unknown today if not for a woman named Rosa Parks.

Some members of the lesbian, gay, bisexual, and transgender community will say that they are too busy fighting their own stigma issues to participate in the recovery advocacy movement. Remind them of a most remarkable human being (and lesbian woman) who dreamed in 1944 that she could change the way a nation viewed alcoholism and the alcoholic. Tell them how Marty Mann built an organization that opened the doors of treatment and saved hundreds of thousands of lives. Tell them her legacy is today being threatened.

Some will say their background disqualifies them. Remind them of Jerry McAuley and Malcolm X whose religious conversions, recoveries from addiction, and activism were born in a jail cell. Tell them how each of these men, separated by a century, went on to lead thousands into lives of sober self-respect and dignity.

Some will say they are ill-suited to put a face and voice on recovery. Remind them that the greatest social movements have been sparked and supported by the most imperfect of people. Remind them that their face and their voice will be part of a choir of thousands who like themselves owe a debt of enormous gratitude.

Some will say that they and their families would be injured if they stepped forward. Acknowledge that stigma is real and that we don't need everyone in recovery to play this public role. Remind them that there are hundreds of ways they can support this movement outside the view of the camera. I have had the pleasure of being with many of you in your local communities these past few years, and I have had an opportunity to observe your work. We don't need all individuals and families in recovery for this movement to succeed, but we do need a deeply committed vanguard. You have been that vanguard and I want to close by honoring your passion and your perseverance. It is time for us to leave here and to go back to our communities. It is time for us to leave here and create the future of recovery in America.

Many stories have been passed down as part of the oral history of the civil rights movement, and I would like to close with one I first heard in 1967. It was of a day in a Southern city in which hundreds of people were marching in defiance of a court order. When they reached a crest of a hill what faced them ahead was a sea of baton-slapping police officers, barely restrained police dogs, and a phalanx of photographers and television cameras. It is said that a terrified silence fell over the marchers as each marcher visualized what was about to unfold. The spell was broken by the weathered but calm voice of one of the oldest marchers who said clearly and simply, "Let's go make some history." Our meeting here has been important only to the extent that we leave here and sustain this movement in communities all across America. So I leave you with these words, "Let's go make some history."

My words may have played no role in what happened afterwards, but many of those present did exactly what I was calling for. My words were chosen to heighten self-consciousness of ourselves as a national movement. My hope was that those spoken words would help us rise above our own limitations and face the coming challenges of mounting and sustaining a new recovery advocacy movement in America.

Recovery University

My travels across the United States as a trainer and consultant exposed me to many wonderful people and institutions, but one trip, a 2001 visit to Lubbock, Texas, stands among my most vivid memories. My host was Dr. Carl Anderson, a tall, white-haired, honey-voiced rancher who also headed the Center for the Study of Addiction at Texas Tech University (TTU). "Dr. A.," as he was then known by his students,

335

started a program for people in recovery to work on their college degree in a recovery-conducive environment. The program combined financial scholarships, individual mentoring, academic coaching, and recovery support groups held in the program's Serenity Center. I was awed to see so many joy-filled students in that program and to learn that their collective grade point average was a full point higher than the student average. I was struck by their bland disregard of some of the drinking revelry around them—a wisened "been there, done that; have more important things to do" attitude and the purpose and discipline that marked their lives.

It was worth the trip to watch Dr. Anderson with his young protégés (praise to one, tough love to another, quiet advice to others, and shared laughter with all). However, this is not a story about the achievement of one man, but a story of how one man's vision became a recovering community and how that community became a center of academic excellence. It is also a story about how one man inspired many people (mostly those impacted by and recovering from addiction) to financially invest in the future of young people in recovery.

Every time I question whether my individual efforts can make a difference, I think of Dr. A. and the lives he touched on that West Texas campus. No one who has witnessed the intensity of those students could ever doubt the proposition that one individual can change, if not the world, that portion of the world he or she can reach. Consider the possibility that you were born to do one special thing in this field. Do you have an inkling of what that might be?

Dr. A.'s work was nested in a larger history of recovery schools. The first collegiate recovery schools were founded at Brown University (1977) and Rutgers (1983) and the first recovery high schools rose unnoticed in Maryland and South Carolina, with the then more notable programs, including Sobriety High (1986), PEASE (Peers Enjoying a Sober Education) Academy (1989), and the Gateway Program (1992). This network of school-based collegiate and secondary recovery programs were linked by the founding of the Association of Recovery Schools in 2002. I later had the pleasure of co-authoring an article with Dr. Andrew Finch on the history of the recovery school movement. Sometimes, we serve a movement by recognizing it and honoring its leaders.

Words Matter

As I became more interested in the sources of stigma and the forces that sustained it, I became intensely interested in language and wrote an essay suggesting that leaders of the new recovery advocacy must choose their language carefully. I also recommended that certain words be abandoned. I wrote the following in 2002 about the application of the term "abuse" to alcohol and other drug-related (AOD) problems.

Of all the words that have entered the addiction/treatment vocabulary, "abuse" is one of the most ill-chosen and, as Mark Keller once characterized it, pernicious. First of all, to suggest that the addict mistreats the object of his or her deepest affection is a ridiculous notion. Alcoholics do not "abuse" alcohol (mixing Jack Daniels with fruit punch does come to mind here) nor do addicts "abuse" drugs. Addicts, more than anyone, treat these potions with the greatest devotion and respect.

In addition to being technically incorrect, references to alcohol/drug/substance "abuse" drip with centuries of religious and moral censure. In 1673, Increase Mather, in his sermon, "Woe to Drunkards" proclaimed that alcohol was the "good creature of God" but that the "abuse of drink" was "from Satan." Terms such as alcohol abuse, drug abuse, substance abuse all spring from religious and moral conceptions of the roots of severe alcohol and other drug problems. They define the locus of the problem in the willful choices of the individual, denying how that power can be compromised, denying the power of the drug, and denying the culpability of those whose financial interests are served by promoting and increasing the frequency and quantity of drug consumption.

Abuse has long implied the willful commission of an abhorrent (wrong and sinful) act involving forbidden pleasure, e.g., the historical condemnation of masturbation as self-abuse. The term has also come to characterize those of violent and contemptible character—those who abuse their partners, their children, or animals. It was the weight of this history that led the National Commission on Marihuana and Drug Abuse to criticize the term "drug abuse" in 1973. The Commission suggested that "continued use of this term with its emotional overtones, will serve only to perpetuate confused public attitudes about drug using behavior." The term gained even greater prominence following the Commission's report.

337

To refer to people who are addicted as alcohol, drug, or substance abusers misstates the nature of their condition and calls for their social rejection, sequestration, and punishment. There is no other medical condition to which the term "abuse" is applied. If we truly believe that addiction is a serious health problem, then why do we continue to have departments and centers of substance abuse? The terms abuse and abuser should be now and forever abandoned in discussions of people with severe and persistent alcohol and other drug-related problems.

Referring to AOD problems in terms of "abuse" is an example of how we unthinkingly absorb language and ideas by osmosis that become part of the prism through which we view ourselves, those we serve, and the world. I deeply regret the extent to which that phrase entered my vocabulary and wish I could now delete it from all my early writings.

Making claims that the "abuse" language did considerable harm was a serious accusation, but was there any real scientific evidence of such harm? The answer was no—until 2010. Dr. John Kelly published a series of elegant studies in which he presented case studies of people with serious alcohol and drug problems and asked his study respondents (drawn from various helping professions) how they viewed the person profiled and what actions needed to be taken to resolve this problem. The respondents were split in half with one group getting case studies describing the Mr. Williams in the case study as a "person with a substance use disorder" and the other half of the respondents received a case study of Mr. Williams described as a "substance abuser." All other details of the case studies were the same. What Kelly found was when Mr. Williams was a person with a substance use disorder, the case study elicited compassion and recommendations for treatment, but that when Mr. Williams was a substance abuser, the case study was more likely to elicit moral judgment and more punitive responses.

So, did the ranting and writing of a recovery advocate or the clear conclusions of an addiction scientist change the use of "abuse" and "abuser" in the field? I will leave it to those of you reading this in the future to make that judgment.

Recovery as a Heroic Journey

As my role as historian and cheerleader for the new recovery advocacy movement continued to evolve, I searched for stories and metaphors that would help motivate people in recovery to get involved in advocacy work. One of the most powerful metaphors I used was that of recovery as a heroic journey. I conveyed this metaphor through numerous speeches and in a two-part article that was posted in 2002 at numerous recovery advocacy websites and published in many advocacy newsletters and magazines. The following is an abridged version of that first piece.

In his classic work, *The Hero with a Thousand Faces*, Joseph Campbell described a dominant myth pervading the world's cultures. Campbell noted that, in spite of their myriad variations, mythic stories of the heroic adventure shared a common structure: the hero's departure, the hero's transformation by great trials, and the hero's return. Campbell's portrayal of the heroic journey beautifully depicts the metamorphoses of addiction and recovery while at the same time posing provocative questions about the final stage of the recovery process.

The beginning of the hero's tale is the call to adventure. Here the yet-to-be hero, often a person of little note or a community outcast, responds to a call from beyond his or her parochial world. To answer this call requires leaving what is familiar to enter regions of "both treasure and danger." The call to adventure marks a great separation from family and community and an entry into an unknown world.

As the adventure unfolds, the hero encounters numerous trials, tribulations, and tests of character. Eventually, the hero experiences an ultimate test. Here, the hero is "swallowed into the unknown, and would appear to have died." But the hero, often with the aid of a personal guide, finds a way to escape, whether from the labyrinth or the monster's belly. The death experienced by the hero turns out to be, not a death of the body, but a living death of the ego. In this transformation, the hero recognizes and embraces new sources of power and understanding and is reborn into a new consciousness and relationship with the world. The central part of the heroic tale involves the acquisition of new knowledge that turns out to be as much rediscovery as discovery. Campbell notes: "the powers sought and dangerously won are revealed to have been within the heart of the hero all the time."

According to Campbell, the most difficult stage of the hero's journey is the return home. Returning home is a stage of re-entry into the community that was left behind, reconciliation between the hero and the family/community, and a stage of service when the hero delivers the gift of their newfound knowledge to the community. To complete the heroic journey, the hero who left the community as a seeker must return as a servant and teacher. Campbell notes that the task of fully returning is so difficult that many heroes fail to complete this final step of their journey.

Obvious parallels are present between the processes of addiction and recovery and the structure of the hero's tale. The recovery stories of hundreds of thousands of people share striking similarities to Campbell's myth of the hero. My primary purpose for exploring this similarity is to explore one aspect of this comparison: what the hero's return to the community implies as a task of late stage recovery. Campbell's discussion raises the question, "Have recovering people returned to their communities to share the boon (gift of knowledge) of their adventure?" Returning to the community calls not just for a physical and social re-entry into the community, but also for acts of reconciliation (healing the wounds inflicted upon the community, forgiving the community for its own transgressions), and giving something of value back to the community. For the heroic journey to be completed, for the hero to reclaim his or her citizenship in the community, those debts and obligations must be paid. Left unpaid, the hero's final act of fulfillment remains unconsummated. Left unpaid, the community loses experience and knowledge that could enhance its own health and resiliency.

The boon of the heroic journey can be offered individually through acts of restitution, by carrying a message of hope to others (sharing one's "story"), and by modeling the lessons contained in the boon (practicing recovery principles in our daily lives). And yet the questions could be asked: Have recovering people as a group fully returned to their communities or are they hiding within those communities? Are recovering people as a group reaching out or have they escaped into the comfort and security of their own sobriety?

The stigma of addiction—the price that even those in long-term recovery can pay in disclosing this aspect of their personal history—leads many recovering people to "pass" as a "normal," scrupulously hiding their recovery journey from members of the larger community. Some recovering people live a socially cloistered existence, interacting almost exclusively with others in recovery. Does such isolation constitute a failure at re-entry, a missed opportunity for reconciliation, and an abdication of the responsibility to teach and serve the community?

These questions are not easy to answer because recovering people and their styles of recovery and styles of living are extremely diverse. Some recovering individuals have achieved Campbell's stages of re-entry, reconciliation, and service.

If recovering people have not fully returned to their communities, it is as much a cultural failure as a personal one. It is the cultural stigma—the very real price that can be exacted for disclosure of recovery status—that is a primary culprit here. It is time for a new recovery advocacy movement that, by removing the cultural stigma that continues to be attached to addiction/recovery, can open the doors for recovering people to return to their communities. It is time recovering people shared the boon of their recovery, not just with others seeking recovery, but with the whole community.

A new recovery advocacy movement is afoot in America that promises greater contact between recovering people and the larger community. Recovering people around the country are again creating grassroots organizations aimed at supporting recovery through advocacy, community education, and recovery resource development. The participants in this New Recovery Advocacy Movement, while responding to critical community needs, are finding in their recovery activism a way to complete their own personal journeys. They are finding ways to return and serve their communities.

If you feel like it is time to complete your recovery journey and for you to fully return to the community, find out how you can be part of your local recovery advocacy organization. If there is no local recovery advocacy organization, begin talking with others in recovery about how you might start one. It is time recovering people came home—individually and collectively.

Many in recovery reach a stage where their addiction is reframed from a curse to an experience that brought an immeasurable gift into their lives. Perhaps it is time that, in Campbell's terms, recovering people identified and communicated the exact nature of that gift to the world. Perhaps it is time the heroic journey of recovery was completed.

The "Boon" of Recovery

When I first presented the above piece in 2002, it sparked much discussion about how recovering people could return to their communities and the exact nature of the gifts they could give to their local neighborhoods. Discussion of the latter question prompted me to write a second part that is abridged below.

The most obvious gifts of knowledge that recovering people can bestow on our communities are our stories—stories that unveil the experience of addiction, stories that communicate the reality and hope of full recovery, and stories detailing how such recovery can be initiated and sustained. Five ideas about recovery need to be inculcated within communities across America.

1. *Addiction recovery is a reality—it is everywhere.*
2. *There are many paths to recovery.*
3. *Recovery flourishes in supportive communities.*
4. *Recovery is a voluntary process.*
5. *Recovering and recovered people are part of the solution; recovery gives back what addiction has taken.*

Those alone are worthy gifts, and ones that the New Recovery Advocacy Movement is calling upon recovering people to give to their communities. Larger, more difficult-to-define gifts may exist that could benefit communities across the world. Such gifts are not about how to recover from addiction, but rather what recovery from addiction has taught recovering people about life and how to live it. Recovering people could bestow many gifts on the larger society.

Many recovering people reach a stage in their recovery where addiction is reframed from a curse to a gift-bestowing blessing. Civilians (those not in recovery) who have had close contact with recovery groups have often lamented that it is too bad one has to be an addict to reap the benefits of recovery. The endless application of recovery programs to problems other than addiction surely suggests something of value here that far transcends their original intent.

For years I have been asking those in long-term recovery what they most value about their recovery experience. Most surprising is the number who describe living a better life, rather than sobriety, as their greatest achievement. Their responses reveal more about how to live than how not to drink or use other drugs. Collectively, these voices say that, through their close encounters with death (of body or self), they have come to understand both the fleeting transience and preciousness of life, and, as a result, the importance of living every moment as a gift to be cherished and lived to its fullest. Those confronting terminal illnesses have often shared a similar observation. What makes those in recovery unique is that they constitute what might be called a Lazarus Society or a Phoenix Society of men and women who, in the face of utter personal destruction, have not only survived but have been reborn, often with decades of life to live, to serve, to teach. The members of this Society, in their most retrospective moments, speak of the experiences and aspirational values that became important in their lives through the experience of addiction recovery. They speak of the importance of:

- Living in the present (Acceptance)
- Paying attention (Awareness)
- Listening (Empathy, Respect for Elders)
- Recognizing oneself in others (Identification; Unity of all People)
- Relating (Connectedness)
- Creating community (Participation, Belonging)
- Acknowledging limitations and imperfections of character (Self-knowledge, Humility)
- Believing (Faith, Hope)
- Staying focused (Vision, Centeredness)
- Accepting limitations of time (Patience, Perseverance)
- Paying debts (Restitution)
- Saying "I'm Sorry" (Forgiveness)
- Saying "Thank You" (Gratitude)
- Telling the truth (Honesty)
- Telling one's story (Witness)
- Respecting privacy (Discretion)
- Keeping promises (Fidelity)
- Laughing (Humor)
- Celebrating (Joy)
- Avoiding complications and distractions (Simplicity)
- Doing one's duty (Responsibility)
- Giving and helping (Service)
- Accepting differences (Tolerance)

The stories of recovering people also speak of what they have come to believe are the poisons of the human spirit: such things as self-deception, self-conceit, self-centeredness, jealousy, bigotry, resentments, anger, gluttony, avarice, and callousness.

This all stands as an interesting blend of surrender and assertion, reaching inward and outward, reconstruction of self and, perhaps in the future, the reconstruction of communities. The recovery message embraces the ethic of personal responsibility—the power of personal action—while simultaneously affirming the power of acceptance and surrender and acknowledging that the most important things in life cannot be achieved alone but only in the context of relationship. If that sounds contradictory, an appreciation of such paradoxes is also part of the boon of recovery.

The New Recovery Advocacy Movement is calling for recovering people to return to their communities and deliver the boon of recovery. The first task will be that of recovery education and advocacy, but a day may come when recovering people will pass on the deeper lessons of that boon to the larger community. On that day, the community will have received a great gift. On that day, recovering people will have come home. They will, in Campbell's terms, have completed their heroic journey.

Underbelly of a Movement

My lifetime has been marked by some of the most significant social movements in American history—movements that stopped wars, championed the rights of the historically disempowered, and forged the beginnings of a new relationship between humans and their global environment. And there are the movements directly affecting my life's work. At the opening of my career, I witnessed the fulfillment of the modern alcoholism movement's decades-long drive for community-based treatment of alcoholism, and, in the closing years of my career, I participated in the early stages of the new recovery advocacy movement. My life has been a living laboratory that offered many opportunities to observe and participate in these movements. The nobility of these movements and what they achieved can obscure the primitive processes that often mark the internal realities of these movements.

Movements are messy; they can draw the best and worst people and draw the best and worst from those who participate in them. They are a dance of competing agendas and conflicting personalities, and individuals and relationships can be wounded in the struggles within

344

these movements. Enormous benefit can come from involvement in social movements, but such movements also pose dangers.

Be careful out there, and be sure to take care of yourself while you are changing the world.

Courtesy Stigma and Personal Witness

The stigma attached to addiction, addiction treatment, and even addiction recovery is extended professionally and socially to those who choose to work in the addictions arena. Erving Goffman, the premier stigma theorist, referred to this as *courtesy stigma*—discredit extended to families and others closely linked to people with addiction disorders. It is common for addiction counselors and recovery support specialists to encounter courtesy stigma. This can take the form of other health and human service professionals looking askance at those who would choose to work in the addictions field or in the responses of civilians when introduced to us. The phrases "I could never do that kind of work" and "it must take a special person to help THOSE people" may express the civilian's respect for those who counsel people with addictions, but I suspect these phrases can also convey the civilian's suspicion about the mental status of anyone who would choose such work. Such reactions are also a way for civilians to emotionally distance themselves from such problems.

Put simply, those of us who work in the addictions field elicit discomfort because of our association with these problems. Such discomfort does have its moments. I must confess a certain delight in observing the varying reactions of people at a social reception who introduce themselves to me with slightly or very slurred speech and a drink in their hand and then ask what I do for a living. Two common responses to such situations are an effort at bootlegged therapy—the whispered request for a free consultation about a family member or friend—and a defensive justification of the drink in their hand followed by rapid flight. Both the whispered consultation and the nervous exit are examples of courtesy stigma.

Such encounters with courtesy stigma can be irritating and contribute to the professional and social closure of those working in addiction treatment. Through such closure, we progressively isolate ourselves from the larger community and associate only with each other. It took some time for me to recognize the positive potential in such professional and social encounters. And it came to me through the scientific evidence about stigma reduction. It turns out that one of the most effective ways to reduce the stigma attached to addiction, treatment, and recovery is through personal contact between citizens who have not experienced these problems and citizens who once experienced but no longer experience such problems. In short, social stigma flourishes where no contact exists between those who stigmatize and the stigmatized. Personal contact breaks down such stigma, particularly when the contact is personal, cooperative rather than competitive or conflicted, and when the encounter is a positive experience.

What that means for us is that those who are targets of courtesy stigma, such as family members and those who work as professionals or volunteers, can also serve as antidotes to stigma. We do that through the act of witnessing—sharing our testimony about the potential and reality of long-term addiction recovery. Every such encounter should leave those we meet with a more human view of those addicted to alcohol and other drugs and more hopeful about their future. By becoming a carrier of the recovery message, you can become a stigma killer. Have you killed any stigma recently? Or are you avoiding situations where you may encounter courtesy stigma?

Honoring the Future

There was a point in the history of the New Recovery Advocacy Movement that I became concerned that I was moving from a historian of that movement to a leader of that movement. Requests to speak to local groups were coming in from all corners of the country. I was keynoting national advocacy conferences and was being asked to represent the movement in meetings with federal and state agencies. My writings had helped stir the movement and document its evolution, but there was a period when people mistook me for that movement.

My predicament reminded me of Alfred Korzybski's observation that "The map is not the territory." I was the chronicler of the movement, not its leader, but I must confess that the calls of recognition and praise from one's peers are seductive. All of us warm to that kind of visibility and attention, and yet I knew that this role for any sustained period would wound me and wound the movement. I recalled the struggles other leaders had experienced with such a role. I recalled

346

Bill Wilson's efforts to save AA from himself and the role Charles Dederich played in the implosion of Synanon. I gave considerable thought to how to disengage myself from a role of central leadership without disrespecting those making the requests and without hurting the movement to which I was deeply committed.

Recognizing this risk, I began to temper my role and to talk with key people about the need for leadership development and leadership succession planning at all levels of the movement. Several leadership development initiatives unfolded that brought a large cadre of new grassroots leaders to the fore and allowed me to return to a more appropriate role of historian/elder. It was time for regional, state, and local leaders to assume leadership at a higher level, but there were questions about how to facilitate this transition.

On one day when I had done three interviews about the New Recovery Advocacy Movement, it dawned on me that others should have been doing those interviews, but to achieve that, they had to be blessed for this role by existing leaders inside the movement and garner increased visibility outside the movement. The idea I had to facilitate this was to do an interview series with these existing and future leaders as a way of achieving these twin goals. I discussed the idea with Pat Taylor at Faces and Voices of Recovery and we launched the advocate profile series in which she and I interviewed some of the leading recovery advocates from around the country.

The advocate profile series was a true pleasure. I got to know many of these incredible individuals much better, and the interview series heightened the visibility of these individuals as leaders and conveyed the depth and rich diversity of the recovery advocacy movement. The other thing this series did was that, by increasing the number of visible leaders, it diminished the vulnerability of those in leadership positions by moving the focus from one or two figures to a large cadre of such figures. The time I spent interviewing people like Stacia Murphy, Joe Powell, Lisa Mojer-Torres, Don Coyhis, Andre Johnson, Phil Valentine, Bev Haberle, Jim Gillen, Merlyn Karst, Mike Barry, Walter Ginter, Carol McDaid, Bob Savage, John Shinholser, Tom Hill, Tom Coderre, Patty McCarthy-Metcalf, Scott Strode, Michael Botticelli, and others was sacred time. I felt a passing of the torch as these interviews were completed and posted on multiple websites. There were also interviews I did with persons like Johnny Allem on the eve of his retirement from the Johnson Institute in which I felt I was honoring lifetimes of commitment and achievement.

I'm telling this story to emphasize the importance of finding ways to contribute so that the contribution is more important than your acknowledgement as its creator. The most ephemeral rewards come in the form of praise and plaques; the most meaningful rewards come in seeing a changed world and knowing you stood with thousands to make that happen—that you did your part. That's what it's all about—doing your part. That requires stepping up, but sometimes it also requires stepping down. (New leaders can only rise when space is created for them to fill.) Stepping down can also constitute an act of service. Stepping up or stepping down? Which do you need to do at this moment? Are there existing and aspiring leaders that you could honor? How could you best do this? Could you do it today?

Stigma and Leadership

A strange phenomenon occurs within social movements organized by and for those who have been stigmatized and disenfranchised. What stigma does at its most primitive level is challenge one's worthiness and right to exist. It teaches us to hate ourselves and to see ourselves as without value and visibility. That self-hatred is so deep that we are taught to also hate those who share our stigmatized status. Rather than confront the source of our devalued status, we project our self-hatred and anger on others like ourselves. Oppressed minorities are much more likely to express violence against themselves and their own kind than express violence toward their oppressors, in spite of the dramatic culturally visible incidents of the latter. This ingrained self-hatred creates a paradox within social movements.

First, members of oppressed groups long for a movement that will free them from their oppressed status and long for the emergence of charismatic leaders to spark and sustain such a movement. On the other hand, oppressed people are inherently distrustful of indigenous movements and tend to sabotage their own emerging leaders. A member of a professional association for African Americans conveyed this to me once by his observation that, "We [the association] don't elect leaders; we elect victims." His comment reflected the way in which anyone who achieved a visible leadership position was subject to jealousy, distrust, criticism, and all-to-often extrusion from the leadership role. It is only the surviving leaders of successful movements that are later reified and memories of their earlier maltreatment airbrushed from history.

The scapegoating of leaders that is so often a dominant element within indigenous social movements is at its most extreme an act of cultural suicide—a killing of one's collective future. Why would groups act out such a drama? It is quite simply because they have been programmed to believe they have no right to exist. It is because they believe they have no right to the hope the leader is offering. It is because they too easily believe the lies spread by dominant institutions to discredit movement leaders. The crucifixion of the leader protects the dispossessed from one more cycle of disillusionment and the agony of dashed hopes. It is better for a people to blame themselves and destroy rising hope than face the horrific truth that the whole world is conspiring to, or complicit in, an effort to kill them as a people. It is tragically ironic that movement leaders face as many challenges to their credibility from inside the movement as they do from the larger culture. The great leaders understand the dynamics of such imposed self-hatred, absorb challenges from their followers, build their followers' sense of self-value, and later encourage self-forgiveness for prior acts of stigma-driven sabotage.

Shredded into "A Million Little Pieces"

In 2003, James Frey published an emotionally wrenching memoir of his addiction and recovery experiences entitled, *A Million Little Pieces*. Spurred by the book's selection as an "Oprah Winfrey Book," it went on to sell millions of copies and turned Frey into the redemptive hero of the moment—UNTIL some of the key facts upon which the book was based turned out to be false. Frey was invited back on the Winfrey show where he was confronted about the falsehoods in the book. Frey's public rise and fall contained key lessons for me. The first lesson involved the risks involved in the "I did it my way" approach to addiction recovery—what can be simply an extension of the narcissism and grandiosity that so characterizes addiction. In this state, the process of self-inflation and, at times, inflation by others continues until the slightest prick sends this ballooned ego careening wildly until it crashes.

The Frey incident was a morality lesson for those in the New Recovery Advocacy Movement. Great care needs to be taken in the public presentation of one's personal story. Great care also needs to be taken to avoid a movement whose public image rests on one or two highly visible figures. It is easy to become intoxicated by public recognition and be seduced by media people who are as adept at placing people on high pedestals as they are in bringing people down from them. The risks to individuals involved are great as are the risks to the public image of people in recovery and the movement that represents them.

James Frey contributed to his own shredding, but he offered important lessons to people in recovery who will ever face a microphone. The same shame, and internalized stigma, that rendered James Frey vulnerable for self-aggrandizement and its subsequent consequences is a vulnerability also shared by all addiction professionals. No one working in the addictions arena fully escapes the stain of that influence. The culture which briefly reifies the redemptive hero (the recovering addict or the addiction professional) is also poised to later crucify that heroic figure. These tales are often a collision between personal vulnerability and culpability and the social processes through which cultural stigma gets acted out through the scapegoating of individuals and organizations. Have you experienced or witnessed such scapegoating? Again, be careful out there.

Liberating History and Science

One of the crucial functions of any profession is the control of knowledge. Such control means that ownership of the field's knowledge must be kept only in the hands of those who have been granted membership. Control of knowledge is a means of protecting the financial interests of the profession. Such control has several mechanisms. First, there is the arcane language through which the field's knowledge is communicated that assures that civilians (people not in the professional club) cannot understand the field's core knowledge. This language obscures and obfuscates and assures that people will require the paid services of a professional interpreter. Second, the field communicates its evolving and emerging knowledge through restricted channels. Civilians conducting internet searches for first-hand accounts of research studies are taken to sites which deny them access to studies or charge them inordinately high fees to access articles written in a reference-cluttered language that is rarely understandable.

I spent a good portion of my life mastering this language, learning to write in this stilted style, and measuring my professional progress by getting my words published in these insider journals. I actually believed that this was how you gained power to generate influence. Here's what no one told me: 1) the peer review process guarantees that, with few exceptions, only knowledge within prevailing policy frameworks will be published, 2) ideas that challenge these prevailing policies are published primarily in obscure "fringe" journals, and 3) the insider journals are only read by a small number of people—mostly a closed club of individuals who also write for these journals.

It occurred to me late in my career that perhaps it was time to liberate and extend the field's knowledge. I spent a lot of time thinking about how this might be done. Here are the strategies I settled on. First, I decided that for every article I wrote for a peer-reviewed scientific journal I would write five articles to be published in professional trade journals and newsletters. These venues had the potential to reach a large audience of real people—those seeking recovery and those on the front lines of addiction treatment and recovery support. Where my peer-reviewed articles were published in journals that at best had a few thousand subscribers, my articles in such trade journals as *Counselor* and *Addiction Professional* could each reach more than tens of thousands of readers. The problem was that the former had some permanence: they would be archived in libraries for decades to come. In contrast, the latter had no longevity—they were ephemera—what librarians referred to as *grey literature*. But I thought the internet could solve that problem. And it did.

Beginning in 2004, I began posting all of my recovery advocacy articles on the Faces and Voices of Recovery website. But that still left a lot of material. As my body of recovery-related writing grew, so did the frequency of requests for this or that article. I provided permission to post many of these articles, but the result was a scattering of this work in cyberspace and time spent each day responding to requests. The answer to this dilemma was a simple one: Place the bulk of my written work on one internet site where it can all be downloaded without charge. I began development of this site and it was officially launched in June of 2010. I think of the www.williamwhitepapers.com website as a platform of influence. Do you have a platform of influence? What might such a platform of influence be for you? When the website with my papers was launched, I felt that my work had finally been liberated. Do you have ideas that need to be freed beyond the boundaries of your current reach?

Board Work: What am I doing here?

Each of us must do what we are best suited to do and avoid those things for which we are ill-suited. This proposition has two problems. First, we don't know which category something belongs in until we try it, and, second, what we are suited for doesn't stay consistent across the stages of our life. I had joined the Board of Recovery Communities United, a Chicago-based grass roots recovery advocacy organization in 2002 and later agreed to serve as Vice President of the Board under the Presidency of Dr. Andrea Barthwell. What I didn't know at the time was that Dr. Barthwell would be called to the White House to serve in the Office of National Drug Control Policy, which would suddenly thrust me into the role of President of the Board.

I have worked with volunteer boards most of my professional career and have had the pleasure of serving with some exceptionally competent board presidents. In spite of such exemplary role models, I found myself hopelessly inept in this role. I was constitutionally unsuited for the slow, deliberate, consensus-guided process of board facilitation and was saved from prolonged entrapment in this role only by my own relocation out of Illinois. During this same period, I had agreed to serve on a few other boards and had experienced similar feelings of being poorly suited for board work in these roles as well. In 2004, I decided that I had served on my last board and began turning down all board service requests. I was greatly honored by some requests that came in during this period, but countered that I would be happy to serve as a technical advisor to this or that organization or otherwise volunteer time, but that the board role was not for me. When I made that decision, it was as if some professional weight had been lifted from me. In 2004, I served the National Council on Alcoholism and Drug Dependence (NCADD) in two ways. I volunteered to help write a celebratory pamphlet commemorating their sixtieth anniversary (and offered future help on such tasks), and I declined to serve on NCADD's Board. I believe both decisions served the best interests of NCADD. Sometimes we serve best by what we don't do.

Radical Recovery

By mid-2004, the activism of small cadres of people in recovery across the country inspired me to write something to honor this work. One of the things we can do as a leader (and I view each of you reading this as a leader) is celebrate achievements for which we can claim no credit. My essay to honor this renewed spirit of activism was entitled "Recovery Rising: Radical Recovery in America." Here is an abridged synthesis of that essay.

Radical recovery is the use of one's recovery from addiction as a platform to advocate social change related to the sources of and solutions to community-wide AOD problems....Radical recovery is the discovery that changing oneself and changing the world are synergistic. It is choosing to become the dropped pebble that generates enduring and far-reaching ripples through one's family, community, and world. Put simply, radical recovery is about people in recovery defining themselves as a community; moving beyond self-healing toward social action on issues related to their shared experience; reflecting on the needs of people still suffering from addiction; and forging goals and strategies to widen the doorways of entry into recovery and to enhance the quality of the recovery experience. Radical recovery is making amends and expressing gratitude through the vehicle of social action. It is mobilizing communities of recovery to build relationships of influence with other community institutions. It is a vision to reshape the ecology of addiction and recovery in America.

Radical recovery is family oriented (an extension of family healing), visible and vocal (in offering oneself as living proof of the reality of recovery), and solution focused. Radical recovery brings a sense of urgency, but is grounded in stillness, reflection, questioning, and listening. Radical recovery confronts the social conditions and institutional interests within which AOD problems arise and flourish. Radical recovery is political, sensitive to institutional interests and willing to confront: 1) predatory industries (that promote addictive products to vulnerable populations), 2) community (prison) economies (whose raw materials are young men and women of color and disenfranchised whites), and 3) any treatment leader who views people with AOD problems as a crop to be harvested for personal and institutional profit. Radical recovery respects the importance of professional resources but emphasizes the recovery-initiating and

353

recovery-sustaining power of relationships that are natural (as opposed to professionalized), reciprocal (as opposed to hierarchical), and enduring (as opposed to transient). Radical recovery is not about lobbying for an infinite number of ever-expanding addiction treatment centers. It is about nurturing the development of indigenous recovery-support resources that diminish the need for professionally directed treatment.

Radical recovery is inclusive (in its tolerance and celebration of the multiple pathways and innumerable varieties of recovery experience) and respectful (of the traditions and folkways of various communities of recovery). Radical recovery promotes metaphors of personal and community liberation for historically disempowered peoples and respects the right of communities to generate their own catalytic metaphors. Radical recovery is collaborative. It embraces coalitions of people with shared interests and aspirations involved in kindred causes. The movement within which radical recovery is embraced is interracial and interfaith and brings together people from diverse social classes and personal and professional backgrounds that otherwise share little in common.

It is radical in its scope (focus on environmental as well as personal transformation), radical in its inclusiveness (celebration of multiple pathways and styles of recovery), and radical in its synthesis of social responsibility and personal accountability. People in recovery are looking beyond their own addiction and recovery experiences to the broader social conditions within which AOD problems arise and are sustained. A radicalized vanguard of people in recovery is using personal transformation as a fulcrum for social change. They are living Gandhi's challenge to become the change they wish to see in the world. Those who were once part of the problem are becoming part of the solution.

Prophetic voices are rising from communities of recovery across America. Voices of the formerly hopeless are becoming instruments of personal healing and community renewal and redemption. If you share this call to a larger platform of service and believe that your personal/family story can touch others, come join us. Become part of this movement.

354

Do you see evidence of radical recovery in your own community? What is your perspective on this radicalized style of recovery? Do you feel a personal pull toward this movement?

Eulogizing the Living

In January 2005, I traveled to Hartford, Connecticut to speak at a retirement celebration for Bob Savage. Bob had lived a full life as a social activist and addiction treatment professional, but was called out of his first retirement to found the Connecticut Community of Addiction Recovery (CCAR) in 1997. CCAR went on to become one of the most dynamic grassroots organizations within the new recovery advocacy movement. I often referred to CCAR as the "north star" of the movement because of their many innovations: large recovery celebration events, focused recovery advocacy actions, anti-stigma educational campaigns, a network of recovery support centers, their pioneering work in recovery coaching, their articulation of core recovery values, and the unique relationship with their state agency that had pushed the state toward the development of a "recovery-oriented system of care." Bob had been in the thick of all of this.

The celebration for Bob was one of those wonderful evenings that no one wants to end. As I listened to the praise and loving chides heaped on Bob and what his second life had wrought, it dawned on me how rarely we honor the living heroes and heroines among us in the treatment and advocacy communities. I resolved that night to use part of the time and energy I had left in this field to eulogize such individuals through my speaking and writing. Perhaps you could join me in this pledge. Respect for elders is a diminishing value within the western world. Who in your professional life deserves such respect and honor? Is it time you expressed those sentiments to them and to the world? It is time we eulogized the living.

Eagles and Chickens

In September of 2005, a draft of the book *Alcohol Problems in Native America* that Don Coyhis and I had written (blessed by the editorial gifts of Richard Simonelli) was presented to a gathering of Native American leaders from across North America. What was needed

355

at that moment was a metaphor or story that could be used to convey the rich content of the book. Don Coyhis expressed our work through the story of baby eagles whose parents had been shot and who were raised by chickens to believe that they were chickens. The eagles continued to live as chickens until they met a wise owl who laughed at their chicken-like antics and educated them to their true nature as eagles. Don then went on to illustrate how Indians are eagles who have been taught that they are chickens. The following is his elaboration of that metaphor taken from the foreword of the book.

In this story, the eagles forgot who they were when they lost the guidance of their parents. We, as Indian people, forgot who we were as we lost our world to genocidal wars, epidemic disease, forced dislocations from our lands and the forced loss of our children to Indian boarding schools. Cut off from our history and cultural traditions, a race of sober eagles was defined as drunken chickens. Lies and labels deformed our view of ourselves and our view of Indians as a people. We were taught that our alcohol problems were an expression of our inferiority. We were told that we were alcoholics by birth—that if we drank alcohol, we would inevitably become an alcoholic. We were told that we are born with an insatiable craving for alcohol, that we are hypersensitive to alcohol's effects, and that we are prone to violence when intoxicated. We were told, in short, that a love of alcohol was part of our Indian nature.

We were taught to poison ourselves and then we were blamed for our own self-destruction. The Wellbriety Movement is asking us to reject these destructive lies. The Wellbriety Movement is asking our intoxicated brothers and sisters, "Why are you acting like a chicken when you are an eagle?" Being drunk is not the Indian way. It is not an effective protest. It is a form of personal and cultural suicide. It is time Indian People rejected alcohol, not because some Indians develop alcohol problems and alcoholism, but because alcohol is a symbol of efforts to exploit and destroy us as a people.

When you return home to your people, spread the truth about our true nature. Tell the people to cast off the lies that have been told about them. Invite them to write a new chapter in our history—a chapter written not with words, but with lives lived in Wellbriety. We will destroy the "Drunken Indian" stereotype with every sober breath we take. We will call upon Indian nations and Indian families to detoxify themselves from the poison that was injected into our histories. We will

356

*sweat this poison from our bodies and our minds and rediscover the
essence of ourselves as Indian People. The stereotype of the drunken
Indian is the image of the chicken that has been foisted upon us. The
eagle is the symbol of our sobriety and strength as a people. It is time
we declared clearly and boldly: We are not chickens; we are EAGLES!
We must teach our children that they are not destined to be chickens;
they are destined to be EAGLES! Our new history begins today!*

Confirming the power of Don's metaphor, Native children
attending the conference put on a skit of their transformation from
chickens to eagles. The skit was one of the emotional highlights of the
conference. Never underestimate the power of metaphor and story—or
the wisdom of children.

Communities of Recovery in Action

Robert McKnight, in a most provocative book entitled, *The
Careless Society: Community and it///s Counterfeits*, argues that most
communities are untapped reservoirs of hospitality. He contends that
the professionalization of compassion (professionals taking over
support functions historically provided by nuclear families, extended
families and kinship networks, neighborhoods, churches, and labor
unions) has weakened rather than strengthened support systems and that
what we as a country need is not more or larger social agencies but
greater community cohesion. He calls on human service agencies to tap
such indigenous resources and do only for each community what that
community cannot do for itself. Applied to the world of addiction
treatment, that would mean that professionally directed treatment would
not be the first line of response to alcohol and other drug problems, but
the safety net for the community. The first line of support would be
indigenous recovery support structures such as families and natural
social networks, recovery mutual aid groups, peer-based recovery
support services, and church-based recovery ministries. But could the
natural community really step forward to provide such support?

A superficial scan of these indigenous supports would lead one
to suspect they could not, but there is a hidden network of organizations
and a deep service ethic that when aroused can generate enormous
support. As August gave way to September in 2005, the nation watched
horrified at the devastation of Hurricane Katrina, including the breach
of the levees that had stood as the last protective shield for the City of

357

New Orleans. That horror intensified as images continued of chaos and desperation along the Gulf Coast. The response by federal and state authorities seemed agonizingly slow. The last group one would expect to demonstrate speed and efficiency in response to such horror would be a national network of recovering alcoholics and addicts, but here is what happened.

On September 2, 2005, I received a phone call from Samantha Hope-Atkins, the founder of Hope Networks, expressing the overwhelming needs Hope Networks was facing trying to respond to the local needs of recovering people in the aftermath of Katrina. Many recovering people had lost their homes and everything in them. Hundreds of recovering people had been displaced due to the destruction of recovery homes. The network of recovery support meetings had disappeared in tandem with community destruction, evacuation, and resettlement in shelters far from the Gulf Coast. People in medication-assisted recovery had lost access to methadone and other medications. Addicts were in acute withdrawal and no treatment resources were available.

The list of needs was long, but Samantha said two needs were immediate: drug-free housing for those displaced and (to my surprise) recovery literature to offer solace to people as they went through the earliest days of rebuilding their lives. She asked if I might help send out an appeal for help getting these resources. In response, I sent out 40-50 emails to recovery advocates and others in recovery from around the country who I thought might be of assistance. Within hours of those email transmissions, I began receiving responses from all parts of the United States and Canada noting that materials (from people's own personal copy of the Big Book to boxes of books and recovery literature spanning multiple recovery fellowships) were being shipped to Samantha's headquarters in Baton Rouge. At the same time, offers of drug-free housing poured in via emails from across the country. Recovering people, anguished by what they were witnessing, responded instantaneously when the call for help reached them. Robert McKnight is right; the community is a reservoir of untapped hospitality. What untapped resources exist in your community that could help individuals and families in recovery? Is it time to extend a request for help to these resources?

Best of Times, Worst of Times

At the end of each year, I try to take personal stock of the past year and also try to assess what kind of year it was for the worlds of addiction treatment and recovery. In some cases, 2006 was a remarkably good year. In September, more than 40,000 people participated in more than 500 separate recovery celebration events, signaling the growing size and power of the recovery advocacy movement. And yet I was troubled by a series of highly publicized events that signaled the continued stigmatization of alcohol and other drug problems.

- The year opened with the public flaying of James Frey for embellishing key facts in his recovery memoir, *A Million Little Pieces;* the nonstop media coverage on Frey conveyed the implied message that people in recovery were as much liars as those actively addicted.
- Actor Mel Gibson was arrested for drunk driving and attributed his anti-Semitic rant during his arrest to his rekindled alcoholism. He fled to rehab.
- Actor Robin Williams relapsed after many years of sobriety and re-entered treatment. His years of recovery had not been a focus of media coverage, but, as is typical, his relapse was (as was his suicide in 2014).
- Congressman Mark Foley lost his congressional seat following exposure of his sexually explicit emails to congressional pages. His public response was the announcement that he had an alcohol problem and that he was checking himself into alcoholism treatment.
- Tara Conner, Miss USA, faced possible loss of her crown before agreeing to go to rehab after publicly confirming reports of underage drinking and drug use. At the time, the extent of her addiction and whether she actually had an addiction, was unclear in media reports—further muddying public understanding of addiction, addiction treatment, and addiction recovery.

How do you read such contradictory messages from the culture? Through the recovery process, contradictory attitudes and behaviors often co-exist. The same is true as cultures transform themselves. It is important to monitor the direction such cultural ambivalence is tipping. Sometimes, doing so is impossible to read or predict.

Let's Go Make Some History

Johnny Allem of the Johnson Institute (JI) called in 2006 with a proposal to assemble my recovery advocacy writings in a book that would stand as something of an early chronology of the New Recovery Advocacy Movement. Although, much of this material had been posted on various recovery advocacy websites and published in a variety of recovery advocacy newsletters, he felt that having these documents assembled with new introductions would add further momentum to the movement they honored. I agreed to pursue this project with the understanding that the papers would remain in public domain so they could continue to be reproduced and that all proceeds from the book would go to support the advocacy activities of JI and Faces and Voices of Recovery. The book came out in August of 2006 under the title *Let's Go Make Some History: Chronicles of the New Addiction Recovery Advocacy Movement.*

Pulling together my early writings on the new recovery advocacy movement seemed a fitting way to consolidate whatever legacy I would leave that movement. It also stirred my own thinking about who would take over the role I had played in the early history of this movement. Those meditations led to continued explorations of how to heighten the visibility of existing and emerging leaders of this movement.

Shame Revisited

In 2007, the recovery advocacy movement was progressing beyond anyone's expectations. Thousands were marching in recovery celebration events and each year the number of new local grassroots recovery advocacy organizations grew exponentially. I was being invited to speak across the country and my advocacy essays had just been published by the Johnson Institute. From pulpits and podiums I was calling on a vanguard of recovering people and their families to stand together and declare their existence in this culture. I wrote about how such public disclosure of one's recovery status could be done respectfully and tastefully without violating the anonymity traditions of Twelve-Step programs. The "coming out" of recovering people was signaled by buttons, bumper stickers, license plates, T-shirts, sweatshirts, hats, posters, and other assorted movement paraphernalia. I was given such tokens everywhere I traveled, transferring items to the Illinois Addiction Studies Archives and keeping some duplicates for my own pleasure. I proudly donned such trappings at addiction conferences and recovery advocacy meetings.

And I wore them at home. Florida is T-shirt and shorts country so I often slipped on a recovery T-shirt to hang around the house or work in my bamboo garden. On a day, like hundreds of others, I was wearing one of my favorite T-shirts—one given me by a group of children that had a child's rainbow painting on it below a child's printing of the words "Happiness is Recovery." It was a beautifully designed shirt and one that had taken on special meaning to me. On this particular day, my wife asked me to run to a nearby grocery store to pick up a few items for dinner and, without thinking, I slipped off my Happiness is Recovery T-shirt, slipped into a nondescript T-shirt and headed to the store. A few moments down the road, I suddenly realized what I had done. It was a piercing moment of self-awareness. With all my bluster about making recovery visible and public, I still experienced some embarrassment related to that status, still feared the judgments of strangers, and feared that the recovery message on my clothing would be read with incomprehension or disgust. And this was deeply ingrained shame experienced by someone who had been drug-free for decades and who was challenging people in recovery to put a public face and voice on recovery.

The stain of shame penetrates deeply. We can scrub it from our skin, emotionally expiate it, and declare it gone. And still it seeps outward through our pores from deep within us. It tells us we are unworthy. It tells us we have no right to be. It calls us names and makes us sweat and blush with embarrassment. It whispers that we do not deserve full citizenship. It looks for judgment and contempt in the eyes of others. It dwarfs and silences us. Can you recall experiencing such feelings? Do you still experience such shame related to your own history or your close association with people recovering from addiction? One reason people need connection to a community of recovering people is to regularly purge such poison from our systems. The experience of community is the ultimate balm for shame.

Connecting the Dots (Recovery Community Building)

Big stories and little stories make up the history of addiction treatment and recovery. Sometimes the big stories are not apparent until you begin seeing the larger pattern that the small stories are forming. I am sometimes slow to see such patterns, but one became strikingly apparent to me in late 2007. For some time I had been interested in the movement to create recovery homes in communities across the United States—particularly the growing network of Oxford Houses. These self-supported, self-run homes represented something quite distinct from the often treatment-sponsored halfway or three-quarter way houses that had preceded them. I had been interested in and written about the growth in recovery high school and collegiate recovery programs. I had been interested in the growth of small recovery industries that employed recovering people who often had little, if any, legitimate work history. I was interested in the growth of recovery ministries in general and particularly the emergence of recovery churches. I was interested in the rise of recovery cafés (particularly in the UK). I was also interested in the emergence of recovering writers, musicians, artists, and others who expressed their recovery experiences through their respective crafts and interests. Connected to all of this was a new recovery advocacy movement that was generating new service institutions and service roles. BUT I had looked at these in isolation without seeing that all of these activities were a new form of recovery community building.

Seen collectively, they represented something without precedent. First, they were unfolding outside of, or at least on the far periphery of, the multi-billion dollar treatment industry. Secondly, they were an outgrowth of the recovery community itself, but a far more diverse recovery community than that term usually implied. Third, they represented the kind of institution building that occurred on the heels of the civil rights movement, the women's movement, and the Gay rights movement. As I began to see these many trends as a whole, it occurred to me that the future of recovery in America might well be more influenced by what was occurring outside of addiction treatment as what was occurring inside treatment. Where treatment offered a pathway of entry into recovery, these new developments were offering a world in which one could recover. In 2012, I documented these developments in a book chapter co-authored with Drs. John Kelly and Jeffrey Roth that was also published in the *Journal of Groups in Addiction & Recovery.*

What are the little stories that you see unfolding right now? If you connect the dots, are they forming a larger pattern? If so, what is the import of that larger story?

The Other Side of the Pond

In the spring of 2008, I received a flurry of emails from England, Scotland, and Wales about my recovery writings and their influence on efforts to launch a recovery advocacy movement in the United Kingdom. It was really quite exhilarating. Several mornings a week, I would have fresh emails updating me on the progress of these UK efforts. A year later in March 2009, I joined Keith Humphreys, research scientist from Stanford, and Pat Taylor, Director of Faces and Voices of Recovery, on a trip to the UK to meet with various government representatives, and I presented a series of lectures on recovery advocacy and recovery management.

The 2009 trip to England and Scotland forged many relationships that have extended to today and marked the beginning of connections between the US and UK recovery advocacy movements. While the movement in the UK was in its formative stages, I must confess to feeling great excitement at receiving news of the first UK recovery marches in September 2009. Images from the Liverpool recovery march were particularly moving to me. The 2009 trip also solidified relationships with key people in the UK recovery movement, one of the more important of which was with Dr. David Best. In the years following our first meeting, David and I collaborated on a number of important recovery-focused research studies.

Hossein Dezhakam and Congress 60 in Iran

The 2009 trip to the UK was also noteworthy for having met Mr. Hossein Dezhakam, leader of the Congress 60 recovery community in Iran. Hossein approached me after my presentation at an addictions conference in London and asked me through his interpreter if we might continue to communicate about issues of common interest. I readily agreed, and Hossein and I began what has become a sustained professional collaboration and personal friendship.

When Mr. Hossein Dezhakam became addicted to alcohol, hashish, and opium, he applied his training as an engineer to experiment with ways he could break his addiction to these substances. After multiple attempts, he stumbled on a method of tapered pharmacotherapy using tincture of opium that led to his successful recovery. In 1998, he founded a community, Human Revivification Society (Congress 60), to help others seeking recovery from addiction. There was initial resistance to the use of opium tincture (OT) in the treatment of addiction, but this changed as the number of people achieving stable recoveries grew within Congress 60.

Congress 60 is today organized into branches (16 in Tehran and 22 in other Iranian cities) and around six key roles: *Guardian* (founder/director), *Didehban* (14-member parliament of Congress 60 responsible for overall policy and planning), *Marzbans* (a seven-person executive team), *Mosafer* (travelers, those seeking treatment and recovery from addiction), *Hamsafar* (companions, family members, and friends of each traveler) and the *guides* who supervise the treatment process.

Recovery within Congress 60 is depicted as a three-stage journey: 1) using reparative medicine (opium tincture) for 11 months, 2) a drug and medication-free process of physical, mental, and emotional rejuvenation and self-discovery, and 3) a perpetual spiritual process of understanding the order and mystery of the universe. The first two stages are viewed as sufficient to overcome addiction, with the third viewed as a heightened level of spiritual development and community service.

One of the most unique aspects of Congress 60 is its use of sports, and more recently, music and the arts, in the recovery process. Each week, travelers and companions are involved in such competitive sports activities as soccer, volleyball, rugby, archery, badminton, table tennis, and bodybuilding. Teams representing Congress 60 in archery, rugby, dart, and traditional bodybuilding have made it to National Levels of competition in Iran. The entire Congress 60 community is also involved in numerous community service projects.

My regular correspondence with Hossein Dezhakam is now approaching its ninth year and has been a wonderful experience. I have been privileged to profile Congress 60 in one of the leading addiction journals and to have collaborated on studies of Congress 60 methods— most recently their efforts to integrate smoking cessation into their larger addiction recovery framework.

Hossein and I have found a special brotherhood that transcends the religious, political, and cultural barriers that could have easily divided us. Our communications have also given me a unique window of understanding about how recovery initiation and long-term addiction recovery, if they are to succeed, must be firmly nested within unique cultural environments, and that approaches that work within one cultural context might not work and may even do harm within another cultural context.

Are there communications you could begin that would push you outside the political, religious, and cultural windows through which you view the world?

Recovery is Contagious

In the spring of 2010, I was asked to give a talk at the annual celebration of the Northeast Treatment Center (NET) in Philadelphia—one of the City's most dynamic treatment programs. I spoke at this event a few years earlier and enjoyed it immensely so readily agreed to attend again when I received the invitation from the NET Consumer Council. It was one of those noisy, boisterous recovery celebration events with everyone dressed in their finest, filling the room with conversation and laughter. When it was time for me to speak, I looked out over the room and, after a few remarks of thanks for the invitation to be there, I was inspired to put words on an idea that had been percolating in my mind since an earlier meeting with the NET outreach teams—a group of current and former persons served by NET involved in street outreach not unlike that I had pursued 30 years earlier. The idea was the contagiousness of recovery. Here is part of what I said that night.

Folk wisdom says recovery comes only when we hit our own personal bottom. But recovery did not come to some of you in this room by hitting bottom. Some of you lived on the bottom, and recovery remained a stranger. Some of you were drowning in pain, had lost everything but your life to addiction—and recovery still did not come. When it finally arrived, it wasn't forced on you and you didn't initially choose it. You caught recovery in spite of yourself. And you caught it from other people in recovery—from people here at NET and from people in the recovery fellowships meeting every day throughout this city.

Let me be clear and brutally honest. Some of you did not come to NET seeking recovery. Many of you had never even seen long-term

365

recovery in the flesh—had no idea what it even looked like. Many of you came to treatment not because of the monkey on your back, but the people on your butt. Some of you came looking not for recovery but respite—a break from the life, not an end to it. Some of you came to escape the threat of jail. Some of you came to keep or get back important people in your life. The reasons were many and may have changed every day, but recovery was not at the top of that list. And yet many of you have started what will be a lifelong recovery journey. So how did this miracle happen?

My message tonight is a simple one: Recovery is contagious...And there is no better example of this process than what is happening right here, right now. This night is a celebration of the contagiousness of recovery and the fulfilled promises recovery has brought into our lives. Some of you did not leave the streets to find recovery; recovery came to the streets and found you. And it did so through volunteers of the NET Consumer Council walking those streets. They put a face and voice on recovery. They told you that recovery was possible, and they offered their stories as living proof of that proposition. They told you they would walk the road to recovery with you. Some of you hit low points in the early days of that journey, and it was your brothers and sisters in this room that lifted you back up—who called when you missed group, who, in some cases, went and got you. Many of you were buried deep within a culture of addiction—a way of thinking, feeling, acting, and relating as powerful as the drugs you were taking. The NET community and the larger recovery community of Philadelphia helped you escape and welcomed you into membership in another world—a culture of recovery. And this moment we are sharing together tonight stands as witness to the vitality of that recovery culture.

The contagion of addiction is transmitted through a process of infection—the movement of addiction disease from one vulnerable person to another. The contagion of recovery is spread quite differently—not through infection, but affection. Those who spread such affection are recovery carriers. Recovery carriers—because of the nature of their character and the quality of their lives—exert a magnetic attraction to those who are still suffering. Recovery carriers affirm that long-term recovery is possible and that the promises of recovery are far more than the removal of drugs from an otherwise unchanged life. They tell us that we have the potential to get well and to then get better than well. They challenge us to stop being everyone's problem and to become part of the solution. They relate to us from a position of profound empathy, emotional authenticity, respect, and moral equality—lacking even a whisper of contempt. Most importantly, they offer us love. Yeah, some of us got loved into recovery, and I don't mean in the way some of you with smiles on your faces may be thinking.

We all have the potential to be recovery carriers. Becoming a recovery carrier requires several things. It requires that we protect our recoveries at all cost—recovery by any means necessary under any circumstances. It requires that we help our families recover. It requires the courage to reach out to those whose lives are being ravaged. It requires that we give back to NET and other organizations that helped us along the way. And it requires that in our new life, we try to heal the wounds we inflicted on our community in our past life.

Addiction is visible everywhere in this culture, but the transformative power of recovery is hidden behind closed doors. It is time we all became recovery carriers. It is time we helped our community, our nation, and our world recover. To achieve this, we must become recovery. We must be the face and voice of recovery. We must be the living future of recovery.

So to all who are here tonight—individuals and families in recovery and allies of recovery, I leave you with this message. Recovery is contagious. Get close to it. Stay close to it. Catch it. Keep catching it. Pass it on.

If recovery is as potentially contagious as I suggest above, how could you increase its contagious quality in the settings where you currently serve? How could you become a more effective recovery carrier?

A Personal Redefinition of Recovery Time

The year 2011 was a rough personal time. My first cancer scare and resulting kidney surgery early in the year was followed by what felt like an onslaught of smoking-related deaths of close friends and colleagues. Particularly troubling were my communications with two friends in recovery who led amazing lives of service while literally smoking themselves to death—in spite of repeated unsuccessful attempts to quit. This all came to an emotional head for me at a National Recovery Celebration March in Philadelphia. When I arrived I was asked to go to the "old-timers table" to get a purple sash to wear with other old-timers leading the march. I had done this ritual several times so the ritual itself was not new, but one part of it was. Attached to the sash was a large button upon which each person wrote the number of years they had been in recovery. On impulse that day, I changed the number on my button to "22"—the number of years since I had quit smoking—the last drug I had shed from my life. Lots of people who knew me and had seen the much higher number I had proudly worn in earlier years stared at the sash with expressions of wonder and concern—I'm sure questioning whether I was now acknowledging a previously undisclosed recurrence of drug use.

It all made for interesting conversations that day and the days since. I am tired of burying people who proclaim recovery status and the joys of drug-free living while dying of addiction-related (smoking-related) diseases. Since September 2011, I have included abstinence from nicotine in my own personal understanding of addiction recovery. That decision on my part has not been a popular one in some quarters, but the needless disease and dying of people in recovery have to stop. My decision has forced others to explore their own understanding of recovery and their own relationship to the drug nicotine.

Never underestimate the potential influence of a symbolic act—on yourself and on others. Is there anything you could do to speed the day when nicotine will be forever removed as a celebrated drug within the culture of recovery?

Recovery around the World

My increasing involvement with recovery advocates in the UK between 2009 and 2011 was quite inspiring. In that time, I had started interviewing recovery advocates throughout the US for a new section of the Faces and Voices of Recovery website. Early in 2011, it dawned on me that it was time to extend this work to interviews with recovery advocates around the world. I worked with Pat Taylor to create a small committee to guide this effort and began the interviews later in 2011. What the process did was broaden my understanding of how diverse cultural contexts shape recovery opportunities and styles of recovery, but I also was amazed to find this common thread of people wanting to give back through their recoveries what addiction had once taken from them. It seems this desire to reach the still suffering is part of the universal DNA of addiction recovery.

What also intrigued me was that people from diverse racial, religious, political, and economic backgrounds found common ground with each other—sometimes even as their countries were at war with each other. It made we wonder if the world might have a great deal to learn from people in recovery whose own delusions of superiority had been so brutally destroyed before they came to embrace their own imperfect humanity. It is ironic that the world can be tearing itself apart and yet common ground can be found among people in recovery expressing their gratitude for the simplest of life's blessings. In our preoccupations with treating addiction pathology, we can overlook the simple but profound lessons buried within the experience of recovery. Those are lessons worth studying for all of us.

Community Recovery

The name of Dr. Arthur Evans, Jr. has been mentioned several times in these pages. It is hard to imagine how I could have done my most important work without his invitation to assist him with the recovery-focused transformation of Philadelphia's behavioral health care system. As that effort proceeded through the opening decade of the 21st century, an unexpected shift in our work occurred that we began to articulate through the concept of *community recovery*. We had promoted personal and family recovery from our earliest work together, but by 2010 we found that the community itself had become our client. We came to understand that, as we were building new recovery support institutions, bringing isolated elements of the community into relationship with one another, and promoting programs like public recovery murals, we were actually helping the community itself heal. In a series of articles, Arthur Evans, Roland Lamb, and I tried to convey this broader vision. Here is how we described community recovery in our first paper on the subject.

> *Community recovery is a voluntary process through which a community uses the assertive resolution of alcohol and other drug (AOD)-related problems as a vehicle for collective healing, community renewal, and enhanced intergenerational resilience.* Community recovery is more than the personal recovery of community members; it involves strengthening the

connective tissue between those with and without such problems while restoring and sustaining the quality of community life.

Community recovery is *voluntary* in the sense that it involves a rising community consciousness (acknowledgement and clear definition of problems), community commitment, and community action. These three critical steps must rise from within the community and cannot be externally imposed. The stages of community recovery parallel the stages of personal and family recovery: 1) recovery priming (experiencing—suddenly or incrementally—a catalyst for change), 2) initiating a process of healing and renewal, 3) achieving sustained changes in community relationships, roles, rules, and rituals, and 4) enhancing the long-term health and quality of life within major community institutions and the community as a whole.

Community recovery is a *process* in the sense that it must unfold and be sustained in a prolonged if not permanent manner. It is not an event or one of a series of special projects. The factors that sustain community recovery are often different than the factors that initiate community recovery. The ultimate test of the community recovery process is not the mass recovery of one generation, but breaking intergenerational cycles of problem transmission and imbedding personal, family, and cultural resistance and resilience as an enduring intergenerational legacy within the deepest fabric of a community.

Community recovery is *assertive* in the sense that the diminishment of alcohol and other drug-related (AOD) and broader problems occurs as a result of concerted, collective action rather than a process of attritional drift (via the maturing, extrusion, or death of those community members with severe AOD problems).

The *resolution* of AOD-related problems reflects a broad spectrum of outcomes across neighborhoods, families, and individuals. These outcomes include the complete cessation of AOD use, reduction of AOD use to non-problematic levels, reduction of patterns of AOD use that pose the greatest threats to public health and safety, and the reduction of peripheral effects of AOD use on families and neighborhoods. The resolution aspect of recovery is measured by what is subtracted from family and community life.

370

Collective healing, renewal, and resilience are aspects of recovery measured by what is added to family and community life. These outcomes include the enhanced health of individuals; the repair of strained or severed relationships within the community; the renewal and rise of indigenous leaders; the enhanced health of key community institutions; intergenerational connectivity; and the enhanced resilience of individuals (particularly children, adolescents, and transition age youth), families, and neighborhoods.

The *prognosis for community recovery* is influenced by the ratio of problem prevalence, severity, and complexity to the level of community recovery capital. *Community recovery capital* encompasses the scope and quality of resources that can be mobilized to initiate and sustain a community recovery and revitalization process. People in personal/family recovery are an important source of recovery capital that can be mobilized to serve as recovery carriers in their daily interactions within the community. With rising recovery capital, push forces out of addiction (experienced and feared pain and consequences of AOD use) become balanced with pull forces for addiction recovery (attraction to the promises of recovery as exemplified in the lives of recovery carriers).

There are *multiple pathways and styles of community recovery and renewal.* Successful strategies and tactics for community recovery and renewal must achieve a community/cultural fit. Each family/neighborhood/community must find personally and culturally meaningful metaphors that help them reconstruct a new recovery-based community identity (story) within which four questions are answered:

- Who and what were we before these problems peaked?
- What happened to us as a result of these problems?
- What sparked the recovery process?
- Who and what are we now and who and what are we becoming?

As you read these words, did you have the sense that your own community is in need of a recovery process? What might you do to inspire a vision of community recovery?

Recovery Landscapes (Space)

Addressing alcohol and other drug (AOD) problems at a community level involves shrinking addiction spaces and expanding recovery spaces. The latter is happening at an unprecedented rate around the world, based on the growing awareness that addiction recovery requires more than a personal decision. It requires a recovery-conducive world, including physical and social environments within which personal and family recovery flourish. Recovery advocates are trying to create that world by expanding the recovery space within local communities. In this context, we are witnessing the growth and diversification of recovery mutual aid fellowships and the spread of recovery advocacy organizations, recovery community centers, recovery residences, recovery schools, recovery industries, recovery ministries, recovery cafés, recovery-focused sporting events, and innumerable projects related to recovery and the arts (e.g., writing, theatre, and film). Recovery community building is occurring at a level of intensity never before seen in history.

How many spaces exist within your community where addiction thrives compared to the number of recovery-friendly spaces? A young woman arrives home following weeks cloistered in an addiction treatment facility. As she steps out of her doorway for the first time, where will she go? Will she find spaces in which her fragile recovery status is welcomed, celebrated, and strengthened? Or will she find. . . ?

Recovery and the Media Revisited

It is a rare addiction professional who does not have ambivalent feelings about the media. We recognize the enormous power of the media to dispel myths and educate the public while simultaneously cringing at its power to perpetuate old myths and create new ones. Unending drama in the addiction stories and a progressive decline of such soap operas in recovery are everywhere. It is little wonder which of these stories the media so frequently feeds upon. Addiction professionals can themselves be caught in the media feeding frenzies—called upon as experts to add a 30-second quotable line for an article or newscast covering the latest drug panic. What I have learned is a simple principle of such involvement: the more rationally objective your statement, the greater the likelihood it will end up on the editing floor. What we are asked for as a field by the media is rarely our knowledge; we are much more likely to be asked for the pithy quote that will help feed public alarm and fuel pre-existing stereotypes. One must recall from our earlier discussion that the ultimate aim of all media channels is not to educate but to sell, so each media outlet, in order to sell, competes for the public's attention by speaking in the loudest and most alarmist tones.

So why does the media so rarely tell the story of recovery? Long-term recovery, by intent, eschews the drama of active addiction. For media adrenaline junkies, recovery speaks too gently, too humbly, too simply. It speaks, not of excess and crisis, but of balance, simple pleasures, gratitude, and the joy of service. For those in recovery coaxed to the microphone, the details sought most aggressively are not the story of what happened after sobriety and sanity but the pain, chaos, and harm to others during active addiction—the drama. It is little wonder that people in recovery, particularly those in long-term recovery, often feel used after such interviews and make vows to avoid future encounters with the media. Personal visibility and recognition in a stigmatized arena can make one as much a media target as a media darling. Be careful out there!

Body of Work

I began writing in the mid-1980s when it became evident that the turnover of the addiction treatment workforce would not allow me to influence the long-term course of the field through conference presentations and training workshops. My focus then shifted toward extending my words to audiences far beyond those I could reach with my voice. Much of this early writing focused on immediate needs of the field such as issues of organizational health, ethical decision-making, and innovations in addiction counseling. As my work took on greater recovery-orientation, I realized I was at such a late stage in my career that I would not be available to support what would be a long-term process of transforming the core philosophy and practices of addiction treatment and recovery support services. At that point I became focused on—and still am—creating a body of work that could support this evolution long after my physical presence within the field. In short, I

373

began writing for the future as well as the present. That brought a level of detachment in knowing that I could create a body of written work that could carry my ideas into the future.

One advantage of creating a body of written work for the future was that it could separate people's thoughts about the message from their feelings about the messenger. That strategy also made it easier for me to progressively disengage from more visible professional and public roles by forging a higher purpose to which I could allocate my time. At an even more personal level, the "create a body of work" strategy offered me a plan for completing a legacy for new generations of addiction professionals and recovery advocates. As I sought to complete this body of work, a question loomed: If it is time for me to disengage from my public role in this movement, are there others ready and willing to carry this work into the future? I found the answer to that question during a trip to Boston.

Meeting the Future at Harvard

In late 2011, Ernie Kurtz was notified that he had been selected to receive and deliver the 2012 Norman Zinberg Memorial Lecture at the annual addictions conference hosted by Harvard Medical School's Department of Psychiatry. When Ernie could not make the event because of health problems, he arranged with Harvard for me to present the lecture in his place. It was a great honor for me and a duty to repay Ernie for so much support he had given me over the years, but another experience during that trip overshadowed the privilege of speaking at Harvard. A young recovery advocate and documentary filmmaker, Greg Williams, contacted me weeks before my lecture at Harvard to ask if he might film my presentation and interview me for the film he was preparing on the recovery advocacy movement. I had heard Greg's name many times in discussions of up and coming recovery advocacy leaders, but had not met him before our encounter in Boston.

I met Greg and his film crew at Boston's recovery high school the day before the Harvard lecture and spent the afternoon with him and his team. Working with Greg that day and the following day at the lecture was an intensely moving experience. In my era, most people entered recovery at midlife and spent much of their subsequent years clearing out the debris from years of addiction. Few in that era entered recovery as young as I did. But here in 2012, was a bright, articulate, and deeply committed young man in recovery who had the potential of decades of recovery advocacy work.

My encounter with Greg called my attention to the large number of young people entering recovery in their late teens and early twenties and what that could mean to the future of recovery around the world. In my trip to Harvard, I had the opportunity to honor a long-standing leader in the field and to meet the future of the field. Are there individuals around you who are also part of that future? What can you do to nurture their dreams and offer them guidance?

Tithing Time in "Retirement"

A series of health problems in 2011 and 2012 convinced me it was time to end my full-time employment with Chestnut Health Systems (CHS). The leaders at CHS were gracious in offering me retirement via an emeritus status that would allow me to continue my affiliation with them in an uncompensated role. The emeritus role allowed me to keep writing with the continued support of my CHS research assistant and tech people. But then another idea came to me about a new behind-the-scenes role I could play in the recovery advocacy movement. It involved continuing to do some writing projects under contract for various organizations with my fees for this work being paid to Faces and Voices of Recovery and other recovery advocacy organizations. This allowed me to carry on doing much of the work I loved at a level my health would allow and provide financial support to the recovery advocacy movement. I came to think of this as tithing time for the movement and began to think of how others might do something similar.

Those of us working in addiction treatment and recovery support have been deeply blessed by this field. Those blessings raise the question of how we can best give back to the field—above and beyond the paid duties we perform. Is tithing time outside your paid role an option for you? If your work in and commitment to this field is more than a paycheck, how are you demonstrating that commitment?

Movement Disengagement

As we age, the time comes to re-evaluate our role in professional endeavors and larger social movements. In the spring of 2015, I made the decision to take another step in my withdrawal from professional/public life. I had already ceased traveling and making presentations, but I had continued to give speeches through the aid of internet technology and had continued to field media interviews about everything from recovery history and research to drug policy issues. My decision to cease these activities was prompted by two things. First, my memory, which had served me so well for so long, was slipping. In recent presentations, I had found it harder to retrieve names and dates that in the past had flowed easily from my lips, and when I later listened to these presentations, I found an occasional error of fact that I had shared. Put simply, these presentations no longer met my standards of quality; it was time to end them.

A second influencing factor was that when listening to the presentations later, I noticed that I lacked the emotional control that I had long ago mastered in these situations. The recent presentations were at times too emotionally intense—demonstrating an anger and impatience with progress in key areas, as if I was running out of time and needed these changes to happen NOW! There's a fine line between the strategic use of emotion as an advocate and the loss of emotional control. The former moves people and prompts them to reach out to you; the latter repels people and leaves them fleeing in discomfort. My conclusion: Others were doing a more effective job in these roles, and it was time for me to give them up and retreat to the shelter of my writing desk.

As I made this decision and let go of these other activities, my impatience subsided and allowed me to experience the awe of what had been unfolding before my eyes these past months. The film, *The Anonymous People*, directed by Greg Williams and released in 2013, was winning awards and sparking the further cultural and political mobilization of people in recovery and their allies. More than 100,000 people participated in public recovery celebration events in 2014 in the US. The first national recovery rally was held on the Mall in Washington, DC on October 4, 2015. The advocacy movement was growing internationally far faster than I could have predicted. Young People in Recovery was flourishing as an organization and promising a new generation of recovery advocacy leaders.

The Comprehensive Addiction and Recovery Act was moving through both houses of Congress—legislation later passed that supported the long-term development of recovery support resources in local communities. Recovery was becoming more firmly embedded as the organizing center of behavioral health care in the US, with an increasing number of states and local communities extending acute care models of treatment to models of sustained recovery management nested in larger recovery-oriented systems of care. In December 2015, Michael Botticelli, Director of the White House Office of National Drug Control Policy appeared on *60 Minutes* in an interview that was authentic, passionate, and historic—speaking of his own recovery and the new policy shift in viewing addiction as a public health rather than a moral or criminal problem. Weeks earlier, Tom Hill, another long-tenured recovery advocate, had been appointed Acting Director of the Center for Substance Abuse Treatment. Then Tom Coderre, another leading recovery advocate, was appointed to serve as a Senior Advisor and Chief of Staff at the Substance Abuse and Mental Health Services Association (SAMHSA).

These events were indicative of what was also happening around the country at state and local levels. A key goal of the recovery advocacy movement was to enhance recovery representation at all levels of decision-making within the alcohol and drug problems arena. It was clear in 2016 that recovery representation was increasing at the national, state, and local tables where such decisions were being made. In 2016, Greg Williams' documentary, *The Anonymous People,* was followed by a second film, *Generation Found.* It highlighted the growth of recovery high schools and alternative peer groups to support young people in recovery. Like his first film, *Generation Found* screenings served as an organizing tool to expand local recovery support services. I found myself feeling like a proud father when my wife and I were able to view a premier showing of this movie with Greg and other recovery advocates.

Such iconic events within the history of the recovery advocacy movement would have been unthinkable only a few years earlier. Fully appreciating the momentum of these changes allowed me to experience a heightened humility and recognition that the recovery advocacy movement now had a life of its own and did not depend on any single individual, including me. Identifying these changes led me to realize that my continued participation in activities I no longer excelled in could hurt that movement. As noted earlier, sometimes one serves best by stepping down rather than stepping up.

An aging cadre of recovery advocates who, like me, will be stepping down from roles they have filled these past years. If you are among the former, are you ready to relinquish your place to create the space for a new generation of advocates? If you are among the younger generation of advocates, are you ready to step up to fill their shoes?

Chapter Fourteen
Recovery Management & Recovery-oriented
Systems of Care (1998-2017)

My involvement in the New Recovery Advocacy Movement was paralleled by my championing a radical redesign of addiction treatment. In this chapter, we will explore my call to shift addiction treatment from models of acute biopsychosocial stabilization to models of sustained recovery management nested within larger recovery-oriented systems of care. The stories and discussions here should provide opportunities for you the reader to reflect on your own experiences with addiction treatment, regardless of the role or roles that brought you in contact with such treatment.

Resignation of a Hero

By the late 1980s and early 1990s, it was obvious to me that something of great value had been lost in the rush to professionalize addiction treatment, but I had yet to find the words that capture the essence of what had been lost. Those words came from a long-time friend in the field who I encountered before speaking at a statewide addictions conference in Minnesota. I was thrilled to see a man whom I had always considered one of the true "war horses" in the field. He was well-known for his tireless duration of service and his refusal of promotions on the grounds that he wanted to stay on the frontlines working with individuals and families affected by addiction. When I greeted him, it was obvious that something was afoot. When I inquired how he was doing, he said the following.

> *I know this will surprise you, but I have made a decision to leave the field. It is just getting harder and harder to feel good about what I am doing. It's not my program; it's the field. I feel like I'm in a world that cares more about whether a progress note is signed by the right color of ink than whether people are actually*

making progress in their recovery. I feel like we are becoming people- and paper-processing institutions rather than people-changing institutions. I'm in a world where alcoholics and addicts are repeatedly exploited for financial profit in treatment programs that have no long-term recovery vision. I've found another job to support myself and my family until I retire. I'm going to come back into the field as a volunteer, because I think I will be a more effective servant in that role than in my current clinical role.

These were the words I had been searching for. The field was in many ways better than it had ever been—more programs, bigger budgets, beautiful buildings, a professionalized staff, and greater than ever cultural visibility. And yet one of my dear friends was telling me that the field we had both grown up in was losing its soul.

Within days, I was telling his story around the country. As I did, people at all levels of tenure in the field and widely varying roles shared with me how much they identified with his feelings. In my subsequent conference presentations and in numerous writing venues, I called for a process of renewal through which we as a field could get re-centered on the service ethic that was the core of who we were as addictions professionals. That message struck responsive cords, but I still felt there was something in front of me that I was not grasping. It took an encounter some years later in Dallas to name that missing something.

An Epiphany in Dallas

In the late 1990s, a recovery advocacy organization invited me to Dallas, Texas to talk about the history of addiction treatment and recovery in America. In responding to such requests, I often arrived early enough before my presentation to interview any old-timers I could locate about their early experiences in jails, treatment institutions, and mutual aid societies. In Dallas, I had arranged to interview a number of old-timers about the early history of treatment in the Southwest, and was fortunate to have a number of people with decades of sobriety and a considerable knowledge about the relationship between AA and early treatment institutions in the Southwest.

After touring the AA clubhouse and interviewing this distinguished group, we took a break, and Searcy W., the oldest of the old-timers there, asked me, "Bill, what is this research stuff you do?" I explained that I worked out of an addictions research institute and that we spent most of our time conducting treatment follow-up studies to scientifically evaluate the effectiveness of addiction treatment. I proudly noted that we had a few studies that were going to follow people for five years after treatment. He then mused, "Five years? Very impressive," and then asked me, "What does your research tell you about characters like us (waving an arm to include the other old-timers)?" It was a stunning question. I had to admit, that from the standpoint of science, we knew almost nothing about such long-term recovery. I finished my interview and my professional talks in Dallas, but Searcy's probing question haunted me in the weeks following my visit.

Searcy's question came at a time I was trying to sort out what remaining contributions I could make to the field. I continued to reflect on this when I heard of Searcy's death that next year. I resolved that whatever time I had left in my career I would dedicate to answering his question. I realized that, as a field, we could fill whole libraries with what we knew about psychoactive drugs and the processes and consequences of addiction. We also know a great deal about specialized addiction treatment and its short-term effects. But what do we know about the solutions? It was time I and the field expanded the knowledge base from a sole focus on the problem and its related clinical and social interventions to the lived process of recovery experienced every day by several million individuals and their families. It was time to shift my focus of attention to the prevalence, pathways, stages, and styles of long-term addiction recovery.

What I did not fully realize at the time was how much this shift in focus would profoundly change my view of a field I had already worked in for more than 30 years. My epiphany in Dallas was the first step in a process of professional rebirth with far-reaching effects that I could not have envisioned at the time. It created a clarity of purpose through which all my subsequent work was filtered. Issues unrelated to this recovery focus, I progressively weeded from my professional life, while casting a broad net in hopes of aligning myself with opportunities to shift the field's focus towards long-term personal and family recovery. Once that clarity of focus was achieved through an irrevocable commitment, unexpected opportunities arrived as if by plan. This confirmed my belief that few things are as essential to success as clarity of purpose. As you look at the span of your professional activities, what is your primary purpose?

The Behavioral Health Recovery Management (BHRM) Project

In 1998, on the heels of my epiphany in Dallas, Fayette Companies (Peoria, Illinois) and Chestnut Health Systems (Bloomington, Illinois) were awarded a contract to apply the concept of chronic disease management from primary health care to the improved treatment of behavioral health disorders. Mike Boyle and Russ Hagen, the CEOs of Fayette and Chestnut, asked if I would head this project. I declined the project lead role, but said I would take the lead on the technical work on the addiction side if Mike would handle the administrative tasks and provide leadership on the mental health side. That began a sustained partnership that profoundly changed my own life and may yet change the field of addiction treatment.

Our first task in the new project was to name it. I liked some of the new technologies emerging from various disease management projects in primary health care, but I thought the term "disease management" was an ill-chosen one for what we were attempting to do. The term had come to convey ways professionals managed people with chronic illnesses to reduce the excessive costs those patients incurred from serial acute episodes of medical re-stabilization. I suggested that we refer to our proposed approach as "recovery management" rather than disease management and that the focus should be on how the addictions professional could enter into a long-term recovery support partnership with those persons with severe alcohol and other drug problems. My vision of recovery management was that the person doing the managing was not the professional, but individuals and families seeking and in recovery. Professional helpers, rather than directing this process, were instead consultants and sources of encouragement. In response to the suggestion that no one would know what the term recovery management means, I argued with a mix of optimism and grandiosity, "They will in three years."

My argument struck a responsive chord with Mike and others and the new project was christened Behavioral Health Recovery Management (www.bhrm.org). BHRM provided the incubation chamber for all the work I would do on recovery management years after funding ended for this pilot project. I had no idea at the time that

Mike and I and others would spend the rest of our careers defining recovery management and conducting experiments on how clinical practices in addiction treatment would change within this model to improve long-term recovery outcomes. Framing that work as "disease management" would not have had the influence as did the focus on "recovery management." Naming something has power. Name carefully.

A Disease Concept for the 21st Century

One of the most controversial ideas in the history of the addictions field is the proposition that alcoholism/addiction is a disease. In the early days of the Behavioral Health Recovery Management (BHRM) project, we explored the idea of addiction as a disease—a chronic disease—and its implications for the design of addiction treatment.

In a series of five articles in *Counselor* spanning 2000 and 2001, I reviewed the birth and evolution of this concept, identified the core ideas of the proponents and opponents of the disease concept of addiction, and predicted that the concept's future hinged on the development of a more clinically and culturally dynamic and more scientifically defensible conceptualization of alcohol and other drug problems. I called for a new disease concept that would:

- *forge consensus on a language that can be used to differentiate types and intensities of alcohol- and other drug-related problems,*
- *shift from an alcoholism model to a more encompassing addiction model,*
- *carefully map the conceptual boundaries of addiction disease, defining the conditions and circumstances to which it should and should not be applied,*
- *place alcoholism/addiction within a larger umbrella of alcohol- and other drug-related problems,*
- *portray addiction as a cluster of disorders that spring from multiple, interacting, etiological influences and that vary considerably in their onset, course, and outcome,*

383

- *define the complex inter-relationships between addiction and other acute and chronic disorders and champion integrated models of care for clients and families experiencing multiple problems,*
- *define the roles human will and personal responsibility play in the onset, course, and outcome of alcohol and other drug (AOD) problems,*
- *celebrate the variety of styles and pathways of long-term recovery, and*
- *view addiction as a chronic rather than acute disorder and incorporate the principles of chronic disease management that are being used to understand and manage other chronic health disorders.*

It's undeniable that the concept of "disease" had provided alcoholics an organizing metaphor for personal change and given America a framework for organizing a response to her alcohol-related problems. However, a question still exists of whether additional or alternative metaphors would reach a larger number of those suffering from severe AOD-related problems and provide a more effective framework for organizing broad social responses to the prevention and management of AOD-related problems.

Anyone spending any time in the addictions field will need to become a student of this centuries-long debate and formulate their own conclusions related to three questions: 1) Is the declaration that addiction is a disease scientifically true? 2) Is the disease concept of addiction clinically useful, e.g., is it metaphorically true (makes sense out of experiences that are otherwise inexplicable)? 3) Does the disease concept of addiction work as an organizing paradigm for AOD-related social policy, stigma reduction, and service planning? What are your answers at the moment to these three questions? Whether you choose to characterize addiction as a disease, disorder, illness, malady, problem, behavior, or a choice, what are the implications of this characterization upon those affected by AOD-related problems and the families and communities in which they are nested? If we really believed that this condition in its most severe forms was a chronic condition, how would we treat it? That's the central question my colleagues and I began to ask.

Creating Space in People's Lives

One of the challenges of doing long-term follow-up studies of people leaving addiction treatment is achieving a high enough follow-up rate to assure the scientific integrity of study findings. Until the 1990s, follow-up rates of 70% were thought to be good and many published studies had rates far lower than that. That information changed in the 1990s as new technologies were pioneered that consistently generated follow-up rates above 90% even in 5+ years follow-up studies. Achieving such rates was an astounding accomplishment.

One of the pioneers in this area was a colleague of mine from Chestnut Health Systems, Dr. Christy Scott. Dr. Scott created numerous innovations to consistently achieve 94-95% follow-up rates in the studies she directed. When I asked the key to this success, her answer surprised me. She said, "You have to create space in the lives of the people you are following. We have learned how to create that space, be positively valued in that space, and maintain our space in their lives over an extended period of time." She then described the emphasis on relationship building during the engagement stage, the continued atmosphere of respect and positive regard, and highly systematized efforts to remain in contact via ongoing phone contacts and personalized cards on holidays and birthdays.

Through my collaboration with Chris on various projects, I was able to get to know those who managed the cases—the interviewers and the trackers (field workers assigned to locate temporarily disengaged clients), and to observe their relationships with the stream of people coming in for follow-up interviews. After some time, I was forced to admit that these research staff had relationships that were more respectful and enduring than the relationships that these same individuals had with addiction counselors and other treatment professionals. As addiction treatment evolves from brief biopsychosocial stabilization to a focus on long-term recovery management, we will have much to learn from those who conduct long-term follow-up studies. Coercion will continue to bring people into addiction treatment, but we will retain relationships after that coercion disappears only if we occupy positive space in their lives. We have much to learn about how to do that. This would not be the last time I would explore the role of "space" in addiction recovery. What space do you and your co-workers occupy in the lives of individuals and families you have served—in the months and years following the end of formal service delivery?

Recovery Checkups and Assertive Continuing Care

An interesting thing happened in the history of treatment evaluation research. A number of research scientists began to suspect that the mere act of contacting clients at intervals after treatment and asking them how they were doing was exerting unintended (and positive) effects on the outcomes being evaluated. While this may have been good news to the clients who reaped such benefits, it was not good news to the scientists who prided themselves on objectively measuring treatment effects rather than creating such effects via their own research procedures. It turns out that those being monitored do better than those who are not, and they do better in the precise spheres of their lives being monitored. Such effects occur even when there is no intended clinical component of the follow-up interview and when the interview data is collected by persons with no clinical training.

The lesson here is the power of post-treatment monitoring/support and a larger lesson about the importance of setting goals in behavioral terms and measuring progress on those goals. Under the tutelage of my Lighthouse Institute colleagues, Drs. Mark Godley, Susan Godley, Mike Dennis, and Christy Scott, I have come to think of this as a mantra, "define it, measure it, monitor it, reward it." That principle is the key to client adherence to post-treatment recovery self-maintenance activities and to achieving fidelity to clinical protocol for treatment and post-treatment recovery management activities performed by ourselves or others. The Godley studies of assertive continuing care for adolescents and the Dennis and Scott studies on post-treatment recovery checkups for adults exerted a profound influence on the Behavioral Health Recovery Project (BHRM) project and my own thinking about what long-term recovery support could and should look like. It is not enough to propose an idea of merit; we must find venues in which such ideas can be rigorously tested. And only rarely can that be done without partnership with others.

Organizational Courage: The Case of Dawn Farm

My first encounter with Dawn Farm in Ann Arbor, Michigan was in the early 1990s through my mentor, Ernie Kurtz, who was then serving on Dawn Farm's board. Since that time, I periodically visited the Farm while I was in town for work with Ernie. My initial impression of Dawn Farm was that of a traditional therapeutic community in a farm setting—hard to get in and hard to stay in. But, like most TCs, those who did make it through achieve long-term recovery and often turned into quite remarkable human beings. I had done a few speaking engagements for Dawn Farm staff, so was not surprised to get an invitation from Dawn Farm's Director, Jim Balmer, to speak at a 1999 community meeting he was organizing. What I was unprepared for was the message that followed mine.

Jim reviewed the history of Dawn Farm to a group of invited stakeholders, including current and former Dawn Farm clients, family members, staff, board members, referral sources, and funding source representatives. Jim then reviewed a string of decisions over the years that, with the best of intentions, had narrowed the doorway of recovery for Dawn Farm clients and isolated Dawn Farm from both the recovery community and the larger community. He stated that Dawn Farm had begun a process of self-inventory and invited those present to participate in this process. Speaking on behalf of his organization, Jim said, in essence, *We have made mistakes. We will atone for those errors in attitude and action. Will you join us to help shape a more recovery-focused approach to addiction treatment?* And then he opened the floor to the audience to share their views of Dawn Farm and how it could improve the quality of its services.

I don't think I have ever witnessed an act of greater professional and organizational courage as what Jim did that night. I reflected later how similar it was to the process of personal recovery. Jim and Jason Schwartz, Dawn Farm's Clinical Director, began a long process of organizational transformation that night that has extended to the present. It began with openly acknowledging institutional wounds, limitations, and imperfections. It also involved inviting resources and relationships beyond Dawn Farm in this sustained process of organizational change. Organizations need to recover too. That night Dawn Farm affirmed that recovery from professional and organizational arrogance was possible. It was a night I will never forget. Almost two decades later, Dawn Farm is still being guided by that recovery vision. Organizations like Dawn

Farm have been laboratories for me to study the role of community in recovery.

Many of my writings with Ernie Kurtz on linkage between professional treatment and long-term indigenous recovery support resources were influenced by witnessing Dawn Farm's recovery-focused transformation process. Do you have connections to organizations through which you can test your beliefs about addiction recovery?

Taking it to the Streets

We as a country do not respond to other public health epidemics by waiting for infected people to come to us. Why do we do so with addiction? If we now reach out to find and treat people with diabetes, breast cancer, heart disease, and a host of other medical conditions at their earliest possible stages of development, why do we wait until people addicted to alcohol and other drugs have so much pain in their lives that they are finally forced to reach out to us? If we treat epidemics of sexually transmitted disease by assertively locating and treating those exposed, why don't we do that with addiction? If we are truly concerned about the problem of addiction, why aren't we sending workers into the neighborhoods where addiction is most pervasive? I did that as a streetworker nearly half a century ago in one community before that role disappeared. Why can't we do it today in thousands of communities? Why do we wait for people to destroy themselves, damage their families, and injure their communities before we intervene? Is it because we as a culture still feel these individuals are not worthy of such rescue? Such disregard can be embraced with a smug attitude of contempt until we realize that the person who has not been reached is someone we love or someone who could injure someone we love. Stigma and smugness kill. Addicted people are decaying and dying. Is it time we went and got them?

An Invitation from the UN

The call came out of the blue. Would I write a chapter in a report being prepared by the United Nations Office on Drugs and Crime, Sustainable Livelihoods for Social Rehabilitation and Reintegration Working Group? My affirmative response came not as an affirmation of my competence to take on this task as much as the belief that this was a project that would stretch me by allowing me to step out of the uniquely American context in which nearly all of my professional work had been rooted. And that is precisely what it did.

As the days unfolded on this project, I worked my way through stacks of books and articles on addiction, treatment, and recovery in other countries and talked to numerous sources. I was again humbled by the recognition that my knowledge was a mile deep but an inch wide. I knew a great deal about addiction and recovery in the United States, but what did I know about such problems in India, South Africa, Europe, or Australia? I had considerable trepidation as I pondered this question, and it was only the encouragement of committee members that tipped the scales toward an agreement to take this on.

Over the coming months, I immersed myself in the world literature on addiction and recovery. What I found was that patterns of addiction, approaches to treatment, and the pathways of long-term recovery varied dramatically depending on where you were standing on the planet. After so many years in the field, it was humbling to realize how bounded my knowledge was by geography and culture. It reinforced for me how carefully we must place limitations on what we perceive to be the truth about addiction and recovery. Every time I have extended my experience into a new clinical population or a new culture or another country, I have been forced to step back and redefine some of my most basic understandings about alcohol and other drug problems and their resolution. And in that process I developed knowledge that improved my understanding of ALL those seeking help for alcohol and other drug (AOD) problems. Is it time your knowledge was stretched? What reading, travel, or communications with others would facilitate that stretching process?

Treatment Works? Taking on a Sacred Slogan

Sloganeering has a long history in the alcohol and other drug (AOD) problems arena as a means of promoting or stigmatizing drug use, advocating particular cultural policies toward drug use, and conveying particular definitions of the nature of AOD problems. The ideological and financial backlash against addiction treatment through the late 1980s and 1990s left treatment advocates on the defensive. It was in this climate that the slogan, *Treatment Works,* became the central organizing slogan of the addiction treatment industry. There was much to commend the slogan. It was short and catchy, celebrated those whose lives had been transformed by professional treatment, and honored treatment practitioners and their organizations. Something bothered me about the slogan, and it took some time to sort out the source of that discomfort.

In 2004 and early 2005, I posted and published a paper challenging the use of this slogan. I argued that the slogan 1) erroneously conveyed the existence of an entity called "treatment" that was consistent in character and quality across the United States, 2) perpetuated a single, professionally-directed pathway to AOD problem resolution, 3) failed to acknowledge individuals who resolve AOD problems without professional intervention or who are harmed by professional treatment, 4) justified the prevailing acute care model of intervention (analogous to treating a broken arm) that was unsuitable for most people with severe AOD problems, 5) misrepresented the highly variable and complex outcomes of addiction treatment, and 6) shifted the responsibility for recovery from the addicted/recovering person to the treatment professional.

I argued that the slogan *Treatment Works* should be abandoned and replaced by a cluster of messages that shifted the emphasis from the intervention (treatment) to the desired outcome (recovery), extolled the importance of personal choice and responsibility, celebrated multiple pathways of recovery, affirmed the supportive roles of family and community in the recovery process, and incorporated catalytic metaphors drawn from diverse medical, religious, spiritual, political, and cultural traditions.

I knew that this would not be the most popular article, but I knew that such an article could be best written by someone with a long history as a treatment advocate. Authored by someone outside the field, this article would have been discounted as one more "treatment-bashing" article. Authored by myself, I thought there was a chance to spark serious discussion inside the field on the central messages we need to convey to our local communities and the country about addiction treatment. This writing was a reaffirmation that our job is to tell the truth about treatment, not sell it as snake oil. And we must tell that truth to multiple parties: our own staff, patients and families, allied professionals, policymakers, and the public. History has taught me that any misrepresentation of fact to promote addiction treatment in the short run has the potential to mortally wound the field in the long run.

"Stop Kicking People out of Addiction Treatment!"

Several clinical practices in modern addiction treatment are likely to stimulate the "What the hell were they thinking?" question among future historians. At the top of my own nominations would be the practice of "administratively discharging" clients for essentially confirming their diagnosis. This practice most frequently involves discharging someone for alcohol or other drug use after he or she has been admitted to addiction treatment. Although sometimes referred to as "therapeutic discharge" and conceptualized as a motivational wake-up call, there is no scientific evidence that this practice has any positive influence on long-term recovery outcomes. Although I had thrown untold people out of treatment for this perceived volitional infraction, I became convinced that this type of administrative discharge was illogical and therapeutically counterproductive. Here was my chain of thinking.

We admit an individual for what we allege is the disease of addiction, the essence of which is the inability to refrain from alcohol and other drug use in spite of escalating consequences and the loss of control (the ability to moderate or cease drug use once it has begun). Lacking any definitive diagnostic test, we base our diagnosis of this disease on the client's self-reported history of inability to abstain and/or loss of control. We explain to the client, family members, and employers that the history of failed promises and resolutions is not a manifestation of weak character or immorality but a symptom of the disease of addiction. We argue that persons suffering from this disease require treatment rather than punishment or abandonment. Having successfully won this argument, we admit the individual for treatment of this disease and as part of that admission request that the individual refrain from alcohol and other drug use. We further state that he or she could be discharged for alcohol or other drug use—the central symptom of the disease that is being treated. When such use occurs days, weeks, or months into this treatment, the client is administratively discharged ("kicked out of treatment") for becoming symptomatic.

Let's compare this with the treatment of other health conditions. First, asking a patient to not exhibit symptoms of their disorder as a condition of entry into treatment is unthinkable on the grounds that such symptoms are not under the patient's volition or control. Second, expelling a patient during treatment for exhibiting a symptom of the disorder being treated would be unthinkable. Third, the appearance of symptoms while treatment is under way is a sign that some aspect of the treatment is not working and that the treatment protocol needs to be adjusted—not terminated.

In 2005, I asked several colleagues to collaborate on a paper on the subject of administrative discharge. We researched, wrote, and published this paper in *Counselor* with commentaries from many leaders in the field in hopes it would reach a broad audience and spark a reassessment of the field's policies on administrative discharge. And it did spark considerable response. That response came not in the form of letters to the editor of *Counselor,* nor in a sudden flurry of emails and phone calls. It came over a span of months in reports of some programs using the article as a handout for all their staff, and others changing their administrative discharge (AD) policies shortly after reading the article.

The best way I know to exert positive change on a field is to act as if we have the power to do just that. Is there a deeply established or new practice within your service setting that you feel is not only ineffective but harmful? Is it time you acted as if you had the power to change that practice?

A Recovery Revolution in Philadelphia

I had resolved to get off the road, to get some of my legacy writing done that had been on my "To Do" list for years. I had declined speaking and consultation requests for months, but in the closing weeks of 2005 a special invitation arrived from Philadelphia. Dr. Arthur Evans had taken over the city's Department of Behavioral Health and called with a challenge to help transform the city's treatment system via the recovery management approach that I had been promoting around the country. (Arthur previously worked with Dr. Tom Kirk in the State of Connecticut pioneering a broad spectrum of innovations in addiction recovery support.) Arthur said, "What we do here can make a difference, and it can make a difference for the whole field. Help me take your vision and make it a reality in Philadelphia. Use us as your laboratory." How could I say "no" to that? After all, this was the birthplace of the Revolutionary War and the birthplace of addiction medicine—the historical home of Dr. Benjamin Rush. What better place is there to start a revolution in addiction treatment?

The pivotal beginning of this project began for me the second week in February 2006. In four days, I participated in non-stop meetings with the leadership of the Department of Behavioral Health, addressed 300+ members of the city's recovery community, met with local recovery advocacy organizations, conducted a full day workshop for 700+ frontline addiction treatment staff, met with local addictions researchers, and outlined the principles, promises, and pitfalls of recovery management to 200+ treatment agency administrators. In my years in the field, I had helped with many interventions on individuals and organizations, but this was the first time I felt like I had helped stage an intervention on a city.

That visit marked the beginning of a consultation relationship with the City of Philadelphia that continued through 2014. And it did, as Dr. Evans promised, serve as a laboratory to test the key ideas that have been the core of my writings on recovery management and recovery-oriented systems of care. I owe a great debt of gratitude to Dr. Evans and key members of his leadership team, but I owe an equal debt to all of the individuals and families in recovery, representatives from community and faith-based organizations, and addiction treatment providers in the City of Philadelphia. Whatever contributions I have made related to recovery management and the development of recovery-oriented systems of care are a gift to the field from Philadelphia. How do you thank and pay tribute to a whole city?

RM and ROSC at GLATTC

On the heels of the invitation from Dr. Arthur Evans, Lonnetta Albright, Director of the Center for Substance Abuse Treatment's Great Lakes Addiction Technology Transfer Center (GLATTC), invited me to write a series of papers and monographs on recovery management for GLATTC (work that continued from 2005 through the fall of 2016). I did not know at the time just how profoundly these twin invitations would affect my life. First, they created a pathway for me to extend my career within the field by again morphing my central role in the field—this time from that of a trainer/lecturer and research consultant to that of a writer. Second, it provided a focus that would create what may well be my most significant contribution to the field. Such contributions require a suitable platform that can elicit one's best possible work. My work with the City of Philadelphia and GLATTC provided just such a

platform. Do you currently have a platform to create your best work? Are you using that platform to the best of your ability? Is it time to find a more personally suitable platform?

Recovery Summits

As a new century and millennium opened, I began calling for a shift from pathology and treatment paradigm to a recovery paradigm in my presentations and in my published articles in scientific and trade journals. There was some evidence that this shift was underway. Earlier calls for the rediscovery of recovery (by such individuals as Ollie Morgan and David Elise) seemed to be finally heard. There was a new White House initiated Access to Recovery program announced, Center for Substance Abuse Treatment's (CSAT's) Recovery Community Support Program was growing, a few pioneers were trying to reshape treatment into a "recovery-oriented system of care," the "recovery coach" (or personal recovery assistant, recovery support specialist) emerged as a new role within the service system, and interest was growing in post-treatment recovery support services.

This interest in recovery as an organizing concept reached a turning point in September of 2005. Two "recovery summits" were hosted that month—one by the Substance Abuse and Mental Health Services Administration (SAMHSA)/CSAT and one by Faces and Voices of Recovery. Both summits brought together recovery advocates from around the country, and the CSAT summit included federal policymakers, treatment administrators, and addiction researchers. These events did not mark a true tipping point in the field's conceptual orientation, but they did suggest that such a point might well be reached in the near future. Like the process of personal recovery itself, systems rarely change through a process of sudden conversion. Such change is more likely to be extended over a prolonged period of time with elements of old and new co-existing. Also like recovery, the process can be quite messy. At its core, the addiction field is struggling to define a science and technology of change—for persons and organization and, yes, for itself.

Defining Recovery

In 2006, I received an invitation from John Schwarzlose and Tom McLellan to participate in the first consensus conference of the newly created Betty Ford Institute. The purpose of the conference was to see if a group of tenured addiction researchers and recovery advocates could come up with an operational definition of recovery. The charge on the surface seemed a simple one, but I knew better. I had been working for two years on a paper entitled "Recovery: Its Definition and Conceptual Boundaries" and knew that any attempt to define recovery touched on some of the most controversial issues in the field. I finished a draft of this paper and was delighted to have the major questions I posed in the paper serve as an organizing framework for the conference. My delight was not that my answers to these questions would be adopted by the conference—we actually excluded my recommendations and definition from the version of the paper distributed to conference participants. My delight was that this group of distinguished intellects would push my thinking on these issues to a greater depth.

The questions I took on in the paper included: *1) Who has the authority to define "recovery" at personal, professional, and cultural levels? 2) Should the term "recovery" be applied only to the resolution of particular types of alcohol and other drug (AOD) problems? 3) What are the essential, defining ingredients of the recovery experience? 4) Does recovery from a substance use disorder, by definition, require complete and enduring abstinence? 5) Does recovery, by definition, require abstinence from, or a deceleration of, all psychoactive drug use? 6) Does the use of prescribed psychoactive drugs disqualify one from the status of recovery? 7) Is recovery something more than the cessation or deceleration of alcohol and other drug problems from an otherwise unchanged life? 8) Is recovery an all or nothing proposition or, as with other chronic health conditions, something that can be achieved in degrees? 9) Must recovery be conscious, voluntary, and self-managed? 10) What are the temporal benchmarks of recovery? (When does recovery start? When is recovery self-sustainable and durable? When, if ever, is recovery complete?)* My paper and the other commissioned papers were published in 2007 in a special edition of the *Journal of Substance Abuse Treatment* along with a draft consensus document.

The highlight of this whole experience for me came on the last day of the conference. Nearly all of the discussions of recovery by this distinguished group had focused on defining recovery as a primarily intrapersonal process. The exceptions to this were two speakers from Alkali Lake, British Columbia, Charlene Belleau and Fred Johnson, who were present because of the work the Betty Ford Center was doing in this Canadian First Nations Community. In their presentations, the Alkali Lake speakers talked of recovery as a process shared by the individual, family, and community/tribe. My discussions with Charlene Belleau and Fred Johnson helped refine my own thinking about this issue, and Charlene helped me visually portray this by centering recovery within three overlapping circles designating individual healing and health, family healing and health, and community healing and health. These three circles were then placed within the Medicine Wheel that portrayed two things: the dimensions of these changes (physical, emotional, mental, and spiritual) and the life cycle over which they occurred (child, youth, adult, and elders). The moment that Charlene and I sketched this figure on a napkin over lunch, I realized this was the most comprehensive and integrated understanding of recovery I had been able to achieve.

In the months following the conference, the papers from the conference joined the ranks of the most downloaded articles in the history of the *Journal of Substance Abuse Treatment* (JSAT) and were widely discussed in the field. But the greatest value for me was a penciled sketch on a napkin. The little things really can be the most important.

Recovery Capital

Much of my career had been focused on the acquisition of knowledge about the pathology of addiction and the clinical assessment of such pathologies as experienced by individuals and families. The shift to a greater recovery orientation in my work was marked by an equal shift in focus from personal/family/community deficits to personal/family/community assets. The challenge was that the field had provided few ways to conceptualize or measure such assets. In the 1990s, Robert Granfield and William Cloud introduced the concept of "recovery capital" to refer to the quantity and quality of internal and external resources that one can bring to bear on the initiation and maintenance of addiction recovery. Their work was a leap forward in my own work and my interest in how the interaction of problem severity and recovery capital shapes both the prospects of recovery and the intensity and duration of resources required to initiate and sustain recovery. I later had the opportunity to work with William Cloud on a primer on recovery capital written for addiction professionals, work with Dr. Alexandre Laudet on studies of recovery capital, and to collaborate with two UK researchers, Drs. Teodora Groshkova and David Best, on a recovery capital scale (full and brief versions) for use as a tool in clinical assessment and recovery planning.

In our work with individuals and families, it is important not to get so caught up in ameliorating the number and severity of presenting problems that we ignore the larger and more important agenda of developing internal and external assets. While the former may provide a brief respite from pain, it is the latter focus that provides the foundation for long-term recovery and garnering the promises such recovery can bring. So, the next time you evaluate someone whose problems seem absolutely overwhelming to them and to you, explore the often hidden assets that have allowed this person to survive to this point. Such assets and those they can add to it are the keys to their future and your clinical effectiveness.

The Neurobiology of Recovery

In the late 1990s, Dr. Alan Leshner, Director of the National Institute on Drug Abuse (NIDA), launched a public education campaign via the mantra, "Addiction is a brain disease." Dr. Nora Volkov followed Leshner as Director of NIDA and continued this campaign. Leshner, Volkov, and other scientists crisscrossed the country showing slides of brain scans illustrating the new neurobiological breakthroughs in the understanding of addiction. Their essential message was that the brain gets hijacked by powerful psychoactive drugs in ways that compromise human will and the ability to "Just say no." This campaign had the best of intentions, but I worried that getting the citizenry to believe that the aberrant behavior of the addict was a function of a diseased brain did little to make those recovering from addiction more socially desirable—more attractive as a mate, friend, neighbor, or employee—and that it might actually increase stigma attached to the addicted and those in recovery. I suspected there was a thin line between seeing someone as brain diseased to brain deranged to dangerous.

In late 2007, I penned an essay entitled "The Neurobiology of Recovery" in which I raised this concern and suggested two propositions:

1. communicating the neuroscience of addiction without simultaneously communicating the neuroscience of recovery and the prevalence of long-term recovery will increase the stigma facing individuals and families experiencing severe alcohol and other drug problems, and
2. the longer addiction science is communicated to the public without conveying the corresponding recovery science, the greater the burden that stigma will be.

I went on to call for a recovery research agenda that would include studies of the neurobiology of addiction recovery.

This essay grew out of a larger understanding that had come to me—that portraying addiction-induced individual, family, or community pathology without also conveying assets and potential resiliencies could inflict significant harm. (The historical portrayal of Native American alcohol problems with no reference to resilience and recovery within Indian communities is a classic example of lying and wounding by omission.)

In the case of addiction research, I felt any presentation of the neurobiology of addiction should also be able to answer such critical questions as:

- To what degree does neurobiology influence who recovers from addiction and who does not achieve such recovery?
- What is the extent to which addiction-related brain pathology can be reversed through the long-term recovery process?
- What is the time period over which such pathologies are reversed in recovery—days, months, years?
- What role can pharmacological adjuncts, social supports, and other services play in extending and speeding this process of brain recovery?
- Are there critical differences in the extent and timing of neurobiological recovery related to age of onset of

use, duration of addiction career, problem severity and complexity, age of onset of recovery, gender, genetic load for addiction, developmental trauma, ethnicity, primary drug choice, and other potentially critical factors?

Sometimes articulating what we don't know is as important as declaring what we do know. My hope is that by the time you are reading this that such questions will have been answered. Can you think of other examples in which individuals, families, or whole communities have been harmed by portraying their pathologies without reference to their stories of resilience and recovery?

Asking the Right Questions

Between 2005 and 2009, I authored and co-authored a series of papers chiding National Institute on Alcohol Abuse and Alcoholism (NIAAA) and the National Institute of Drug Abuse (NIDA) for failing to pursue a recovery-focused research agenda. Each article introduced an area of concern shared by individuals and families in recovery, noted the lack of research to address those concerns, and then listed a series of research questions that needed to be answered in that area. The series posed critical questions about the prevalence, pathways, and styles of recovery; the effects of recovery on the resistance and recovery prognosis of children of addicted and recovering parents; the extent and timing of neurobiological healing within the recovery process; and questions related to addiction recurrence after a prolonged period of recovery.

My central point in this series was that we as a field knew a great deal about addiction and about particular treatment interventions, but we knew comparatively little about <u>long-term</u> recovery from addiction. The central contribution of this series beyond making that point repeatedly was the questions that were posed. Sometimes you don't need answers to make a contribution to the field; you can just ask the right questions—and keep asking them until someone listens.

The addictions field needs people who ask questions inside the field's prevailing conceptual box and people who ask questions outside that box. What are the most striking questions about addiction, treatment, and recovery that have arisen in your own work? Is it time you raised those questions in a more formal way? Answers are important only to the extent we have asked the right questions. What are the most important questions you could ask?

Confronting Confrontation

In 2006, Bill Miller and I shared a book signing at a state addictions conference in Arizona. I had long considered Bill one of the true scholars and gentlemen of the addictions field—a man whose insight and productivity was matched only by his personal integrity. As we chatted about our current projects, he asked me about the historical roots of the use of confrontation as a therapeutic orientation in addiction counseling. I knew parts of that history—particularly the confrontation techniques of America's early therapeutic communities, but I acknowledged that I suspected there was much more to this story.

After the conference, I began piecing together disparate pieces of this history and contacted Bill to see if he would collaborate on an article on the history and scientific status of so-called therapeutic confrontation. He agreed and we prepared an article that we published in *Counselor Magazine*—a choice that reflected our desire to reach the largest possible number of addiction counselors. The article, published in the fall of 2007, traced the history of confrontation from the theories of Kolb and Tiebout through the therapeutic communities and fringe psychotherapies of the 1960s to the evolution of its use in Minnesota Model alcoholism programs. It then summarized the best studies on confrontation, noting the lack of evidence for its effectiveness and evidence for its potential harm. The article ended as follows:

> *It is time to declare a final moratorium on the use of harsh, humiliating confrontational techniques in addiction treatment. It is time to lay to rest once and for all the arrogant notion that we should or even can dismantle other human beings and then put them back together in better and wiser form. With impressive consistency, research tells us that authoritarian confrontation is highly unlikely to heal and may well do harm, particularly to the more vulnerable among those we serve. Within this context, such confrontational treatment is professionally unethical, and is doubly problematic when used with coerced populations such as*

court-ordered or employer-mandated populations....It is time to conduct a historical self-inventory of such practices, admit that these practices were ill-chosen, end their use, make amends where we can to those injured by such practices, and embrace different practices that are more effective and more respectful. There is now a strong science base for addiction treatment, and a related menu of evidence-based treatment methods that provide ample alternatives....As is true for our clients, it is painful sometimes to face reality and change our ways. But it is time, long since time, to wash our hands of authoritarian confrontation, and to listen instead to the co-therapist we have within every client.

This article triggered many communications of appreciation in the weeks following its publication. Some were from other researchers (e.g., Tom McLellan), but most were from clinical directors and front line counselors who simply wanted to say thank you and that an article declaring a moratorium on such techniques was long overdue. Most important among these were emails from counselors who reported that the article was forcing them to rethink their use of such methods in their counseling. I suspect there were many readers who did not like the article, but who found it harder to go back to their usual confrontational style of counseling. We've all had learning experiences so penetrating that it was impossible to go back to our routine patterns of thinking and behaving—at least without a new level of consciousness and discomfort. Can you recall such an awakening that you experienced or provoked in others?

The Science of Recovery Management

As colleagues and I promoted recovery management around the country through our writings and conference presentations, we began to get the inevitable push back from those with vested interests in the existing system of care and from those who quite appropriately asked us the tough questions. We often heard things like:

- "We're already recovery-oriented. That's what we've been doing all along."

401

- "This is nothing new; RM and ROSC are nothing but old practices couched in new buzz words."
- "Recovery management is the flavor of the moment. Next month it will be something different."

People had the inevitable concerns that dollars would be taken from primary addiction treatment and reallocated to post-treatment recovery support services—cries that we risked "throwing the baby out with the bathwater." And there was the confusion and consternation from all the new language—*recovery* (new definitions), *recovery management*, *recovery-oriented systems of care*, *communities of recovery*, *recovery community organizations*, *recovery checkups*, *peer-based recovery support services*, *recovery coaching*, *recovery capital*, and *recovery planning* (as opposed to treatment planning), to name a few.

Such questions and concerns were expected and a natural part of the systems transformation process. Another more important question arose that was not so easily addressed. After a decade of trying to promote evidence-based practices in addiction treatment, addiction professionals inevitably asked, "Does addiction science support recovery management? Is this an evidence-based practice?" Of course, recovery management (RM) is not a technique or a particular modality of treatment; it is a philosophy of how to organize pre-recovery, recovery initiation, and recovery maintenance (and quality of recovery) support services. But in 2007 and 2008, I began to define all of the changes in clinical practices that flowed from the RM philosophy and to systematically review the scientific literature related to these practices.

The resulting project turned out to be what a long-term AA member characterized as a "searching and fearless" inventory of addiction treatment. Under the sponsorship of three organizations, the project took on a life of its own and became one of the most challenging exercises of my career—how to synthesize conclusions from hundreds of scientific studies of addiction treatment and recovery and communicate them in a language understandable to front line addiction professionals, addiction treatment managers and administrators, policymakers, and private and public purchasers of addiction treatment. The resulting monograph—*Recovery Management and Recovery-Oriented Systems of Care: Scientific Rationale and Promising Practices*—was released in the fall of 2008. It remains the most pivotal piece of writing I have done on RM and recovery-oriented systems of care (ROSC). Here is how RM and ROSC were defined in this monograph.

> *Recovery management is a philosophy of organizing addiction treatment and recovery support services to enhance pre-recovery engagement, recovery initiation, long-term recovery maintenance, and the quality of personal/family life in long-term recovery.*

> *The phrase recovery-oriented systems of care refers to the complete network of indigenous and professional services and relationships that can support the long-term recovery of individuals and families and the creation of values and policies in the larger cultural and policy environment that are supportive of these recovery processes. The "system" in this phrase is not a federal, state, or local agency, but a macro-level organization of the larger cultural and community environment in which long-term recovery is nested.*

The principles and practices I set forth in the 2008 monograph were later beautifully captured in Dr. Kevin McCauley's 2016 film, *Memo to Self: Protecting Sobriety with the Science of Safety.*

The 2008 RM and ROSC monograph generated a lot of responses both in the United States and abroad, particularly in the United Kingdom. Of all the comments on the monograph, none touched me more than a short note from Keith Humphreys who wrote, "You have taken a million threads and woven an intricate and beautiful prayer mat for the field." His comment completely captured the process of this project—the massive effort at synthesis and sense-making—and my own deep hopes that the monograph would move the field to deep reflection and renewal.

The process of creating such a work involved a period of withdrawal and extreme focus—months of reading, thinking, and writing—then re-emergence to engage people in discussions of the draft I had circulated for review. I've always thought of this process as one of incubation. My best work has come from a combination of periods of isolation followed by intense discussions with people capable of critically challenging and extending my ideas. I view my writing as a highly personal process and yet a highly social process that produces a product that is only as good as the degree and quality of this isolation

403

and interaction. How could you cultivate opportunities for and an environment conducive to creative incubation? Do you have people who can offer a thorough critique of your work? If not, where could you find such people? What ideas have you injected into the field that sparked initial resistance? How did you respond to such resistance? What lessons have you learned about working through such resistance?

"I am a Human Being"

In early 2009, I made a regular consultation visit to Philadelphia—an exhilarating marathon of morning to evening meetings and site visits crammed into each three-day visit. On the third day, I helped review the one-year progress of four new programs funded to provide outreach and treatment services for addicted people with histories of prolonged homelessness and failure in traditional treatment programs. The new programs no longer looked like traditional programs. They had moved from chaos—knowing what not to do but not yet knowing what to do—to clarity. These communities were now marked by assertive outreach and engagement, nontraditional treatment, an expanded menu of recovery support activities, an emphasis on empowerment and choice, and continuity of contact over time, including assertive post-treatment follow-up and reengagement of all people prematurely leaving the program.

One of the most poignant moments in my meeting with staff and clients was when clients told their recovery stories and what had made these programs different than those that had long failed to engage them. In telling his story, one client who I will call Tyrell waved a small photo ID and declared, "I am a human being: I have an ID and a birth certificate." I had never heard anyone declare his or her somebodiness with such clarity and passion. No ID is a special dimension of the lives of many homeless people. No ID means you have no connections, that no one has your back, that no one will miss you, that you have no identity, that you are invisible, that you lack value. And if you are also a man of color, it means you are particularly vulnerable and expendable. This man, who I feared by his physical appearance might be dying, was fighting to become visible.

Interestingly, this was not the end of my encounter with Tyrell. After the "I am a human being" declaration, I talked with Tyrell after

404

the meeting about his hopes and aspirations. He described his years of addiction and homelessness and the new hope he felt about his future as he tried to rebuild his life one step at a time. On this day Tyrell was dressed in a suit to represent himself well in the meeting. I explained to him that I often give my ties away to individuals like himself as a token of best wishes for their continued recovery, and I asked if he would accept the tie I was wearing as a gift. He graciously accepted. It was a personal and touching moment.

Many months later, I was invited back to Philadelphia to keynote the Mayor's annual Making a Difference Dinner in which local organizations and individuals were honored for their work helping individuals and families achieve long-term recovery from addiction. Hundreds of people attended the social reception prior to the dinner, but the image that caught my eye was Tyrell standing back in the crowd trying to get my attention. He was dressed to kill and lifting the tie I had given him in the air so I could see it. He had moved from being nobody to being Tyrell. As it turns out, that was not the last time I saw Tyrell. In the spring of 2010, I spoke at Northeast Treatment (NET) Centers recovery celebration dinner and who should I see there but Tyrell. He told me that he had gotten a place of his own and that he was continuing to come to groups at NET to support his sobriety. He literally beamed with pride describing his progress. I expect there will be other chapters to this story. Never underestimate the power of taking specific interest in those who seek to better themselves.

Wounded Systems: A Meditation on Parallel Process

My work to help elevate the recovery orientation of Philadelphia's behavioral health care system provided endless opportunities for observation and reflection. In 2008, Roland Lamb, the Director of the Office of Addiction Services, asked that we spend some time reflecting on how to restructure relationships throughout the service system. As we proceeded to conduct focus groups on the status of these relationships, a striking image emerged. Power-based relationships that were governed by real or implied threat and control had long-pervaded the addictions field from top to bottom. Whether viewing relationships between federal and state agencies, state and local agencies, agency leadership and direct service workers, or the relationships between direct service workers and clients and families, focus groups revealed an underlying tone of paternalism, disrespect, and, at times, outright contempt.

The theme that emerged was that of control. Clients are controlled by counselors, who are controlled by supervisors, administrators, and boards, who are controlled by state, federal, and private funding and regulatory agencies, who are controlled by the larger political entities to which they are accountable. Competition, conflict, and struggles for status, power, and resources dominate these relationships. From clients to macro system administrators, the system consisted of closed tiers, with those in each tier viewing the tiers above and below through a perceptual lens of deficits and an attitude of condescension.

Such relationships may be inherent within hierarchical systems, but Roland and I suspected that this was magnified tenfold in systems dealing with highly stigmatized issues and stigmatized groups of people. The distrust and disrespect that pervades intrasystem behavioral health care relationships may well reflect the internalization and institutionalization of the social stigma attached to addiction and mental illness.

As discussions in Philadelphia continued with stakeholders at all sectors of the service system, there was growing consensus that a new recovery-focused philosophy was needed not only for clients and families but for the system as a whole. Several emerging tenets of that philosophy emerged, including the following core ideas:

- We (individuals) are all wounded (imperfect).
- The elements of the service system and the service system as a whole are wounded (imperfect).
- The service system and its practitioners have taken on some of the characteristics of the disorders they are expected to treat, e.g., denial, projection of blame, grandiosity, self-centeredness, preoccupation with power and control, and manipulation.
- We all need to recover—individually and as a system of care.
- We need to recover together.

I think the points of understanding Roland and I forged from the turbulent process of systems transformation are some of the most important of my professional career. Are you in a system that needs to recover? How might you serve as a catalyst of such recovery?

Peer-based Recovery Support Services

One of the most visible components of recovery management is the development of peer-based recovery support services. In fact, such services became such a symbol of recovery management (RM) and recovery-oriented systems of care (ROSC) that many treatment organizations added such services as a loosely attached appendage and then claimed this appendage as evidence that they were now a "recovery-oriented system of care." By 2007-2008, an avalanche of questions poured in on recovery support services, peer and otherwise, with particular interest in the newly christened recovery coach role. In response, I was asked by the Great Lakes Addiction Technology Transfer Center and the City of Philadelphia, to prepare an extensive paper on what was known about such services historically and from the standpoint of scientific evaluation. The result was the 2009 monograph, *Peer-based Addiction Recovery Support: History, Theory, Practice and Scientific Evaluation.*

Research for the new monograph underscored for me just how different peer-based recovery support services were from what had become the more professionalized role of addiction counseling and addiction medicine. The former were characterized by quite different theoretical constructs (e.g., experiential knowledge, wounded healer, helper principle), different role responsibilities, different relational models (including different standards of ethics and etiquette), and different sources of accountability. In 2011, the Betty Ford Institute hosted a consensus conference on recovery support services. This event reflected the growing interest in defining and distinguishing these services and describing how they were being used as adjuncts and alternatives to the formal addiction treatment system.

As my research into recovery support services and particularly into the emerging role of the recovery coach continued, I was struck by the reactions of addiction counselors to this new role. First, many addiction counselors were threatened by the new role and charged that recovery coaches were practicing counseling or therapy without a license. Ironically, this was the exact charge levied against addiction counselors by psychologists and social workers in the pre-professional era of addiction counseling. Second, I could not help but note the number of addiction counselors who expressed interest in this new role (until they found out it was generally unpaid or underpaid). The interests came from counselors who were overwhelmed with paperwork, who felt like the personal authenticity within addiction counseling had been bled out of the role, and who felt like the increased brevity of addiction counseling had led to its disconnection from the processes of long-term addiction recovery. To such counselors, it seemed like the recovery coach role contained some of the exact ingredients that had been lost, or at least diminished, within addiction counseling. I have heard similar concerns raised by social workers, psychologists, nurses, and physicians—all concerned about the growing depersonalization within their roles. It seems that the helping professions are mourning the lost authenticity and human connections that were once so integral to their roles.

The critical questions seem to be how we can remain in that zone of authenticity and effectiveness and avoid creating service relationships in which both service providers and recipients feel like they are objects on an assembly line. When that has happened historically, lay and professional renegades have birthed new roles and alternative systems of care. Could that be what is happening with peer recovery support services? If so, what are the future risks that could accrue through what will inevitably be efforts to professionalize and commercialize this new role and the recovery support organizations in which they are nested?

Recovery-Oriented Methadone Maintenance

During 2009, more than 260,000 people a day received methadone in the United States as a medical treatment for opioid (at that time, primarily heroin) addiction. Like many people in the field, the subject of methadone has always stirred deep feelings in me. In my writing on recovery management and recovery-oriented systems of care (ROSC), I had skirted but not directly addressed if or how methadone maintenance treatment (MMT) fit into recovery management (RM) or ROSC service models. By mid-2009, I and my co-authors had produced five monographs on RM and ROSC. It was time for me to face MMT and address the deepest roots of the controversies surrounding MMT and define as clearly as possible my own views on the relationship between MMT and long-term recovery from heroin addiction.

I pursued this work in two stages. The first was a paper on reducing addiction-related stigma with particular reference to medication-assisted treatment and recovery that I prepared for the Philadelphia Department of Behavioral Health. The second was a series of three papers co-authored with Lisa Mojer-Torres on recovery-oriented methadone maintenance (ROMM). The first paper reviewed the history of MMT with a particular focus on the early recovery-focused, person-centered model of care that viewed heroin addiction as comparable to other chronic medical disorders, described the corruption of this model during its federal/state regulation and widespread replication, and then outlined recent efforts to define a recovery-oriented model of MMT. The second paper addressed the question of how recovery is defined and which, if any, people in long-term medication-assisted treatment could be considered in recovery or recovered. The third paper outlined proposed changed in approaches to MMT to increase long-term personal and family recovery outcomes. The papers required reviewing hundreds of studies on MMT. In a period of four months, I learned more about MMT than I had learned in the previous 40 years I had spent in the addictions field.

As Lisa and I sent out the first outlines and early drafts of these papers, I received questions and cautions from many quarters. Was I sure I wanted to take on this issue? Was I worried what my authorship of these papers would do to damage how various communities of recovery and professional groups viewed me and my work? Weren't there other more important (and safer) issues I could take on? Others wrote pledging their support to help me get through the responses they suspected would follow my release of the papers. Lisa and I had three goals for the papers. First, we wanted people to take a fresh look at methadone and the history of methadone maintenance treatment. Second, we wanted people who had denied people in medication-assisted recovery the status of recovery to reconsider this position. Third, we wanted to challenge Opioid Treatment Programs (OTPs) around the world to increase their recovery orientation.

One of the side-benefits of this project was that it provided an opportunity to work with some remarkable MMT advocates (e.g., Walter Ginter, Joyce Woods), physician pioneers (e.g., Drs. Mary Jeanne Kreek, Bob DuPont, Jerry Jaffe, Herb Kleber, Ed Senay, Bob Newman, and Tom Payte), and MMT policy leaders (e.g., Mark

409

Parrino) whose collective careers spanned the birth and evolution of methadone maintenance in the United States.

At first, the response to the 2010 release of these papers was one of silence. Then Lisa and I began to hear rumblings about the monograph's potential importance at the same time points in the monograph were attacked from the ideological poles—from those objecting to our legitimization of the role of medication in recovery, from those working in OTPs who feared we were setting too high a bar for service practices, and from harm reduction (HR) advocates who feared the value of HR might be lost in this new recovery orientation of MMT and that "recovery" was a euphemism for pushing patients out of methadone treatment.

The saddest aftermath of the ROMM monograph was the death of Lisa Mojer-Torres in April 2011 from a recurrence of ovarian cancer. In the days following her death I understood why she had obsessed over every word in the monograph. She, more than I, recognized this would be her final testimony. It reminded me that everything we say or do could be our own final legacy and that we should never assume we will have the chance to correct or clarify our words in the future. Every spoken word, every key stroke on the computer, every act could be and should be thought of as a final testimony. Lisa lived that in our work those final months. Before her death, Lisa was honored for her work as an advocate by the American Association for the Treatment of Opioid Dependence (AATOD). In 2012, I was awarded AATOD's Friend of the Field Award for my collaborative work with Lisa.

If there is a single person who bridged the chasm between the world of medication-assisted treatment and American communities of recovery, it is Lisa Mojer-Torres. Since her death, I have worked with Lisa's husband Rolando, Walter Ginter, Joycelyn Woods, Mark Parrino, and others to build on Lisa's contributions. Are there legacies you are helping to carry forward?

Passing the Torch

Interest in recovery management (RM) and recovery-oriented systems of care (ROSC) heated rapidly during early 2010, spawning requests for training and consultation within the Center for Substance Abuse Treatment's 14 regional addiction technology transfer centers (ATTCs). To aid these requests, the national ATTC office hosted a meeting of 14 regional teams in Tampa, Florida in August 2010. This Recovery-Oriented Systems of Care-Training of Facilitators (ROSC-ToF) was intended to build regional capacity to respond to RM/ROSC-related training and consultation requests. The three days of training had a sense of history about them—a feeling that those present might mark the crystallization of a long-term movement to transform addiction treatment in the United States and beyond.

As the meeting unfolded over the course of three days, I found myself thinking about meetings as if I were seeing this event from a great height and distance. From this perspective, I inevitably compared this event to what had been a virtual lifetime of meetings. And I wondered about the value and import of all these meetings and which, if any, earned the designation of important or historic.

As the months accumulated following this meeting I had begun to fear that this meeting like so many others would leave no lasting imprint. But by 2011, communications began to filter in on what was unfolding around the country as a result of what we had started in Tampa. Successes in launching local projects. Successes in influencing state policies. Successes in garnering new funds to support recovery support services. Personal successes of the ToF people assuming greater leadership roles within their states. The planted seeds promoting this long-term recovery support perspective were sprouting around the country and moving across its borders.

I had to smile at my own lack of faith. Planted seeds must have time to germinate. What seeds are you waiting on? Give them time. The issue may not be others' lack of activism; it may be our lack of patience.

How many people are in recovery? How are they doing?

For years, I had been clamoring to every National Institute on Drug Abuse (NIDA) and National Institute on Alcohol Abuse and Alcoholism (NIAAA) figure I could corner about the need for periodic recovery prevalence surveys that could answer basic questions related to the rates of recovery in both community and clinical populations. Woefully failing in that effort, I decided in 2011 to review every existing study I could find that offered any answer, no matter how tentative, to these questions. The result was a monograph analyzing 415 studies published over the span of a century. I was not the best person to conduct such analysis. I had not done that level of statistical analysis since I was in school 35 years earlier, but I pursued it out of a sense of frustration. I figured that if the findings received some visibility, more qualified scientists would be forced to look at the issue, if for no other reasons, to test or refute my conclusions. Sometimes we can aid progress by being a foil—stimulating work out of our own imperfect efforts. Sometimes we just have to do SOMETHING—ANYTHING to get things moving forward.

As part of this larger effort, I also collaborated on the design of a survey of recovery prevalence in Philadelphia and its six surrounding counties. That published study further confirmed the substantial prevalence of people in recovery (almost 10% of the adult population), but it also included much more somber findings. When we compared the health profile of adults in recovery to adults in the general population, we found that those in recovery had far more health problems and far less access to health care resources. Those of us in the addiction treatment business have a tendency to see our work completed when people initiate addiction recovery. What we fail to recognize is the physical, emotional, relational, and economic baggage that people carry with them into the recovery process and the role addiction professionals can and should play in enhancing global personal and family health in long-term recovery. What would addiction treatment and recovery support look like if we fully understood this?

Writing a Revolution

There are many forms of activism. The activist must choose methods that constitute a personal fit and refine or change those methods over time. I began writing about recovery management in 2000 at a time when most of my efforts to transform the design of addiction treatment in the US consisted primarily of speaking. As my physical ability to travel declined, I relied more and more on the written word. I initially wrote a long series of papers aimed at quite different audiences—peer-reviewed scientific journal articles, articles in professional trade journals, and innumerable papers posted at treatment and recovery advocacy websites. The articles grew into a series of eight monographs on various aspects of recovery management and recovery-oriented systems of care (Now available as the two-volume book set,

412

Recovery Monographs). And finally, I co-edited a book with Dr. John Kelly of Harvard (*Addiction Recovery Management: Theory, Research and Practice*) that included chapters from some of the leading theoreticians, practitioners, and researchers working in the area of addiction recovery management.

What this body of work did collectively was create a groundswell of interest that slowly penetrated the field's consciousness and then its policies and practices. Each article, each monograph, each book—and each lecture, each scientific study, each telephone call, each meeting, each consultation—added weight to the argument that the successful resolution of severe, complex, and chronic addiction required far more than tweaking the existing acute care model of biopsychosocial stabilization.

When people began citing my own unattributed words back to me, I knew that this shift was well underway and that those of us who had started this crescendo of change were no longer the drivers of this change process. It now had a life of its own. None of this was a solo achievement. All of the critical activities had been done in tandem with others, but this exercise did convince me that one could start and support a revolution in thinking, policy, and practice with the written word. It takes a lot of people to write a revolution, but someone has to stroke the first keys. Each of us is shaped by the history in which we are nested, but each of us also has a chance to create history by participating in movements for change within our professional and personal lives. What aspects of your current environment are calling you to activism?

The White House

Tom McLellan was officially nominated by President Barack Obama in April 2009 (and sworn in on August 10, 2009) to serve as Deputy Director of Demand Reduction at the White House Office of National Drug Control Policy (ONDCP). Tom confirmed this news to me by email and Keith Humphreys, one of the premier recovery research scientists, shared with me that he would be working as Tom's assistant at ONDCP. This was a rather stunning moment for me. I had been a critic of national drug control policy for so long that I literally was spellbound by the sudden possibility that such policy would be led by individuals I had the utmost respect for and who would bring to their

413

work impeccable scientific credentials, prolonged careers in the addictions field, and strong understandings of recovery. Even more surprising was a subsequent call from Keith in the late summer of 2009 informing me that ONDCP was considering a recovery initiative. When I hung up the phone from talking with Keith, I sat in quiet self-reflection and amazement. A day had come in my life that I never thought possible. I had just talked to someone calling from the White House who wanted to explore how the President of the United States and his staff could support addiction recovery in America.

In January 2010, I interviewed Tom McLellan for a new "Pioneer Series" I was publishing in *Counselor*. The series provided some of the true heroes of modern addiction treatment with an opportunity to pass lessons learned to a new generation of addiction professionals. When my interview with Tom was finished, he surprised me with a proposal of his own. He shared that an Office of Recovery was going to be established inside ONDCP and that he wanted me to think about the possibility of heading it. I followed this brief conversation with a set of questions that would help me decide whether I was physically and mentally capable of serving in this role and how it might be reconciled with existing commitments that I had.

I did not hear from Tom in the weeks that followed our initial discussion and before I could get to Washington, DC to meet personally with Tom, I heard that he and Keith were both resigning from ONDCP—Tom proclaiming that he was "ill-suited to government work." The public announcement of his resignation occurred on April 16, 2010, and two weeks later I met with him and several ONDCP staff to explore potential strategies of an ONDCP Office of Recovery. In particular, we discussed how this Office might help:

- celebrate the growth and diversification of American communities of recovery;
- reduce policy barriers to long-term addiction recovery;
- mobilize individuals and families in long-term recovery in support of local prevention, early intervention, treatment, and recovery support efforts;
- develop and disseminate treatment models that incorporate prolonged recovery support and assertive linkages between professional and peer-based recovery support resources;

- formulate an addiction recovery research agenda; and
- facilitate international information exchange on creative and effective approaches to long-term addiction recovery support for affected individuals, families, neighborhoods, and communities.

As I left Washington, DC, I still had a sense of exhilaration from our discussion of what was possible but a deep sense of demoralization knowing that the two people in the country perhaps best equipped to implement such a strategy were leaving ONDCP. The work Tom and Keith began did survive under the effective leadership of Michael Botticelli. Most such change efforts are leadership relay races sustained by pressure from below to move such ideas as recovery management (RM) and recovery-oriented systems of care (ROSC) from rhetoric to reality. Are you pushing?

The Real RM and ROSC Pioneers

My colleagues and I had built a body of recovery management (RM) and recovery-oriented systems of care (ROSC) literature in the opening decade of the 21st century, but innumerable questions remained about how these models of care and community organization could be implemented in diverse cultural contexts. To answer that question, I began interviewing RM and ROSC pioneers from around the country across diverse community settings and cultural contexts. These interviews, which span 2007-2016, allowed those in leadership at federal, state, and local levels to share their experiences with RM/ROSC implementation and what they had learned from these processes. As the interviews continued—now surpassing 35 posted interviews, I was humbled and left in awe at the deep dedication of the people attempting this work. Rather than obsess over all the obstacles to change, here were people who simply did it in spite of all those obstacles. Few things in my career have inspired me more.

Precovery

For years, I have written about the need for what I have called recovery priming—identifying, engaging, and motivating people in need of addiction recovery. In fact, my earliest days as a "streetworker" more than four decades ago focused specifically on such work. But during those years, I lacked the experience to fully conceptualize this process. During 2012 and 2013, I maintained a sustained meditation on what precisely happens within the years, months, and days that precede conscious recovery initiation. What became evident was that, for many people, the recovery process begins well before the day of last drug use, but little attention has been given to this period of recovery priming that unfolds during active drug use. I came to think of this period as *precovery*. Reviewing over four decades of personal and professional experiences working with active drug users transitioning into recovery, I concluded that the first day of abstinence was not the first milestone of recovery initiation but the outcome of a movement towards healing and wholeness that has in many cases been unfolding for quite some time.

Precovery involves several simultaneous processes: physical depletion of the drug's once esteemed value, cognitive disillusionment with the using lifestyle (a "crystallization of discontent" resulting from a pro/con analysis of "the life"), growing emotional distress and self-repugnance, spiritual hunger for something in one's life of greater meaning and purpose, and (perhaps most catalytic in terms of reaching the recovery initiation tipping point) exposure to recovery carriers—people who offer living proof and a contagious hope for a meaningful life in recovery. Collectively, these precovery processes reflect a progressive synergy of pain and hope.

Unfortunately, it can often take decades for these processes to unfold naturally. If a conceptual breakthrough of note is present in the addictions field in recent years, it is that such processes can be stimulated and accelerated. Today, enormous efforts are being expending to accelerate precovery processes for cancer, heart disease, diabetes, asthma, and other chronic disorders. We as a culture are not waiting for people to seek help at the latest stages of these disorders when their potentially fatal consequences can no longer be ignored. We are identifying these disorders early, engaging those with these disorders in assertive treatment and sustained recovery monitoring and support processes. What are you and your program doing to accelerate these precovery processes for those in the earliest stages of their addiction careers? Imagine what it would mean to these individuals, their families, and their communities if we could even cut their years of addiction in half. What we lack as a culture is not the technology to achieve that goal but the collective compassion and commitment to do it.

Recovery and Harm Reduction

Another area of contention encountered in my recovery management (RM) and recovery-oriented systems of care (ROSC) work was the question of if and how the large menu of harm reduction (HR) strategies could and should be integrated into the redesign of addiction treatment. This, of course, included the question of HR-oriented medication strategies, but it also encompassed a far broader range of potential strategies that had long been heatedly debated within the addictions field. In 2013, Dr. Arthur Evans, Roland Lamb, and I co-authored a review on harm reduction and recovery management and described how their respective philosophies and service elements were being creatively integrated within the City of Philadelphia. This review was later followed by a series of published/posted interviews with people like Dr. Alan Marlatt, Dr. Andrew Tatarsky, Dr. Marvin Seppala, Howard Josepher, and Ken Anderson who were attempting similar efforts from around the country in diverse service settings and among diverse service populations.

I drew two things from these experiences. First, I was saddened by the vitriol that so often characterized the polarized debates within the addictions field—so much heat, yet so little illumination. Second, I was inspired by what could happen when dedicated people set aside apparent ideological differences to build collaborative teams focused on the needs of people at different developmental stages of addiction and recovery. What emerged in place after place was a simple understanding that multiple subpopulations of people with highly varied and distinct needs exist and that each of these individuals may require different services and supports at different stages of their addiction, treatment, and recovery careers. That longer term perspective provided a framework for the integration of HR within RM and ROSC system transformation efforts. Are there indications of such integrated efforts in your community? What actions might you take in your role to support such efforts?

Pushback

The advocacy movements of the mid-20th century birthed formal service "programs" that became "agencies" and then "businesses" that evolved into a multi-billion dollar industry. I began to fear that this new industry and those who led it were becoming addicted to money and regulatory compliance. The question for those of us on the front lines of this industry then became how to rise above conditions that could blunt our ability to carry a message of experience, strength, and hope. A second question was how we could rise above the paper, the procedures, the personalities, and the politics to become a catalyst of change.

For those who can rise above our own imperfection and the imperfection of the systems in which you work, this field offers you moments in which you can directly participate in the transformation of another human being. There is nothing in the field more sacred than such moments. For me, advocacy for recovery management (RM) and recovery-oriented systems of care (ROSC) served as a means to forge such a contribution and to maintain fidelity to my reasons for entering this work so many years ago.

Challenging prevailing clinical and business practices in that process, however, did not go unnoticed. Some attacked me for "bashing" treatment and betraying the field. Such criticisms hurt, given my tenure in the field. But they also clarified the nature of my commitments. My personal and professional commitments were never ones of mindless devotion to the institutions that make up this field. They were instead to the individuals and families those institutions were founded to serve. If I challenge the field's institutions, it is out of my belief that they are falling short of that mission. Treatment organizations should not be held to a standard of perfection, but they should be held accountable to fidelity or infidelity to their founding mission.

Many days passed when I felt all I was doing was shouting into an empty cave. I only heard back the echo of my own voice. I still have days when I wonder if I am a Don Quixote masquerading as someone whose voice makes a difference. Such "Am I making a difference?" questions haunt people at all levels of this field. Wounded people need hope, but they also need the truth: about themselves, their family members, and the power, limits, likely outcomes, and the potential for unanticipated consequences of professional interventions. Silence on such matters is not golden.

Leaving Philadelphia

In the spring of 2014, I ended my decade-long consultation relationship with the City of Philadelphia. Health problems prevented regular trips to that wonderful city, and my work had morphed into phone consultations and writing papers on various aspects of the continuing recovery-focused systems transformation process. When I accepted the consulting position, Dr. Arthur Evans, Commissioner of the behavioral health system, offered me an opportunity to use Philadelphia as a laboratory to test for what I was writing about recovery management and recovery-oriented systems of care. Over ten years, I did just that, enjoying the City, its people, and learning beyond what words can express. All of that made ending my service there very difficult. My so-called "retirement" had occurred eighteen months earlier, but ending the Philadelphia work was my deepest realization that my professional life was entering its final chapters.

I was not the only consultant working to aid the systems transformation process in Philadelphia, and I left this role with the sense that others would not be able to fully come into their own until I, through my disengagement, created the space for them to flourish. As I look back today, I am deeply moved by the energy and skill with which others now carry this banner in my absence. Sometimes the best thing we can do for others is to step aside to give them space to grow. Are you filling space that others could now fill? Are you approaching the time to let go of the present and reach out for new ventures?

The Future of RM and ROSC

The journey from idea and vision to implementation and institutionalization of a new approach can be a most difficult one and hard to evaluate, given the discontinuities and disruptions that inevitably mark the life of large social systems. So after investing most of my late career in altering the model of addiction treatment care in the United States, it is fair to ask two questions: 1) Will this effort make a real difference in the future of addiction treatment and recovery? 2) Was it personally worth the effort?

To the first, I say that the final chapters have yet to be written in this movement to assure availability of long-term recovery support for individuals and families affected by the most severe, complex, and enduring alcohol and other drug problems. It will have made a difference if such problems are treated at earlier stages within more accessible, affordable, and effective systems of care and if extended recovery support becomes as routine as the prevailing five-year monitoring and support protocol following cancer treatment.

To the second, I would answer an unequivocal "Yes." There are critical issues that arise within the historical context in which each of us work, and few things are more exhilarating and fulfilling than personal involvement in shaping the fate of these issues. In the face of progress, we can look back to feel we played a part in that. In the face of failure, we can look back knowing we did what we could. Either way, we can look back knowing we were involved in the issues of our day. Do you have such a sense?

Chapter Fifteen
The Field, the Profession, the Person

In this final chapter, we will explore some of the issues that arose within the addiction treatment field over the past half century and see if we can mine some lessons learned from these episodes. In these reflections, we will shift from a focus on individuals and families affected by addiction and models of clinical care and social support to explore some of the professional practice issues faced by addiction counselors, other addictions professionals, and by recovery support specialists. I will also offer some miscellaneous reflections on the interface between our personal and professional lives within this most interesting and unusual of career choices.

The Ethics of Affiliation

The following were common events during my early years in the addictions field. An alcoholism education campaign funded directly or indirectly by the alcohol industry. Alcoholism representatives sitting on the boards of local alcoholism councils. Studies of various drugs published in scientific journals and presented at professional conferences whose authors' work was subsidized by pharmaceutical firms that manufacture the drugs. Published studies in which investigator affiliations with these companies are not clearly declared. Treatment programs offering all expenses paid "education tours" to employee assistance representatives and other referral sources. Tobacco companies donating money to local "drug abuse" councils. Local councils on problem and compulsive gambling funded in great part by contributions from gambling casinos or other sectors of the gaming industry. These types of situations were such a part of the landscape that it took me some time to reflect on their influence and the ethics of such practices.

In 1998, Prevention First in Springfield, Illinois asked if I would help facilitate a dialogue among leading prevention organizations on the ethics of collaborating with alcohol, tobacco, and pharmaceutical companies. We assembled more than 75 people representing community-based prevention programs, state prevention agencies, and larger public health entities such as the American Medical Association.

Using small discussion groups, structured questions, and scales to report group consensus, we were able to take the pulse of the field on key questions related to what we came to call *the ethics of affiliation.*

The consensus conference participants concluded that the missions of the alcohol and tobacco industries were in inherent conflict with prevention organizations and that the potential for mission corruption was great when prevention agencies entered into relationships with these industries. Even those who espoused hope of changing alcohol and tobacco industry policies admitted that the David and Goliath nature of this relationship made such influence unlikely. Conference participants found many core ethical values relevant to decisions related to such relationships. The *freedom and autonomy* of prevention organizations to advocate on key alcohol policy questions could by undermined by financial linkages with and potential financial dependence upon organizations that manufacture, distribute, market and sell alcohol, tobacco, and pharmaceutical (ATP) products. The values of *fidelity and loyalty* demand that prevention organizations not weaken their fiduciary promise to serve their communities. Forum participants expressed fears that this promise could be compromised for personal/institutional self-interest via acceptance of money from the ATP industries. They were concerned that accepting funds from ATP industries in support of prevention initiatives could potentially do more harm and injury to the community than the good that could be potentially achieved through such monies.

In short, participants believed potential iatrogenic effects from collaborations undermine the prevention message and inadvertently empower ATP companies to more effectively promote their products, thus violating the ethical value of *nonmaleficence.* Finally, participants were concerned that soliciting/accepting funds from ATP industries, while helping prevention organizations in the short run, could injure these same organizations in the long run, violating the ethical value of *self-interest.* This exercise deepened my understanding of the ways in which professional judgments can be compromised by ill-considered decisions that create real or perceived conflicts of interest.

So how do we make such calls? Several questions have served me well in deciding to whom I will and will not lend my name and presence. The questions are: 1) What are the interests of those requesting my involvement? 2) Are these interests in conflict with my personal/professional values? 3) Would my involvement with these parties help or harm my future work within the addictions field and the organizations with whom I am currently affiliated?

Ethics is about what we do or fail to do and the effects of those actions or inactions on others and on ourselves. It is also about who we are standing with and the effects those relationship choices have on the world and ourselves. Are you standing close to any organization that heightens your ethical discomfort?

Death by Atrophy and Absorption

After the numerous program closings in the early 1990s, the addiction treatment field seemed to be growing again in the late 1990s. I attended conferences with growing numbers of new faces and asked the sponsors how this could be in light of program closures. The answer was that addiction treatment was being added as an appendage to other systems. People were present from prison treatment programs, re-entry programs, specialized probation programs, and drug courts. Public Welfare specialists attended who were running treatment tracks linked to public assistance. Public health specialists were there who were focused on HIV/AIDS and other addiction-related disease management, and medical personnel were there who were involved in brief screening and intervention in primary health care settings. Child welfare specialists attended in great numbers—they filled roles in treatment tracks for addicted mothers with histories of abuse or neglect of their children.

Seen as a whole, it appeared the addictions treatment field was growing, but that perceived growth has a more complex story. The field was growing at its periphery at the same time its core was shrinking. If that trend continues, the field could disappear with the lingering illusion that specialized addiction treatment services continue to be available. Take a few moments to reflect on recent developments in addiction treatment in your local community and in your state. What are the degrees of growth and shrinkage at the core and at the periphery of the field in your city and state?

A Leadership and Workforce Crisis

Many things led to the virtual collapse of America's first network of addiction treatment institutions. One of those factors was the aging out of the field's leadership and failure to address the issues of leadership development and succession planning. The leaders who had birthed the field in the 1860s and 1870s and nurtured that field to maturity in the 1880s and 1890s simply were not available to respond to the threats to the field in the opening decades of the 20th century. The field might aptly be described as having died, in part, of old age.

As briefly referenced earlier, by the mid-1990s, I was convinced that this death by aging could be replicated if we as a field did not address this challenge of leadership and workforce development. In every sector of the field—policy, administration, clinical services, research, training—critical positions were filled with long-tenured and talented individuals who would be leaving in mass in the opening two decades of the 21st century. The clock was ticking and little had been done to create a new generation of leaders or to recruit a new generation of front line workers.

I tried to sound the alarm about this issue for several years in diverse speaking forums and in a series of articles. The first of these articles, entitled "The Coming Leadership Crisis in Addiction Treatment" was published in 2002 in my regular history column in *Counselor*. It recounted an earlier leadership crisis that had contributed to the collapse of America's first network of inebriate homes and asylums in the opening years of the 20th century. It then profiled the current aging of the addictions field's workforce and called for a sustained process of succession planning, leadership development, and workforce recruitment.

The second article co-authored with Lonnetta Albright of the Great Lakes Addiction Technology Transfer Center, was published in *Addiction Professional* in 2006. It challenged aspiring leaders in the field to: 1) fully commit yourself to the field, 2) orient yourself to the field, 3) develop a personalized leadership vision, 4) study the great leaders, 5) expect obstacles, 6) expand your educational and experiential credentials, 6) actively participate in professional associations, 7) cultivate professional mentors, 8) participate in formal

424

leadership development initiatives, 9) build networks of influence, 10) recognize and actively manage toxic personal and organizational processes, 10) strengthen your character, 11) conduct yourself as a role model, 12) create a personal leadership plan, 13) continually re-assess yourself, and 14) study and engage the next generation.

Other personal responses to this issue included efforts to recruit and mentor new trainers and writers in the field through two books (*The Training Life* and *The Call to Write*) and increased time mentoring those I saw as up and coming leaders in my specialty areas. The latter included collaborations (with Bob Carty, Felicia Dudek, Bruce Joleau, Mark Sanders, Joe Rosenfeld, and Pam Woll) to develop training of trainer workshops for aspiring trainers that were presented for many years through various addiction professional associations and the addiction technology transfer centers. Writing this book is an attempt to offer a final gift to those who will follow me.

The field did respond to these calls with various leadership and workforce development initiatives. Participating in various leadership development institutes was a source of great satisfaction to me in the opening decade of the new century. Whether the field's response was sufficient enough will have to be judged by those reading these words in the future. If you were to look at the "big picture" of the field today, what emerging workforce needs do you see? What role could you play in acknowledging and responding to these needs?

Rituals of Disengagement

As the addictions treatment field evolved from a social movement to a profession and then a business, considerable effort was made to elevate how we screen, select, hire, orient, and train new people entering our organizations. But little time has been devoted to the creation of rituals of disengagement that help people leave in ways that enhance their own health and the health of the organization. This is particularly true for long-term employees. Disengaging can be particularly troubling when it involves a person who has been central to the life of an organization and the field. I have encountered a number of situations in which organizations wrestled, often quite awkwardly, about how to structure the final contributions and disengagement of such individuals. In 2006, Russ Hagen and I co-authored an article aimed at organizational leaders in which we suggested nine prescriptions to guide this process of disengagement: 1) time your exit, 2) deal with leadership transitions openly, 3) define leadership transitions in terms of opportunity, 4) develop an exit strategy, 5) create leadership development and succession plans, 6) develop leaders at all levels and in all positions, 7) solidify your legacy, 8) pass it on (Mentor), 9) arrange a proper goodbye, and 10) get out of the way (find new pathways of service).

This is an issue that should be of concern to all of us. Remember, with persistence and good fortune, the time will come when you will face this dilemma and opportunity.

The Ethics and Etiquette of Drug Use

I experienced many times in my career when I tried to spark broad discussion of a particular issue related to the ethics or professional etiquette of addiction counseling. None of these issues was more challenging than the question of how the addiction professional's personal alcohol, tobacco, and other drug (ATOD) use affected his or her professional practice. This issue was difficult for a variety of reasons.

First, many recovering people worked in the field. Thus, the question of how recovery status and particular pathways and styles of recovery could aid or inhibit the counseling process was relevant. Also, I wondered how biases learned in particular cultures of addiction and recovery could spill forward into our work as professional counselors.

Second, some working in the field did not bring a personal or family history of alcohol and drug addiction. How could the ability to maintain one's own relationship with alcohol inadvertently breed attitudes of incomprehension and contempt toward those who lacked such powers of control? For this same group, what were the ethics and etiquette of private and public drinking and drug use? And the giant issue of smoking within the field continued to unleash strong emotion at every turn as a professional practice issue.

It took a long time for me to accumulate observations and sort out what I thought needed to be said on these issues. I interspersed comments in various speeches and workshops over the years, but it wasn't until 2006 that I addressed this subject in a focused manner. The result was an extensive essay that was published by the Great Lakes Addiction Technology Transfer Center and later published in

Alcoholism Treatment Quarterly. This article achieved its goal of stirring discussion in the field and it offered guidelines on a broad spectrum of issues related to ATOD use (or non-use) by addiction professionals. The suggested guidelines included the following:

1. Respect the fishbowl effect that accompanies work in a status- and stigma-laden field.
2. As a professional leader, seek not a life of perfection, but a life of reasonable congruence between the field's core values and your daily conduct.
3. Filter decisions related to disclosure of your ATOD use history, your recovery status, and your pathway(s) of recovery initiation and maintenance through the values of honesty (tell the truth), discretion (protect your privacy), and, for those in Twelve-Step recovery, the tradition and spiritual principle of anonymity.
4. If you are in recovery, cultivate and sustain mechanisms of recovery maintenance separate from your professional life.
5. Rigorously evaluate your own past or current relationships with ATODs, their role in your decision to work in the addictions field, and the congruence or incongruence between those relationships and your service responsibilities.
6. Use your personal/family ATOD-related history and your broader life experiences to enhance mutual identification and acceptance in the service relationship, convey hope and encouragement, and model skills essential to recovery self-management.
7. If you drink alcohol, use discretion related to when, where, and under what circumstances you drink; the amount you drink; and how you conduct yourself while drinking ("the night has a thousand eyes").
8. If you work within an organizational culture that promotes excessive ATOD consumption, cultivate an outside-of-work support system to neutralize the influence of that culture, develop a sobriety-based support network within this setting, and explore relocation to a healthier organizational environment.
9. If you are consuming over-the-counter or prescription drugs with psychoactive effects or side effects, communicate this status to your clinical supervisor and/or a trusted professional

peer, with the request that they help monitor your performance for any untoward effects.

10. If you are in recovery and have resumed ATOD use, you have a professional responsibility to immediately report this change in status to your clinical supervisor; evaluate the effect of this changed status on your clinical performance; and seek immediate help to prevent future harm to yourself, your clients, your organization, and the integrity of the field.

11. If you wish to return to the field in a clinical role after ATOD use and a re-stabilization of your recovery, your chances are best if you demonstrate your willingness to meet the highest standards of supervision, e.g., your willingness to: 1) re-enter the field on a probationary status, 2) accept any requested limitation of duties, 3) participate in a formal impaired professionals treatment program, 4) provide random urine drops, 5) provide verification of counseling participation, 6) provide verification of participation in recovery mutual aid meetings, and 7) have a professional peer mentor.

12. If you are using illicit drugs, evaluate the potential effects of such use on those to whom you are personally and professionally accountable.

13. Adhere to all current legal, professional, and organizational standards related to ATOD use.

14. Immediately declare to your supervisor any pre-existing relationship with a potential or admitted client (or a client's family member) with whom your past alcohol and other drug (AOD) use or related activities could affect the client's feelings of safety and comfort receiving services at your organization.

15. Remain cognizant of how your reasons for using ATOD influence your attitudes toward, relationships with, and biases related to treatment goals and methods for each client.

16. If you are addicted to nicotine and working as an addictions professional, you have a responsibility to initiate and sustain recovery from that addiction, and to keep seeking personal/professional support until that goal is achieved permanently.

17. Disclose your past or present ATOD experiences and decisions with clients only if that disclosure is clinically strategic, brief, appropriate for the developmental stage of the service

relationship, and restricted to past material over which you have emotional control.

Does your review of these guidelines reveal any areas where you need to take action?

This work was an example of how to serve the field by throwing oneself into the fray even when it is likely to stir controversy. The issue is not whether everyone likes what you say. The issue is whether your involvement in a particular issue helps move the field forward. A sacrifice in short-term popularity may well serve your organization or the field in the long run. Are there such issues about which you have felt the need to speak out? Are you willing to take the heat for asking the field to confront these issues?

An Eloquent Silence

One of the challenges of developing one's craft in the addictions field—or any field for that matter—is learning when to speak and when to be silent, when to make statements, and when to ask questions. Each of us has a style of communication that constitutes our personal zone of comfort. Sometimes, that zone must be extended to enhance our professional effectiveness. As someone whose mind has always been in a racing mode, my mouth is prone to move at that same pace. During much of my early career, I thought that my influence upon others came from the words I spoke and the ideas I conveyed. I viewed spoken words as the medium through which my influence and my career would advance. The result of this orientation is that one spends most interactions formulating thoughts and speaking rather than listening and reflecting. In the middle of my life, I spent most of my time talking from one professional pulpit or another trying to change the world with my words. I think of this as the noisy stage of my life.

Over the past ten years, I have reached a quiet period of my professional life in the sense that, as I have acquired greater knowledge over my career, I find I am speaking less. When people contact me now for guidance, I find what they need most is not my voice but my ears and my empathy. A few years ago, I had the opportunity to participate in a meeting filled with many speakers who I had long known and mentored at different times. I felt a deep sense of satisfaction to see how each had found his or her own voice. It dawned on me later that I had

429

not spoken a word during the meeting and yet had the sense that I had been more eloquent in that meeting than in any conference keynote address I had ever given. Perhaps we are most eloquent when we speak through the lives of others. Who are you speaking through?

A Woman's World (Feminization of the Field Revisited)

The addiction treatment field's transition from a man's world to a woman's world unfolded slowly and steadily over the course of my career. Many things influenced that transition: the professionalization of the field and the need for increased academic credentials, the resulting reduced percentage of recovering men working in the field, the salary structure of the field, and the development of new programs that attracted many women into the field. What do you think are the most important factors that have increased the representation of women working as addiction professionals?

Through my history column in *Counselor*, I tried to celebrate the feminization of the field. I authored and co-authored five important pieces. The first told the early story of addiction, treatment, and recovery among American women. The second identified more than 60 women who had made significant contributions to the addiction treatment and recovery fields. The third told the history of treatment services for women at three institutions: Hazelden, Caron Treatment Centers, and the Betty Ford Center. A fourth article, published in *Addiction Professional* in 2007, was a tribute to Mrs. Betty Ford commemorating the 25th anniversary of the opening of the Betty Ford Center. This was followed by an article of tribute to Dr. LeClair Bissell, an addiction medicine pioneer and long-time field activist who died in late 2008.

When I entered the addictions field in the 1960s, special efforts were underway to recruit and retain women. As I leave the field, similar efforts are underway in some settings to recruit and retain men. It's amazing how things can change over the course of a single career. What changes have you witnessed since entering the field?

Honoring Institutional Leaders

The first publication of *Slaying the Dragon* in 1998 and a long series of follow-up articles on the history of the field firmly linked my name to any discussion of the history of addiction treatment and recovery. What that did was open opportunities for me to help capture the history of many of the institutional pioneers in the addictions field. I began a series of articles on the history of addiction counseling that led to a regular history column in *Counselor Magazine*. The next opportunity came when I was asked to write brief institutional histories of the National Council on Alcoholism and Drug Dependence (NCADD) and the Christopher B. Smithers Foundation for inclusion in the *Alcohol and Temperance in Modern History* published in 2003. In 2004, I was approached by Stacia Murphy, then President of NCADD, with a request to write a short booklet on the history of NCADD to help celebrate the organization's 60th anniversary. I collaborated with Ames Sweet of NCADD on writing this history and tribute.

In 2006, I was approached by Ron Hunsicker, then CEO of the National Association of Addiction Treatment Providers (NAATP) with a request to write a history of NAATP for its 30th anniversary as an organization. That project provided me the opportunity to interview many pioneers of private addiction treatment in the United States. My years working primarily in the public sector had given me only a cursory understanding of private addiction treatment. Through the NAATP project, I realized more deeply than I ever had the many branches of the field of addiction treatment and how hard it was to grasp the field as a whole. In 2010, I started a new "Pioneer Series" of interviews in *Counselor* in which I interviewed some of the field's pioneers in such areas as policy, research, treatment, and harm reduction. Those interviews expanded my sense of the "field" and the remarkable group of people who have committed their lives to working in it.

Which branches of the field do you know the least about? How could you increase your understanding of these other arenas of addiction treatment and recovery support services?

431

Eye of the Hurricane

My life ran smoothly during my years spent traveling as an addictions trainer and conference presenter. Blessed by good health, I missed only a day or two of work over a span of fifteen years. My personal and family lives were fulfilling and predictable. My work at Chestnut Health Systems remained engaging but not overwhelming, even during and after my relocation to Florida. All of this gave me the illusion of power and control over my life. That illusion was shattered in 2004 when a hurricane named Charley that was supposed to go elsewhere made an unexpected right turn into Charlotte Harbor and wrought devastation on the quaint communities surrounding my home. The days without power and phones, months of dealing with insurance companies and contractors, and thousands of dollars in unplanned expenses reminded me of the many things in my life over which I had no control. It also reminded me that the health and peacefulness that had pervaded my life was a precious gift that could change in a moment.

My wife and I worked through the aftermath of Hurricane Charley as best we could, and I missed only a few scheduled conference presentations. But I re-entered my work with a sharpened awareness of things around me. I seemed to see more clearly, feel more deeply, and act with an unprecedented sensitivity to what I was doing and experiencing. Charley was a wake-up call—a message that I could take none of the joy and predictability in my life for granted and that I could not even take my life itself for granted. Charley added a degree of heightened focus to my life and a greater commitment to finish tasks that I thought constituted an important legacy to the field. What I also didn't realize at the time was that this experience would prepare me to help respond a year later to the needs of recovering people displaced by the devastation of Hurricane Katrina on the Gulf Coast of Louisiana and Mississippi.

What experiences in your life have brought pain and disruption in the short run, but unexpected gifts in the long run? What unfinished business in this field remains uncompleted for you? Is now the time to move that work forward? Is it possible that something you are going through right now is preparing you for something in the future that is beyond your imagination?

Lessons from the Women in my Life

Things that inspire our work can come from many places, including events in our personal lives that inject fresh energy or perspective to our professional service activities. I have been blessed by incredibly strong women in my life—a now 94-year-old mother whose service ethic knows no bounds, sisters who have mirrored her efforts to be helpful to others, and a wife for whom my admiration grows daily. With that as a backdrop, I received an important lesson from my daughter, Alisha, as I watched her respond to a learning disability that had made her early school experiences frustrating and painful.

Getting Alisha's condition diagnosed early was an important breakthrough. She was taught that she could learn, but that it would take approaches different from her peers. That was a nice way of saying she was going to have to master some special learning techniques and work harder than other students to progress through her school years. And that is what she did. She fought through the frustration and personal insults and simply wouldn't give up. She became an expert on her own style of learning. She mastered what it took for her to listen and comprehend and how she needed to approach homework assignments and exams. She sought out consultants who offered guidance on how to master new and difficult tasks, but she took personal responsibility for that learning. Her attitude was that it was her problem and therefore had to be her solution. She faced that problem head-on and did it with a grace and style that touched me deeply.

I wish I could take some credit for her remarkable attitude and how it guided her through high school, college, a master's program, and most recently, completion of a doctoral program, but I have been more of an admiring bystander than a coach in this process. I am in awe of her ability to just keep on keeping on. I am in awe of her courage. When I face difficult challenges, I think of how tenacious she was in the face of her frustration. She is my role model. (In May 2011, Alisha White completed her PhD in English Studies at Georgia State University. I cannot describe the pride I felt on that day of her persistence and the woman she had become. She currently teaches at Western Illinois University.)

Sometimes inspiration is right under our noses; we just must see it. Are there examples of courage, fortitude, and creativity that

433

exist close to you that you've failed to fully appreciate and acknowledge?

A Case Study in Integrity

Dr. William Miller is a person whose body of lifetime work I greatly admire. One episode taught me something about his character and about the meaning of professional integrity. Dr. Miller had long demonstrated an interest in spirituality which always surprised me a bit, given his reputation as a hard scientist. Buried among his hundreds of publications, one could find pieces on Biblical perspectives on alcohol use, spirituality as an untapped force in treatment, and conversion-like experiences so profound that they can serve as a catalyst for long-term addiction recovery. I had greatly admired the meticulously crafted, peer-reviewed articles summarizing his scientific studies and the piercing scientific analysis he brought to his many published commentaries, and yet lurking there in the background was Bill's fascination with the power of religious and spiritual experiences. That such orientation and interest could co-exist in the same man was something of a fascination to me.

The next chapter in this saga begins with Bill's retirement as Distinguished Professor of Psychology and Psychiatry at the University of New Mexico. Yet, he continues involvement in hand-picked projects. The Robert Wood Johnson Foundation honored Bill's achievement with an Innovators Award that provided him funds to study a topic of his choosing. The subject Bill chose was the influence of integrating spiritual guidance into addiction treatment on post-treatment spiritual practices and recovery outcomes.

In 2009, I was asked by Dr. Tom McLellan, then Editor of the *Journal of Substance Abuse Treatment*, to write a commentary on the results of Bill's work. When Tom briefly described the design of two controlled studies, I immediately recognized these studies as the most scientifically rigorous and elegant investigations of spirituality and addiction treatment that had been completed. I expected to read findings that provided the scientific support for integrating spirituality as an evidenced-based practice in addition treatment. And I suspected that was what Bill had set out to test and suspected he would find. But the plot thickened when the paper arrived for my review.

The design of the studies was even more rigorous than I expected—subject pools big enough to provide lots of statistical power, cohort assignment to treatment as usual plus the tested intervention or treatment as usual without the intervention, an intervention design that gave experimental subjects a choice of 13 different spiritual disciplines, manualized delivery of a 12-session intervention focusing on those disciplines chosen, careful selection and training of staff delivering the intervention, rigorous fidelity monitoring, good follow-up rates, and interviewer blinding to whether subjects were in the control group or intervention group. As I said, quite rigorous and elegant. And the results revealed no measurable effects of the spiritual guidance (SG) intervention on recovery outcomes.

So what do we take from this? Other studies on spirituality and recovery will follow these initial efforts led by Bill Miller. But what does this tell us about the man? How many treatment professionals would publish a study concluding that a treatment intervention they passionately believed in simply had no measurable effects? The publication of Miller's SG study is professional integrity at its finest. This is science at its best—why science must test most importantly what we view as most self-evident. Science is as much about discovering what does not work as discovering what does work, with whom, and why. That's another lesson I learned from Bill Miller.

A Good Week (On Professional Passion)

Sometimes I lament the loss of passion and vision in the addictions field. When it transitioned from a social movement to a professional field to a health sector industry to a profit-focused business enterprise, much of the passion was bled out—or I should say extruded out (counseling of old-timers who didn't fit the new world), screened out (failure to hire newbies perceived as having too much passion), and trained out (the depersonalization of addiction counseling). Now, before I break into a rant about the "good old days" (Don't you hate it when old people do that!), let me remind you as I've noted in these pages that the old days weren't that good and much is wonderful about the contemporary field. And let me say further that the laments of old-timers are often our way of mourning our own lost sense of importance. But some days and weeks remind me how blessed the future of this field can be. This was one such week (November 2009).

435

I have worried that the best and brightest were no longer considering the addictions field as a frontier of challenge and creativity within which one could make great contributions. Then I discovered the writings of Stephen Bamber, a young doctoral student from the UK, who has unlimited potential for such contribution: brilliant insights, lucid arguments, and writing that flows like music. I soaked up every word in paper after paper from his young career and knew with an unexpected sense of joy that people like Stephen would far surpass what I have tried to achieve through my writing if they can sustain their focus on recovery as a subject for sustained advocacy.

I have worried that those of us who have spent much of our time translating research to practice were aging out of the field, leaving a potentially widening chasm between the worlds of research, clinical practice, and peer recovery support. Then I received a DVD to preview—one of dozens I regularly get in hopes of an endorsement or a positive published review. Most are a great disappointment—great production with little content or reasonable content with poor production value. But this week came *Pleasure Unwoven*, a DVD that was the brainchild of Dr. Kevin McCauley. The DVD provided the clearest synthesis of the neurobiology of addiction I have ever seen. It left me breathless. Exceptional content, amazing clarity in explaining a complex science, visual images from Utah that made we want to pack my bags and start driving west, and the personage of Dr. McCauley who may well soon qualify as the field's most skilled addiction educator. People like Dr. Kevin McCauley will far surpass what I was able to do on the road speaking for 25 years and that knowledge makes it easier to make peace with having retired from that road work.

I have also come to understand that I am not a passive bystander in this generational transition. When I recognized the depth of Dr. Kevin McCauley's potential contributions, for example, I ask myself how I might widen his pathway of future contributions. To do this, I sent copies of *Pleasure Unwoven* to key people of influence within the field. That led to an invitation to write a review of the DVD for *Alcoholism Treatment Quarterly*, and to write a letter of nomination to receive the 2010 NAATP Michael Q. Ford Journalism award. Hearing that Kevin would receive the award was a special moment for me—an experience of influence well-spent and encouragement well-deserved.

I have wondered if the passion of today's recovery advocates will be devoured as the movement is pushed towards professionalization and commercialization. This week I worked with

436

Lisa Mojer-Torres on a series of papers on medication-assisted recovery. She squeezed this work in amidst side effects of her cancer treatments. In the face of that, how can I raise questions about lost passion?

This week I worked with David Childs, one of the leaders of South Carolina Faces and Voices of Recovery, to plan a recovery event there early next year. David was calling from his car on the way to a work appointment in an industry so high tech I couldn't even understand his description of it. He, like a legion of others across the country, leads and supports the recovery advocacy movement on a volunteer basis. I so enjoyed the call, his delight with the plans for the coming meeting, and his excitement about a vision of peer-led recovery community centers all over South Carolina. His joy was infectious. It reminded me that no one can think he or she leads this movement or that it will not thrive without their presence. David's call made me wish for a long life, not to just contribute to this movement, but to witness the future that David and others will be creating.

The good old days got us here, but what of the days ahead? Now, those are going to be something worth watching and, for many of you reading this, worth saying you were a part of. Yes, it was a pretty good week. Passion is still running deep and still disturbing others as it always will. Those concerned with the still-suffering will always be pushed to the frontier and be a source of disturbance for those whose passion for service, if it ever existed, has been diverted to defending and promoting personal and organizational interests. Keep pushing.

Looking Back: Best Moments; Worst Moments

In looking back over the past four decades, the best moments within my professional life were not when I was standing to receive an award or when I received some unexpected financial advancement. They have instead been in the quiet, intimate emotional encounters with those who have just felt the spark of recovery or at times alone when I was writing words that I hoped would help change the world. The fact that many of my best moments were working on projects for which no one was paying me suggests the need to maintain a professional identity and mission that transcends identification with a particular organization or even identification with the field at a particular point in time. The structures of our current employer and those that make up the field constitute the stages on which our professional drama must be written. They are not ends in themselves to be blindly served.

My worst moments were not the wounds experienced as I witnessed the lethal trajectory of failed efforts at recovery, although these are among the most painful experiences in my career. The worst moments for me were times I fell victim to my own pettiness, when I felt jealous of others' achievements, when I felt resentment that my own work was not more widely recognized, when I was more preoccupied with myself than my message. One of the challenges for all of us is to find a way to use our assets as instruments of service while keeping our egos out of the process as much as possible.

In 2011, Ernie Kurtz and I began an extended conversation about the role of self in recovery. We were struck by what appeared to be two different styles of recovery—one involved an assertion of self and the other a transcendence of self. The very same might be said for contributions in the addictions field. We clearly have personalities marked by characteristics often associated with addiction: narcissism, grandiosity, preoccupations with power and control, etc., and some of these individuals have made significant contributions to the field. But those I most admire contributed to the field while exhibiting a style of ego-deflation that is characteristic of many people in recovery. Once again, the process of helping people recover from addiction seems to parallel the process of recovery itself.

Nowhere is the need to keep our own ego out of our work more evident than in the counseling relationship itself. We are not the source of healing; we are the guide that helps each person we serve find that source. In my journals, are the words of Albert Schweitzer:

> *The witch doctor succeeds for the same reason all the rest of us succeed. Each patient carries his own doctor inside him. They come to us not knowing that truth. We are at our best when we give the doctor who resides within each patient a chance to go to work.*

That "doctor inside" is not ego but something far greater—the essence of the human spirit or, as others might suggest, the seed of God. It is that inner fire that the best counselors awaken.

Order out of Chaos

There is a thread in these musings that is worthy of identification. Much of my professional life seemed pretty chaotic and unplanned as I was moving through it, particularly the first two decades. But in looking back on it today, it has a perfect order, as if each step was necessary to prepare me for the next. Even key milestones, such as going back to school, while appearing to have been clear decisions on my part, were greatly influenced by chance meetings and opportunities. And the jobs I took along the way that were such important steps in my development often had more of a feeling of falling out of the sky than something I sought. That has imbedded within me the belief that we each have a path—not destined ahead of time—but created as we live it and that the most important thing we can do with our careers and our lives is to listen to our heart to determine when we are in the center of that path and when we are drifting off of it. In that sense, personal dissatisfaction is one of the most important things in our lives because it tells us we have lost connection with that path and need to find it or create a new path. Personal content and discontent are gauges that need to be closely monitored. What are your gauges telling you today?

On Self-forgiveness

Accepting our own imperfection requires the capacity to recognize and atone for actions elicited from inadequate knowledge/skill or misjudgments or from more deeply imbedded defects of character. I've found a few things that help with this process and would offer the following prescriptions. When you feel jealous of another's achievement, send a note of congratulations. When you resent the lack of acknowledgement of your work, send an acknowledgement to another person and refocus on the needs of those you serve. When you are wrong or make a mistake, admit it to yourself and another person, learn from it, and keep moving forward. (The work is too important to wallow in self-recrimination.) The guiding mantra is: "Admit mistakes, delete negative behaviors, forgive yourself, get back to work—it's really not about you." I still have to regularly recite this mantra to myself.

439

The Value of Shedding

There have been times in my life when I needed to take a first step in a new direction but was loaded down with so much clutter in my life that such a first step was impossible. Several points in my life occurred when I have tried to figure out how I got so loaded down. We live and work in a culture of consumption—a culture of acquisition. We are programmed to acquire money and things and status, and those of us in service work are prone to acquire an ever-expanding list of responsibilities. As a result, our life can become exceptionally over-extended. Many of the times I have felt most trapped occurred when I had lost the capacity to control my willingness to take on additional responsibilities.

We have talked in these pages about the need to add new people and activities at critical times in our careers/lives, but a point for present consideration is the value of shedding. Careers and lives can be measured not only by what we add, but also by what we subtract. Are there too many possessions in your life? Are there people who are injecting poison in your life? Are there people who are slowly sucking the energy and hope from your life? Are there duties that have become unachievable or unbearable? Are there roles or organizations that it is time to exit? Moving forward requires space. What do you need to move out of the way? What people, activities, and things do you need to shed from your life to lighten your load?

The Addict and the Person: Masked and Unmasked

Historically, helping professionals have viewed those addicted to alcohol and other drugs with contempt. An idea at the center of this contempt is that "the addict" in their most depraved state is the revealed "real person"—unmasked by drug-induced disinhibition. The addictions field has always taken a different view—one that saw the "real" person in the personality and aspirations of the recovering addict. The difference between the specialized addiction treatment field and other clinical disciplines who have attempted to treat the addict can be demarcated by whether the addict is viewed as Dr. Jekyll or Mr. Hyde. Is Dr. Jekyll the authentic person or a mask of normalcy? Is Mr. Hyde the real self or a mutation induced by poison? Those who have played a special role in the history of addiction recovery have long cherished the belief that alcohol and drugs made good people bad and evil people more evil, and that sobriety-mediated redemption was possible for both.

This view has been expressed in many ways, but none more eloquently than at a workshop I was conducting on career development for addiction counselors. One of the exercises I included asked participants to generate a vision statement of what they wanted to achieve before ending their career in the addictions field. One of the women responded as follows when participants were asked to share their responses: "I want to work with the children of addicted parents. I want to teach them that they can hate the disease and still love their parents." That says it all. The disease or disorder or problem (or whatever you call it within your philosophical framework) is not the person.

A Question of Courage

The political climate that rippled into the addictions field in the early years of the new century was oppressive beyond anything I had ever experienced. Certain words could no longer be used in conference presentation titles or reports to government agencies. Invitations to speak came with the proviso that I not talk about certain subjects. Rumors filtered through the research community of scientists whose grants had been cut following presentations of research findings that were not politically palatable. As someone frequently speaking in front of large audiences, I was hyperaware of the price I could pay by the messages I conveyed or failed to convey. I refused to accept invitations that came with blatant or veiled efforts to censor my remarks, but I did turn down many requests to speak on topics that I knew were political lightning rods. My greatest concern was the effect my words could have on organizations with whom I was associated. Besides, I rationalized, many of these subjects were diversions from my focus on recovery research and recovery advocacy. It was only a question of time before a request came in that would pit my fear against my desire to break the silence induced within this oppressive atmosphere. The request arrived just before Christmas in 2006.

The request came from Dr. Gary Fisher, founder and director of the Center for the Application of Substance Abuse Technologies at the University of Nevada. His request was straightforward: "I have written a book on the failure of the war on drugs and I would like you to consider writing a forward for it." Well, here it was. The manuscript that arrived for my review was well-researched, well-argued, and well-written. It was a call for reasoned discussion and a plea to escape the polarized choices set up by equally rabid drug warriors and drug legalizers. I knew immediately that it was a book that would make a lot of people mad on both sides of the political spectrum. The warriors would discount the book as an invitation for drug use and the rabid reformers would say the book did not go far enough. After considering a long list of creative excuses why I would not be able to write the forward, it became clear to me that now was the moment to break my own silence and add my name to those calling for a fundamental re-evaluation of national drug policy. The forward was written and *Rethinking the War on Drugs: Candid Talk about Controversial Issues* was published in September 2006.

The response to *Rethinking the War on Drugs* (and my introductory comments) was one of utter silence. It was as if Gary had never written his book and I had never offered my support of it. That silence was pregnant with meaning. Once again, I was reminded that drug policy is not established through a process of rational debate nor is it changed through such a rational process. No, drug policy is a much more primitive process—one that is much more about racism, sexism, social class, and intergenerational conflict, xenophobia, industrial (licit and illicit) profit, and political manipulation than it is about the public health of American citizens. How naïve and silly of me to think that drug policymakers would read a book documenting the failed performance of those policies, admit their ill-considered passage, and change them. How self-indulgent of me to think that people at that level would even read, let alone be concerned, about a few hundred words I had written on American drug policy. Any delusion of self-importance I had feigned or believed was shattered with this reminder of my lack of access to the arena in which the big dogs play.

A Return to Eagleville

In the spring of 2006, I was contacted by Jim Baker, a board member of Eagleville Hospital in Eagleville, PA, with the news that the board of the hospital wanted to bestow on me the Eagleville Award, an acknowledgement given annually to someone who had made a significant contribution to the addiction treatment field. The award was quite special to me because of my collaborations with Dr. Don Ottenberg and Dr. Jerome Carroll of Eagleville during the early 1970s. Don had been a source of great inspiration to me in my early career and one of my earliest role models. He had exceptional academic training, but drew his authority from his character and his propensity for penetrating observations and candid truth-telling. Don had passed on a few years before my visit with the Eagleville Board, but I felt his presence during my visit to Eagleville in June of 2006. It made me wonder if others who visit Chestnut Health Systems in the years to come would similarly feel my presence. If we are lucky, maybe that is a legacy we leave our organizations and our field—a presence that reminds people that there are people who spent their professional lives delivering the field into their hands.

The message I extended to the board and staff of Eagleville on June 4, 2006 was a challenge to extend the reach of treatment beyond the Eagleville campus and beyond the short time of their involvement with clients. I tried to convey an image of treatment as an extended health care partnership marked by continuity of contact in a primary recovery support relationship. Rather than simply thanking them for the honor of the award, I challenged them to forge a new institutional identity that acted as if they really believed that addiction was a chronic disorder. I used the analogy that when colleges and universities had become too isolated from their local communities, there were calls to create "universities without walls." I challenged the board members of Eagleville to create treatment without walls. I think Don would have liked that.

Are you leaving an imprint on the organization and community in which you are working? What lingering presence do you hope will remain after you leave? Are there places to which you need to return to finish old business?

A Question of Personal Power

Over the course of my career as a trainer, I learned an important lesson about power in the context of interpersonal relationships. What I sought was a platform of mutual respect that could lower resistance (an inevitable outcome of the power differential between audience and speaker) and enhance engagement, communication, and the subsequent learning process. What I discovered was that this often required an adjustment in my own perceived level of power. In some circumstances, my own perceived power needed to be increased and, in others, my power needed to be decreased. For example, when I was training high-status professionals (e.g., physicians, judges, or high-ranking military officers), I made sure that, lacking such credentials, my introductions to such audiences emphasized my formal education and training, my past work with related organizations, and my familiarity with their history and culture. In other settings, such as speaking to various recovery community organizations, I asked that such introductions not include my academic credentials but instead emphasized my direct experience with my subject matter, e.g., my work with recovery advocacy organizations around the country. I discovered as I interacted with audiences that power could be increased or decreased by altering such things as manner of dress, the style of presentation (e.g., degree of formality), or altering how I drew on my own expertise or the expertise of my audience.

Sometimes, you will want to increase your power, and sometimes, you will need to diminish your power. That applies to therapeutic and training encounters, but it also applies to all other human interactions. When our power is too high, it breeds envy, competition, and resistance; when it is too low, it can invite disrespect and invisibility. Both extremes can impair engagement and invite aggression. A good habit to get into is that of checking the measure of your perceived power and making adjustments as needed.

The Legacy Project

Early in our careers, we are too committed to action and in possession of too little self-awareness and awareness of the history of our profession to give much thought to what personal legacy we would like to leave the field. But with the accumulation of years, an awareness that our days in the field will end develops and we realize the field will go on in our absence. Often toward the end of our careers, we give thought to what positive imprint we would like to leave—some final contribution to the future of our organization, our community, or the larger professional field. My own preoccupation with legacy began early—in part because my work in the field was such a big part of my life and because of my own uncertain life expectancy. Rather than leave my potential legacy to chance, I wrote out what I called my "Legacy Project."

What I did first was identify what I saw as the major needs of the field. I then picked those that I thought I might be able to contribute to. The topical areas I chose included outreach and engagement, clinical supervision, the special treatment needs of women and adolescents, professional ethics, the history of treatment and recovery, and personal and organizational health. Within each of these areas, I then tried to figure out how I could make my mark in that area. It served as my own evolving "to do" list. When something was completed, I added it to the plan as an accomplishment. When a need appeared, I listed it and added a "to do" task under it. A key to my productivity in the field is this project that has now been in place for more than 35 years.

As a new century began, I asked myself what I could do within my remaining years that could influence the future of addiction treatment and recovery. After considerable reflection, I settled on the following major professional goals:

- Shift the governing idea within the field from a focus on the problem (addiction) and the proposed clinical remedy (addiction treatment) to a focus on the lived solution (long-term personal and family recovery) and the lessons that can be drawn from the millions of people in long-term recovery,
- Extend acute care models of addiction treatment to models of sustained recovery management nested within larger recovery-oriented systems of care,
- Promote the growth and diversification of recovery mutual aid societies,
- Promote the development of new recovery support institutions in the community space beyond addiction treatment and recovery mutual aid, and
- Help culturally and politically mobilize people in recovery and their allies via the birth and maturation of a new recovery advocacy movement.

I replicated such legacy goal-setting in my mentoring of others. For example, Mark Sanders and I have met each year for many years to review and refine his annual professional goals. I think that ritual has contributed significantly to what he has been able to do for the field, and confirmed for me the power of formal goal setting. Perhaps it is time to consciously begin to shape or consolidate your own legacy.

You can contribute to the field in a number of ways. Many people aspire to do that one big thing that will stand as a contribution or generate fame or fortune. Some people do make such singular contributions. But a more common pattern of contribution is from those who leave their imprint on a field through a collective body of work spread over the course of their life. That work may or may not be visible to others or garner great public attention, but great achievements are built on the backs of those whose names will be lost to history. We do not all have to be stars to contribute and to know that our lives have made a difference to the individuals, families, and communities we serve. Is it time to think about the type of contribution you would like to make? What can you do now to start your own Legacy Project? Starting small with one or two goals might work to help you gain momentum.

Meeting Jean Kilbourne and Others

In the spring of 2005, I was asked to keynote a conference celebrating the anniversary of the founding of the National Council on Alcoholism and Drug Dependence (NCADD) in St. Louis, Missouri. One of the joys of presenting at lots of conferences is that you get a chance to meet many pioneers within several areas of the field. On this day, I heard Dr. Jean Kilbourne speak on the targeting of women by the alcohol, tobacco, and pharmaceutical industries. Her presentation was riveting both in the scope and depth of her research as well as in her exceptional presentation skills. In the months that followed, we exchanged communications about our mutual interest in the history of addiction and recovery among American women. Those exchanges led to collaboration on an article that generated wide responses from recovering women and service professionals around the country.

As I now reflect back on this collaboration, I recall how close I came to not approaching Jean about working together on this project. My hesitancy came out of my own self-consciousness about approaching someone I greatly admired. I have had to chastise myself throughout my career and goad myself into action to move into areas of service that involved collaborations with others whom I admired but did

446

not know. My infernal shyness in making these initial contacts served neither myself nor the field and stood as an obstacle that even at this late stage of my career I must continue to conquer. I have developed my own self-talk to help push me into action. The mantra says simply, "Stop obsessing and just do it!" With that, I pick up the phone or send an email I've written in my head far too many times. It really is that simple. Sometimes you just have to do it!

An Embarrassment of Riches

Receiving praise from one's professional peers is a source of confirmation that one's vision and work are making a difference. In the summer of 2006, I was stunned to get a letter from the American Society of Addiction Medicine (ASAM) informing me that I was to be awarded the John P. McGovern, MD Award for "outstanding contributions to the field of Addiction Medicine." The award was presented at the ASAM annual meeting and also involved a brief lecture by myself on the history and future of addiction medicine. As the date of this award drew near, I couldn't help but think of the many unsung heroes in the addictions field who have never been called to a podium and thanked for their commitment, competence, and enduring contributions. I vowed to use the ASAM award to acknowledge some of those unsung heroes who had influenced my own career. In the days before the award, I sent emails and letters to many people thanking them for their contributions to my own growth and acknowledging that any praise for what I had achieved was unspoken praise for the role they had played to make that possible.

As I stood that day to accept the award, I felt this network of influence standing with me, for the award that day was not for my work, it was for our work. That was the same attitude I embraced when a few weeks later Griffith Edwards, editor of the international journal, *Addiction*, requested that I participate in their interview series of notable contributors to the addictions field. Here again was an opportunity to thank those who had exerted such an influence on my own development and contributions. Who do you need to thank for making possible the contributions you have made, are making, or will make?

But that was not the end of the sudden flurry of recognition. In October 2006, I received notice of having been awarded a lifetime achievement award by NAADAC: The Association of Addiction

447

Professionals and a week later received the Jeff Luke Servant Leadership Award from White Bison for service to the Native American Wellbriety Movement. The latter was one of the most remarkable experiences of my life—receiving the award in an honor ceremony led by Horace Axtell, a Nez Pierce Elder, with sage smoke fanned over me with eagle feathers while an honor song was being sung—all in front of a standing audience of Native American Wellbriety leaders from across North America. Words cannot convey the power of this experience. A few hours later, Don Coyhis and I signed and distributed copies of the just-published *Alcohol Problems in Native America: The Untold Story of Resistance and Recovery—The Truth about the Lie*. It was an amazing day.

And yet something in this flurry of recognition was unsettling. I had worked hard to suppress my ego and to cultivate an attitude of humility through my writing and speaking and yet here was a flood of recognition that focused not just on the content of my work but on me as a person. The personal nature of this recognition was something of an embarrassment and seemed a threat in some unidentifiable way. My early sense of being flawed had fueled my desire for recognition and sparked envy when I saw others stand to receive awards at professional conferences. I had acknowledged such feelings and had made peace with service for the sake of service and work for its own innate pleasure, only to then have recognition come that I no longer expected or desired. This is so typical of the paradoxes of the long-term recovery experience: you are most likely to receive the thing you are seeking at the same time you stop the frenzied search for it. When I talk this way at home, my wife calls me "Grasshopper" (for my younger readers, this was the moniker given Caine, the central character in the television series, *Kung Fu*, whose philosophical musings sounded at times like slips from fortune cookies.)

Sustaining contributions to a field and one's own emotional health over a lifetime require a delicate balance. We must find sufficient sources of acknowledgment to keep us engaged, motivated, and productive. At the same time, we have to manage periods of excessive acknowledgment that shift the focus of what we do from those we serve to ourselves. In the wake of the above acknowledgment, I received a request to be part of an Elders Project of the Connecticut Community of Addiction Recovery—a video recording of people in long-term recovery and what they had learned about the recovery process. I was deeply honored by this request, but declined (actually postponed) my involvement in this project until I felt I could absorb the experience. I also initiated a new project with Faces and Voices of Recovery to interview local recovery advocates that had potential to rise to the level of regional and national advocacy leaders. This was a conscious effort to expand the scope of those identified as "recovery advocacy leaders" and to diminish my own visibility. Between these excesses of invisibility and the spotlight lies a zone of peak effectiveness and service. The challenge is to find ways to remain in that zone. Can you recall periods of such peak performance and health? How close or far are you from that state today?

In this flurry of accolades that came my way in 2006 and 2007, one of the most memorable and meaningful occurred off the public stage. I received a letter from Dr. Jerome Jaffe whose distinguished career in the addictions field included heading the Illinois Drug Abuse Program and serving as President Nixon's Drug Czar. As a historian of addiction treatment, I consider Jaffe one of the most influential figures in the modern history of addiction treatment. Prior to receipt of his letter, my few encounters with Dr. Jaffe consisted of brief introductions at a few addictions conferences. Dr. Jaffe's letter included the following:

> *I took your book from the shelf, began to read and was amazed, excited and grateful all at the same time. It is a work of remarkable scholarship that is so exceptionally well written that in the past weeks I often returned to re-read some passages. I know of no other work on treatment quite like it....*

Part of the reason Dr. Jaffe's words were so meaningful was that I had become stuck in several of my writing projects. I seemed acutely preoccupied with the question of whether my writing was making any difference. The words began to flow again after the receipt of Dr. Jaffe's letter. Never underestimate the power of passing on acknowledgments to others. To whom could you send such a message today? What difference might it make in their life and the life of our field? Dr. Jaffe taught me just how much such a communication can mean.

449

Service across the Life Cycle

The challenge of managing a long career is that you are evolving as the field itself evolves. Those parallel processes create the potential for great service opportunities as well as periodic opportunities for a mismatch between personal needs and the needs of the field. The evolution of self and the field requires constant adjustments in the relationship between person, organization, and the larger field. When this fit is perfect, we experience deep satisfaction and the field receives the best gifts we have to offer. When mismatched, we risk disillusionment and disengagement and can even do injury to our organizations and the field.

The implication here is the need for continued self-inventory and active and continuing negotiation of one's role within an organization and the larger field. As I pass my 70th birthday at the time of this writing, I am acutely aware that what I bring to the field today is different than when I was 25. Today, I bring greater knowledge and experience, but less energy, stamina, and time. Today, I am aware that assets and limitations are ever changing. I am aware that I can no longer think of personal visions that will take decades to achieve. I once knew that I could outlive and outwork adversaries that were blocking what I saw as needed change. That is no longer true.

Much of my early career was about building professional power. My middle career was about how to best use the power that I had accumulated. Today, I am focused on how to transfer that power to others and to negotiate a graceful disengagement from my activist agenda. That is not to say that I will not continue to contribute to the field, but that I will do so in quieter, less visible ways. And yet somewhere in the days ahead, if I am blessed with those days, I will need to figure out a way to say goodbye to the field. Or maybe my sustained silence will be such a goodbye.

Where are you in this professional life cycle? How are your assets and vulnerabilities changing? What is it that you need to do at this stage of your life and career?

450

A Most Complicated Man

Throughout my life and career I have met people who defied categorization—people whose complexities and contradictions challenged any transient sense that I knew their essential character. These complex characters included family members, friends, co-workers, and acquaintances who captured my attention and stayed in my life long enough for cracks to appear in the image they projected to others. What distinguished these individuals was that others could hold such widely disparate perceptions of them.

In early 2008, I attended the funeral of one of the most enigmatic of such persons—a man who drank and smoked himself into a mere shell of the man's man he had once been. As I traveled to his funeral, I recalled many things about this man that would have justified him dying alone with his body unclaimed. I thought of his drinking escapades, his womanizing, his abandonment of his family and multiple wives, and the undercurrent of violence that made many, including me, suspect that his final demise would likely not be a serene one. He was self-centered and vane, charming, and manipulative (an exploiter), but above all a survivor. I thought of his shattered family roots—of abandonment and poverty, stories always told with a smile of survival while living under a bridge as a child, of his brothers' many scrapes with the law, and his own escape into the military and into a first marriage that graced him with a period of working class respectability, but a respectability that could not forever contain darker demons within him.

But the darkness that eventually claimed this man is not the whole story. People came to the visitation and funeral in large numbers to pay their respects to him. There were family members, friends, neighbors, union members, church members, and even staff members from the nursing home in which he had spent his final months. They came to honor their shared laughter and his friendship, generosity, and service. There also were the members of the military honor guard who bid him final thanks on behalf of a country grateful for his contributions in World War II.

Who really was this person they came to bid farewell? I tried to answer that question as I watched the genuine grief in their faces and

451

listened to them recount stories of how his life had touched theirs. And in their responses I understood that this man—my father—was not a bad man or a good man, but a man in whom good and bad lived together in perpetual disharmony. To reduce him to one or the other is to lie by omission. Each time I think of him, I am reminded that good and evil co-exist within each of us, and yes, within me. We become good not by the absence of evil, but by acknowledging and rising above this ever-present shadow and linking ourselves with people who elicit the best within us.

Creative Collaborations

In 1999, I was asked to do a regular history column in *Counselor Magazine*. I had no idea what a marathon venture this would be or that it would provide such an important outlet through which I could regularly communicate with addiction professionals all over the country. Those of us who wish to change the world must find a platform of influence through which such change can be affected. That platform of influence can come in many forms: a role, one or more key relationships, a visible project, a presentation, a paper or book, a website, or any other way we can find to let the universe know we are here. How would you define your own platform of influence? If you have difficulty defining it, perhaps it is time you began consciously planning and constructing such a platform.

About eight years into my regular *Counselor* series, I developed the idea of collaborating with other key people in the field on a series of co-authored articles that would explore the new frontiers of the field. These collaborators included some of the field's leading pioneers, researchers, clinicians, and recovery advocates. I thought of these articles as the "change the world" series, but a funny thing happened along the journey. By involving others in my efforts to change the world, I found myself changing under their influence. Some of these changes were subtle while others were somewhat dramatic. These changes came from ongoing dialogue and from reading the complete writings of those with whom I was collaborating. I think the freshness of the learning that went into these collaborations helped extend the power of their influence on the larger field. But in setting out to change the world, I also changed myself. How could you extend your influence through key collaborations? Choose your collaborators carefully

452

because some will reshape your ideas and character and some may connect you to a now unseen destiny that awaits you.

"On the Corner" and "Keeping it Real"

One of the things I learned in my early years of personal recovery and my professional work as a streetworker and addictions counselor was the importance of "keeping it real." What that meant to me was staying grounded in the realities of both addiction and recovery. When I met the detoxified, cleaned up heroin addict who exuded great personal charm and profuse promises of reform, I reminded myself that this same individual had brutalized family, friends, and community through his or her years of active addiction. Keeping it real was knowing that such evil and such good can co-exist in the same person—that the addicted person, the treatment persona, the young "pigeon" in recovery, and the recovery elder are all metamorphic stages and that my encounter with any one of these personas was not the whole person—not who the person had been or could become. When I met the most degraded and profane addict, I reminded myself that this same individual in recovery could and would achieve things beyond my capacity to envision. And I knew it was important to stay connected to people whose lives offered testimony that such transformative recoveries were not just possible but a living reality for millions of individuals and families. Keeping it real was seeing that potential within the ugliness of active addiction.

"Keeping it real" is possible only, as my friend, Roland Lamb, always reminded me, if we stay working "on the corner"—stay close to the realities of addiction and recovery regardless of our role. How close to the corner are you at this moment in your professional or volunteer service work? Close contact with the corner—active addiction and early recovery—can heighten your helping sensitivities but it can also grind you down—overwhelm you with its pain and emotional rawness. A healing balm can be found in contact with people in long-term recovery. Do you have opportunities to witness afresh the rawness and drug-fueled frenzy of active addiction? How close are you today to the long-term lived solution to addiction? Is it time you were re-sensitized and replenished through such contacts? Draw deeply from those wells.

453

Treading Water

Motivation has rarely been a problem in my professional life. Regularly renewing our commitment to the field and those it serves and keeping multiple projects going at once provides engaging activity for us most of the time. But some days (or stretches of days, weeks, or months), our motivation seems to abandon us. Sometimes, we can overcome this situation through a sheer assertion of will; other times, recapturing our motivation is not so easy. As I have noted several times in these pages, such periods of lost energy, productivity, and satisfaction constitute an important source of feedback that something in our life has moved out of balance or that we have made an unrecognized developmental shift that requires our attention.

Sorting out all of this is not easy, and one is left with the question of what to do in the interim. Sometimes we can get lost and can't move forward without getting a clearer vision of the direction we are going. We may have to tread water for a time, scan the horizon, and refocus ourselves before starting out again. The hardest thing is to accept such moments with faith that a process is unfolding that will reveal itself in its own time. Sometimes it's enough just to stay afloat. It's okay if you feel like you are just floating at the moment. Trust the process.

What would Mel do? (Keeping My Eyes on the Prize)

I have met some remarkable human beings in my more than four decades working in the addictions field, and many of them have helped shaped my own character. One of the most important of these individuals is Mel Schulstad. Mel got sober in the early 1970s and entered the alcoholism field a few years later. He went on to become a co-founder of the National Association of Alcoholism Counselors in 1974, the precursor to NAADAC: The Association of Addiction Professionals. He was a central figure in the professionalization of the role of the addiction counselor in the United States. Mel served as a friend and mentor for many years. Having just passed his 92st birthday as I write this, Mel only recently retired and remains an astute observer of the addiction treatment field. We just finished co-authoring an article, so even now he is not exactly retired.

Mel has long been one of the key people who kept me grounded during the high and low points of my career. It was a complex relationship in many ways. There were days he felt like a father to me, days we were brothers and comrades in arms, and days he served as professional role model and mentor. At other times, he felt like an all-in-one confessor/teacher/sponsor/guide. Perhaps more than anything, he exemplified how to work in this field as a person in recovery and how to stay focused on the recovery mission when a thousand distractions compete for our attention. I can't count the number of times I have asked myself, "What would Mel do?" Do you have a Mel in your life? If so, cherish and nurture that relationship. If not, begin your search for such a person. We all need a guiding star.

Postscript: Mel Schulstad died January 6, 2012, at the age of 93. A tribute to his life and work is posted at www.williamwhitepapers.com

Mr. Bill or Dr. Bill?

In early 2009, my longtime friend and colleague, Mark Sanders, called to inform me that the Addictions Study Program at Governors State University (GSU) in south suburban Chicago had nominated me to receive an honorary doctorate from the University. I was the first person to be nominated for this honor by the Human Services Department, and Mark and others at the Addictions Studies Program worked hard on the nomination application. The nomination itself meant a great deal to me—perhaps because of my own ill-fated diversion away from doctoral studies in my early twenties and my daughter's own enrollment in a doctoral program at the time of my nomination. The whole experience made me nostalgic for a period of my life pregnant with unlimited possibilities.

Mark called me the day after Thanksgiving 2009 to share his disappointment that the selection committee had not chosen me and had instead selected a former Cubs baseball pitcher. My first response was to giggle at the poetic justice of this, given my status as a rabid Cubs fan and to then think that this was the gods' way of reminding me not to take myself too seriously. The work we do is incredibly important, but sometimes we need reminders to cast away any rising delusions of self-importance. The key is to keep the focus on service rather than self, even if we've got a pretty good fastball.

Dr. Nelson Bradley Redux

Dr. Nelson Bradley was a central figure in the development of the Minnesota Model of chemical dependency treatment—first at Willmar State Hospital and then at Lutheran General Hospital's alcoholism treatment unit (the precursor to Parkside Medical Service's national chain of addiction treatment programs). I first met Dr. Bradley at Lutheran General in 1973 as part of a small team of people from Bloomington, Illinois seeking a treatment model that could be replicated or adapted to the needs of our community. Dr. Bradley introduced us to Dr. Jean Rossi, Rev. John Keller, Jim McInerney, and many of the other staff at Lutheran General. Dr. Bradley exhibited a unique blend of humility and graciousness that softened and humanized the intense passion he had about the treatment of alcoholism and its importance to the country. I remember reflecting on the way home that these traits were an admirable combination and that I would be well-served to try to emulate them in my own work in the field.

On October 23, 2009, I received word that I would be awarded the National Association of Addiction Treatment Providers' 2010 Dr. Nelson J. Bradley Lifetime Achievement Award. News of the award reminded me once again of that initial meeting with Dr. Bradley and how influential he had been in my life. The program of Alcoholics Anonymous has existed for nearly 75 years on the principle of attraction: "If you have decided you want what we have and are willing to go to any length to get it...." Throughout my career, I have been drawn to people who conducted their personal and professional lives on that same principle. Dr. Bradley was a person who had many qualities I wanted. He influenced many people in the addictions field through his insights into addiction and recovery, his long career, and the sheer power of his personality. I am one of those grateful people.

As I reflected on the award that bears his name, I realized that it stood for, not so much a personal achievement on my part as the success of a movement. I was but a link in the chain of that movement, as was Dr. Bradley. Perhaps you are, or will be, another such connecting link. All it takes to kill a movement is one generation that fails to accept the torch from the outstretched arms of the field's elders. The future of addiction treatment and recovery will be shaped by how well we extend that torch of leadership and by those who accept or forsake that torch. Can you feel yourself reaching?

Sunday Night Calls

I cannot recall when I first met Dr. Tom McGovern of Texas Tech University in Lubbock, Texas. It feels like he has always been in my life. Tom is one of the unsung heroes in the professionalization of addiction counseling and the long-time editor of *Alcoholism Treatment Quarterly* (ATQ). Tom encouraged me to submit many of my early papers on the history of recovery in America for publication in ATQ, and we came to be good friends over the years. He also relied on me to help peer-review articles submitted to ATQ or to write reviews on books he thought were of importance to the field. Tom did a lot of the work on ATQ on Sunday afternoons and evenings and did much of that work by phone—calling to request this or that. The Sunday evening calls came to be something of a tradition at my home. When the phone would ring on Sunday evening, my wife would say, "That must be Tom McGovern calling," and she was usually right. Tom is that rare embodiment of goodness and kindness and one of the most ethically sensitive people I have ever met. He has been a steady influence in my life, and these pages would not be complete without an acknowledgement of what he has meant to me and so many others. One would think a "work call" on Sunday night would be a source of great irritation, but seeing his number on the incoming call log always brings a smile to my face. Besides, I suspect Tom considered those calls more as a service activity than work. I came to see them the same way.

Working in the addiction treatment and recovery support arenas requires technical guidance, but it also requires, at its best, connection with sources of goodness. Do you have such sources in your life?

Person behind the Profession: Website Lessons

Here's the problem. You have created a body of written work, but you are so busy creating that you have little time to organize that written work in ways that: 1) you can find it, and 2) other people can easily locate it. The answer seemed simple enough to nearly everyone around me: you need to organize your papers on a website. I had already done some of that by placing some of my recovery advocacy papers on the Faces and Voices of Recovery website, but that still left me

457

responding to requests every day for a copy of this paper or that paper. That process should not have been difficult, but it occurred far too often and was like looking for the needle in the proverbial haystack. So I overcame my resistance to the idea of a website and in June of 2009 contracted with family members to help me create a website.

I worked my way through a lifetime of papers, selecting and formatting those that seemed of potential interest historically or relevant to the current state of addiction treatment and recovery. As the amassed papers got posted, it seemed that this project was moving toward completion, but those who first reviewed the site had other ideas. It was their consensus that, as one suggested, "Your writings are there, but you are not." Their feedback revealed what I had long known about myself—a comfort with the product of my labor but a discomfort when that attention turned to myself.

My friends and colleagues coaxed me to reveal more of myself on the site—to convey the person behind the papers and books. To achieve this, I had to work through periods of self-consciousness. As I responded to suggestions that the site needed to contain photos of myself over the course of my career, it seemed that my images detracted from the ideas contained in my writing. It took some time to be convinced that the ideas needed context and that such context was made up of the life and the personal and professional world I had occupied. After a year's work, the site went live June 6, 2010.

As I reflected on this boundary between the person and the professional, it became clear to me just how personal our work in the addictions field is—regardless of one's role. The work is personal because the issues of addiction and recovery are so personal. Those issues reflect the darkness and light in each of us, and as such, the person is the medium of the professional work. Credibility in the addictions field, regardless of one's academic and professional pedigrees, always comes down to the nature of our character and our relationships. The medium of our work is the profession AND the person.

To enhance the quality of what you can professionally contribute to this field, spend as much time developing your personal as well as your professional credentials. No matter what you achieve, the question will remain, do we live what we speak and write. How we conduct ourselves in our daily lives affirms or revokes our words. Those who seek our counsel have a right to know who we are as professionals, but they also have a right to a glimpse of who we are as a person. The former process involves questions of credibility; the latter involves questions of integrity and authenticity while maintaining clear boundaries of privacy. The trick is finding the balance between abdicating presence of self in our work on the one extreme and inordinate preoccupation with self on the other.

A Meditation on Death

A few years ago, country singer Tim McGraw had a hit song entitled, "Live Like You Were Dying." The song is essentially a story of a man who learned to fully live only when he found out he was dying. The refrain of that song played in my head in early 2011 when a CT scan ordered by my physician revealed what appeared to be renal cell carcinoma. The urologist to whom I was referred suggested monitoring it over time due to its small size, but my general practitioner and an oncologist I consulted for a second opinion were both adamant that it should be surgically removed and the surgical specialist agreed after reviewing the CT scan. What complicated the prospects of surgery were electrical problems in my heart stemming from my earlier excessive drug use. My arrhythmia and the propensity for my pulse and blood pressure to drop under the influence of anesthesia made surgery a potentially dicey adventure.

Facing the potential of my life ending provoked a reappraisal of just how blessed my life has been and reflections on the most important things on my list of unfinished business. It was six months from my original diagnosis until the pathology report following kidney surgery revealed that the tumor on my kidney was benign: not cancerous. Eight months later, I was diagnosed with prostate cancer and underwent prostate surgery in May of 2012. All of this underscored for me what a full life I had been blessed to live and also reminded me of those things I still wanted to accomplish.

Someone once told me that cancer was the best thing that ever happened to them. At the time, I thought they had lost their mind. Today, I understand what they meant. Live, love, and contribute as deeply as you can. Every day really is a gift.

What Cancer Taught Me about Addiction Treatment

Adversity is a seductive invitation to self-pity. Cancer, like other unwelcomed challenges experienced in my life, provided such an invitation. But adversities provide opportunities as well as pitfalls. None of us escape adversities in our lives, but there really is something to the old saw, "When life gives you lemons, make lemonade." Cancer was far more than an assault on my cells; it was a test of my character. Cancer provided invaluable lessons regarding my personal vulnerability and my need for better self-care—lessons of great import to someone both other-directed and action-oriented. The loss of bladder control in the weeks after my surgery forced me to once again confront limitation and powerlessness and brought humility and humiliation in equal measure—also valuable experiences for those of us fixated on controlling our own daily destinies. My need to rely on others, particularly my wife, forced me from the role of caring for others to the role of being cared for. I was forced to abandon efforts to bend life to my will and accept the limitations that cancer and healing imposed. And yet paradoxically, in that experience of acceptance, I found a way to transfer self-pity into something of great value.

For years I had been advocating that addiction in its most severe forms be recognized as a chronic disorder and treated on par with such chronic conditions as cancer, diabetes, asthma, and heart disease. My arguments were drawn from my studies of addiction and models of disease management for chronic illnesses. My writings on these topics were exercises in thinking. What my cancer and its treatment provided to me was a far deeper and more profound understanding of the differences between cancer treatment and addiction treatment.

Recognizing this opportunity, I turned my cancer treatment experience into something of a research project with me as the sole subject. The result was a paper suggesting a number of ways that addiction treatment could be improved by incorporating dimensions that were standard practice in cancer treatment. I used my experience with cancer treatment as a source of deep meditation about how differently we treat cancer and addiction. If we really believed addiction was a chronic disorder on par with cancer (and other chronic primary health disorders), we would provide every person seeking assistance:

- Clear and consistent communications regarding the intrapersonal, interpersonal, and environmental factors that contribute to the development of a substance use disorder.
- An assessment process that is comprehensive, transparent, and continual.

460

- Objective data upon which a substance use disorder (SUD) diagnosis is based with normative data for comparison to the general population and to other patients being treated for SUDs.
- Objective information on the severity (stage) of the SUD.
- Objective information on treatment options matched to the type and severity of the SUD.
- A declaration of potential professional/institutional biases related to diagnosis and treatment recommendations.
- A menu of treatment options before making a final decision on the course of treatment.
- Access to the experiential knowledge of former patients who have experienced a variety of SUD treatments and who represent diverse pathways and styles of long-term recovery management.
- Personalized refinements in treatment-based assessment data and individual responses to initial treatment.
- At least five years of monitoring and support following completion of primary treatment.
- Assertive re-intervention and recovery re-stabilization in response to any signs of clinical deterioration.
- A long-term, person- and family-centered recovery support relationship based on mutual respect that is free of contempt or condescension.

It really is that simple. If we believe that addiction in its most severe forms is a chronic disorder, then let's treat it like we really believe it. We don't get to pick all the cards we are dealt in life, but we can choose how we play them. Adversity can be transformed into achievement; the call to self-pity can be shunned and transformed into a call to service. Adversity is a call for both self-assertion and self-transcendence. Are there cards of injury or sorrow you have been dealt that could be turned into instruments of self-learning and service to others? Wouldn't playing the cards this way be better than the alternatives?

On Chameleons, Caterpillars, and Butterflies

One of my favorite people on earth is Roland Lamb, who I have had the pleasure of working with for many years in my collaborations with the Office of Addiction Services in Philadelphia. Roland comes from a long line of Baptist preachers and it shows. He can preach with the best of them. Roland has a mantra that he constantly refers to in speeches and conversations. Whether in responses to a query of "How are you?" or from the speaker's platform, Roland regularly declares, "The struggle continues…but victory is certain." Such a slogan is fitting for the man who Dr. Arthur Evans chose to be the point person of the recovery-focused transformation of Philadelphia's addiction treatment system.

Roland also likes to point out the differences between chameleons and caterpillars. Chameleons quickly adapt and blend in to the changing environment, whereas caterpillars draw inward and then transform themselves to emerge as a fundamentally new being. Roland draws several lessons from all of this. The chameleon, like many people and many systems, hides its true nature behind superficial, surface changes in its appearance. Boasting itself as the epitome of change able to adapt instantly to any environment, it changes nothing but the superficial shades of its skin. Such alterations convey the appearance of change but do not constitute any substantive change in character or functioning. In contrast, the caterpillar's unattractive adolescence and lumbering carriage reveals nothing of its future beauty and grace. Gazing on the butterfly's brilliance and fanciful flight provides no clue to what transformations were required to create such a spectacular creature. Roland's vivid metaphor readily sparks questions for each of us. At this moment, am I a chameleon or a caterpillar? Or am I a butterfly? Ultimately, it is up to those we influence or fail to influence to make that determination.

On the Value of Endurance

On a day struggling to catch up with lost work time due to recent surgery, an email arrived announcing that I had won the 2012 Voice Award for Lifetime Achievement presented by the Substance Abuse and Mental Health Services Administration (SAMHSA). My first reaction was that my life must be close to over—given the accumulation of acknowledgements entitled, "lifetime achievement." My second reaction was not about this particular award but that this combined with others perhaps signaled that I had reached a goal set long ago to try to personally and positively influence the future of addiction treatment and recovery in America. I also realized that I had worked for more than two decades in the field before ever receiving any such acknowledgement from my professional peers, and yet received numerous awards and honors in decades that followed. Such acknowledgements came not from a singular achievement but from slowly becoming an icon of long-term commitment and endurance within the field. Like the marathons we discussed earlier, just finishing a career in this field is something to be honored. I hope you will be able to experience moments in which the field looks back on your career and says, "Job well done. Thank you."

As I reached my 65th birthday, I began asking myself the question, "How have people in the toughest roles within this field sustained themselves for decades of activism? I don't know any role more publicly and professionally thankless than those who have advocated for the rights of methadone patients and sought to elevate the quality of methadone maintenance treatment. One such individual I have long admired—even when we disagreed on some important issues—is Dr. Robert Newman. I interviewed Dr. Newman for my "Pioneer Series." In a later communication during the summer of 2012, I asked Dr. Newman how he had sustained his advocacy for methadone maintenance for so long. Here was his response to my question: "I consider the OPPORTUNITIES associated with some day winning the fight to be vastly greater than the CHALLENGES involved in continuing to wage the battle." That just about says it all.

(Postscript: In January 2013, Dr. Newman announced to friends and colleagues that he would be ending his role as Director of Beth Israel Medical Center's Baron Edmond de Rothschild Chemical Dependency Institute. At the time of this writing, he continues to be active in the field.)

Dream Reach

If dreams are about wish fulfillment as some most famous shrinks have suggested, there is no question that I miss my contact with addiction professionals and recovery advocates across the world. Since I stopped traveling and lecturing, my dreams have been filled with new presentations and new conversations. Some of these dreams include struggles to effectively present (dream-expressed preoccupations with my declining physical and mental abilities), while others are filled with recently developed ideas or new findings from just-completed studies. What is interesting is the length and level of detail in these dreams. No longer being able to travel, I still find myself reaching out to those I served for so many years of my life. So if you should ever have a dream of attending a conference in which I appear as a speaker, listen closely because it may be me reaching out to you in my own dreams. Who's to say that couldn't happen?!

Recovery Blogs

Brevity is not my strength as a writer. And yet my wife Rita and others have long encouraged me to write for a wider professional and public audience. Do shorter, less technical pieces, she and others coached. Other than my regular columns in *Counselor* spanning more than 15 years, I had not found a format to do such writing. But after my website was launched in 2011, it occurred to me that a regular recovery-themed blog might provide a medium for such short missives to the world. So on July 13, 2013, I posted my first blog and have been posting a blog each week since. I have friends who have retired and made a complete break from involvement in the field, but such did not seem a good fit for me. The blogs have been a way to stay mentally and emotionally engaged in the field even as I disengaged from nearly all of my past involvements in the field. This may, in part, be my way of saying that one can leave this field without abandoning it. The blogs will stop at the point that I feel I have run out of things to say or lost my ability to say such things clearly, but for now, they remain my connection to kindred spirits in the field.

On Paying Respect

My long-time mentor, Ernie Kurtz, died January 19, 2015, of pancreatic cancer. He had refused all further treatment many months earlier knowing that such treatment would mean little in extending his life and could well worsen the quality of his remaining life. Ernie remained intellectually active through the final months of his life, working on numerous projects. We were invited in 2014 to contribute an article on AA for the international journal, *Religions*, to which we, at Ernie's insistence, agreed. We chose to focus the article on secular spirituality within AA, drawing themes from works Ernie had earlier co-authored with Katherine Ketcham (*Spirituality of Imperfection* and *Experiencing Spirituality*). Ernie's mind remained incredibly sharp in the months we worked on this paper, even as the cancer ravaged his body. We completed final corrections on the paper on a Thursday and Ernie died the following Monday. I was in awe of the courage and acceptance with which Ernie faced his impending death and equally in awe of his discipline to continue his work until the very end of his life. His passing was one of the greatest personal losses of my life and one of the great losses to the field.

On April 22, 2015, a memorial service was held for Ernie in Ann Arbor, Michigan at Dawn Farm—the local addiction treatment program that Ernie had long supported. Attended by 100-150 people, those attending included people representing diverse pathways of recovery and individuals in recovery longer than most US citizens have lived. Also striking were the elders of recovery history in the US and Canada. Those present shared tributes and memories of Ernie and statements of shared respect and affection were read from countries (e.g., Israel and Iran) known to agree on very little. What was most striking to me was that those present represented a community that Ernie himself had helped create. He was a connector, and many of those present knew each other only through Ernie's mutual introductions.

There is an inherent sadness in memorial services as we grieve those we have lost, but some can also be deeply meaningful, as was Ernie's. Those who gathered in Ann Arbor for his service did so as an act of homage, humility, and gratitude. It was our way of saying that we were better people as a result of Ernie's life and work and as a result of the friendship and service that he extended to us. The next time an opportunity comes to pay such tribute, take it. Paying respects really is about paying a debt with one's respect.

Graceful and Ungraceful Disengagement

Funny and not so funny things happen to some of us as we age— things that can embarrass us and tarnish the reputation of those with whom we are associated. (This same thing can happen during periods of personal or professional distress.) After 2010, even as I was professionally disengaging, I was upset with myself about some incidents and my professional performance. One of my strengths had always been an encyclopedic memory that allowed me to do full-day workshops without the need of notes. But recently, I found myself unable to retrieve information from my memory or later realized I had made an error in information that I had provided. I had also always been able to do a reasonable job of demarcating my role as a professional trainer and my role of advocate, yet increasingly found my advocacy bleeding into my professional presentations. I had worked hard as a presenter to maintain emotional control and carefully temper the language used in my presentations, yet found occasional profanity slipping into my presentations. I had always been a high energy trainer whose speech patterns could sometimes quite strategically mimic those of a country preacher, yet found myself less and less in control of when I moved into this style of speech. In short, I was less and less in control of myself during presentations and interviews and as a result began to ponder how I could do harm to my own reputation and the institutions and movements that I represented. That concern led to the decision in 2015 to end professional presentations, media interviews, and to, in short, retire from my public professional life—even while continuing my recovery research and writing activities.

Periodically, I was drawn back into doing a major writing project, like an article for a peer-reviewed journal. Such was the case with the article noted earlier that I did in 2016 with Drs. Marc Galanter, John Kelly, and Keith Humphreys for *Alcoholism Treatment Quarterly*. I was quite pleased that the article was rapidly accepted with minimal revision requests and felt a bit of pride after its approval that I still had "my stuff"—until the proofs came back from the copyeditor with 45 requested corrections—acronyms not spelled out, text citations not in the reference list, and names spelled differently in the text citation and reference list. That rather humbling episode convinced me that I was indeed losing my "mojo" and that I needed to add articles in scientific journals to my list of deleted activities.

As noted earlier, sometimes we serve best by stepping back rather than stepping up. Again, the question is not just what we need at a particular point in our lives, but how those needs and how we meet them affect the larger arena in which we serve.

Tying Up Loose Ends

When I retired from full-time work, I continued to consult part time on various recovery initiatives, but I began to phase these activities out after 2014. The last of these major contracts was my work with the Great Lakes Addiction Technology Transfer Center (GLATTC) that had supported much of my writing and training on recovery management over the past decade. I communicated to GLATTC Director, Lonnetta Albright, that I would end this contract in the fall of 2016. That last year was quite enjoyable as most of the work involved collaborations with my wife, Rita Chaney, who had served as my research assistant in recent years doing everything from transcribing interviews to helping create chronologies and bibliographies related to spiritual, secular, and religious recovery mutual aid organizations. Our final product those last months included completing a series of interviews with addiction treatment and recovery pioneers and finishing a topically categorized, 150-plus-page recovery research bibliography that we hoped would support future research on addiction recovery. I had assembled the recovery research bibliography over a span of four years, and Rita completed the meticulous work of formatting and proofing the final product before it was submitted and posted at www.williamwhitepapers.com.

Completing the recovery research bibliography was a special experience for me. First, Rita had been so supportive of my writing efforts for all these years and it was fitting that we would finish this last product together. (And there was the special pleasure of Rita and I working together on this.) Second, it seemed a fitting final contribution to my recovery research activities—a way to summarize all that the scientific world had revealed about addiction recovery to date, with the full awareness of how much remained unexamined. My hope was that pulling this together and placing it in the hands of future researchers would speed the fulfillment of a recovery research agenda that would make a real difference in the lives of individuals, families, and communities. That focus was where I started and it seemed a most fitting way to pay it forward.

A Time to Listen

After I disengaged from a weekly menu of speaking engagements and active research, an interesting thing unfolded. People from around the country and from other countries asked if they could come to Florida to seek my guidance on this or that project or just to meet me and share a cup of coffee. Such meetings became a regular part of my post-retirement life. And as I reflected on these meetings, it occurred to me that what these travelers were seeking had little to do with what ideas or suggestions I could share with them. Instead, most of these meetings involved the person sharing their personal and/or professional story. They did not need me to comment on it. But they did need me to hear it, or to experience themselves sharing it with me, or to be able to say to others that they shared their life and work with me.

It was in such meetings that realization dawned that I had moved into another phase of my life, an iconic symbol to which pilgrimages could be made for purposes of affirmation or recommitment to a cause. And the value to such meetings came not in the words of affirmation I could offer, although such words were freely given, but rather in the simple act of listening. It was intriguing to me that people expressed how much they gained from meetings in which I shared so few words. Many brought a nervousness and self-consciousness to the encounter that left them trying frantically to condense all they had considered saying into what must have seemed rapidly ticking minutes.

A related event occurred as 2017 opened in the midst of great political turbulence in the United States: I was invited to participate in a meeting of people interested in researching, preserving, and presenting the history of addiction recovery mutual aid in the United States. I had stopped traveling years earlier so the meeting was scheduled close to my Southwest Florida home. And I had not made a professional presentation in more than three years, but agreed to do a short presentation to this gathered group. After thousands of presentations, this short talk in such an informal meeting should not have posed much of a challenge to me, and yet it seemed to take on great significance to me as the date approached—a fact my wife observed days before I acknowledged it. When the night arrived for the opening of the event, my 45-minute presentation went fine but a most interesting thing happened immediately after I finished speaking. I simply lost my voice, really lost it, leaving me able to offer only a soft whisper or brief squeaking response for the following two weeks. I had rarely ever experienced any loss of voice in my decades of presentations, but found myself in the remainder of this meeting and the days that followed only able to listen and observe. Now was this attack of acute laryngitis simply a random medical anomaly or was something more important afoot? I'm not sure, but it seemed numerous events in my life coalesced to suggest that my season of speaking had passed and that it was again time for me to circle back to the beginning of my career, an earlier season marked by the core acts of listening and observing. As one of my favorite songs suggests:

> *To everything (turn, turn, turn)*
> *There is a season (turn, turn, turn)*
> *And a time to every purpose, under heaven. . .* (From
> *Turn, Turn, Turn [To Everything There is a Season]* by
> Pete Seeger, performed by The Byrds and others)

Dragon's End

When I was writing the closing chapter of *Slaying the Dragon* in 1997, I struggled to extract personal meaning from this history that would be of benefit to those who would read the book long after my passing. I offered many reflections, but I think none more important than these closing thoughts that seem appropriate to include here to help move us toward closure of these musings.

> *So what does this history tell us about how to conduct one's life in this most unusual of professions? I think the lessons from those who have gone before us are very simple ones. Respect the struggles of those who have delivered the field into your hands. Respect yourself and your limits. Respect the addicts and family members who seek your help. Respect (with a hopeful but healthy skepticism) the emerging addiction science. And respect the power of forces you cannot fully understand to be present in the treatment process. Above all, recognize that what addiction professionals have done for more than a century and a half is to create a setting and an opening in which the addicted can transform their identity and redefine every relationship in their lives, including their relationship with alcohol and other drugs.*

469

What we are professionally responsible for is creating a milieu of opportunity, choice and hope. What happens with that opportunity is up to the addict and his or her god. We can own neither the addiction nor the recovery, only the clarity of the presented choice, the best clinical technology we can muster, and our faith in the potential for human rebirth.

Wounded Healer

One of the foundational concepts within the history of recovery support is that of the *wounded healer*—the notion that people who have survived a particular illness or trauma might use that experience as a foundation to help others in similar circumstances. This idea, first introduced by psychoanalyst Carl Jung and later amplified by Henry Nouwen and others, provides a rationale for the legions of recovering people working in addiction treatment organizations and filling service roles within addiction recovery mutual aid and recovery advocacy organizations. Carried to extreme, it was posited that only an addict could help another addict. Through the course of my career, that proposition was challenged by my experience of people in recovery who were not effective healers and people who lacked personal or family recovery experience who were exceptional healers. All humans are wounded, but only those who find ways to transcend such wounds seem to possess these healing qualities.

In his history of Alcoholics Anonymous, Ernie Kurtz noted many non-alcoholics who had played important roles in the history of AA—Dr. Silkworth, Sister Ignatia, Sam Shoemaker, Willard Richardson, Frank Amos, Dr. Harry Tiebout, and Father Ed Dowling, to name a few. Ernie described how these individuals did have something in common.

Each, in his or her own way, had experienced tragedy in their lives. They had all known kenosis; they had been emptied out; they had hit bottom....whatever vocabulary you want. They had stared into the abyss. They had lived through a dark night of the soul. Each had encountered and survived tragedy (Not-God: A History of Alcoholics Anonymous, p. 143).

Wounded healers, regardless of recovery status, enter helping relationships with others with conscious awareness of their own healed and healing wounds. Such awareness allows us to serve others from a position of emotional authenticity, learned humility, and moral equality. Over the course of the last half century, I was at my best when I maintained that awareness and at my worst when I lost it. We are indeed all wounded, and what we can bring to the most wounded among us is our presence, our compassion, and our testimony that survival is possible and that a life of meaning and purpose can be found on the other side of such experiences.

The Sweetness of Daily Life

Aging brings far more challenges than I could have anticipated, but within these challenges a calm sweetness is present in daily life that remained out of my conscious awareness during my earlier years. So, today on the brink of my seventh decade of life, I share a most peaceful life with a woman I love, blessed by two wonderful children and other warm family ties, and a daily life of reading, reflection, writing, and seeking out pleasurable activities in Southwest Florida. I continue to be involved in various recovery research and recovery advocacy activities as time and energy allow, but I limit these far more than in earlier years. I feel a deep satisfaction in what I have survived and what I have given. I am drawn more to the desire to finish this life well—hoping for a final chapter filled with as much dignity and grace as I can muster. Interestingly, I have little fear of death at this time of my life, other than the anticipated sadness over lost time with family and friends and my intense curiosity about what will continue to unfold in the world in the years ahead. If death arrives today, I will breathe my last breath with a smile in my heart knowing just how much fun this whole thing has been and that the world is perhaps a little bit better because I lived in it. What more could anyone ask as we take our last breath? I leave the future of addiction treatment and recovery in your hands and wish you Godspeed on that continued journey.

About the Author

William ("Bill") White, Emeritus Senior Research Consultant at Chestnut Health Systems, has a Master's degree in Addiction Studies from Goddard College and has worked in multiple roles in the addictions field since 1969. Bill has authored or co-authored more than 400 articles, monographs, research reports, book chapters, and 21 books, including *Slaying the Dragon: The History of Addiction Treatment and Recovery in America; Let's Go Make Some History: Chronicles of the New Addiction Recovery Advocacy Movement;* and *Addiction Recovery Management: Theory, Research, and Practice* (co-edited with Dr. John Kelly). For the past 25 years, his work has focused on mapping the prevalence, pathways, styles, and stages of long-term addiction recovery. Bill's sustained contributions to addiction treatment and recovery in the United States have been acknowledged by numerous awards from such organizations as the National Association of Addiction Treatment Providers, the National Council on Alcoholism and Drug Dependence, NAADAC: The Association of Addiction Professionals, the American Society of Addiction Medicine, the American Association for the Treatment of Opioid Dependence, Harvard Medical School Department of Psychiatry, Faces and Voices of Recovery, Young People in Recovery, and the Association of Recovery Schools. Bill's collected papers can be found at www.williamwhitepapers.com. Bill lives with his wife, Rita Chaney, in Punta Gorda, Florida.

43535587R00275

Made in the USA
Lexington, KY
29 June 2019